AFRICAN PHILOSOPHY
IN SEARCH OF IDENTITY

African Systems of Thought

General Editors
Charles S. Bird
Ivan Karp

Contributing Editors
James W. Fernandez
Luc de Heusch
John Middleton
Roy Willis

AFRICAN PHILOSOPHY
IN SEARCH OF IDENTITY

D. A. Masolo

Published in association with the

International African Institute, London

Indiana University Press

Bloomington and Indianapolis

Edinburgh University Press

199.6

MASO

First published in 1994 by
Indiana University Press
601 North Morton Street, Bloomington, Indiana 47404
and
Edinburgh University Press Ltd
22 George Square, Edinburgh

© 1994 by D. A. Masolo

Manufactured in the United States of America

Library of Congress Cataloging-in-Publication Data

Masolo, D. A.
    African philosophy in search of identity / D. A. Masolo.
        p.   cm. — (African systems of thought)
    "Published in association with the International African
Institute, London."
    Includes bibliographical references and index.
    ISBN 0-253-30271-4 (cloth : alk. paper). — ISBN 0-253-20775-4
(pbk. : alk. paper)
    1. Philosophy, African. 2. Africa, Sub-Saharan—Intellectual
life. I. International African Institute. II. Title. III. Series.
    B5375.M38   1994
    199'.6—dc20   93-15353

1 2 3 4 5 99 98 97 96 95 94

British Library Cataloguing in Publication Data

A CIP record for this book is available from the
British Library
ISBN 0 7486 0496 0

Contents

*To my family for their great endurance,
and to the memory of our dearest and best friend,
sister and daughter Jane-Pauline Audi.
May her fortitude and strong sense of self
be a motivation to us all.*

Acknowledgments

I OWE A SPECIAL debt of gratitude to many friends who have contributed to the completion of this book. To Ivan Karp for his special friendship, encouragement, and resourcefulness during the preparation of this work through its various stages, and for initiating the idea of this book from its original notes and drafts; to V. Y. Mudimbe, Paulin Hountondji, and Kwame Appiah for agreeing to read the drafts of the manuscript, and for their most constructive suggestions and criticisms; to Henry Odera Oruka and E. S. Atieno-Odhiambo for their leadership, guidance, and helpful criticisms during many years of enriching collegiality; to Hellen Oluoch for her admirable patience and competence and the care with which she typed the various versions of the manuscript; to Janet Rabinowitch of Indiana University Press and to Elizabeth Dunstan and David Parkin of the International African Institute (London) for their encouragement and for believing that the project was possible. Finally, to my friend and wife Christine and to the children, Marvin, Leiz, and J-P before her most sudden departure, for their great understanding, companionship, encouragement, and endurance during the long preparation of the whole project.

AFRICAN PHILOSOPHY
IN SEARCH OF IDENTITY

1 Logocentrism and Emotivism
Two Systems in Struggle for Control of Identity

THE BIRTH OF the debate on African philosophy is historically associated with two related happenings: Western discourse on Africa, and the African response to it. This dialogue has taken many forms and has discussed a variety of topics and ideas depicting the individual's role and impact in the shaping and control of one's identity and destiny. At the center of this debate is the concept of reason, a value which is believed to stand as the great divide between the civilized and the uncivilized, the logical and the mystical. The debate evolved as claims and counterclaims, justifications and alienations, passed between the two camps: Western and non-Western. To a large extent, the debate about African philosophy can be summarized as a significant contribution to the discussion and definition of reason or what Hegel called the spirit. Indeed, it is commonly referred to as the "Rationality debate."

The focus on reason may not be obvious to many, particularly to students and those unacquainted with philosophical abstraction. For this reason we felt it would be helpful to map out the course of the debate so as to provide a historical background to many of the issues and problems discussed in African philosophy today. The background should help, we believe, to illuminate the development of the discussion to its present complex state.

Philosophical Foundations

When Aimé Césaire published the *Cahier d'un retour au pays natal* (English translation rendered as *Return to My Native Land*) in 1939, he introduced in and through it two new concepts which would later turn out to be key to the discourse on African identity and determinant of a new course in the francophone production and representation of knowledge about black Africa and its diaspora. The first of these concepts was "negritude," which Césaire is credited with inventing as a neologue in the *Cahier*. In this famous poem, Césaire uses the word "negritude" six different times to conceptualize the dignity, the personhood or humanity, of black people.

The second concept is captured by the word "return," which appears in the title of the poem itself. Closely related to the concept of negritude, the idea of "return" gives the dignity, the personhood or humanity, of black people its historicity; it turns it into a consciousness or awareness, into a state (of mind) which is subject to manipulations of history, of power relations. It is this idea of "return" which opens the way to the definition of negritude as a historical commitment, as a movement. In the *Cahier*, then, the word "return" has two meanings, one real, depicting Césaire's historical repatriation to a geographical or perceptual space, Martinique; the other metaphorical, depicting a "return" to or a regaining of a conceptual space in which culture is both field and process—first of alienation and domination, but now, most importantly, of rebellion and self-refinding.

Today, this "return" is a deconstructivist term which symbolizes many aspects of the struggle of the peoples of African origin to control their own identity. Historically, the call for a "return to the native land" was only one of the many revolutionary expressions of the then rising black militantism, nationalism, and Africanism. Retrospectively, it had both a metaphorical and a historical significance for its readers. It was both an ideology and a full-blood call.

For many black people, slavery and slave trade had provided the context for the need for a social and racial solidarity among themselves. Solidarity was their strength and a weapon with which to counter Westernism's arrogant and aggressive Eurocentric culture. Césaire's "return to the native land" was therefore a symbolic call to all black peoples to rally together around the idea of common origin and in a struggle to defend that unifying commonality. To Césaire, negritude meant exactly this—a uniting idea of common origin for all black peoples. It became their rallying point, their identity tag, and part of a language of resistance to the stereotype of the African "savage."

The details of this intellectual struggle have been well explained by V. Y. Mudimbe in his book *The Invention of Africa* (1988). Mudimbe's work is a powerful genealogy of African *episteme* as a product of a complex interplay of different forms of Western power, political and cognitive, which, in Mudimbe's view, succeeded in alienating and objectifying Africans as "the other." We strongly share this view. Mudimbe destroys the bases of present discourse as part of Western epistemological assumptions about the standards of rationality. The irony is that he presents no alternatives to Africans. Like most of the powerful structuralist philosophers who have influenced him, Mudimbe gives a brilliant structural historiography of African culture to the present day. His reliance on Michel Foucault places him in the same untenable position as other poststructuralist thinkers who attempt to deconstruct their own episteme. Richard Harland writes as follows about this problem:

> The dilemma that Foucault is coming up against at the end of *The Order of Things* and the end of *The Archeology of Knowledge* [two books which underlie Mudimbe's drive] is a problem that hangs over all the earlier Superstructuralists. It is easy enough for the theory of epistemes to encompass the thought of other historical periods; but when it encompasses the thought of our own

present-day period, it also encompasses the thought of the thinker of the theory of epistemes. The power of received social discourse suddenly becomes an embarrassment when Foucault himself has to submit to its control. It is a classic case of a deterministic theory that reflexively determines itself out of existence.[1]

Black peoples wanted to reaffirm their culture, derogated and nearly destroyed by Westernism, slavery, and colonialism. The black race had to heed to a refinding, redefinition, and reproclamation of itself. In this context we may refer to the celebrated paragraph of Langston Hughes in the journal *The Nation* of 23 June 1926, where he says:

We, the creators of the new black generation,
want to express our *black personality*
without shame or fear
If this will please the whites, much the better
If not, it does not matter
We know ourselves to be beautiful
And also ugly
The drums cry
The drums laugh
If this will please the whites, much the better
If not, it does not matter
It is for tomorrow that we are building our temples
Solid temples as we will ourselves know how to
construct them.
And we will keep ourselves straight
On top of the mountain
Free in ourselves.

The significance of this poem is that it was a response to the specific ideological attitude—the Western white attitude—that intended to annihilate black culture and black civilization.

This Western attitude had started as a mere cultural bias, supported loosely by a racist orthodox biblical ideology. But it gradually grew into a formidable . two-pronged historical reality: slavery and slave trade on the one hand, and academic expressions on the other. The academic expressions were made by prominent European scholars, among them the philosophers Immanuel Kant (in *Von den verschiedenen Rassen der Menschen* of 1775) and Georg Wilhelm Friedrich Hegel (in *Lectures on the Philosophy of World History*, English translation 1975). In the above work, Kant had endeavored to explain the emergence of different races in relation to the various natural causes bearing on them in different geographical regions of the world. According to him in this work, the original human species was white, appearing as dark brown. The black race, he believed, had emerged as a result of humid heat beating on the skin of the original species. Kant's other mention of the black race was made on the occasion of his review of Johann Gottfried von Herder's *Ideen zur Philosophie der Geschichte der Menschheit* of 1785. In this review, Kant suggested that for a credible general natural history of mankind, there was need for Herder, as for any other author writing from a philosophical point of view, to compare various sources on every race, especially those which appear contradictory. As his example, Kant says that from various sources it is possible to demonstrate that the (indigenous) Americans and blacks are a spiritually decadent race among other members of the human stock.

Kant's remarks and ideas can be understood in context. The eighteenth century was a period of great cultural revitalization and power consolidation in Europe. This revitalization and consolidation often took the form of self-comparison with other peoples in the areas of culture and history. Frequently, Africa was a ready example of the opposite of the desirable heights already attained by Europe. In history, anthropology, philosophy, and religion, Africa was described as utterly inferior to Europe. According to Hegel, in *Lectures on the Philosophy of World History*,

> The characteristic feature of the negroes is that their consciousness has not yet reached an awareness of any substantial objectivity—for example, of God or the law—in which the will of man could participate and in which he could become aware of his own being. The African, in his undifferentiated and concentrated unity, has not yet succeeded in making this distinction between himself as an individual and his essential universality, so that he knows nothing of an absolute being which is other and higher than his own self.[2]

Hegel often depended on the outdated historical and missionary literature of Herodotus and mission reporters. After Hegel, perhaps the most popular proponent of African mental inferiority was the French philosopher and sociologist Lucien Lévy-Bruhl in his famous works *Les Fonctions mentales dans les sociétés inférieures* (1910) and *La Mentalité primitive* (1922).

Let us understand Hegel's position. His project in the philosophy of history was to identify and explain the idea of history. History, he contended, was a process of change through the intervention of reason in the world. Through reason man knows and transforms his reality in a continuous dialectical manner. In these transformations culture is born. By the power of dialectical reason, this culture is itself in constant dialectical motion through the conflict of contradictions. For Hegel, then, reason is the infinite idea which realizes itself in the chainlink of its finite moments. It is not just a logical structure, but also historical reality since, according to his preface in the *Philosophy of Law*, "all that is rational is real," and vice versa. Reason therefore identifies itself with the reality which is its own creation. Reason is also history as a dialectical process in the transformation of this reality.

From this background, it is clear that for Hegel culture was the concretization of reason in its historical moments. To identify the signs of cultural change was to identify the intensity of dialectical reason at work in the world. From this position, it appears, Hegel easily inferred that where there was "no culture" there was no reason. It is obvious that Hegel defined culture itself in terms of the European cultural standards of the time, as the "series of external forms" in which the idea of the spirit displays itself.

According to Hegel, "The stage of self-consciousness which the spirit has reached manifests itself in world history as the existing national spirit, as a nation which exists in the present . . . [and that] nation's character consists simply in the form and manner in which it appears in world history and takes up its position and stance within it."[3] Subsequently, Hegel discusses the natural context or the geographical basis of world history and compares the contributions and stances of various geographical regions of the world to world history.

Sub-Saharan Africa fared poorly in this comparison. "In this main portion of Africa," Hegel said, "history is in fact out of the question."[4] In Africa life is not a manifestation of dialectical reason but of "a succession of contingent happenings and surprises. No aim or state exists whose development could be followed. . . . "[5] Africans live in a state of innocence. They are unconscious of themselves, as in the natural and primitive state of Adam and Eve in the biblical paradise before the emergence of reason and will. Africans are intractable. The condition in which they live is incapable of any historical development or culture. They have no history in the true (Hegelian) sense of the word.

There are two important points to note in Hegel's definition of history and culture. First is the central role of reason as the subjective tool with which man creates and orders the world, and as the objective reality which dialectically manifests itself as an imposition over the natural spirit through cultural change and development. Hegel's philosophy is logocentric. Civilization, which for him is "the world" from the human point of view, begins only with the mind's power of drawing conclusions and of determining right and truth. Second, Africans are excluded from this fundamental value. They have no reason. Because they lack reason, they also lack history, development, and culture.

Hegel's thought, widely described as objective idealism, is part of the legacy of the great intellectual revolution in seventeenth-century Europe. In this period, people were overwhelmed, as a result of the Newtonian synthesis, by the vast power of the human mind. The ability of human reason to discover and, indeed, to create universal law was a new revelation. Analyze-synthesize, said Newton. Thinkers followed this prescription literally, such that the Age of Reason and Enlightenment which arrived by the eighteenth century was primarily one of intense criticism of existing institutions and the projection of new systems ruled by rational law. The scientific conception of the Renaissance period removed as causes of natural events all supernatural forces. Galileo Galilei, a leading figure of the period, taught that scientific explanation consists of stating the conditions of any event and showing how the event depends upon the conditions. This is how Hegel himself had tried to explain history; Hegel says that "In our language, the word 'history' combines both objective and subjective meanings, for it denotes the *historia rerum gestarum* as well as the *res gestae* themselves, the historical narrative and the actual happenings, deeds, and events—which, in the stricter sense, are quite distinct from one another."[6] For him, then, history was a scientific explanation.

Since Hegel's time, an appreciable amount of intellectual effort in studying African peoples has been dedicated to solving the problem raised by Hegel's provocative doctrine regarding the definition and roles of Reason as the governor of the world and of history, and regarding his exclusion of Africans from it. Divergent schools have sprung up around different views on this issue. Is reason historical or ahistorical? In either case, what are its manifestations? Among twentieth-century philosophers, perhaps Lévy-Bruhl has been the best-known exponent of the historical view with his theory of the *prelogical*, which he sets forth in the two works mentioned above. In anthropology the question of reason and its role in sociocultural transformations of reality was critically discussed by the evolutionists, particularly by Edward Burnett Tylor and Lewis Henry Morgan. Both Tylor and Morgan advocated the notion that human nature is already charted and is composed of specific features that are universally shared. In this sense, they differed fundamentally from Hegel. While they affirmed the psychic unity of mankind, however, they denied to members of other cultures the full range of products of that psychic unity, such as science. In other words, while they affirmed that the reasoning capacity is the same in all humans, they also affirmed that there are considerable differences in the levels of what different societies have done with ideas. The differences, according to them, are sociological rather than epistemological.

So, while ideas have led to advanced material and social transformations in the Western world, they have done less in some societies, and even almost nothing in others. Michael Polanyi says almost as much in his *Personal Knowledge* when he compares what Evans-Pritchard says of the Azande to what scientists do with alternative theories in the laboratories in the Western world. According to Polanyi, it is not that the Azande do not develop or realize alternative theories to the usual ones in their pattern of explanation. Rather, as scientists frequently do in the West, they ignore or brush such alternative theories aside in order to let life go on. This is because, says Polanyi, "Our formally declared beliefs can be held to be true in the last resort only because of our logically anterior acceptance of a particular set of terms, from which all our references to reality are constructed."[7]

In religion, one dares say that the entire missionary project took the Hegelian doctrine as its basic assumption. The ahistoricist school, on the other hand, was greatly influenced by the structuralist tradition founded by the sociology of Émile Durkheim and enlivened by Ferdinand de Saussure and Claude Lévi-Strauss among others. To this school belong such people as Marcel Griaule and Germaine Dieterlen among the French-speaking anthropologists, and E. E. Evans-Pritchard in England. Africans have also had their share of participants in this debate. The separation between the ethnophilosophy school and its opponents roughly runs along the differences between the historicist and the ahistoricist evaluations of the nature of reason and its roles.

However, the controversial descriptions of African thought systems are best associated with Lucien Lévy-Bruhl rather than with Hegel. Lévy-Bruhl dedicated nearly all the last thirty-nine years of his life to the study of African ways of thinking, or primitive mentality as he called them. Because of this interest, he studied them primarily from the logical point of view, examining the structure and order of reasoning procedures in the systems of thought and belief of primitive societies.

According to Lévy-Bruhl, the nature of the individual's thinking pattern is influenced and determined by the collective representations of his society. These representations are, in turn, shaped by the social institutions. Long acquaintance with scientific institutions molds people into thinking logically and procedurally. The prescientific age, on the other hand, was marked by attribution of explanations to supernatural and occult powers. According to him, human societies can be classified into these two broad types—the civilized and the primitive—with two and opposed types of thought springing from each. From every stage of institutional development emerge a corresponding epistemology and a corresponding morality.

Lévy-Bruhl's position therefore proposes a moral relativism. This moral relativism has its correspondence and development in the epistemological relativism which is so evident in the studies of primitive mentality. Such epistemological relativism denies any identity in time of the human spirit and the unitary character of the logical form of thought. His point was, therefore, that while the modern man makes his judgments by means of the principles of identity, the primitive man is dominated by collective representations and realizes a mystic participation or relationship with his object. He is prelogical.

The theory of the prelogical compares two systems of inferential practice, Western and non-Western. Western inferential practice, Lévy-Bruhl thought, is invariably dependent on the naturalist view of material causality and is supported by observation. This type of inferential practice is what is called in logic the conditional argument (If p then q), in which the consequent must be *seen* to inescapably derive its validity from the precedent. In contrast to this, Lévy-Bruhl thought, primitive mind does not base its inferential practice on sufficient grounds supported by observation. Rather, it always introduces unrelated factors into the explanation of experience. Instead of saying, for example,

If p then q
But p
Therefore q

primitive reasoning process will usually run something like

p and q if x
But p and q
Therefore x

where x is indeterminable, arbitrary, and alterable at will. It is not subject to observation. Lévy-Bruhl's point is that the introduction of x into the second set is inexplicable and lies outside the "normal" patterns of factual relationing in explanatory processes. It is beyond reason, as is demonstrated in the first premise of the second set, which he thought was contradictory. At best, he thought, it was mystical.

The point addressed by Lévy-Bruhl is certainly an important one. But also obvious is the mistake that he made in his generalizations about societal patterns of reasoning. Because science had gained solid ground in influencing Western epistemological criteria for and definitions of truth, he thought *every* Western person was scientific in this sense and *at all times*. And similarly, he thought that because there were syllogistic problems in the discourses or statements about certain aspects of life in non-Western societies, they were present in all aspects of non-Western life. Toward the end of his life, however, Lévy-Bruhl realized and attempted to rectify this mistake in logic in his own thought.

In successive works, Lévy-Bruhl tried to soften his prelogical thesis. In *Les Carnets*, a work written toward the end of his life and published posthumously in 1949 (translated into English as *Notebooks on Primitive Mentality*, 1978), he at least expresses his intention to modify his earlier position. In a modified form, he contends that the question is not so much about a historical contraposition of two different logics as it is of the affirmation of the coexistence of two mentalities in man, of two forms of experience, one naturalistic and the other mystical. In the savage it is the mystic mentality that prevails. For this mentality certain incompatibilities (which may not necessarily be logical contradictions), which naturalistic European experience would reject as impossible, can in fact coexist. For example, Lévy-Bruhl argued, the savage does not regard magical facts as impossible, or magical judgments as nonsensical. For him (the savage) all is possible to a magician. In such a case, from Lévy-Bruhl's revised point of view, a logical contradiction would exist only if the word *impossible* had only one, univocal sense, which, as he now realized, it does not have. The only problem therefore appears to be that Europeans, in contradistinction to the savage, use the word *impossible* in relation to facts which refer to the general conditions of experience. What this means is that when he is not involved in judgments of magic and supernatural power, even the savage, like the European, when immersed in the practical conditions of everyday life, also rejects the absurd and the impossible, making recourse to naturalistic experience.

Whether theoretically acceptable or not, the application of the Hegelian views to the study of history, anthropology, philosophy, and religion promoted what became the popular European view of Africans as people with inferior forms of religion, law, economy, government, technology, and logic. The assertive European philosopher and Christian arrogated to himself the "duty" and assumed the mission to pull "the Negroes (up) within the range of culture" (Hegel).

The famous Martinican philosopher, psychiatrist, and political revolutionary Frantz Fanon used Hegel's dialectical principle to explain history rather differently. According to Fanon, history is a process within which cultural ideologies abolish each other through alienation. In this sense, cultures are usually defined on the basis of discriminatory categories like race or other social units such as ethnicity or class. But race, ethnicity, class, and similar discriminatory classifications are themselves ideological concepts whose contents shift with the variables of required alliances and targets in social relations. To paraphrase Fanon in Mudimbe's words, history is the dialectical process of the politics of otherness. For Fanon, therefore, supremacy in intercultural and intracultural relations depends on the ability to demonstrate one's preferability over others. This preferability is not judged on the basis of what is rationally or theoretically acceptable, but on the basis of what is emotionally and "pragmatically" satisfying. Any form of cultural supremacy is the function of a successful process of discrimination. The world is full of examples of this: Christian vs. non-Christian; developed vs. developing; capitalism vs. socialism, etc. These portray the world as a stage for continuous cultural tensions and competitions. The world is one big collection of active and emotive dialectical relations, in the sense of cultural strifes, whether explicit or implicit. It is in this way too that Africans became an invention of Western discourse. They became *The Africans.*

In this respect, the expressions of pre-Hegelian white attitudes toward blacks, the Hegelian expression itself, and the entire legacy after him achieved two things: first, they made the emotive relations explicit and, second, they made these relations active by setting their dialectics in motion. In this context, by emotive relations we mean those attitudes based upon value judgments held mostly by missionaries and Western travelers in Africa before and after anthropology was established as a science. Their notes contain such value judgments about Africans as "primitive," "evil," "savage," etc., which, to our view, are not empirically justifiable. The evolutionist theory expounded by Herbert Spencer, Edward Tylor, and Lewis Henry Morgan seemed to give such judgments even greater credibility under the guise of scientific explanation.

Black literature emerging in the United States in the early 1900s considered a response to such value judgments a matter of urgency and priority, for they were considered to be at the base of the social (segregation), political (disfranchisement), economic (labor exploitation), and cultural (discrimination) problems which the Negro faced in America and worldwide. The aim of this literature was to correct the image of the Negro. This literary activity went side-by-side with what is largely known as the civil rights movement. For both, the cultural demand has been for equal treatment with other citizens, or, better, with other racial groups. However, there was also a difference between them. The civil rights movement aimed at securing the black man's constitutional rights along political and economic lines. Its concern was with the problems of the black man as an American. The literary activity, on the other hand, was a universalist movement. Its aim was to rehabilitate the image of the black man wherever he was; it was the expression of black personality. This literary movement came to be known as the Harlem Renaissance, a predecessor of the more widely known cognate, negritude.

Negritude was the black francophone version of this expression of black personality. The Harlem Renaissance gave negritude both its form and its content. The form was poetry and the content was pluralism, as expressed in Langston Hughes's poem cited above. This value of pluralism was built around an ontology that accepted diversity or otherness without hierarchical judgments of human worth on the basis of racial and cultural characteristics.

Theories of racial pluralism as an ontological constitution of humanity were a commonplace of Western thought in the mid-nineteenth century. Black thinkers, on the other hand, found it a liberalizing concept. To W. E. B. Du Bois, for example, each race is striving, "in its own way, to develop for civilization its particular message, its particular ideal, which shall help guide the world nearer and nearer that perfection of human life, for which we all long, that 'one far off Divine event.' "[8]

Among African Americans, the theory of ontological designation by race goes back to Rufus Lewis Perry (1833–1895), considered by many[9] to be the first Afro-American to make efforts at professional philosophical writing. According to Perry in his *The Cushite or the Descendants of Ham* (1893), race "was not a social creation, but providently ordained. Race pride held ontological status. Black, yellow, and white races were separate and equal types . . . and each type a constitutive component of being."[10] Senghor's later epistemological paradox would in fact incarnate this existentialist race ontology.

To characterize negritude as a legitimate origin of philosophical discussion in Africa, we must therefore trace its origins and roots to these writings on race by African Americans in the United States, especially in the 1920s.

The African reaction to Europe dates as far back as the time of slavery in the fifteenth and sixteenth centuries, and realized itself in the defense of African humanity (at times) in a type of apology for Africa. The humiliating situation to which the slaves were subjected, under the claim of their inferiority, determined the rise of a dichotomy between the racial values of whites and those of blacks that in a way lingers even to our day. In other words, there was a clash between a violent, racist, expansionist, and imperialist Europe on the one hand and a powerlessly resistant and reactionist Africa on the other. Or, as the creators of negritude would later put it, a tough, individualistic, competitive, violent, and materialist European civilization armed with science and technology was at war against the sweet and human but weak African civilization. In other words, the two formed a thesis and antithesis vis-à-vis each other. In these circumstances, it is no historical coincidence that a cultural movement such as the Harlem Renaissance expressed an eagerness to correct the mistakes, sometimes even violently, and to reestablish the truth.

The movement or ideology that opened the windows to the consciousness of a personality and a cultural heritage going in ruins began among Africans in the diaspora rather than among those on the African continent.[11] According to Maria Carrilho in her *Sociologia della negritudine*, "The particular condition of the Africans of the New Continent [the Americas], who found themselves to be invariably both black and slaves at the same time, no doubt provoked . . . the birth of that collective sentiment of uneasiness, of that togetherness of inferiority complexes that [often] led Blacks to dream, not of blackening the white, but of whitening their own [black] skin."[12]

In confrontation with the racism of the white community, the first need of American blacks was that of redeeming their own dignity, trodden underfoot for centuries, to confirm the lack of foundation for discrimination and to regain self-identity. According to M. Cook, "They became conscious of the fact that among all the ethnic groups that populated the United States—the Anglo-Saxons, Italians, French, Germans, Hebrews, Spanish, etc.—only the blacks suffered the brainwashing that led them to believe that they were naturally inferior and not to have a history. In order to fight this deep inferiority complex, it was necessary to reestablish the truth."[13]

This is not entirely correct. It was not the black man who had the inferiority complex. The category of inferiority, born out of dialectical relations with whites, was imposed upon him to accept as his own. So also, the onus was on him to prove and reaffirm his worth.

Among the names that may be listed under this resistance literature is that of Edward Wilmot Blyden, who was also the first writer to use and defend the phrase-concept of "African personality."[14] Blyden was also the progenitor of *panafricanism*, "conceived not as a provoked black racism to oppose the arrogant white racism,"[15] but rather "as an opposition to any form of racial prejudice and social chauvinism and as a catalyst to a constructive solidarity among all Africans . . . and to form a 'dynamic political philosophy' and a guide of action for the Africans of Africa who were beginning to make the first bold bases for the movement of national liberation."[16]

Like the writers of negritude, Blyden projected to found and build his human dignity on his cultural and historical past. In *Race and study* (Freetown, 1895), Blyden explicitly called for the return to this glorious black past:

> "For each one of you—for each one of us—there is a special duty to accomplish, a terribly necessary and important job, a job for the race to which we belong . . . there is a responsibility that our personality, our belonging to this race, presupposes. . . . The duty of every individual and every race is to struggle for its own individuality, to maintain it and develop it. . . . Therefore honour and love your race for yourselves . . . if you are for yourselves, for if you abdicate your personality, you will not have left anything to give to the world. Neither will you be happy nor of any use, and you will have nothing to attract and fascinate other people because with the suppression of your individuality you will also lose your distinctive character. You will also realize then that having abdicated your personality you will also have lost the special duty and glory to which you are called. In truth you will be denying the divine idea—god—and sacrificing the divine individuality; this is the worst type of suicide."[17]

Like Perry and Du Bois, each in his own way, Blyden too was echoing the idea of racial pluralism as the foundation of world history.

This passage also indicates that Blyden was both a puritan and a separatist. He advocated the reestablishment of "pure" black values and opposed any ideology of cultural change. In this way he too reached the mark of racism then typical of the Western world. While Du Bois believed in the achievement of complete equality for American blacks in their American context, Blyden, like his successor Marcus Aurelius Garvey, was convinced that the Negro would never achieve such equality by integrating himself. The Negro had to develop separately. Immediately after World War I, Garvey set out on an ambitious—and perhaps also unrealistic—campaign to lead and return all black peoples back to their African homeland. At a congress organized by him in New York in August 1920, he proclaimed himself the first president of the so-called newly created African Empire, "The United States of Africa." In contrast to Du Bois, whose influence had remained purely intellectual, analytical, and gradualist, and who therefore appealed mostly to the intellectual elites among the blacks, Garvey's personality and ambitions had influences mostly in the heart of Harlem among the more militant black families of the ghettos. Although his campaign was short-lived,[18] his flamboyance prepared the ground for a new school of black writers and poets between the years 1920 and 1930. Blyden and Garvey were the founders of the Harlem Renaissance movement. Members included Claude McKay, Langston Hughes, Jean Toomer, Countee Cullen, and Sterling Brown, among others. All these people saw Africa, with its rawness and anchorage to bare natural forces, as an essential antithesis to the domineering industrial civilization of the white world.

Agewise, McKay belonged to an older group, the group that included Alain Locke and Du Bois. But the themes, the radicalism, and the style of his work, particularly in *Home to Harlem* and *Banjo*, put him closer to the younger group. Locke and Du Bois were people who had made it to the ranks of the middle-class bourgeoisie and were widely considered as leading intellectuals and men of culture who had risen above the ravaged life of Harlem. Generally, they regarded McKay's work with suspicion. In their opinion, McKay had allowed himself to fall into the trap of producing knowledge about black people for consumption by white readers as a cheap means of lifting himself out of the perennial pecuniary problems he had. They often treated McKay with contempt, sometimes imposing their own editorial changes on McKay's works and publishing them without consultation with him. In return, McKay frequently poured venomous countercriticism on black intelligentsia, particularly Locke and Du Bois, accusing them of tragic misguidance and impotence in their attempts to imitate white middle-class culture which they nonetheless fell short of. He was particularly stinging on Du Bois, whom he described as lacking the artistic qualifications to critique his work.

McKay's *Home to Harlem* and *Banjo* reveal images and impressions that capture the bare and harsh realities of life for black people, those in Harlem and drifters abroad. McKay had experience of both. The sense of truthfulness and the undisguised representation in these works appealed to and inspired the younger group. They saw in them the image of distinctness of race as revealed by the plight of its majority.

Like Garvey's dream, their imaginative apprehension of Africa as a homeland to return to was short-lived. They replaced the desire of a physical return to Africa with another zeal—the zeal to reestablish relations with the earth, no longer with Africa as a spatial and sociocultural entity, but with the metaphysical rhythm of nature and the cosmic forces. As a result, their works began to take a relatively more general universal and metaphysical (if not mystic) orientation and historically immediate or lived approaches and characteristics. Claude McKay, for example, says the following in his *Banjo*:

A black man, despite his education,
is able to preserve the closest relations
with the rhythm of the primitive life of the earth

And may be his failure in the organization
of the modern world
Was the true force that saved him
from the miserable thing
commonly known as the Whites.[19]

It is believed by some writers[20] that this quotation from McKay is basically implicit in the conception of negritude as expressed by Aimé Césaire in his *Cahier d'un retour au pays natal* when he eulogized the black people as

Those who invented neither powder
Nor the Compass
But who ecstatically leave themselves
to be carried away
Toward the essence of everything
Not caring about dominating [others]
but good at the game of the world
The flesh of the flesh of the world
The throbber of the movement of the world itself.

In that short paragraph (of McKay) we find a prelude to what would in the later years constitute the essence of negritude. This time around, McKay had a different message. Although he still believed that in order to refind the authentic black personality one must return to African origins, this return now need not be physical, but merely imaginative or intellectual. Nonetheless, he still expounded the cult of difference as an essential characteristic of black identity. This difference is conceived as a certain emotive attitude before reality. And by this McKay already anticipates the key point of negritude—the rhythm that inserts man into the cosmos—which will be at the heart of Senghor's doctrine. This cult of difference was opening itself, for the poets of the Harlem Renaissance as it did for Blyden and Du Bois, to a view of the future, to a mission entrusted to the black race. And that mission consisted of offering to the world her lost paradise, that is, a new sense of the human, a new humanism. And with this aspiration, negritude was ushered in.

But Césaire himself seems to have a different conception of his own neologism, *negritude*, from what the enthusiasm of identity developed it to be. More recently, James Clifford writes that "It is too familiar as a literary movement and as a set of 'positions' in an ongoing debate about black identity, essentialism, and oppositional consciousness. Negritude, in many of its senses, has become what Césaire never wanted it to be, an abstraction and ideology."[21] Césaire himself, in an interview with Lilyan Kesteloot, affirms that negritude has been blown by interpretations beyond what he originally meant it to be:

It has tended to become a school, to become a church, to become a theory, an ideology. I'm in favour of negritude seen as a literary phenomenon, and as a personal ethic. . . . In addition, my conception of negritude is not biological, it's cultural and historical. I think there is always a certain danger in basing something on the black blood in our veins, the three drops of black blood.[22]

It is quite evident that Césaire tries hard to dissociate himself from the runaway but more popular version of negritude advocated by Senghor, perhaps for political or practical reasons, if there is any meaningful difference between the two. Even in the work of René Ménil,[23] "who was Césaire's main contact with surrealism in the thirties and who participated in both of the formative group endeavours, *Legitime defence* and *Tropiques*," writes Clifford, "the negritude of Léopold Senghor and that of Césaire are clearly distinguished. The former elaborates a 'backward-looking idealism,' a falsely naturalized, consistent African mentality that tends to reinscribe the categories of a romantic, sometimes racialist European ethnography. Césaire's Caribbean negritude, by contrast, rejects all essentialist evocations."[24]

It ought to be added here, however, that, as Clifford and René Depestre do correctly point out, it was written before the neologism was muted that the neologism would eventually take diverse evolutionary paths in its historical interpretation. For, while Césaire talks of only "three drops of black blood" in his veins, Senghor and other non-*métis* Africans boast a full-percentage purism which could have opened them more toward an ideology of essentialism. Because of these diverse realities, the Senghorian evolution of negritude and its heirs can claim a legitimacy equal to that of Alejo Carpentier, Jorge Guillén, Jorge Amado, César Vallejo, Julio Cortázar, René Marquéz and other creolite heirs of the Césairean negritude.

When Amadou Mactar Mbow addressed the First Pan-African Festival of Algiers in 1969, he said that "If the word [negritude] belongs to Aimé Césaire, and if Senghor has been its most heeded poet, the thing, however, came into being in black diaspora. This revindication movement was called Harlem Renaissance in the United States of the 20s [by Du Bois, Cullen, Hughes, Toomer]; Indigenism in Haiti in 1925 [by Jean Price-Mars, Jacques Roumain, Carl Bronard, Jean Brierre, et al.]; and Cubanism in Cuba [with the generation of Nicolas Guillén]."[25]

The Politics of Rationality

While the followers of Blyden and Garvey in the United States were busy writing the rebellious poetry of Negro renaissance in the 1920s, a different event was taking shape in Europe, especially in Paris. Leading European artists such as Vlaminck, Apollinaire, and, later, Picasso had discovered and exposed black art; the jazz and blues and the world of Afro-American music and dance were beginning to win the admiration of non-African artists and aestheticians, not because they were beautiful but more so because they were different. According to Clifford, this marked the beginnings of surrealism or, more precisely, the ethnographic surrealist attitude,

> a belief that the other (whether accessible in dreams, fetishes, or Lévy-Bruhl's *mentalité primitive*) was a crucial object of modern research. Unlike the exoticism of the nineteenth century, which departed from a more-or-less confident cultural order in search of a temporary *frisson*, a circumscribed experience of the bizarre, modern surrealism and ethnography began with a reality deeply in question. Others appeared now as serious human alternatives; modern cultural relativism became possible. As artists and writers set about after the war putting the pieces of culture together in new ways, their field of selection expanded dramatically. The "primitive" societies of the planet were increasingly available as aesthetic, cosmological, and scientific resources.[26]

He also writes about the postwar surrealistic passion for exotic African art:

> The postwar passion for *L'art nègre* fostered a cult of the exotic artifact, and the carved figures and masks of West and Equatorial Africa satisfied perfectly a European fetishism nourished on cubist and surrealist aesthetics.[27]

Each epoch has its own turnovers, I suppose, for something similar to the postwar ethnographic surrealism is taking place under our very noses today in the name of a new form of pragmatism (in the broad sense of the word) called postmodernism. Like surrealism, postmodernism depicts a growing boredom with and rejection of the formalistic scientism, positivism, and even rigorous and systematic philosophizing. Against these qualities postmodernism recommends, to use Richard Rorty's words, the need to dephilosophize the conversation of mankind and to make wider openings to cultural pluralisms. Postmodernism wants to view knowledge basically as discourses, representational paradigms, or forms of metaphors while considering schools of thought as "communities of discourse" which need greater cross-cultural and interdisciplinary rapprochement rather than fragmentation as the more promising way to achieve a greater understanding of all aspects of reality. These new turnovers have brought controversial but certainly very interesting and fruitful discussions on the roles of metaphysics and epistemology in philosophical valuation as discussed in the works of such influential postmodernist philosophers as Richard Rorty, Hector-Neri Castañeda, Hilary Putnam, Donald Davidson, and A. J. Mandt, for example. The method they use is the deconstructive hermeneutics launched recently by Jacques Derrida.

As in the case of ethnographic surrealism, postmodernism is essentially a surge (not an oppositional one) against absolutist thinking, against another form of establishment, against analytic philosophy with its scientist / foundational / positivistic principles. In postmodernism everyone has a point, there are no centers and margins. Africans, feminists, and other perspectival units can all have a voice. In other words, the postmodernist picture of society is one in which every human potentiality is given free rein. Its episteme is structuralist, as is now so clearly outlined in the works of Michel Foucault. The worry is, however, that even the present postmodernism, like surrealism before it, might only be another form of temporary fashion or exoticism, comparable at its worst to the more mundane hippy movement of the seventies, a cooling moment to create an introspective awareness for the positivistic realist tradition perhaps. In this sense, despite its depiction of the need for a greater intellectual cultural outreach, postmodernism, like surrealism, leaves unperturbed Martin Hollis's "model of man." At its best, however, postmodernism must be made into an even stronger need for checking the absolutist excesses of scientism.

By contrast, ethnographic surrealism had a more concrete bearing on Western considerations of African history, literature, and art, especially in France between the two world wars. Even in the literary world, much was taking place. In 1927, Maurice Delafosse made a study of West African history and discovered that the African medieval age had been in many respects comparable to the European.[28] From his studies he drew the conclusion that not only had the pretext of black intellectual inferiority of Lévy-Bruhl not been proved, but also that the contrary could be found.

The African medieval age was the period of the great African empires. These empires not only demonstrated a high degree of statecraft, but also included great centers of learning, such as Timbuktu, Gao, and Jenne. Subjects taught in these universities included both religious and scientific disciplines: Islamic studies, history, philosophy, architecture, government, geography, etc. Such evidence must have led Delafosse to deduce that, in fact, African civilizations in the medieval age must have been superior to many others in the world. At this point, one is tempted to ask how, then, did such a great civilization fall into inertia? As if consciously, the answer to this question was to be given later by Leo Frobenius.

Also in 1927, Georges Hardy revealed in another work the disastrous consequences of European influence in Africa, especially in regard to the African religious heritage.[29] Frobenius himself had held a similar belief about the primitivizing effects of Europe over Africa, arguing that Africans became barbarous (uncivilized) only as a consequence of the arrival of the whites on the continent. He discovered in West Africa the remains of an ancient civilization which he deduced to have connection with the ancient Egyptian civilization.[30] According to Frobenius, cultures are like living organisms, in the biological sense that every culture is subject to the laws of the organic world, springing up like seed, growing, and attaining its apogee at maturity. It is man's environment that is of decisive significance in the development of a culture, for it alone is able to move him. That is why Frobenius regarded environment as a factor of overriding significance and recognized the primary bond between every culture and its location,

while the factor of race seemed unimportant. He thus attributed differences between various cultures largely to the differences in environmental conditions. All
cultures rise and fall, traversing three stages (youth, maturity, and old age), comparable to a life curve. In 1931, the well-known French ethnologist Marcel
Griaule—joined later by Germaine Dieterlen, with whom he published monumental works on the Dogon and Bambara ethnic groups of West Africa—began
his ethnological expeditions among the Dogon. People like Georges Balandier[31]
had also studied and published some of their findings on African social and cultural status.

Even more recently, African scholars themselves have tried to demonstrate
Africa's central role and contribution to the genesis of human civilization. In *The
African Origin of Civilization* (1974), Cheikh Anta Diop argues that many social
and cultural practices, in their old and in modern forms, owe their origin to
Egypt. Such practices and systems include totemism, circumcision, kingship language, cosmogony, agriculture, social organization, and matriarchy. The arguments presented by Diop sometimes sound like a joy dance in the shadow of
Egyptian grandiosity, an eagerness to prove a point rather than a thorough presentation of facts. His argument can be put as follows:

1. Egypt has been cited and recognized as the origin of and leader in many
   forms of human civilization.
2. Many of these forms of civilization originating in Egypt have closer
   affinity with similar forms in upper Africa than they have with their
   Indo-European and Semitic counterparts.
3. Egyptians and Africans are the same people and are originators of world
   civilizations.

Diop bases his arguments on the monogenetic theory of culture, and picks
"the Heart of Negro Lands" as the location of the cradle. The choice sometimes
sounds too arbitrary, and so leads him into making rather sweeping statements.
He says, for example, that "No less paradoxical is the fact that the Indo-Eu-
ropeans never created a civilization in their own native lands: the eurasian plains.
The civilizations attributed to them are inevitably located in the heart of Negro
countries in the southern part of the Northern Hemisphere: Egypt, Arabia, Phoe-
nicia, Mesopotamia, Elam, India."[32] Despite the weakness of his arguments,
Diop represents one form of the African response to Western discourse on Africa, and the African eagerness to explain the contrary view.

Diop's starting point is that Eurocentric writings on Africa, in anthropology
and history, are ideologically tainted and vexed with racial prejudices. Theories
of origin, evolution, and human nature are—as they have appeared in Eurocentric literature—matters of cultural awareness more than they are part of scientific
literature. Diop's major focus and significant contribution is therefore to interrogate Eurocentrism in its pretensions as a dependable source of knowledge of

other (non-European) cultures and peoples. Thus, despite the controversies and disagreements regarding his theses, Cheikh Anta Diop has contributed to a major focus of contemporary discourse—the production of knowledge as a source of power against Others. On the whole, Diop's writings on the origins and evolution of the human species do not jump the bounds of what constitutes major points of concordance among paleontologists. His point, then, rests on demonstrating the double role of science: as a source of knowledge, but of knowledge that also marginalizes Others. Thus, like the science, history, and literature he critiques, Diop too ends up inventing a new Africa with Negroid Pharaohs in Negroid Egypt. His objective is to demarginalize Africa by placing it at the center of human evolution, and hence controversially conjuncting the monogenetic theory of human origin with that of geographical culture precedence. He rewrites African historiography and repairs the ruptures in the knowledge of Africa as a historical continuum from antiquity to modern times.

Along the same vein is the thesis of Henry Olela. Contrary to the Hegelian attempt "to subscribe to the argument of the European or Asian origin of any cultural traits of merit found in Africa," Olela states that it is a "fact that even the ancient Greeks themselves often credited Africa with being the source of foundations of philosophical knowledge."[33]

According to Olela, the lands of North Africa and the island of Crete in the Mediterranean Sea were once inhabited by peoples who moved north from around the Sahara region as a result of the expansion of the desert almost 2,500 years before Christ. Even the inhabitants of ancient Egypt were the descendants of the Gallas, Somalians, and Maasai. The Cretans of African descent, according to Olela, kept close ties with their Egyptian compatriots and established a flourishing culture around the Mediterranean.

For Cheikh Anta Diop, it had been sufficient to counter the Hegelian legacy by demonstrating that Egypt was part of Africa both culturally and historically. Since Egypt was known to be the cradle of many aspects of world civilization, by extension, then, for Diop the whole of Africa shared in Egypt's leadership in cultural genesis.

With Olela, the cradle is carried even further south. For him, civilization moved northward from black Africa, engulfing both Egypt and the surrounding regions of the Mediterranean through descent and diffusion. For Olela, then, to talk of ancient Egypt (which he calls Sais) is to talk of ancient Africa. Ancient Egypt, Olela contends, "was the intellectual center of the world. Their speculation covered the whole realm of human knowledge including pure mathematics, ethics, astronomy, mathematics, science and medicine." In the field of mathematics, one of the ancient African texts, the Rhind Mathematical Papyrus, "was written during the reign of King A-User-Re in 1650 B.C." and copies were made around the year "1800 B.C. [*sic*] by the scribe A'hmose."[34]

Notice the date of the Papyrus! It is written long before the birth of the first acknowledged Western philosopher, Thales of Ionia (ca. 640–ca. 546 B.C.), and even longer before the first Western mathematician, Pythagoras of Samos (ca. 580–ca. 500 B.C.). According to Olela, then, it was the African mathematical concepts, especially their "geometrical maxims or theorems, which were later directly adopted by the Greeks. There are at least five such basic propositions which found their way to Greece after the voyages of Thales, Pythagoras, and Euclid . . . and their lessons from the Egyptian seers."[35] But even more striking is the following paragraph:

> Because of their mathematical knowledge, the Ancient Africans of Sais were able to calculate the height of a pyramid as well as the distance of a ship in the ocean from a given point on land. But in the history of philosophy written by Eastern philosophers, these two discoveries have been falsely attributed to Thales. Euclid adopted the ancient African method of determining the distance of a ship at sea (Euclidean Theorem 1.26).[36]

Even modern natural science, Olela contends, is only a recent development based on ancient African science. Parts or some aspects of this science are found in the Edwin Papyrus, which dates as far back as between 5000 and 2000 B.C.

In the field of philosophy, Olela identifies four important schools of thought —the school of Heliopolis; the school at Hermopolis; the school of Thebes; and the school at Memphis—which must have influenced ancient Greek philosophy. With reliance on R. T. Rundle Clark's *Myth and Symbol in Ancient Egypt*,[37] Olela concludes that it was the ancient Africans of Sais who first identified the basic elements of reality which emerge later in pre-Socratic Greek thought.[38] Likewise, Plato adopted and developed the doctrine of the immortality of the soul from the Egyptians.[39] Of Aristotle, Olela writes the following:

> He went to Egypt with Alexander the Great. He had access to priestly material in the Temples and he freely acquired books from the Library at Alexandria. He adopted the Egyptian notion of the *unmoved mover*. Creative process developed from disorder (chaos) to order. This process was performed through *mind* and *word* . . . or pure intelligence. He also adopted the doctrine of the soul as discussed in the *Book of the Dead*.[40]

It is curious to notice the semblance between Olela's argument and the Dogon and Bambara doctrines about the primordial chaotic state of the universe and the *gla gla zo*[41] process through which order replaced disorder as *Nommo*, the word, shaped the universe into its present form. But to Olela and Cheikh Anta Diop, this would probably only corroborate the hypothesis of the ancient African origin of the basic presuppositions in the history of philosophy.

The project of these two works is significant to the history of African philosophy. Although very recent, they amplify the rediscovery of arguments started and developed during the Harlem Renaissance, although with a difference. The

Harlem tradition was eager to reclaim reason for Africa by modifying or totally rejecting its Hegelian monopolistic definition. Their project was one of a parallel coexistence of two separate but equal forms of reason. The theme of parallel coexistence became a central premise for black and Jewish American minority philosophers, notably W. E. B. Du Bois, Alain Locke, and Hannah Arendt. The Diop-Olela tradition, on the other hand, made its reclamation by a reductive argument which saw Western and modern African reason as developments of ancient black African civilizations diffused to the rest of the world from Sais (ancient Egypt). In conclusion, then, Olela states: " . . . the contemporary African philosophy is moribund if it does not take into account the 'history of African Philosophy' which takes us back to ancient Africa (Ancient Egypt, Egypt, etc.). Once the Black Western philosophy will take a new dimension, the monopoly of philosophy by the Greeks will have a turn."[42] And, as if to deal the last blow to the Hegelian bias, he quotes from George James's *The Stolen Legacy*:

> Now that it has been shown that philosophy, and sciences were bequeathed to civilization by the people of North Africa and not by the people of Greece; the pendulum of praise and honor is due to shift from the people of Greece to the people of the African continent . . . that the Greeks were not the authors of Greek philosophy, but the people of North Africa . . . [43]

This thesis has recently been strongly supported by Martin Bernal in a work entitled *Black Athena: The Afroasiatic Roots of Classical Civilization* (1987) in which he argues that Greece is quite aware of her indebtedness to ancient Egypt for the civilization and scholarship for which Greece has falsely been praised and honored. During the past two hundred years, between 1785 and 1985, Bernal argues, documents asserting or testifying to this borrowing from Africa on the part of Greece have been systematically destroyed.

In a recent review of Bernal's book, G. W. Bowersock affirms the truth of Bernal's findings. According to Bowersock,

> Bernal has done his homework thoroughly. . . . Bernal is well aware that people who say the kinds of things that he is saying tend to be dismissed by the establishment as cranky or worse. I hope that this will not happen in his case. It is important, at least in this early stage of the debate, to separate the issue of the actual truth or falsity of ancient traditions concerning Egyptians and Phoenicians in Greece from the systematic and indisputably racist efforts of modern historians to deny those traditions.

Bernal shows, conclusively as Bowersock admits, that the present Western perception of Greece as the cradle of the dominant Western culture is a false consciousness at best and, at worst, a deliberate but false ideology and plot artificially pieced together between the late eighteenth century and the present. "Whatever happens [with Bernal's stated objective to shatter the false European cultural pride and arrogance]," concludes Bowersock, "Bernal's first volume [entitled *The Fabrication of Ancient Greece 1785–1985*] must be judged salutary, exciting, and, in its historiographical aspects, convincing."[44]

Bernal states that his work has two distinct purposes: the scholarly and the political. In regard to the first purpose, Bernal's work can be said to have its undeniable strengths in scholarship; it displays his own very admirable preparations in the classics, in modern languages of wide geographic diversity, in history, and in archaeology. This personal background puts Bernal in an enviable position of privilege as a researcher in the sociology of knowledge. The work is accomplished through what appears to be a meticulous and patient analysis of an enormous corpus of detailed and sophisticated data on the civilizations of the Mediterranean region. This makes Bernal's work an interesting addition to Mediterranean and Middle East studies in general and to Egyptology in particular. It illustrates the richness of the Mediterranean region as a boiling pot of cultures, as a region where movements of peoples back and forth, across and around the Mediterranean shores and their immediate hinterlands produced some of the most dominant brands of human civilization, with enduring traditions down to our own times. In this respect Bernal's work deserves fair attention from the practitioners of the disciplines and area studies whose boundaries the work straddles. This evaluative focus on either the credibility of the data and hypotheses or the analytic plausibility of Bernal's work lies beyond our disciplinary confines. His own statement (p. 73) that the work "raises many interesting new questions and generates hundreds of testable hypotheses" defines the legitimate desire to place the work under scholarly scrutiny. This openness to scrutiny, he declares (p. 73), "is precisely what differentiates fruitful radical innovation from sterile crankiness." It is almost predictable that Bernal's work will be subjected to such scrutiny as part of the rules of the trade.

However, Bernal's work has dimensions which make it a target also for scrutinizers who practice outside the strict confines of history, archaeology, or the classics. It has a political purpose, which is, he says (p. 73), "to lessen European cultural arrogance." Whether this is an achievable or useful purpose is yet to be seen. All will depend, we believe, on how the scholarly purpose fares in its reception.

Black Athena appeared at the height of a new multicultural and academic turn whose main focus has been to deconstruct, decenter, demythologize, deideologize, and dehegemonize Western-produced knowledge by creating and empowering alternative points of reference and alternative discourses. It is this postmodern project in Bernal's work which defines its political purpose. Yet Bernal argues that he enters the domain of Eastern Mediterranean studies as an "outsider" and so lacks the ideological mud and emotional investment of the guardians of the Eurocentric status quo. This claim to objectivity has provoked two emotional outbursts, one in defense of Afrocentricity and the other in defense of Eurocentricity.

It is pertinent to distinguish between two projections of Afrocentricity. One is that which restricts itself to the definition of the basic premises which (should) inform African discursive formations by drawing from African conceptual and perceptual realities. This projection of Afrocentricity deconstructs the politics of Eurocentric power/knowledge which has created images of Africa as its marginal Other, but this projection remains cogent and noncombative. Its ideology is unpronounced. The other projection, however, is one which openly declares its anti-Eurocentric war through its theory of Western conspiracy to replace Africa as the genesis of modern civilizations. This projection is built on a variety of historical premises which include a loose sense of PanAfricanism and on the claim to restitute the genesis of modern civilizations to its rightful claimants by writing the "correct" histories. It is this second, "historically correct" projection of Afrocentricity to which Bernal claims his work belongs. The leaders of this projection of Afrocentricity ascribe to Bernal's work a legitimating authority for claims which are not altogether within scholarly confines. I say "not altogether within scholarly confines" because the outbursts of Afrocentrists frequently lack just what is required for discourse in a scholarly framework.

Then there is the perspective which views Bernal's work as only another addition to the list of theories of white conspiracy. This is the position held by Mary Lefkowitz in her long article "Not Out of Africa: The Origins of Greece and the Illusions of Afrocentrists."[45] She classifies *Black Athena* together with Cheikh Anta Diop's *The African Origin of Civilization*, George G. M. James's *Stolen Legacy*, Yosef ben-Jochanan's *Africa, Mother of Western Civilization*, and John G. Jackson's *Introduction to African Civilization*. She also likens Bernal's project to that of Marcus Garvey, although the latter was not a scholar and so lacked the kind of authority with which Bernal persents his own project.

As these two types of reactions show, it is the political purpose of *Black Athena* which has received quicker attention, at least to this point. To this situation there are two simple things that can be said. First, that Bernal's scholarly purpose deserves separation from the political mud. Its strengths and weaknesses can still be discussed within a scholarly framework and in a manner that is both interesting and productive. Second, that the strengths of Afrocentricity, if any, lie in the political rather than in the scholarly domain, and have so far been presented in a manner that is both uninteresting and unproductive.

Another critical commentary on Bernal's work is in spectacle form. It is a film produced by California Newsreel and bears the same title as Bernal's work itself, *Black Athena*. The eminent scholars who speak in it also suggest, like Mary Lefkowitz, that Bernal selects, carefully and uncritically, only the kind of evidence that supports his Afrocentric agenda.

Cristina Brambilla writes:

In such a climate and fervor of African rediscovery, the young black students [in Europe] must have felt themselves wrapped in responsibility, for . . . it was not just a matter of re-evaluating the past civilization, but a matter of re-living and manifesting it today . . . ; not just a matter of being oneself (i.e., African or Caribbean), but of being so at this given time in Paris and in the midst of the Whites.[46]

Negritude and European Philosophy

Within philosophy, and particularly in France, young African students were experiencing a time of formidable challenge to Cartesian rationalism.[47] In the surrealist areas, which most of them frequented, they came into contact with neo-Freudian theories and the revelation of a mysterious life that took place in the subconscious realm and determined the observable superficial (outward) life. In the attempt to reach that inner reality in man, surrealism abolished all barriers between logical thought and dreams, the conscious and the unconscious, the individual and his surrounding world. At the same time, the existentialist movement was also advancing its appraisal of the mystic contact with being. In style it turned toward a description of the spontaneous life of man as the window through which we see being, as Heidegger proclaimed. The history of human life represented for existentialism the endless unfolding of the meaning of being, according to Karl Jaspers. This surrealist and existentialist hostility to the scientistic systematicism and rationalism of Hegel and Descartes, respectively, found a special liking in the heart of negritude, as Aimé Césaire would later write in the following powerful verse in which he identifies Western logocentrism as an instrument of discriminating against others:

Reason I will sacrifice you to the evening wind.
You call yourself the language of order and system?
For me you are the crown of the [colonial] whip
But there are the raw contraband goods of my laughter
My treasure made of saltpetre
Because we hate you
You and your reason
Because we identify ourselves with the *dementia praecox*
Our treasures are therefore the self-thinking madness
The madness that shouts
The madness that frees itself.[48]

The historical point of meeting between the African students in Paris and the personalities of the rebellious Afro-American poets of the Harlem Renaissance came between 1931 and 1932. During this time, a Martinican group led by Paulette (or Andrée) Nardal founded and published six issues of *Revue du Monde Noir* (*The Black World Review*), a bilingual review to which leading exponents of the black movement contributed articles. In addition to the exchange of views in the review, frequent meetings also took place between Africans, Antilleans, and leading Afro-American intellectuals in Paris. In a doctoral thesis on "Alain Locke and the Negro Renaissance," Clare Bloodgood Crane says:

> Senghor wrote that from 1929 to 1934 he and his fellow African students "had contact with the Negro-Americans through the intermediary of Mademoiselle Andree Nardal . . . [who] ran a literary salon where Negro-Africans, Antilleans, and Negro-Americans met." This salon . . . "was frequented notably by the celebrated Professor Alain Locke."[49]

Thus the influence of the Harlem Renaissance upon the birth of negritude was not only from a distance; it was also direct, through personal contacts.[50] From these contacts a movement erupted among black students in Paris. The movement had two separate wings. One, led mostly by the radical students of the Antilles, took the form of a political class struggle in which they vowed to fight against the bourgeois Christian and capitalist Western world through surrealism and communism. Their criticisms of the Western world were made through their paper *Légitime Défense*, published for the first time in Paris in 1932 by Etienne Léro. The other wing, led by the Guyanese Léon Damas, the Martinican Aimé Césaire, and the Senegalese Léopold Sédar Senghor, was much more a cultural movement than a political one (at least at the beginning). While for the founders of *Légitime Défense* political revolution had to precede cultural revolution, for Senghor and his friends politics was but one aspect of culture.

The effective impact of negritude on the black intellectual elites took place only after World War II, despite the fact that Léon Damas had already published his *Pigments* in 1937 and Aimé Césaire his *Cahier d'un retour au pays natal* in 1939. The Second World War appears to have enlightened black intellectuals and militants in a very special way, as Senghor himself confessed to have had a new experience of what Africa must truly be, and it was not the Africa idealized in the poems. "Two years before the war," Senghor said in 1949, "I was still immersed in the drunkenness of the reign of childhood, of the rediscovered *negritude*."[51]

After the war these black intellectuals discovered that it was not possible to build the new negritude only on literary and artistic values, but rather that it must reflect an economic and social evolution by integrating, in an active articulation, the scientific progress of Europe; that it must become a dynamism and a movement; that an African culture had to become a symbiosis of different elements. Senghor, therefore, and in contrast to other exponents of negritude, called for a harmonious integration of black and white values as the basis of the new "African personality."

Senghor had defined culture as the "psychic constitution that, in every people, explains their civilization. In other words, *it is a certain way*, particular to every group, *of feeling, thinking, expressing and acting.*" And this "certain manner" or character is the symbiosis of geographical, historical, racial, and ethnic influences. According to Senghor, the confluence of geographical, historical, racial, and ethnic determinants makes every race different in expression from another. Every race has a fundamental ontological difference from all other races. It is this new negritude, and partly the influences of Gobineau and Teilhard de Chardin, which led Senghor to his famous saying on the epistemological difference between white people and black people; that is, between two systems or modes of thought, one ratiocinative or logocentric, the other emotive:

Emotion is black as much as reason is Greek.

(L'émotion est nègre comme la raison hellène.)

For Senghor, the European is a man of will, a warrior, the bird of prey, pure look, or staring, who differentiates himself from his object. He maintains that object at a distance, immobilizes and fixes it. Armed with the instruments of precision, he dissects it in ruthless analysis. Animated by a will to power, he kills the other and reduces it to a mere instrument for practical purposes. He *assimilates* it. According to Senghor, the European mind considers the universe as an essentially determined, ordered system intelligible to the contemplative and indifferent observer whose primary concern is to discover the natural laws that govern all beings. In this domain, the role of reason is paramount as the power that guides human activity. Man is the *res cogitans*, and his object the *res cogitata*, and truth is the *precision* in the relationship between the cogitative activity and its object—that is, *adaeguatio rei et intellectus*. As is easily noticeable, the center of this epistemology is the *cogitative act* or reason, not as a passive state or faculty, but as an active and aggressive effort to assimilate the object.

In contrast to the cogitative white, the black man is completely different in Senghor's view. He is a man of nature. Traditionally, he is thought to live in, with, and by nature. He is a sensualist, a being with open senses and without an intermediary between subject and object; he is himself subject and object at the same time. He feels more than he sees. It is in himself, in his body, that he receives and tests the radiations emitted by objects of knowledge. He dies to himself to be reborn in the other. He is not assimilated, but assimilates and identifies himself with the other. "This does not mean that the black man has got no reason as others make me say," responds Senghor, "but rather that his reason is not discursive but synthetic; it is not antagonistic, but sympathetic. This is another way of knowing. While the European reason is analytic by utilization, that of the black man is intuitive by participation."[52]

This escape toward the object, Senghor says, is animated by reason. And quoting Marx, he writes, "reason has always existed but not in the rational form." Yet, for Senghor, the African still remains essentially characterized by the emotive faculty—which is not the negation of reason, he warns, but another form of knowledge that nevertheless substitutes for pure reason in the knowing process. That which moves the black man is not the exterior aspect of objects, but rather the essence, or, better still, the *surreality* of nature.

> Water moves him, not because it washes, but because it purifies; fire not because of its heat or colour, but because of its destructive power. The bushes, which dry up and become green again, are symbols of life and death. This is because the exterior aspect of objects, in order to be grasped in its particular singularity (or peculiarity) is but a sign or symbol of the ESSENCE of the object. . . . This implies that the black man is a mystic.[53]

The influence of more than one European school of thought can be traced through these lines from Senghor's works. First there appears to be what Robert Goldwater calls "emotional primitivism," in which the merit of so-called primitive art is that it expresses feeling unmediated by the restrictive and crippling cognitive structures (rational refinements) of the West.[54] Then, in Senghor's metaphysics or mystics of pure essences, there is his preference for the phenomenological school of Edmund Husserl and the existentialism of Martin Heidegger and Karl Jaspers over the sociologically leaning phenomenological analyses of Jean-Paul Sartre. Senghor therefore defends the theory of an African mode of thought as characteristically and essentially different from "the" Western mental scheme, the former surrealistic or mystical, and the latter realistic and objective (scientific).

Even if at times elegantly and eloquently decorated with rhetorical theories borrowed from events connected with leading leftist histories, Senghor's version of negritude has been charged with being a reactionary movement and of being apologetic to the neocolonial culture and imperialist activities of European expansionism. Perhaps the most elaborate of such charges is in Marcien Towa's *Léopold Senghor: Negritude ou Servitude?* (1971).

Despite these charges, the impact of Senghor's epistemological existentialism has been far-reaching. It has been at the roots of the doctrine of African socialism, especially the version expounded and tested by Julius K. Nyerere. In *Some Aspects and Prospectives of African Philosophy Today* (1981), I argued that the failures of Nyerere's *ujamaa* were due, more than anything else, to the poor sociological assessment of the causes of the apparent communalistic "attitudes" in African traditional social relations. This poverty of realism is itself dependent upon another historical conjunct: the intellectual atmosphere prevalent in the 1930s and 1940s and which was so uncritically sympathetic to African traditional situations at the expense of the rising expectations of the African masses. Negritude was itself one of the legitimate children of this atmosphere, alongside neo-Marxism and existentialism. These doctrines, says Mudimbe, had one factor in common: "rediscovering Marx, Freud, and Heidegger, [they] critically re-evaluated the significance of links existing between objectivity and subjectivity, history and reason, essence and existence . . . emphasizing diversely the pertinence and the importance of subjectivity, unconscious existence, relativity of truth, contextual difference and otherness."[55] Taking the communalistic phenomenon of African traditional society as a given, Nyerere proceeded to build upon it a social-political structure—the *ujamaa* system. It is my belief that this epistemological naïveté contributed significantly (although only partially) to the problems of Nyerere's ideal state.

Although Senghorian epistemology pervaded African theological and philosophical works of the 1960s and 1970s, there was an additional influence strongly in play: the Second Vatican Council and its aftermath. Vatican Council II was itself greatly influenced by phenomenology as a new intellectual quest. Through the council, phenomenology gave the church a new theoretical conceptualization, a theological adaptation which was meant to serve the practical, pastoral renewal of the church and, ultimately, of contemporary mankind. In the words of John F. Kobler, "Vatican II was an international demonstration-model of this [phenomenological] methodology as used by an intersubjective community in a corporate and constructive way for renewal purposes in the best tradition of Husserl."[56] Out of the council emerged a powerful mixture of scholastic and phenomenological descriptive styles. So "When the bishops returned 'to the things themselves' as individualized in each one's concrete experience, they each entered their personalized realm of the *mysterium fascinans* as the ultimate ground of religious and human *meaning for them*,"[57] a return to the sources to achieve an in-depth renewal, both philosophical and religious.

In the African context, to use Mudimbe's observation, this new spirit of renewal centered around the "question about the legitimation of an exploratory inquiry: how to reconcile a universal faith (Christianity) and a culture (African) within a scientific discipline (theology) which is epistemologically and culturally marked."[58]

Today, this phenomenological approach is best and most prolifically represented by the Zairean school of Kinshasa, both in philosophy and in religious studies. In philosophy the school is led by Jean Kinyongo, Marcel Ntumba Tshiamalenga, Oleko Nkombe, and B. Ngoma, and also includes the works of the Nigerians Kane C. Anyanwu, Chekwudum Okolo, I. C. Onyewuenyi, and Theophilus Okere. In religion the school is led by Vincent Mulago, Alphonse Mushete Ngindu, Joseph Ntendika, and others, and also includes the Kenyan John S. Mbiti, the Cameroonians Jean-Calvin Bahoken and François Lufuluabo, and the Burundian André Makarakiza, to mention just a few.[59]

Sartre and Negritude

Until the writing of "Orphée Noir," negritude had existed among the black students of Paris more as a state of mind and poetic literary theme than as a theory and program. It found its first systematic definition in the "Orphée Noir," the preface by Jean-Paul Sartre to Senghor's *Anthologie de la nouvelle poésie nègre et malgache de langue française* (1948).

The essay took as its point of departure a parallel analysis of the situation of a white proletariat and that of a black man, both being exploited by the capitalistic structure, and added in conclusion that the two sets of oppression, though essentially the same, were conditioned by diverse historico-geographical factors. In fact, Sartre says, the black man was a victim of such oppression primarily because he was black. His self-awareness should therefore take into consideration first of all the questions of race, not of social class. If the struggle of the proletariat and that of the black man are to have a single conclusion, all the same the final unity which will bind all the oppressed has to be preceded in the colonies by what Sartre called "the moment of separation and of negativity; such anti-racist racism is the only way by which to abolish racial differences."

For Sartre, therefore, negritude was born out of a precise historical situation. It was a response by the budding black intellectuals in Paris who felt the need to react to the imposition of a strange and alienating European culture. According to Sartre, what was important for black people was to die to European culture in order to be reborn in the Negro soul. Negritude was therefore an act of creation and construction. For him, it is not merely a matter of knowing, or of withdrawing into the self as if in a trance, but rather a matter of *discovering* and *becoming* what one authentically is. Negritude was therefore a project or plan of action. It was not enough to feel oneself black, it was also necessary to realize oneself as such.

According to Sartre, therefore, negritude had two dimensions: objective and subjective. The first, which was expressed through the customs, art, songs, and dances of African peoples, was the goal toward which the modern poet was returning voluntarily and consciously in order to arouse once more the immemorial instincts. In so doing, the poets were trying to take on the negritude of their people. Subjectively, negritude is the living and creative symbolism of African civilization as can be found in the quest for the lost paradise. It is passion. Perhaps these distinctions pull an important curtain between Senghor and Césaire, with the former poised more toward an essentialist (ontological) definition of negritude and the latter leaning more toward a negritude seen as a literary phenomenon and as a personal ethic.

In his distinction of the two aspects of negritude, Sartre also distinguished the two Africas present in the movement. One was constituted of the old and dead past. The other is new: the created and invented Africa of the renaissance, of negritude. To Sartre, therefore, Césaire, as poet, does not describe negritude passively as a painter would, but rather he makes it; his work is creative.

Negritude, Sartre said, with its surrealist method, had broken through the superficial logical reason and was leading man to the reign of instinct and the unconscious, the realm of presence and belonging which Sartre defined as "a certain attitude of affection in regard to nature," the being-in-the-world (Dasein) of the black man, a rejection of the *Homo Sapiens*.

The black man had been humiliated by being turned into a slave. Slavery alienated and killed his authentic existence and expression. And negritude, as a movement aiming at overcoming the ills of this phenomenon of slavery, was therefore no longer only a state, nor a mere existential attitude, but a becoming, a making. The contribution of the blacks to the evolution of humanity is no longer only a taste, a rhythm, or a piece of authentic primitive instincts. It is a dedicated enterprise, a patient construction, a future, or a time of dialectic progression in which the white is the thesis and negritude the antithesis. Negritude moves toward a synthesis, a world without races. It is a passage, not a point of arrival, a means, not an ultimate end in itself. And concluding, Sartre writes:

> A painful myth yet full of hope, Negritude, born out of evil yet saturated with a future good, is as lively as a woman who gives birth so as to die, and who feels her own death even in the richest moments of her life, it is an unstable equilibrium, an explosive establishment; a pride that renounces itself, an absolute that is at the same time transitory or finite; for at the same time that it is the annunciator of its own birth and agony, it also captures the existential attitude chosen by free people and lived absolutely even to the dregs. Because it is this tension between a nostalgic past into which the African no longer wholly fits and a future which he will give away to new values, Negritude defends itself with a tragic beauty which will find expression only in poetry.[60]

The Critics of "Orphée Noir"

Among the group of black students preceding that of Senghor, the "Orphée Noir" found its first critic in a Togolese student, Albert Franklin, who made sharp criticisms of those cultural elements which Sartre had claimed to be constitutive of "Negritude-black-essence." Those elements are collectivism, passiveness, and the sense of rhythm in art.

In regard to black intuitive reason, Franklin held that the relationship between man and nature, man and the world, has always been a technical relationship, however rudimentary it may be at any given time. And since it is technical inferiority rather than color which made the blacks victims of the whites, negritude must not be made a magical apprehension of the world. Rather, it is an action, a struggle for progress and for the end of colonialism.[61] Within the environment of Présence Africaine itself, "Orphée Noir" was received with many reservations. Although Allouine Diop recognized the speculative interests offered by the essay and its important historical contribution in inscribing black man and culture into the annals of history, he was still eager to dissociate blacks from the contents of "Orphée Noir." He took exception especially of the phrase that negritude was "an anti-racist racism." Senghor, too, had to rectify this definition of negritude as an anti-racist racism. He asked: "How could we be racists when we have ourselves innocently suffered the tragedy like black hosts of white racism?" The only thing Senghor thought was good in "Orphée Noir" was the epistemological definition of negritude as "a certain affective attitude in regard to nature."[62]

Sartre characterized negritude as a negative moment within a dialectic progress and therefore as a historical moment destined to dissolve and destroy itself into a vaster synthesis. Yet, even this claim was criticized by the exponents of negritude for already dangerously limiting the concept.

Frantz Fanon in particular confessed later that he read such a characterization of negritude with indignation and pain: "When I read those pages, I felt as if they were taking my last chance away from me. Présence Africaine appealed to a friend of the Black peoples, and this friend could not offer anything better than to demonstrate the relativity of their action. Jean-Paul Sartre, in his study, has destroyed Black enthusiasm," he declared.[63] For Fanon, negritude could by no means be described as a mere means bound to die, nor as calling for or giving birth to a new synthesis—a compromise. The new negritude called for by Fanon must take the form of a violent revolution which alone will overcome the dead world of the old negritude and restore the African self fully. Sartre recognizes as much in his later preface to Fanon's book *The Wretched of the Earth* when Sartre says:

> their [Africans'] fathers, shadowy creatures, *your* creatures, were but dead souls; you it was who allowed them glimpses of light, to you only did they dare speak, and you did not bother to reply to such zombies. Their sons ignore you; a fire warms them and sheds light around them, and you have not lit it. Now, at a respectful distance, it is you who will feel furtive, nightbound and perished with cold (when they throw you out). Turn and turn about; in these shadows from whence a new dawn will break, it is you who are the zombies.[64]

Spontaneity, Sartre declared, must give way to a conscious revolution, to action:

> When the peasant takes a gun in his hands, the old myths grow dim, and the prohibitions are one by one forgotten. The rebel's weapon is the proof of his humanity. For in the first days of the revolt you must kill; to shoot a European is to kill two birds with one stone, you destroy an oppressor and the man he oppresses at the same time: There remain a dead man, and a free man; the survivor, for the first time, feels *national* soil under his foot . . . wherever he

goes, wherever he may be, she is; she follows and is never lost of view, for she is one with his liberty.[65]

For Fanon, who frequently paraphrased his ideas in the language of his medical training, there is a specific problem to be solved in the movement of negritude: the disease is alienation, the cause is colonialism, the cure is revolution, and the destiny is freedom, which is the basis of a positive (healthy) humanity. In something similar to Heidegger's metaphysical basis (time) where death is only a door, a means toward being, Fanon presents the theory of violence as the means of achieving this freedom.

In Sartre's reading, Fanon sees violence and possible death as the only valid paths that lead to the synonymity of man with his freedom. The struggle for liberation is a cruel existential drama, full of hard choices which, nonetheless, have to be made. Liberational violence and death produce humanity. Through them new life is born. Sartre writes that

> this new man begins his life as a man at the end of it; he considers himself as a potential corpse. He will be killed; [and] others, not he, will have the fruits of victory; he is too weary of it all. But this weariness of heart is the root of an unbelievable courage. We find our humanity on this side of death and despair; he finds it beyond fortune and death. . . . The child of violence, at every moment he draws from it his humanity.[66]

If these words of Sartre sufficiently reflect Fanon's existentialist analysis of violent liberational struggle as we believe they do, then they also define Fanon's departure from Senghor's brand of negritude. In contrast to the latter, Fanon reintroduces the subject into the center of the quest for identity. For him, identity is not the result of passive appearances as is claimed in the old negritude. The prevailing political conditions in the world, and particularly the political conditions of colonization, clearly dictated for Fanon that identity ought to be defined as constituted of actions which prevent or eliminate political, economic, cultural, and psychological domination. Only violence can truly free the native from his inferiority complex and from his despair and inaction; it is his key to freedom, self-identity, and self-respect.

For Fanon, "spontaneity" had strengths and weaknesses. For him, "spontaneity" is a quality of the lumpenproletariat, their susceptibility to the oppressor's maneuvers against liberation struggle. In this sense, "spontaneity" meant for Fanon lack of political or cultural awareness. A "spontaneous" person is one who lacks a disciplined political standing, and who can therefore be manipulated by any political organization, by the oppressor as well as by the oppressed. He or she is an opportunist. These are the persons who have been conscripted and used in colonial armies against the liberation movements in their own countries—for example, in Algeria, in Angola, and in the Congo. Anybody who believes in "spontaneity" acts in a traitorous manner against the peasant masses.

Fanon thus angrily rejected the "return to the origins" thesis of the old negritude. For him this was but "a futile and desperate attempt by an alienated elite to recapture contact with the masses." He continues:

> But they will not. They will not, because they are creatures of the colonial regimes, and leaders of the western political parties; and also, for the most part, because they do not direct their propaganda towards the rural masses. . . . They do not go out to find the mass of the people. They do not put their theoretical knowledge to the service of the people; they only erect a framework around the people which follows an *a priori* schedule.[67]

These leaders, says Fanon, view the masses with a mistrust that is criminally evident. They are betrayers of the nationalist cause, made to mistrust their own people by colonial strategies bent on the "divide and rule" method of perpetuating their grip on the island colonies. To Fanon, it is the peasantry that precisely constitutes the only spontaneous revolutionary force of a nation, the backbone of a true nationalism, national culture, or national ideology. Here, he again criticizes negritude:

> We must not therefore be content with delving into the past of a people in order to find coherent elements which will counteract colonialism's attempts to falsify and harm. . . . A national culture is not a folklore, nor an abstract populism that believes it can discover the people's true nature. . . . A national culture is the whole body of *efforts* made by a people in the sphere of thought to describe, justify and praise the action through which that people has created itself and keeps itself in existence. A national culture in underdeveloped countries should therefore take its place at the very heart of the struggle for freedom which these countries are carrying on.[68]

Frantz Fanon's is a revolutionary political ideology, since its objective is primarily the achievement of political freedom through the battering of colonialism. But it is also a philosophy, a metaphysics, a critical analysis of the meaning of the being of man through the analysis of his social being. It is a phenomenological ontology, to use an expression from Sartre's philosophy, which had a major influence on Fanon.

In other words, we are branding Fanon as an existentialist. What we have in mind are two facts: First, like the existentialists, Fanon draws a large part of his philosophical thought from the unique concreteness and applicability of personal experience. His philosophy, in a way, is the spelling out of individual commitments. These commitments take their meaning from the fact that they are deeply experienced by the philosopher—in this case by Fanon himself.[69] The pains of these experiences are the subject matter of his two other books, *Black Skin, White Masks* and *For African Revolution*. Second, we are thinking of Sartre, whose thought influenced Fanon in a special way. In his survey of Fanon's political thought, Emmanuel Hansen writes:

In 1947 Fanon went to France to study medicine. He arrived in France when Sartre was at the height of his fame as a writer, a philosopher, a socialist, and an existentialist. And while at the medical school he read the existentialist philosophers: Husserl, Heidegger, and Jaspers. He also read Hegel, Marx, and Lenin. He was greatly influenced by Sartre, especially by his *Anti-Semite and Jew* and later by the *Critique de la Raison Dialectique*.[70]

From these philosophers Fanon inherited key ideas which he was quick to apply to his particular experience: colonialism, alienation (mainly psychological, a concept which he got while working under Professor François Tosquelles, a psychotherapist), revolution, dialectic, freedom, etc. In 1952, Fanon published *Peau Noire, Masques Blancs* (*Black Skin, White Masks*), in which he characterized these concepts in an examination of the inauthentic ontological existence of black people in a white-dominated world, and advocated, under Sartrean influence, existential freedom for blacks, and for all the oppressed peoples of the world.

Fanon was also a committed Marxist. His opposition to the old negritude as an inertia without an end must be evaluated against the background of the Marxist call for a relationship between thought and action, especially as stated in Marx's famous eleventh thesis on Feuerbach, which states that "The philosophers have only *interpreted* the world, in various ways; the point, however, is to change it."[71] Fanon was obsessed with the commitment to change the world in favor of black peoples. It is for this reason that his definition of negritude had to surpass the versions of both Senghor and Césaire. He saw negritude as a historical force.

Fanon saw himself as a thinker with a special mission. Although he grasped and applied the popular philosophical doctrines of his time in his analysis of black experience, he never pursued professional philosophy. His experiences of racism at home, in France, at the front in World War II, and as a medical psychiatrist in Algeria had given him one message: Human value and dignity were in serious crisis. These experiences defined his subsequent mission: to restate and defend human value and dignity at all possible costs. In *The Wretched of the Earth* he writes: "When I search for man in the technique and style of Europe, I see only a succession of negations of man and an avalanche of murders. The human condition, plans for mankind and collaboration between men in those tasks which increase the sum total of humanity are new problems which demand true inventions."[72] In the Marxist fashion, he saw his mission as that of changing the world.[73]

As a Marxist, Fanon did not accept the essentialist theory of thought or of reality. For him, reality is not made up of fixed essences or of fixed identities. Rather, reality is made up of a dialectical process of struggles for identity and self-definition on an equal basis. He rejected the essentialism of negritude as a form of dependent consciousness similar to that of the slave in Hegel's "Lordship and Bondage" paradigm. While Hegel's slave withdraws into the object and submission, Fanon's Negro aspires to be like the master, he aspires toward freedom. This aspiration creates a tension and struggle between the master and the slave who rejects his slavedom. The ensuing struggle is marked with creativity and regeneration. In the words of Gendzier, for Fanon, "It was the tension between an awareness of the mutuality of dependence and the expression of recognition with the implication of equality, that described the course of the struggle which eventually differentiated the person as object, from man as subject."[74] For Fanon, then, knowledge, as a form of consciousness of the self, cannot take place in a passive and essentialist form.

In these senses, Fanon's work sounds like a prelude to the idea of invention so current in the ongoing discourses in the social sciences, particularly in social and cultural anthropology. *Black Skin, White Masks* clearly spells out, in Hegelian terms, the dialectics of the colonialists' creation of their "Other" in the persons of the colonized peoples, in the prototyped image of the Negro. The white man needed his Negro, according to Fanon, to serve as a mirror reflection of what the white man was not. The Negro was a necessary medium for the white man's attainment of self-consciousness. So the white man created in the Negro an indisputable complex of dependence on the white man. In Hegel's terms, "they recognize[d] themselves as mutually recognizing each other." For Fanon, this white man—Negro relationship was a reproduction of a normal existential condition in which "Man is human only to the extent to which he tries to impose his existence on another man in order to be recognized by him. As long as he has not yet been effectively recognized by the other, that other will remain the theme of his actions."[75] Logically and historically, this relationship translates into strife when there is resistance from the Other. To establish the state of reciprocal recognition, there must be a struggle and all the risks that come with it. Yet, only struggle, according to Fanon, establishes the vital truth of recognition as an independent self-consciousness. He cites the following passage from Hegel's *Phenomenology of Mind* to support this dialectical thesis:

> It is solely by risking life that freedom is obtained; only thus is it tried and proved that the essential nature of self-consciousness is not *bare existence*, is not the merely immediate form in which it at first makes its appearance, is not its mere absorption in the extreme of life.[76]

Freedom is central to the thought of Fanon. He saw freedom as a fundamental value for humanity; it is the basic value upon which all other human values must be built. Only in freedom is man able to enact or practice his abilities, intellectual and physical, and hence realize himself. In freedom, in the Sartrean sense, man creates himself. Freedom is the basic presupposition of authentic expression and action. In this way Fanon sides with Sartre in opposing to the rigidity and dogmatism of Marxism wrongly interpreted the insights of existentialism. These insights replace the dogmatic dialectic of Marxism with a critical dialectic that would follow the movement of history itself. In other words, Sartre and Fanon tried to see man not as a hopeless pawn of a dogmatic dialectic, as a passive victim of the "forces of history," but as one who, if not in charge of his own destiny, should at least be aware of it. These "forces of history" had modeled or molded the man of negritude, compelling him into withdrawal and mere exhibitionist demonstration. The man of negritude is a victim of intellectual, cultural, economic, and political castration. In negritude, black people are represented as having felt satisfied with merely singing praises in admiration of each other, exalting their ontological essence—blackness. While black people engaged in this pressure exercise, the cunning white man took advantage of their passiveness and continued to exploit them. This meant that for a black man truth and reality lay in his being-outside-himself, in the practice-inert weight of the reality around him, absolutely depersonalized; thus reduced, he was an alien in his own country. Fanon deplored the Senghorian school of negritude as utterly inadequate for the rehabilitation of black cultures. For Fanon, there was need to shift focus from the ethnic to the national level of concern.

At the ethnic level, the black man's freedom was truly doomed. And it is here that Fanon insisted upon revolution as a means of salvation, for if man was forced to live within certain given limitations, he was, on the other hand, always free to revolt against them.

Violence, according to Fanon, is the instrument of alienation. In all its three (physical, psychological, and cultural) aspects, violence has been ably used by Western powers to alienate and dominate black people. The colonized blacks were alienated both materially and mentally. Hansen writes: "Politically too, the colonized person is alienated. The colonizer controls his political destiny. He is not allowed any meaningful participation in the political processes which affect him. Hence he does not express his authentic existence. . . . This alienation is expressed in terms of a feeling of inferiority, self-hatred and other directedness vis-à-vis the white oppressor. It is also expressed in immutability and the seeking of external reference—that is, white reference—to validate his behaviour" and thinking.[77]

Although it has been important to treat Fanon here in connection with the movement of negritude, his thought rightly belongs to a later and much more critical period than that of the rise of African philosophy.

The transition from Senghor's negritude through Sartre's "Orphée Noir" to Fanon's revolutionism is a paradigmatic model of the kind of dialecticism that Fanon himself advocated. Fanon was born into a new heritage dominated by a feeling of collectivism within the process of racial-cultural salvation and redefinition. While he shared the major premises of this collective experience, he injected into it a new (if not revolutionary) feeling of subjectivism about the role of the individual in the revolutionary undertaking. Fanon considered elitism to have a key role in the revolutionary process. The intellectual and political elites must exist and unite to give leadership to the masses. For him, as much as the masses need to be led into political activism as an uncompromising revolutionary force, they also need to be educated about the proper political and cultural awareness. Collectivism alone, like negritude, he believed, can only lead to a vicious circle.

Fanon must have seen himself as combining the different (but related) roles of intellectual and political elitism. He accomplished the former through his powerful writings and the latter through his political activism in Algeria. More important, however, has been his intellectual activity. Yet, as remarkably clear as was Fanon's role in intellectual activity in general and philosophy in particular, African philosophers neither echoed nor did any serious studies of Fanon's radical existentialism until nearly fifteen years after his death. Instead, African philosophy lapsed back into the descriptive collectivism from which Fanon had so much tried to liberate it.

Jahn's Contribution

Black intellectuals and students were not the only critics who rejected Sartre's analysis and representation of negritude. Janheinz Jahn, another European intellectual who played an equally important role in the definition of African culture, never agreed with Sartre either. For Jahn, Sartre had wrongly interpreted negritude out of the historical situation offered by André Breton's surrealism, which, in its turn, is grounded on the influence offered it by Freudian psychoanalysis. "But in the light of an acquaintance with African philosophy," says Jahn, "it is difficult to see what neo-African poetry could have to do with all this."[78] Although Sartre rightly identified some aspects of "African philosophy," Jahn holds, he failed to dissent sufficiently from Breton's assertions. Sartre saw only a small proportion of this "philosophy." In his analysis of Aimé Césaire's poetry, Sartre had strongly insisted on the personal sensations of "inflexibility" and the desire for revenge, which are individual feelings. Jahn views this emphasis as unimportant, for "in reality the neo-African poet is not primarily concerned about his own ego. He is Muntu, man, who speaks and through the word conquers the world of things." Jahn continues: "As a poet he is the representative of all, and as representative he is a poet. . . . 'Inflexibility' and 'hate' are nothing but forces which he uses; [for] neo-African poetry is Nommo; that is, it is function above all else, and thus the very opposite of surrealism."[79]

In Jahn's view, Sartre only understood, like many Europeans, unrest, reproach, and rebellion in neo-African poetry; "that was what Europe expected; that was to be understood. What was not understood was interpreted as surrealism."[80]

Again to Jahn, " 'Negritude' could not be the phenomenon of a particular time," because not all the poems of negritude are influenced by the historical situation of white racism and colonialism. Negritude was destined to create and make, rather than merely to express. It was an act destined to lift the curfew imposed on the African spirit and on authentic initiative. Negritude, in its Senghorian essentialist definition as the whole complex of civilized values, had always existed, Jahn thought, and its residual African elements are always visible in the past and present works and behaviors of all black people, in Africa as well as in the Americas. The emergence of that body of poetic literature described as "poetry of negritude" is but the expression of these values in foreign languages—in English, French, Portuguese, or Spanish; or, as Jahn often prefers, these foreign languages are turned African such that they no longer appear as English, French, or Spanish. In apparent reference to the free-style poetry of negritude, and to the powerful neologisms of Césaire, Jahn asserted that the language of negritude had in fact become strange even to its original speakers. African literature takes issue with the age and follows the traditional style even in European languages. It assimilates European elements into African conceptions and expressions. What the colonial and racial evils of Europe accomplished, Jahn argued, was not the creation of negritude, for this had always existed; they only opened up a collective consciousness of the self of black peoples.

Yet, like Sartre, and despite his indispensable contribution to the study of African thought, Jahn has remained a victim of some harsh criticism, from Africans themselves as well as from outsiders. In reference to Jahn's book, William E. Abraham, a Ghanaian philosopher, says that

> his [Jahn's] work does not respond at all to depth soundings. It is best described as a piece of journalism. His idea of African culture is of a mixture of Western suavity of Senghor and anything which African politicians and other men of influence may choose to believe of their own past, for, Jahn says, what they believe is what is effective, and for this reason alone must be true, not in any sense of being connected with evidence, but simply because it has been said. . . . Jahn's work has thrusting airs of being sympathetic, but [it is] pernicious."[81]

While Abraham's criticism may be partly justified, there is also some truth in saying that the nature of present African culture is, realistically and historically, the outcome of the contact between "Westernism" and old African traditions. Each has modified the other, such that what we now have is in many ways the "complex" referred to by Jahn as the "new" African culture, the bastard or "half-caste" born of the native-stranger contact. But which human culture, after all, does not possess elements of "foreign" influence? Jahn does not explore the depths of "African philosophy," but what he has done cannot be totally disapproved. He may have exaggerated some of his ideas (as for example when he argues that modern art and dance, both in Europe and in the Americas, owe their origins to Africa, or that Europe has nothing to compare with "African philosophy"), but he argues them with passion.[82]

Jahn thus attributed the residual permanence of the African past in the present to an underlying "African philosophy." He sees the best example of this philosophy in the exposition of the blind sage Ogotemmêli (see below, chapter 3). According to Jahn, then, African philosophy could be said to consist of three structural levels in their historical progression. At the bottom are the beliefs and practices of the people: their religious beliefs and rituals as well as their language and moral codes. This level forms the foundation of discourse because the beliefs and practices produced in it shape or determine the ways in which the people who culturally share them acquire and adapt new perceptions and construct new forms of knowledge. In other words, the basic beliefs, almost universally, are the foundations upon which new realities are erected. The basic beliefs are already there (*déja là*), even as new experiences mingle with them to produce new forms of cultural expression. The second level consists of expositions, chronicles, and explications of the foundational beliefs and practices into a system. These expositions reveal the interconnectedness of the foundational beliefs and practices by giving them a theoretical form and unity. The works of Placide Tempels, Marcel Griaule, Germaine Dieterlen, Maya Deren, Alexis Kagame, and Vincent Mulago are good examples of this level. The works of John Mbiti, Jean-Calvin Bahoken, François Lufuluabo are other inclusions in the trend which has come to be widely known as ethnophilosophy pioneered by Tempels. The third level consists of critical discourses on the first two levels.

The concept of *déja là* (already there) was produced as a critique of the practice of ethnophilosophy. It addresses the absence of the subject as well as the lack of creativity and originality in the works of those who practice simple exposition of the foundational beliefs. Ethnophilosophers themselves limit their role to that of chronicler and translator. As chroniclers they only record what is already there (*déja là*). As translators, however, they achieve a certain degree of creativity because they not only transform the oral into script, but they also give the transcripted thought new linguistic and conceptual forms that make the oral, the *déja là*, theoretically accessible. The question as to whether the *déja là* could in themselves constitute philosophy became a central focus of anti-ethnophilosophy critiques, particularly the works of Franz Crahay (1965) and Paulin Hountondji (1970, 1971, 1972, 1977, 1983).

Jahn of course eagerly analyzed other examples to match his view, for, he said, "at the basis of all this [whole systems of thought, as exemplified by Ogotemmêli's exposition of Dogon worldview and religious system] we find philosophical principles which agree with the analyses of Tempels, Deren,[83] Dieterlen, and Kagame."[84] In this sense not only did Jahn exalt negritude and African culture, but he also became the first historian of African philosophy. And, at least on this level, Jahn's *Muntu* becomes indispensable to any study of African Renaissance.

In conformity with the structure produced by Jahn, Reverend E. Dirven, in a course entitled *Explication philosophique de textes africains* given at the Major

Seminary of Mayidi in Zaire in the academic year 1972–73, divided the history of "African philosophy" into three parts. The first part of this history deals with the conceptual content of traditional worldviews. In critical terms, it questions the philosophical import in the practice of reaffirming the *déja là*. The second part deals with the negations of the philosophical pretensions attributed to the *déja là* by ethnophilosophers; and the third part consists of research into the nature of philosophizing. Here, negritude is not only considered as an important influence on contemporary African thought, it is also defined as a stage in the history of this thought. And Jahn was the greatest exponent of such a position.

Despite the bitter criticisms against both Sartre's and Jahn's works, these writers (and many others who will be mentioned later in this work) launched a respected representation of the Western world's recognition of Africa's presence in world history. This constitutes the second part of the history of "African philosophy" in the Dirven lectures mentioned above. Men of dedication, both Africans and outsiders, began to toil on the exposition of African values under various branches of knowledge. Various commissions were formed by the Unity of Black Writers and Artists, which, in turn, owes its origin to the negritude movement. It is then not a surprise that a Commission of Philosophy was formed, alongside others, at the Unity's first congress in Paris in 1956. But by this time, the existence of "African philosophy," in the ethnophilosophical sense, had already been taken for granted and, on the whole, the negritude movement, the negritude of Senghor, had influenced its origin and given it its form.

Recapitulation

At the beginning, African philosophy did little more than echo the premises which had been expressed by the Harlem Renaissance and negritude movements. Its characteristics became the unreserved and eloquent defense of African traditions, but that defense was "expressed in imitation of the dominant Western culture as the validation standard." The view was that Africa had a duty to accomplish, and this was to identify and define all the material and psychological constituents of her civilization. This was not difficult, since every culture has different aspects that can be classified into these two categories. What was even more important was to redress these material and psychological values in a manner likely to make them acceptable to the highly ethnocentric (or Eurocentric) Western world, by claiming the essential differences of the "pure" African from the "pure" European. By likening themselves to their European counterparts, African intellectuals thought they would make themselves and their cultures at least un-rejectable and un-dominatable by Europeans. The result was a struggle over the control of identity by means of the definition of reason, its nature and its functions. The point of reference of this struggle is the definition of reason as established in the Western Renaissance period. According to this definition, which became the distinctive mark of Western rationality or mode of thought, scientific explanation was seen as consisting of stating the conditions of any event and showing how the event depends upon the conditions, thus consequently formulating universal laws for judging all future events. In contrast to this, the early exponents of the black struggle for identity saw black rationality as consisting in a passive, spontaneous, subjective, and magical or, as Lévy-Bruhl called it in *Les Carnets*, mystical mode of thought.

There was no consensus about the nature of the relationship between these two modes of thought. Neither was there unanimity about the nature of the dispute itself—whether it was about the functions of either, or just about the constitutive nature of each of the two modes of thought. In fact, Lévy-Bruhl tried to indicate the dual nature of the dispute, pointing out effectively that it was wrong to generalize the dispute without regard to the difference between roles or functions of reason and its nature. The dispute has continued to the present day, however, in total disregard of this distinction.

The radical members of the Harlem school defended the view of the separate natures of the two modes of thought and argued that they were independent systems, each founding separate and incommensurable models of rationality. The moderate radicals of the Senghorian school saw the two models of rationality as metaphysically compatible and complementary, although incommensurate. Still others, such as Cheikh Anta Diop, Henry Olela, and Martin Bernal, looked at the whole problem from a reversed point of view: that it is Europe which has arrogantly and illegitimately identified itself with what was originally not its own. They argue that the elements of scientific and mathematical thinking which have become such important identities of Western rationality and factors of sorting out "Others" are indeed historically African in origin. We have said that these claims were made in the spirit of politically disengaged academic practice. But they have lent more credence to outbursts which are not altogether strictly confined within pure academic practice. The works of Diop, and more recently those of Bernal, for example, have been extensively invoked and cited as legitimizing authorities for outbursts of Afrocentrism. Nothing could be more perverse and tainting. However, if the strengths of Diop's, Olela's and Bernal's works were initially seen as fascinating intellectual tactics or strategies of shattering the European illusion of intellectual, cultural, and historical superiority, these works were quickly regressed into a passive and unproductive intellectual narrative. Whatever the solutions to these disputes, the characteristic differences between the identified modes of thought were to prove crucial and determinant factors for the directions which the subsequent discussions in and on African philosophy took.

It is important to note, as we have tried to show above, how African philosophy became a natural child of the disputes between the Harlem Renaissance and negritude movements on the one hand and Westernism on the other over the nature and functions of reason. But Harlem Renaissance and negritude movements were not the only factors to influence the rise of "written" African philosophy. There were other factors in the interplay. The pre-World War II European philosophical movements of neo-Marxism, phenomenology, existentialism, and surrealism,[85] with their general revolt against the Hegelian transcendental objectivism and "system," turned toward a type of irrationalism emphasizing the spontaneity of man's "bare" existence as constituting the search for meanings or essences. And they thereby displayed sympathy for the African cultural situation. African experience offered rich examples of the mythological narratives and unsophisticated religious beliefs and observances which had been given so prominent a position in the existentialist philosophies of Karl Jaspers, Martin Heidegger, and, to an extent, Gabriel Marcel.

To the members of the Senghorian school, therefore, it was obvious that some aspects of African culture constituted a philosophy in the traditional sense. What was important was to inform the Western world about the good news. This was the beginning of putting into writing what was conceived to be already there, the *déja là*—the beliefs of the people, broadly conceived as the basic premises which define and guide customs. In this sense the *déja là* were taken to be the sort of abstractions which form an integral and essential part of any human culture or civilization. In adopting these existentialist analyses, another property was added to the ones already thought of as making up the nature of man: human life, as such, was thought of as constituting a process of interpretation of and giving meaning to the reality of experience. In this sense, existentialist philosophers usually view life as a "search for truth," a spontaneous but valid form of philosophizing.

The writing of this philosophy was considered a matter of necessity. Because the old Western representations of Africans had to be deconstructed, it was necessary that the Western world be informed of the new (or real) truth through a means that it was familiar with: writing. Africans themselves need not be informed, because they already live the "philosophy"; they are the living book of life. This shows clearly the rupture between the written and the implicit versions (if we may call them so) of African philosophy. Thus the written "African philosophy" emerged as part of Western discourse rather than as an African discourse on itself.

The first person to record this "philosophy" was not an African. He was a white Franciscan missionary, Placide Tempels, who probably wrote his little book, *Bantu Philosophy*, in the service of another Eurocentric ambition and interest. After him, however, a host of Africans can be named who have built his ideas into a school of thought or a trend within the study of African philosophy and who fashionably dominated the field until the late sixties. Furthermore, African philosophy as defined by this school is typified by the practice of directly translating African traditional experiences into the categories and language of

European philosophy and other related disciplines. It is largely due to this practice that the school has come to be popularly known as ethnophilosophy.

Although the scholars of ethnophilosophy are still lively and prolific, a new school sprang up after 1965 with a more critical approach to the study of African philosophical thought and practice. Its focus was the critique of the uses and meaning of the word *philosophy* in ethnophilosophical literature. In a larger sense, this debate is unquestionably part of a recent and wider need to deal with the definitional crisis which has faced philosophy as a discipline. As Mudimbe argues, this critique is part of Western discourse, both on itself and on others, because it derives its convictions from and maintains links with the established Western tradition of philosophy and the structures of Western academic philosophical practice.[86] The critiques are part of Western philosophy's new phase of self-questioning. The answer to this issue of the definition of philosophy may not be anywhere near accomplishment—a fact which, in the nature of academic or professional philosophy, is quite acceptable. What is important to note here is the indebtedness of the contrasts between ethnophilosophers and their critics to similar contrasts between, on the one hand, the movements of the Harlem Renaissance and African consciousness of the early 1900s in the Americas and the islands of the Atlantic and the negritude movement started in Paris in the 1930s, and, on the other, the Western scientific/positivistic views of philosophizing. History is never linear and stagnant. So if we today find shortcomings in the theories and ideas formulated at that time, we must appreciate that the early ethnophilosophers initiated something which we are today bound to modify or even reject and replace.

To appreciate fully the historical importance of earlier trends in the African philosophical movement, it is vital to see that movement in relation to its origin—as part of the entire liberation movement based on race. Thus even the extreme cases of Césaire's and Senghor's celebration of madness, emotionalism, and irrationality as essences of Africanism must first be seen as a metaphorical defensive strategy, a rejection of reason and rationality as absolutist forms of Westernism. As Leonard Harris states, in the spirit of deconstructive and structuralist postmodernism, "philosophy is invariably tied to social reality. . . . The mode of doing philosophy, e.g., its methods, dominant issues, questions, and schools of thought vary as society changes."[87] Philosophy is a form of social expression, both vertically (historically) and horizontally (anthropologically). It is in this view that there is need to create a new philosophy to cope with the present. The challenge to African philosophers lies in making philosophy an African discourse.

What is common to all these movements, and directly significant to early developments in African philosophy, is that they all emphasize a sort of philosophy of individual subjectivity. This doctrine goes back to the resurgence of reason in the seventeenth century, but it enjoyed prominence as a subject of philosophical attention first in the philosophy of Søren Kierkegaard. In the rhetorics of the Negro renaissance, in the epistemological paradox of Senghor, this existentialist view blends well with a phenomenological reevaluation of the world torn by strife to the brink of moral and sociocultural disintegration. Convinced that the fragmentation of the world into greater and lesser cultures and humanisms was due to an overly narrow view of human values, the early exponents of African philosophy offer a unique application of both existentialist and phenomenological philosophies for the practical purposes of moral and sociocultural renewal. Philosophy needed a new approach capable of uniting the different cultures and peoples of the world. Out of this new approach would develop a radically new experience and a fresh new attitude toward reality, an attitude quite reminiscent of the Husserlian slogan *Back to the things themselves*. In this mindset, all cultures were to be seen as good in themselves on the basis of internal structural completeness. So black cultures too had to be explained in terms of their unity with each other and with the whole. It was this explanation of unity that was to be called *philosophy*.

This philosophy, as we shall see, was to be marked sharply by its *difference* from others, and the difference of others from it. Whether or not the emphasis of this otherness or difference was not itself further estranging cultures from each other was never debated until the onset of the new school of professional philosophers, probably better called the school of conceptual pragmatists, including Boulaga, Towa, Hountondji, Wiredu, Mudimbe, Odera, Bodunrin, and many others.

This group has persistently argued that an overplay of contextual relativism in philosophy on the basis of cultural differences is a futile exercise that can only progress toward ethnographical narrations. Such developments turn historico-cultural realities into cages of philosophy rather than springboards for creative intellectual exercise. The onset of professional African philosophy thus brings a crucial change in emphasis—the universal. This has proved to be the dominant concern for most members of this school, whether they have been occupied with the questions of the definition of philosophy, as Hountondji is, or with more specialized concepts in philosophy, as Wiredu is. This fundamental debate has been at the center of African renewal. As V. Y. Mudimbe writes, "All of the social and human sciences have undergone this radical experience between 1960 and 1980. Fundamentally, it is based on 'the right to truth' and so far implying a new analysis of three paradigms: philosophical ideal versus contextual determination, scientific authority versus socio-political power, and scientific objectivity versus cultural subjectivity."[88]

The history of African philosophy is therefore the history of Africa in a very special way. It is the history of Africanism in its critical expressions and articulations. This intellectual quest precedes and forms the foundations for the diversified attempts to deconstruct the old colonial sciences. History took the lead in the 1950s, followed by literature in the 1960s and political science and sociology in the 1970s. At the base of the revolutions of the 1960s, of the transfer of intellectual leadership and administrative authority in general to management by Africans themselves, rests this search for new ideas and new forms of abstraction.

2 | Tempels and the Setting of Ethnophilosophy

THE HONOR OF having brought the first piece of literature concerning "Bantu (or African) philosophy" into academic philosophical discussion is attributed to Father Placide Frans Tempels.

Father Tempels's famous work, *La Philosophie bantoue*, is based on his observation of the behavior and study of the language of the Bantu people (the Shaba Baluba of Zaire) among whom he had worked for a number of years. Life and death, as Tempels had observed among both Christian Europeans and the Bantu, seemed to condition human behavior universally. Even the *evolués*, the "civilized" Christians among the Bantu, *return* (fall back) to their old ways "because their ancestors left them their practical solutions to the great problems of life and death, of salvation and destruction."[1] Now these "solutions," which are based on fidelity to magical interpretations of life and on magical practices, are, he says, "conceptions which, in the course of centuries, have persisted and have been embraced by entire peoples."

Tempels consequently suggests that the only satisfactory explanation of this persistence is that these conceptions must be found within a body of logically coordinated and motivated thought, within a "Lore," since no behavior can be universal or permanent through time "if it has not got at its base, a body of ideas, a logical system, a complete positive philosophy of the universe, of man, and of the things that surround him, of existence, of life, of death and of the life beyond."[2]

Having observed the frequent return by the "civilized" Bantu Christians to their old ways of behavior, Tempels sets off to "postulate, seek and discover a logical system of human thought as the ultimate foundation of any logical and universal system of human behavior," since "no live code of behavior is possible unless the meaning of life is sensed."[3]

It would be good, therefore, for those who have been called to live among the "primitives," for the colonials and, in a particular way, for the missionaries, or generally for those people of good will who want to civilize, educate, and elevate the Bantu, to know this system of "Lore" that is the base of their behavior. For, "In effect," he says, "if the primitives have a particular conception of being and of the universe, this proper ontology will offer a special character, a logical color, to their beliefs and religious practices, to their humors, to their law, to their institutions and customs, to their psychological reactions and, more generally, to the whole of their behavior."[4] According to Tempels, anybody working among the Bantu needs to understand their ontology, because even their logic depends on it. Apart from mere physical or chemical explanations of diseases and deaths, for example, the Bantu also no less believe in their "metaphysical" causes. Whoever understands this ontology penetrates into the "soul" of the Bantu. The gulf dividing the blacks and whites will therefore "remain and even widen for as long as we [whites] do not meet them in the wholesome aspirations of their ontology."[5] Ontology, according to Tempels, defines the subject matter and the laws of inference in African discourse.

According to Tempels, all aspects of Bantu customs, including religion and magic,[6] "lie on the unique principle, the recognition of the intimate nature of things, that is to say, on the principle of their ontology. For it is only this philosophical term that can best designate their knowledge of being and of the existence of things."[7] The entire system of Bantu thought based on this ontology is what Tempels calls "philosophy" in his work, though he confesses not to be able to convince his readers—the missionaries and colonial administrators—"that a true philosophy can exist among the natives, and that there is sense in searching for it."[8]

It is important to note two different but related issues in Tempels's definition of what he calls Bantu (or African) philosophy. The first issue concerns his use of the verb *return* to describe Africans' continued regard for their traditional models of belief and knowledge even after their apparent conversion to Christianity. The use of the verb *return* describes Tempels's own position of judgment in a comparison or contrast of two representational images. With it, he declares his stand in the politics of representation. Tempels contrasts two models of belief and knowledge which, for him, are utterly irreconcilable. One includes traditional religious belief systems and magical explanations of life, and is identified with African traditional thought systems. Its opposite, which is identified with Western traditions, puts together Christian religious beliefs and scientific knowledge. The former, for him, is the paradigm of irrationality. From a religious point of view it is marked with darkness, and epistemologically with ignorance. The second mode of thought, on the other hand, is represented as more rational and summary of the destiny of human nature and history; it is characterized by religious light and scientific truth. In this sense, to "return" (from light and truth, acquired through conversion, back to darkness and ignorance) signifies a "fall," or "regression" on the part of Christian converts.

The second issue, which we shall consider later, concerns the use of the concept of ontology to describe what is to be defined as Bantu (or African) philosophy.

The Ontology of the Bantu

Since Tempels was writing primarily for European readers, there are two things that he calls to attention. First, he notes that it is he, and not "the Bantu," who is making an analysis of Bantu "philosophy"; that is, that beginning with their observable behavior and their language, he wants to expose the first and general principles on which these stand, that is, their ontology. In this sense, Tempels attempts to make a distinction between philosophical practice and the domain of ontological existence. While he does the former, the Bantu merely perform as actors in the latter. Second, this ontology, since it is expounded for European readers, will be expressed in Western philosophical terms to make it accessible to its intended readers. This will be done by the systematic exposition of a theory, often preceded by the analysis of those examples (expressions or behavior of the Bantu) from which the theory emerges.

According to Tempels, the Bantu conception of life is centered on one cardinal value, which is life force, or vital force (in French, *force vitale*). "The vital force is the invisible reality of everything that exists, but is supreme in man. And man can reinforce his vital force by means of the forces of other beings of creation."[9] The Bantu talk in terms of either gaining, reinforcing, losing, or diminishing this force. For the Bantu, all beings of the universe possess their proper vital force: human, animal, vegetable, or inanimate.

To talk of inanimate things as having a *vital* force sounds rather strange. It seems that Tempels does not use the adjective *vital* as a derivative of the Latin noun *vita* (in French *la vie*), which means, in its English translation, biological life. In his explanations, Tempels uses the French phrase *la force vitale* to mean a certain property which underlies all things. But this may be an understatement of what Tempels subsequently says of *la force vitale*. To him, force is the very essence of beings. This is why, as we shall see below, he equates being with force (Being = force), just as we would analytically equate "animal + reason = man." This force, according to Tempels, is as much the essence of a mouse, a tree, a cow or a human as it is of a stone, a footprint, soil, or a piece of cloth.

Among the created forces, man stands in the center. Creation is centered on man. The human generation living on earth is the center of the universe, which includes the world of the dead. Through mediums, who serve as a bridge, the living maintain a constant relationship with the dead. The worst misfortune that can befall the dead is the inability to enter into relationship with those still living on earth. Thus, it is when the dead can no longer enter into contact with the living that they are said to be "completely dead."[10] The inferior forces (animals, plants, and minerals) have been created by God in order to help man increase his force here on earth.

The influence of forces on one another is based on three general laws of interaction. First, a person (living or deceased) can directly reinforce or diminish the being of another person. Second, the human vital force can directly influence inferior force-beings (animal, vegetable, or mineral) in their being itself. And third, a rational being can influence another rational being by communicating his force to an inferior force-being. Fortune and misfortune, and all that which has been termed "magic," says Tempels, have their explanation in the foregoing laws and are known and permitted by God.

Tempels's theory of the vital force finds its filiation in the philosophy of Henri Bergson, which is characterized by dualism and dynamism. Bergson's dualist view posits a vital principle, the *élan vital*, in contrast to inert matter. Tempels also makes this contrast when he compares the concept of vital force in Bantu ontology with the static "being" in Greek thought. For Bergson's dualistic philosophy, the world is divided into two disparate portions: on the one hand, life, and on the other, matter. For him, life is one great force, one vast vital impulse, given once and for all from the beginning of the world; the whole universe is the clash and conflict between life and matter; and it is this conflict of two opposite motions of life and matter, rather than natural selection, that accounts for evolution.

But there are also significant differences between Bergson's *élan vital* and the Bantu vital force. First, Bergson's dualism makes a clear distinction between the force and the matter on which it works change. In contrast, the Bantu, according to Tempels, appear *not to be able* to make this distinction; for them matter and force merge into a unity in which force subordinates matter under its dynamism. Being is force, declares Tempels. Second, Bergson's undeterministic metaphysics of the tension between force and matter has the sufficient power or impulse to create. For their part, the Bantu, as described by Tempels, accept determinism by positing the central human role in the determination of the results of the fusions of vital forces.

Bantu Wisdom

The concept of vital force is therefore integrated into all aspects of human life, as the most fundamental base of reality. Wisdom has its significance in relation to vital force. Wisdom means the knowledge of forces and of their effects; it consists of being able to give explanations of certain happenings in relation to their causes. Wisdom is simply "metaphysical" knowledge. Because wisdom is the penetrating knowledge of things in terms of forces and their laws of interaction, it is attributed first and foremost to God. The Baluba say in face of danger, "*Vidye uyukile*," which means "God knows," and which also implies that "the happening has its reason."[11] The knowledge man has of forces therefore derives from God. From God man gets the power of wisdom as he gets the power of "willing." Wisdom is itself force.[12] Because such knowledge of forces is a conception of life, it is a public commodity that preoccupies every individual among the Bantu, though there are some systems of explaining it reserved to people of particular social ranks within the group.[13] This latter kind of wisdom, says Tempels, is different from natural knowledge. "The Bantu distinguish in the visible being between its exterior appearance and the being-in-itself, or the invisible force."[14] But in order to be able to detect the forces in case of danger, more and better knowledge is required. A deeper knowledge of the interaction of forces than the ordinary one possessed by every *muntu* (human) is needed. Hence the significance of "magicians" and "diviners," who are the specialists.[15]

A wise person is one who is able to explain and interpret events in terms of their deeper and metaphysical causes. In so doing, he or she gains access to the solutions of the problems of life. Everyone in the community depends on and looks upon such a person as one who holds the means to happiness. Such knowledge is admired and desired by all. Yet it is also feared at the same time. Those who possess it not only have to bear much responsibility for the welfare of their communities, they also are constant objects of fear and suspicion in cases of misfortune. Those in power regard them, openly or secretly, as potential challengers of their positions. Even in contemporary society, African intellectuals, as repositories of knowledge, have continued to live under this ambiguity of status. As much as his knowledge is needed in the task of construction and development, the intellectual is constantly blamed for unrest and misguidance of the youth and the public in general. In return for his services, he receives mistrust, suspicion, hate, and, not infrequently, detention without trial and even mysterious disappearance.

More than anyone else, therefore, Africans seem to be haunted most times by the Baconian value of knowledge: its power. For many African leaders, knowledge has a paradoxical and magical value, and is consequently paradoxically treated. Although its constructive value is widely acknowledged, its power is feared or even hated; its authority is frequently, easily, and conveniently misinterpreted; although it is good to have it, it is more convenient and stabilizing to stifle it. This is certainly one of Africa's greatest persistent and historically consistent contradictions. Africans hate most what they need most. The suppression of knowledge and the resultant brain-drain remain Africa's foremost cause of underdevelopment and sociopolitical instability.

Bantu Psychology

The section of Father Tempels's book dealing with Bantu psychology, the theory of *muntu*, is of particular interest, as Edwin W. Smith remarks, though it inevitably contains some repetition.

The values seen in Bantu ontology apply also to their psychology. Vital force, increase of force, and mutual influence between forces are the three notions necessary in Bantu psychology. But they must be seen within the context of the three ontological laws that form the base of all Bantu knowledge or wisdom. The world of creation is seen to be centered on man. Man is the most powerful among all created beings. Other, inferior beings are created by God for the mere purpose of helping man to increase his force. But what makes man superior among all nature? According to Tempels, man, the *muntu*, is an active cause, he exercises vital force. Every man is an existent force in himself, a living force. This inner and deep nature of man is the center of his individuality and has, as its outward symbol, "the name of being"—*Dijina dya munda*. Names give individual persons their specific positions within the "community" of forces. By acquiring a name, every person becomes a link in the chain of forces linking the dead and the living genealogies. No one is isolated. Every person makes part of that chain of forces in nature, both active and passive.

Bantu Ethics

Not even morality can be divorced from this ontology, from the ordered unity of beings in the interaction of forces. The value of life is attributed to God as "he who summons it into being, strengthens and preserves it."[16] For all living organisms life is the vital force; hence, to go against the life of another is to diminish his or its vital force. "Every act, every detail of behavior, every attitude . . . against vital force or against the increase of the hierarchy of the *muntu* is bad."[17] Thus, the moral ladder is derived from that of ontology. To defend his rights, *muntu* turns once more to his ontological principles, and hence the consequence of his attachment to his fundamental wisdom and to his "philosophy"; and this knowledge of good and evil, the knowledge of being good or bad, of acting right or wrong, conforms to and agrees with the same "philosophy" and wisdom.

According to Tempels, the moral quality of human actions, in the framework of Bantu ontology, depends on whether such actions contribute to the stability or instability of the hierarchical order of forces. Actions which contribute to the stability of this order are judged morally good, while those which create instability are seen as morally bad. Morally bad acts create disorder in the relations of forces. The actions of a witch who causes illness to his/her victim are a good example of how such disorder is created. The witch's victim gets ill because the witch communicates his or her vital force to other forces with intention to cause harm. In this sense, the witch is both a causal and a moral agent whose actions are believed to be responsible for the victim's fate.

From this point we can move on to another. There might be more immediate causes of the fate of the victim described above. If the victim has been bitten by a snake, for example, the Bantu will certainly recognize as much. But their world is not made of contingent or accidental events. It is a world designed and controlled by intelligence and will. Will, which is the seat of humans' moral quality, makes humans the "real" causal and moral agents for most of the events in their social world. In this sense, a snakebite may be a necessary but not a sufficient cause of its victim's fate, because it lacks intelligence and will. Intelligence designs what the will desires. There must be a "real" causal and moral agent behind the snake—the witch. In the reverse process, the same framework informs us, the cure of the victim will consist of more than just a pharmaceutic remedy. It would require countering, with more potent forces, the causal and moral agency of the witch. Such counteraction restores both order in the hierarchy of forces and moral good in the social space.

The moral character of a person depends on how he treats the forces of other people and things. By virtue of his wisdom he becomes a moral agent, capable of causing good (happiness) or evil (misery) to others. This theory applies to most accusations related to magic and witchcraft. But Tempels does not limit the area of morality only to matters of magic and witchcraft. On a wider scale, it would appear, all acts which bring about indignity, shame, and disrespect in society constitute, in a broader sense, the diminution of the vital force, either of the individuals wronged or of the society in general, as in the case of the violation of a taboo. All such acts, therefore, are subject to moral judgment on the basis of the knowledge possessed by the culprits. Moral responsibility and agency presuppose the maturity and knowledgeability of the subject.

That is, then, the "Bantu philosophy"—constituted, as Tempels says, by the transcendental and universal notions of being or force, of the increase, action, relations, and reciprocal influences between the vital forces of things. According to Tempels, the knowledge of this philosophy represents a new "discovery" of the Bantu, and strives to correct the old Western attitudes and images of blacks. Only by correcting the old attitudes will the good-willed colonial agents be able to understand the Bantu and Africans in general; and only then will they be able to help the Bantu improve their civilization. In a similar manner Christianity will be able to win the "soul" of the black or Bantu, for "the Bantu can be educated only if we [whites] take as a starting point their imperishable aspiration toward the strengthening of life."[18]

In the context of Tempels's other writings, it must be said that *La Philosophie bantoue* is addressed above all to the missionaries, whom Tempels invites into the encounter with the Africans whom they have the duty to evangelize. More still, the book tends to be a rehabilitation of those who had been disqualified as "noncivilized." To be able to lead the Bantu to a true civilization—which to Tempels is nothing but the Christian way of life—the missionaries of good will would have to begin by understanding them *the way they are*, in their "philosophy."

Recapitulation on Tempels

Despite its general celebrity among a large group of African followers, Tempels's book has never been totally free from criticisms of its shortcomings. Perhaps these shortcomings are historically attributable to two different intellectual atmospheres, the "prelogical" theory of Lévy-Bruhl and Tempels's own philosophical background.

As to the first, in the second half of the 1800s, under the influence of the philosophical and sociological writings of Auguste Comte and Herbert Spencer rather than Darwinian theory, research on evolution in the cultural and social fields assumed more precise and dogmatic forms. It culminated in what is called social Darwinism. Its basic assumption is that civilizations everywhere have evolved in a uniformly ascensional manner, from the simple to the more complex, from the homogeneous to the heterogeneous. It was within this theory that Lucien Lévy-Bruhl categorized the "primitive" peoples as "prelogical" or "mystical." To Lévy-Bruhl, "primitive" societies manifested lower levels of mental functions by failing to recognize, in their attempts at explanation, what observation and laws of inference dictate. Instead they chose to regulate their lives by instituting non-empirical—or better, rationally foreign and unacceptable—propositions about observed facts. They were "prelogical" or, at best, "mystical." Lévy-Bruhl had distanced himself from this stance by the time of his death in 1939, as is evidenced by his book *Les Carnets de Lucien Lévy-Bruhl* (1949), published posthumously.

More elaborately, the ideas of Lévy-Bruhl found their refutations in the structuralism of Claude Lévi-Strauss and in the works of the English anthropologist E. E. Evans-Pritchard, especially the latter's famous *Witchcraft, Oracles and Magic among the Azande* (1937). But Tempels appears to take up and develop the theses of Lévy-Bruhl. Tempels himself asserts that though the ideas of primitive societies have undergone, as any human ideas anywhere else do, some sort of evolution, and reached some complexity today termed animism, dynamism, etc., they nevertheless present traces of more pure and simple fundamental ideas concerning religion and "philosophy" in general.

Under this conviction, it is not surprising that Tempels views "magical" practices as some sort of "corruption" of the logically coherent Bantu ontology. These practices, to him, represent "ceaseless deviation through the frenzy of the search for vital strengthening, toward realities that are not life, or toward magical means of strengthening that are claimed to possess higher efficacy."[19] He claims that "the Baluba tell us that the greater number of *manga* or magical remedies are inventions of recent date," and therefore "fortunately this multiplication of external means, efficacious through the power of man alone, ends by revealing its own foolishness,"[20] so that the real "philosophy" of the Bantu, their present ontology today, is a "magical philosophy" of decadence, a tissue of erroneous deductions which suffers from "humiliating practices," and whose guiding principle is the interaction of forces. Yet, ironically, it is from these practices that Tempels deduces, after observation, that the Bantu live their coherent and complete system of ideas.[21]

For a better understanding of our argument, let us state Tempels's major points in the following summary form:

1. First, there is a belief that all beings have or are forces; and that there is a constant interaction between them.
2. This *interaction* is a passive existential property which unites all beings.
3. Man alone, by virtue of his intelligence, is capable of turning this passiveness in the interaction of forces into an active involvement of the cause-effect kind by determining such results as may be desired by him. Such results can be good, as in the case of protective medicines, or evil, as in the case of killing by magic. Those people who *actually* use their intelligence to bring about such results in the lives of other people or their property are generically called magicians or witch-doctors.
4. In order to achieve such results, the magician or witch-doctor *voluntarily* chooses and arranges for the interaction between a specific force that will act as the efficient cause and the force of the victim-to-be. In this case, the efficient cause can be in many possible forms, such as snake, tree, charms, inanimate objects, or even other humans. But the "real" causal agent, that to whom the responsibility for the event can be attributed, remains the subject of will behind the chain of events.

These four points summarize Tempels's view of Bantu ontology. And he continues to say (on p. 91 of the English version of *Bantu Philosophy*), "They [the Bantu] have no other conception of the world. Their philosophy directs all their activities and their inactivities. All consciously, their human behaviour is conditioned by their knowledge of being as force." Between their different conceptual beliefs on the one hand and their behavior on the other, the Bantu show use of "compact logic." Thus Tempels calls Bantu philosophy "critical philosophy."

But again Tempels writes: "Among the contemporary Bantu, we find a universally magical philosophy dominating their thought and, practically, universally received and accepted; but again on the other side . . . we discover some scattered elements of a more sane and more true anterior philosophy that does not know the interferences of ontological influences."[22] What does Tempels mean by "a more sane and more true philosophy"? On page 92 of the English version of *Bantu Philosophy*, Tempels states that "A system of philosophy may be called 'critical' even if it should be proved fallacious." The problem is at the point of departure. According to Tempels, Western philosophy depends for its exact and true concept of being on an experience which includes experimental knowledge. Such experience leads Western philosophers to reach "reasoned conclusions" as opposed to those of the Bantu. In respect of this position, one would immediately wish to ask the following questions about Tempels's thesis:

1. Can one talk of scientific bases of metaphysics?
2. If so, what are the experimental criteria upon which such problems of Western philosophy as the existence of God can be based?

We do not wish to undertake the discussion of these questions here. However, it is difficult to argue that, as a general principle, metaphysical claims are made only as inferences of experimental science. Certainly, there is a way in which empirical science and metaphysics have benefited from each other. Questions concerning the meaning and structure of matter and the universe, questions about the principle of causality, studies of quantity, space, time, motion, the theory of relativity, the space-time continuum, the reality of qualities, activity in matter, quantum mechanics, and so on, are all metaphysical questions which have benefited from new researches and knowledge in science. It is a fact, for example, that modern physics throws much light on the atomic theory of Democritus and the physics of Aristotle. Many of the philosophico-scientific problems treated by the philosophers and scientists of classical times make up the body of the philosophy of nature.

As science developed, however, it gradually became clear which problems could be solved by science and which ones could not. Whereas the seventeenth century knows many thinkers who find their place both in the history of philosophy and in the history of science (Descartes, Leibniz, Pascal, et al.), in the following centuries their number becomes smaller. Philosophy and science in the future go their separate ways. Although the success of science inspired many philosophers in their attempts to establish a philosophy on as solid a basis as science (Hume, Kant, Comte), they realized, as a rule, the different tasks of science and philosophy. As a result of this new reflection on the original value of philosophy (Hegel), the nineteenth century realized also the double character of the system of Aristotle, which, thanks to the historical interest of the century, was studied both in its original Greek and in its many Latin forms. The point we want to make here is that even in disciplines as closely related to physical science as the philosophy of nature, philosophy needs to be clearly distinguished from science.

The revival of Aristotelian-Thomistic thought in recent times was indeed partly due to the realization of the mutual independence of science and philosophy. In this respect, for example, although the belief in magic and witchcraft raises fundamental epistemological questions concerning the concepts of causality (and action) at a distance, it must not be seen as a belief which stems from scientific primitivism and which, on that account, is to be expected to disappear with the acquisition of the laws and doctrines developed by modern physical science. Magic and witchcraft are not primitive science. In fact, metaphysical theories have always thrived upon the view that the world of experience is much wider than what experimental science alone can claim to be able to deal with. In other words, there has always been a separation between the use of the word *experience* in metaphysics and its use in experimental sciences.

Tempels appears to classify Western metaphysics under experimental sciences, and the Bantu theory of forces with the unprovable experience. For this reason, strange as it may be, Tempels characterizes Bantu ontology as "a product of the imagination of the Bantu, a subjective idea which does not correspond at all to reality, and is unacceptable from the point of view of reason, objectivity, and scientificity of the real."[23] It is also clear from the four-point summary above that Tempels wishes to use Bergson's metaphysics of *élan vital* without the latter two points. In other words, Tempels appears to prefer for the Bantu an indeterministic theory of forces similar to that of Bergson. In Tempels's view, it appears, the inclusion of human agency in Bantu ontology allows the entire theory to thrive upon the errors and confusions of the intellect. Hence it is led to prefer bad thinking to good. Our quick suspicion is that Tempels must have realized that he faced both practical pastoral and theoretical theological problems if he accepted the bit of Bantu ontology that deals with the role of magicians and magical remedies in causal explanations. Not only were magical beliefs and practices condemned outright by Christian faith as heathen expressions, but they were also viewed as attributing to man immense powers over things beyond what is generally accepted as the limits of reason in Western scholarship. At the theoretical level, attribution of such powers to man meant for Christian faith that man had access to godly powers—a presupposition opposed to the foundations of Christian theology, which is based on human culpability and powerlessness.

Hegel expresses the same objection to the concept of magic when he discusses African religion in his *Lectures on the Philosophy of World History* (1975). He says:

> We can sum up the principle of African religion in [Herodotus's] declaration that all men in Africa are sorcerers. That is, as a spiritual being, the African arrogates to himself a power over nature, and this is the meaning of his sorcery. . . . Sorcery does not entail the idea of a God or of a moral faith, but implies that man is the highest power and that he alone occupies a position of authority over the power of nature. . . . Man, then, is master of these natural forces. This has nothing whatsoever to do with veneration of God or the recognition of a Universal spirit as opposed to the spirit of the individual. Man knows only himself and his opposition to nature, and this is the sole rational element which the African peoples recognise. . . . (pp. 179–180)

As a result, Tempels thought that he was left with only one practical option: to ridicule the Bantu concept of causality and the role of intelligent forces (human agents) within the general theory of the interaction of forces. But this reduces greatly the flow of thinking within the system of Bantu ontology. More important, this rejection of the role of intelligent forces leaves Tempels's own exposition limping. First he presents the role of intelligent forces as part and parcel of the general ontological laws of reality. Then he extracts this role of intelligent forces from the system as a foolish and recent addition, but he doesn't show the original position into which this recent addition was but an interference.

As if to offer a solution to this void, Tempels attributes the limp to the system itself. He characterizes the system as a peculiarity in the thought of the Bantu and of Africans in general—their own type of ontology, ethics, epistemology, aesthetics, and psychology.[24] However, Tempels's work was to be based on the hypothesis that although "the Bantu did not have a clear and distinct concept of the existence of things, they seemed to conceive them under the concept of force."[25] For Tempels, then, there are two modes of thought or systems of rationality and two philosophical systems derivable from them: one Western, the other Bantu or African. The former is scientific and proper, the latter intuitive, magical, and contradictory.

In this line, Tempels has been highly criticized by many sensitive black scholars. He was criticized by Aimé Césaire, for example, as having followed Lévy-Bruhl and his school by proposing another point in support of the theory of the "prelogical," and as presenting an argument in support of imperialism; for he characterized Africans as people without utilitarian knowledge of reality. Is it possible that the Bantu or Africans are unable to conceive of things in their individual substances,[26] Césaire asked.

The second point is about the equation of the concept of Being with that of Force. There is no doubt that Tempels wrote on "Bantu ontology" under the influence of his own formation in the Aristotelian-Thomistic or scholastic ontology. A. Perbal tells us that Tempels only succeeded in upsetting and disordering the *philosophia perennis* so calmly and ingeniously formulated by the Angelic Doctor. But Perbal mistakenly took this influence as proof that beyond Tempels's elaborations and interpretations, "Bantu ontology" did not exist.

The result of this influence on Tempels was a side-by-side comparison between scholastic metaphysics and "Bantu ontology," on which Kagame, following the same lines, would later make developments. The idea of force was to be interpreted in terms of the theory of being *qua* being. While the scholastic metaphysics talks of being as that which is, the Bantu talk of being as force, or, better still, as that which is force. Being is force, so that "that which is," in the scholastic system, equals "force" in that of the Bantu. While "we have a static conception of being, they have a dynamic one" because, for the Bantu, "being is that which has force." Other alternatives are: "being is that which possesses force," "that which is force or some thing inasmuch as it is force." "Where we would say that [different] beings are identified by their essence or nature, the Bantu would [prefer to] say that forces differ from each other by their essence or nature."[27]

So it is this particular *thing* or existent before me—say, a pencil—with its individuality and particular structure—that the Bantu would refer to as *force*. A *muntu* will call this very thing under consideration "force" while a European will call it "being" or "that which is." This is the part of Tempels's book that has met with most criticism. The mistake which Tempels makes can be demonstrated with an analogy:

I have often held a piece of chalk out in class and asked different students to say "something" about "this thing" in my hand. Almost invariably, I have had students giving answers like this: it is white; it is cone-shaped; it is long; it is chalk (in the sense of its chemical composition), etc. Assuming that at the back of my own mind I believe that there is only one fundamental focus or problem to which every person's attention would be invariably drawn in regard to "this thing," I will definitely make a very stupid mistake in likening those different answers of students as equatable synonyms for the same referent, as synonyms which can be equated in the following way: white = cone-shaped = long = chalk. This equation may make sense in terms of the assumption at the back of my mind, but certainly not in terms of what goes on in ordinary language and human experience.

As Garth Hallett says in criticism of Benjamin Lee Whorf's doctrine of theoretical content in language, "one might as well say that if one person calls a pencil hard and another calls it yellow, hardness is yellowness for one and yellowness hardness for the other. But this is not true. Such two people are not talking of the same thing at all. Their focus is different, that is all. One attends to one aspect, the other to another."[28]

Though Tempels seems at certain points to have "unknowingly" realized this important point, as when he says that to the Bantu being "est ce qui a la force" (is that which has force), which could be completely different from what he says later on, that being "est la force" (is the force), he however deviates from it and continues with his error. Now, to go back to Hallett, "If one person calls a pencil hard and another calls it yellow," continues Hallett, "doubtless that is because the needs and context of the statement called for one focus rather than the other."[29]

Tempels's theory may at times seem convincing, but looked at more closely, it contains many problems. The background of the author, rather than the research, influenced and controlled his conclusions. This does not mean, for example, that the African does not see "man" as such in his physical entity and spiritual qualities; that it is this in fact that they keep on referring to as the "*force existant en elle-même*" (force in-itself) or "*force vivant*" (living force). The Luo often say to a weak child: "Ne oyik dhano to owe biero, kose?" meaning, "Was the human being buried and the placenta left, or what?" What this example shows is that there is a clear notion of the human person as one who has certain natural and practical qualities. They call him "*dhano.*" Yet often as well, they will refer to this same "*dhano*" in terms designating *force vivant* or the like. This does not mean that it is this very concept "*dhano*" which they variantly call by different names, retaining the same meaning—that particular living body that we call "human being." For each of the uses, the point of view simply shifts, and the language therefore becomes different, for this principle of dynamicity, force, or whatever one wishes to call it, is not necessarily equivalent to being as that which is "*in se.*" It does not mean that African thought does not conceive the individuality of being or, in scholastic terminology, substances as beings which exist in themselves, "*in se, non in alio.*"

This perhaps is the key difference between some aspects of African thought and scholastic metaphysics. While the scholastic idea of the substantiality of being ("*in se, non in alio*") is grounded on the static conception of that being, some examples of African thought focus on something other than this "*se*-ism" of being and concentrate on the "be-ing" of existence, the mode or nature of this "to be" of beings, on their communitary category as things that exist "together" and therefore manifest other aspects of this relationship beyond their individual "*se*-isms." This is where the examples given from Bantu and Luo thought try to focus on the tight connection between created beings as things that surpass their individual existence "*in se.*" They see existence as a dynamic and not a static phenomenon. To them, the world is a communion and not a collection of individuals or changeless essences.

But Tempels does not always appear to agree even with this Bergsonian interpretation, as he does not accept indeterminacy in the theory of forces. This leaves Tempels's work highly eclectic if not outright contradictory, as it appears to have been born out of diverse and unrelated pressures, all working to create, in Tempels, a state of appreciation and resistance at the same time.

The Idea of Philosophy in Tempels

There are two senses of the word *philosophy*, but with a good deal of relation to each other. The first sense is usually also called the *ordinary* sense, and refers to some kinds of opinions and commitments to certain ideas or ways of interpreting things, to values and beliefs about the general nature of things. This sense of "philosophy" is quite reflective and can sometimes be "argued" even vigorously. The "arguments" in it, however, are usually also sorts of established opinions, views, and related beliefs which are called upon for justification. This is the sense of philosophy which is usually expressed in the form "my philosophy is . . . " In this sense, philosophy can be held by individuals and be assumed of groups—communities, societies, etc.—as part of the covert culture which is made up of the reasons behind the observable cultural practices and expressions.

In the second sense, philosophy is, to use Antony Flew's expression, what appears as the main subject of most of the writings of Plato, Aristotle, St. Thomas Aquinas, Descartes, Hegel, Kwasi Wiredu, Hountondji, and others. In this sense, philosophy is a commitment to an investigation rather than to any specific idea(s) or opinion(s). It is a study of a variety of subjects from a specific type of approach—an open, rational analysis and synthesis—and can therefore not be expressed in the formula "my philosophy is . . . " Because it is not merely a body of opinions, and does not aim primarily at formulating workable principles, but rather at *understanding*, philosophy in this sense becomes primarily an academic practice, a study, a systematic investigation of ideas.

Although Tempels is widely acknowledged as the father of enthnophilosophy, it is not very clear whether he had used the term *philosophy* in the title *La Philosophie bantoue* in the strong second sense as explained above. However, there is a widespread assumption by those who study Tempels—disciples and critics alike—that he had used the term *philosophy* in the second sense. Had Tempels been understood to have used the term *philosophy* in the first sense, there would have been no need either for the large ethnophilosophical literature in support of his claims, or for the strong criticisms which have come from those opposed to ethnophilosophy. Both camps of Tempels's legacy, however, have drawn their relevance from their acceptance and/or rejection of Tempels's comparison of "Bantu philosophy" with the classic Aristotelian-Thomistic philosophy.

According to A. J. Smet, by far the most widely acclaimed specialist on Tempels, in the earlier (1935–38) publications, before *La Philosophie bantoue*, Tempels had denied the existence of philosophy in the second sense in the Bantu thought system. Smet translates (from Flemish to French) from one of these early publications as follows:

"Pour beaucoup de phénomènes naturels, qui nous frappent, les Noirs ont trouvé une explication: non une explication scientifique, qui satisfait la raison, mais plutôt une représentation fantaisiste qui nourrit leur fantaisie. Cette représentation satisfait quand même les Noirs totalement, parce que leur raison n'a pas encore éprouvé ce besoin de connaître, ou du moins pas ces théories qui dépassent les hommes et qui n'ont rien à voir avec la vie terrestre. . . . Ils se laissent fort peu incommoder par les contradictions entre leurs interprétations de détails d'un seul phénomène naturel."[30]

(Black peoples have found an explanation for several natural phenomena which to us still remain wonders. But their explanations are neither scientific nor rationally acceptable; rather, they are whimsical representations which satisfy their imagination. The reason why people of the black race find such representations entirely satisfactory is that their reason has not yet shown signs of [i.e., attained] the desire for knowledge or at least not those theories which go beyond man and which have nothing to do with practical life. . . . They are not the least concerned about the contradictions which exist in their interpretations of details within any single natural phenomenon.) [my translation]

Although Tempels accepts in this text that the Bantu have an explanation for a number of natural phenomena which remain surprises or wonders to the

[Europeans], this explanation is not scientific. It does not satisfy reason. It is only a whimsical representation. One or two lines later Tempels says that this sort of representation is common to all blacks because their reason has not yet shown signs (*éprouvé*) of the desire for knowledge (*besoin de connaître*). According to Smet, the phrase *besoin de connaître* is derived, in its Flemish original (*honger der weetgierigheid*), from the fourteenth-century Flemish term which was used to translate the Latin word *philosophia*.

In this case, the word *philosophia* could have been used, as Smet rightly suggests, to mean "the spirit of research," the strong desire for knowledge which is manifested through the search for it. It so happens too that this is the classical definition of philosophy understood in the second sense explained above. In this manner, Smet concludes, "in 1935 Tempels denied that philosophy existed in Africa."[31]

Smet argues that Tempels consistently holds this early view throughout his publications which appeared between 1935 and 1938. In these works, Smet further observes, Tempels's use of the pronoun *nous* (we) appears to suggest that he constantly compared the Bantu with *nous autres* (we others, meaning Europeans probably), thus suggesting that he was influenced by and accepted Lévy-Bruhl's concept of the prelogicism of the black people. That Tempels held this view is further supported by his use of the term *anthropomorphe* in the first French edition of *La Philosophie bantoue*.[32] The word is rendered even more clearly in the Dutch version[33] as *homme-animal*. In these years, then, Tempels saw Africans as lacking philosophy in the second sense. But because he held the view that Africans were only savage anthropomorphes, his central belief appears to have been that they were incapable of any philosophy. For him, philosophy was "a universal science" which usually coincides with science as in the Western world. This is the view that was later developed by Robin Horton in a widely debated article published in 1967.[34]

Relying on Tempels's unpublished works,[35] Smet argues that after ten years of missionary work Tempels changed his earlier concepts about the Bantu; he discovered the Bantu as they really are (Fr. *en soi*). So, between the years 1938 and 1940, Tempels collected local proverbs, riddles, stories, song, and fables in which he believed the Bantu expressed their ideas, perceptions, and knowledge about themselves and about the nature of the reality of their experience. At this point, Smet reports, Tempels realized that his *encounter* with the Bantu was an encounter between two different peoples and points of view. He now wished to take the Bantu for what they were. Personally, he had attained a mental revolution, a change of heart. According to Smet, it is this change of heart which Tempels wished to express in his *Bantu Philosophy*—a personal appreciation for a personal encounter! Bantu philosophy was born out of this bizarre and deeply personal experience.

This change of heart does not, however, indicate that Tempels had changed his opinion regarding philosophy and its status in Africa, or regarding the existence in Africa of philosophy in the second sense. Smet himself admits that Tempels's interest in Bantu philosophy was not motivated by the desire for knowledge on the part of the Bantu themselves. The interest was Tempels's, and it was motivated by the objective to evangelize. Thus, although the interest in researching into Bantu thought was motivated by wonder about and desire to know the grounds of Bantu differences from them (Europeans), these motivating conditions belonged to Tempels himself rather than to the Bantu. It was he who was the thinker, and the Bantu his object of study. They were not the wondering and marveling subjects.

To Tempels, then, real philosophy in the second sense remained exemplified in Western philosophy. There was no question about this for him. If this is the case, then Tempels did not use the term *philosophy* in his title *La Philosophie bantoue* in the second sense. This view remains the one maintained by Tempels in the Dutch version of the book.

According to Smet, Tempels revised this view when he revised the Dutch text in 1946, such that, for Smet, from 1946 Tempels attributed to the Bantu the term *philosophy* in the second sense. We argue here, however, that although Tempels attempted to redefine *philosophy* in the terms of the then influential phenomenologico-existentialist thought, as shown in the texts cited by Smet,[36] this in itself does not prove any change in Tempels's earlier notion about the Bantu and their thought. In other words, there is no evidence that Tempels ever attributed to the Bantu "philosophy" in the second sense of the word. For neither the existentialists themselves, at least those most noted for developing the irrational path, such as Heidegger and Jaspers, nor the solicited writers of the famous "Témoignages" [37] ever claimed that the ordinary man, in his existential situation, which is punctuated by spontaneity, ever became a philosopher in the second sense.

According to Smet,[38] Tempels starts his revision by defining metaphysics as both a disciplined science and a profoundly human wisdom. In both senses, Tempels argues, metaphysics basically studies and considers the realities of all things which exist in the universe. And since these realities (of things) are universal and similar throughout the world, it follows for him that also the ideas and notions about them will be similar. For Tempels, metaphysics is a universal science of being in the real sense of the word.

His second premise is that all human reason is directed toward the understanding of the meaning of this metaphysical reality and its different forms of existence. After this, human reason expresses the acquired notions in human terms determined by the prevailing cultural conditions—either in proverbs, riddles, myths, allegories, and other communicative forms, or in systematic scientific definitions. In this case, the knowledge expressed in the intelligence of primitive peoples is therefore not essentially different, insofar as knowledge is concerned, from that of the wise specialists. Both are equal forms of the knowledge of being—metaphysics.

His third premise is that the system of thought that is based on the single and universal idea of being is what is called philosophy. The search for the meaning and truth of being is not a reserve of specialization. It is an existential situation. It is the human condition. This is why Tempels talks of the anonymous expression *"the human reason* expresses."

Many people, including Smet it seems, have wished to express the silent inference from the above premises to the effect that Tempels affirms the universality and equality of philosophy as a search for truth and meaning. But Tempels himself does not make any statement to that effect.

There is no doubt that Tempels's revision certainly makes the 1946 Dutch text slightly different from the earlier versions, at least in spirit. Nevertheless, despite the introduction of the common denominator "philosophy," Tempels still maintained a clear distinction between technical philosophy and what he called deep wisdom. What is important is that Tempels no longer viewed Western philosophy as the universal and paradigmatic system. But even this view is perhaps only apparent. Tempels's revision on his earlier texts on Bantu philosophy may have been occasioned by a changed attitude in him toward a pluralistic view of culture and of philosophy in particular, but Western culture and Western philosophy still remained superior and canonical in his view.

The language of Tempels's revised work is not strange if viewed against the general historico-philosophical background of the time when the revisions were made. The post–World War I continental European philosophy was of mixed events. Although there was the resurgence of scientism, which culminated in the founding of the Vienna Circle during this period, the general continental European philosophy was also greatly influenced by phenomenology and the brand of existentialism professed especially by Heidegger, Jaspers, and Marcel among others. It is not strange that Tempels, like many other Continental thinkers of the time, wanted to insist on a new conception of philosophy. To this school of thought, thinking was not what we call having an opinion or a notion. It was not the same as representing or having an idea. It was not ratiocination, developing a chain of premises which lead to a valid conclusion. Lastly, it was not conceptual or systematic in the sense previously favored by the German idealistic or French rationalist traditions. Thinking was no longer seen as a correlate of science. It was a situation, the natural goal of human expression. This type of thinking is determined both by that which is to be thought as well as by him who thinks. It is a form of remembering who we are as human beings and where we belong. It is a gathering and focusing of our whole selves, of what lies before us, and a taking to heart and mind these particular things before us in order to discover in them their essential nature and truth. Tempels therefore presents philosophy in his revision as a metaphysical situation which unfolds itself in different cultural ways, but philosophy nonetheless. Heidegger himself says the following of metaphysics:

> ... the ontological analytic of Dasein in general is what makes up fundamental ontology, so that Dasein functions as that entity which in principle is to be *interrogated* beforehand as to its Being.
>   If to interpret the meaning of Being becomes our task, Dasein is not only the primary entity to be interrogated; it is also that entity which already comports itself, in its Being, towards what we are asking about when we ask this question. But in that case the question of Being is nothing other than the radicalization of an essential tendency-of-Being which belongs to Dasein itself—the pre-ontological understanding of Being.[39]

Behind this passage is a strong resentment of technical philosophy, especially logical positivism and pragmatism. The noticeable emphasis on the fundamental value of metaphysics says it all. But in a broader sense, as we have already said, the existentialists see the need to redefine philosophy as a discipline. In so doing, the existentialists view philosophy more as a practical enterprise than as a removed specialized discipline. As Jaspers points out, it is practical in that it grows from one's life and one's history. This is not practicality in the pragmatist sense of utility or external applicability. It is the practicality of being engaged with human concerns. In their view, philosophy is a participative reflection, not an objectified rationalization. In *Being and Time* (p. 62) Heidegger says that philosophy is a "universal phenomenological ontology," in that it deals with the way in which being manifests itself to human experience.

Whether the man of experience becomes a philosopher by the strength of metaphysics as defined by the existentialists is difficult to say. On the whole, however, the existentialists sharply criticize the Cartesian epistemological dualism—the subject–object split—as inadequate. According to Heidegger, for example, philosophical thinking is meditative, not calculative. Thinking is questioning, and questioning is a basic human force. For the cogito of Descartes, Heidegger substitutes "waiting" or "contemplation." Sartre calls it "pure reflection," Marcel "secondary reflection," and Jaspers "listening." This was also the period of the height of Bergson's influence and fame, especially in France and Anglo-Saxon countries. For them, the basic object of philosophy is to understand human experience in the world, and the method for achieving this objective is intuition.

The existentialist concern with ordinary and everyday experiences as the focus of philosophy, however, does not suggest that the ordinary man is a philosopher. He is merely told that *his* total experience is important. He is not only a *res cogitans*. He is also a *res corporea*, with feelings, interhuman relations, communication, body, and, above all, life. As in the dualistic epistemology, it is the existentialist who, despite his opposition to the idealist and the rationalist, remains the philosopher, the thinker, while the ordinary man remains the paradigm of the crude "humanism," the archetype of human experience.

If this is true of the existentialists, then it is also true of Tempels's statement about Bantu metaphysics and philosophy. According to this view, then, the Bantu are not philosophers in the second sense of the word. Rather, their experience is the exemplary evidence of the new existentialist definitions of metaphysics and epistemological commitment to self and world.

From this description it is evident that existentialist epistemology recognized the unsystematic, the natural human situation or, as Betrand Russell calls it, the irrational. Although its statements were not made in favor of any particular cultural grouping, the variance of existentialism from the household European scientific tendency and method was a welcome change especially in the view of those who came from the so-called inferior cultures—Africans, Hindus, Chinese, etc. In this sense, Tempels's change of attitude in 1946 toward the definition of metaphysics and philosophy as experience was not in itself particularly directed at elevating the Bantu, except for the fact that they had offered him the firsthand experience of sharing with them the primitive life situation so central to the existentialist epistemological analysis. The 1946 change was therefore important, not because the Bantu became philosophers or were discovered to have been such, but because Tempels converted to existentialism. *La Philosophie bantoue* was Tempels's own philosophy of conversion or the philosophy of a convert. Through this conversion Tempels himself started to appreciate other cultures in general and Bantu culture in particular as different expressions of fundamental human aspirations, attitudes, perceptions, and ideas about the world, life, and their values. It is important to note that Tempels does not express anything more than this post-Victorian anthropological attitude.

In conclusion, then, it can be stated that there is no evidence from what we have said above that Tempels ever talked of Bantu philosophy in the second sense of the term. This idea has, however, been a persistent myth, first created by the monopolist European critics of Tempels, who wrongly thought he had violated the rules and terms of the monopoly, and perpetuated by his African admirers, who rose up eccentrically to defend what did not in fact exist. It has been the latter, rather than Tempels himself, who created the body of literature popularly known today as ethnophilosophy. In other words, they persisted, perhaps due to their misunderstanding of Tempels's position, or out of their own ingenuity, in believing that what Tempels had said of the Bantu was indeed the African equivalent of second-sense philosophy in the West, with differences based on sharp contrasts between Europe and Africa regarding social structure. The merit of Tempels's work in this discourse is that it remains an important point of reference in the ensuing politics of representation or, as Mudimbe calls it, the politics of otherness, centered around the notions of rationality, philosophy, and science.

But this is not to say that Tempels's work can be interpreted in any single and precise way. The influences upon him were multiple and his intentions were extremely unclear and ambiguous. Whether this ambiguity was an intentional historical strategy or accidental will be difficult to ascertain. What is important and perhaps useful to know is the variability of interpretations that emerge from it. In the Western world, defenders of Occidental cultural hegemony and exponents of the Foundationalist school[40] saw in Tempels an abdication and negation of the logocentric definition of philosophy and of the model of man as *homo rationalis* (see chapter 8 below). Others saw in Tempels's work a heuristic exposition of irrationalism which formed part of the antilogocentric methods of the existentialist and phenomenological movements in the West. The "Témoignages" (Testimonies) published in 1947 by some prominent French and French-speaking African intellectuals as prelude to the 1948 Présence Africaine edition of Tempels's book[41] testify to the relatively warm reception Tempels received in these circles. The "Témoignages" portray the Bantu as exemplary evidence of the existentialist subject matter: nonrationalistic, nonscientific (or antiscientific), but highly expressive intuitive discourses highlighting the meaning and richness of life.

Tempels characterizes "Bantu philosophy" as an exception from what he openly regarded as the universal philosophical method which reached its peak in Hegel's logocentrism. Existentialist and phenomenological movements were a challenge to the Western claim to logocentrism as a universal epistemological model. Their influence lay fundamentally in exposing and decoding the significance of basic human relations with reality. To the exponents of these movements, this relationship was not only basic but also more universal than was logocentrism. Against the latter, then, existentialist philosophers prefer what they call "philosophy of life"; they replace the intellect with instinct or intuition as the means for penetrating and grasping reality. Philosophy of life is participative.

According to existentialist philosophers, the logocentric model, or the "system" as they often referred to it, has the tendency of blocking the subject from the complexity of the real under the simplicity of principles. For them, then, the "system" always lacks that which is historical. Its resolutions obscure the inevitable ambiguity, confusion, and incompleteness of human existence; because the "system" was detached from the human beings it was intended to serve, it alienated them from a sense of life as it is lived, and the reality and destiny of the individual were lost. Existence, insofar as it is the unfolding of time, radically escapes the "system" and tends, in general, to lead philosophy to the level of wisdom which, to this movement, is genuinely Socratic in its original task as the "clarification of existence." Philosophy cannot be reduced to a mere "systematic" art of argumentation, they proclaimed. Rather, it is vital—a *manuductio ad sapientiam*.

The return of existentialist philosophy to the immediately lived existence in its *presence* forms the basis of its ontology. Tempels, too, builds upon it. This return proposes (in Heidegger) the unveiling of facticity, which is made possible by the very experience of being that we have before any reflection.

The reception of Tempels among African scholars depended upon how they evaluated the universalizing claims of either the logocentric model or the existentialist discourse. Those who saw the value in existentialism thought of Tempels as a real revolutionary, both in philosophy and in anticolonial discourse. This school of thought was the first recipient of Tempels, and became a very influential source of interpreting Tempels, particularly within ecclesiastical circles. The influence of Vatican II added to its strength. With these backgrounds, ecclesiastical institutions and their actors became major and leading authorities in the practice of explaining and interpreting African thought systems.

Another school of thought among African scholars regarded Tempels's project differently. According to this relatively later view, Tempels's project was a furtherance of the colonial discourse about the "primitives." The exponents of this view saw in Tempels's work a clear separation between scientific thought as identified with the Western world and "primitive" thought exemplified by the Bantu. While the former was the source of progress and domination of reality and others, the latter was the basis of historical inferiority and subservience. Those who hold this view tend to regard Tempels's project as attempting to except Africans from rational practices which define human history and destiny. For them, universalism is to be found in the logocentric model.

3 | Systematic Ethnophilosophy

Marcel Griaule

W E HAVE SEEN that Tempels's book became, especially after its first translation from Flemish into French, a major point of reference for many writers in African studies. In 1948 another important work, *Dieu d'eau, entretiens avec Ogotem-mêli*, by the celebrated French ethnologist—and one of the contributors to the "Témoignages"—Marcel Griaule, was published in Paris. This book, though of a character and style different from that of *La Philosophie bantoue*, still reaffirmed that blacks possessed a system of thought that revealed a system of philosophy, religion, and cosmology similar to that of the Europeans.

Ogotemmêli was an elder of the Dogon people of southern Mali. As a young man, Ogotemmêli had been blinded when his gun accidentally exploded in his face during a hunting expedition as he prepared to fire at a porcupine. Yet, even in such circumstances, Ogotemmêli strongly attributed the accident and his subsequent state to a deterministic notion of fate. This fate had been made known to him earlier through divination, but he chose to ignore it. Divination is an important way of knowing, he remarked, and he had paid a costly price for ignoring its predictions.

In 1931, while Marcel Griaule was on one of his numerous ethnographical expeditions in the regions outlying the upper Niger River in West Africa, he heard of the fame of Ogotemmêli as a man of outstanding wisdom. Griaule sent messengers to search for Ogotemmêli. Upon hearing of Ogotemmêli's willingness to sit for an interview, Griaule set out for the Dogon region of Mali in 1933. *Dieu d'eau* was the result of the meeting and conversations between the two. For thirty-three days Ogotemmêli expounded to the astonished Griaule the entire system of thought of the Dogon people. Unhonored and not aware of his great authorship, Ogotemmêli died in 1962.

Ogotemmêli's recounting of the world system is perhaps too detailed to be given full analysis here. Our main concern is to show its role in and impact on the definition of African philosophy. The system conveyed by the old sage,[1] as Griaule says, belongs to a preserved and higher degree of knowledge and wisdom—a detailed knowledge of the general principles that chain all things together as a single but complex phenomenon. It entails a cosmogony, a metaphysics, and a religion. That the teachings comprise all these is clear from the general character with which the old sage treats the subject, often reserving the specific details to the relevant specialists concerned.

Griaule's work has been subjected to much criticism in ethnological circles, from a variety of viewpoints. The content has been criticized as being too idealistic at the expense of historical dynamism.[2] This criticism also points out the significant methodological variance of Griaule's work from the "traditional" focus of ethnology and social anthropology which emphasizes the practice of "participative observation" by the ethnographer. Such a method, it was assumed, gives the ethnographer the powers of objectivity and control over his or her informants and material. In contrast, Griaule's method pays little attention to the life of the people "as it is lived," that is, to their political organization, economic activities, marriage systems, ritual practices, and so on. For these social anthropologists, Griaule's method constituted a weakness due to his total reliance on translators rather than on direct observation by participation, which is widely practiced in the British and American traditions of fieldwork. But today this does not constitute a particularly serious criticism, because the dialogical method used by Griaule limits, to a certain extent, the practice of representation in which the anthropologist acts as the sole authority. Today the objectivity of the ethnologist is a strongly questioned assumption under the rubrics of the politics of representation. V. Y. Mudimbe's works, particularly *The Invention of Africa* (1988) and *Parables and Fables* (1991), are very good examples of the challenge against the notion of ethnological objectivity. For this reason, Griaule's style is a significant alternative to the Anglo-American model of intensive participant observation. With weaknesses, perhaps, Griaule's style nevertheless institutes the recognition of the authority of informants and defines ethnography as a collaborative and constructivist exercise.

In addition, Griaule's critics are wary of a too perfectly ordered vision of Dogon reality. The product, they argue, is too good to be true.[3] In it, they claim, one sees a mixture of dogonized Griaule and griaulized Dogon. Yet another criticism, particularly by African scholars, has been leveled at Griaule for his emphasis on primitivism, that is, on the traditional at the expense of modern changes in the lives of the Dogon people. But this essentialist characteristic endeared him to Senghor's brand of negritude and its disciples.

In his work, Griaule had charted three cultural regions across Africa: the Western Sudan, Bantu Africa, and a region extending over Cameroon and Chad. Each of these regions, he believed, was characterized by a specific type of knowledge. He considered Tempels's work as significant in its recording of the knowledge characteristic of the Bantu region. His own was the equivalent for the Western Sudan. This knowledge, he believed, was inscribed in language, habitat, oral tradition, myth, technology, and aesthetics. Each of these, as a social reality or practice, is, in its own right, a complete microcosm within a macrocosm, all of them making a progressive formation toward the universal. For Griaule, then, the metaphysic of the Dogon is presented in multiform gradations fitting into larger ones progressively toward the cosmological totality. The residential hut, for example, was a miniature model of the homestead; the homestead a model of the village; the village a model of Sanga; and the entire Dogon region a model of the cosmos. The same pattern applied to the smithy, to the fields, to the kinship system of the Dogon, to the drums, and to cloth texture. All of them are microcosms of the universe. In the same manner of generalization, Griaule thought, according to James Clifford, that "Ogotemmeli and Sanga stand for the Dogon, the Dogon for the traditional Sudan, the Sudan for Black Africa, and Africa for 'l'homme noire.' "[4] Dogon reality, their organization, their drums, and so on, are all stratified because they are derived from a stratified metaphysical vision of reality.

Right from the dawn of all things, from the beginning of the universe and throughout its development to the present time, narrated Ogotemmêli, there are a number of general principles which are essential to this dialectic and which constitute the nature or essence of all things. These general principles can be listed thus: the God Amma, the one God; *Nommo*, which is Word, water, and heat at the same time; the principle of duality; and movement. The nature and role of these principles can perhaps only be shown within the context of Ogotemmêli's teaching, of which we shall now give a general sketch.

The Beginning of Things

That the existence of Amma, the one God, is a "taken-for-granted" first principle and necessary condition for the existence of all other things is clear to us from the manner in which Ogotemmêli begins his discourse. The whole solar system, like the stars which constitute it, came into being by the work of the God Amma, who flung out into space the pellets of earth from which the stars came.[5] God also created the earth, perhaps only in a rudimentary form, leaving its development to the interaction of the principles mentioned above. The earth was feminine. "Its sexual organ is the anthill and its clitoris a termite hill." Amma, being lonely and desirous of intercourse with the creature, approached the earth and united with it, thus giving occasion to "the first breach of the order of the universe." Disorder now followed disorder. From this union, instead of the intended twins, a single jackal was born, also breaching the principle of duality necessary for the development and well-being of things. God, however, united with earth for the second time and the birth of twins restored the regular cycle of duality. These twins, called *Nommo*, developed from water, which was God's sperm that penetrated the earth and impregnated her. The *Nommo* were half men (top half) and half snakes (bottom half). They were also green, which is the symbol and presage of fertility (germination and vegetation).

"These spirits, called *Nommo*, were thus two homogeneous products of God, of divine essence like himself, conceived without outward incidents and developed normally in the womb of the earth. Their destiny took them to Heaven where they received instructions from their father. Not that God had to teach them the Word, that essence of all things, as it is of the world system; the pair were born perfect and complete, so they needed no teaching; they had eight members and their number was eight, which is the symbol of the Word. Their nature was identical with that of the Word just like vapor is identical with breath.

"They were also of the essence of God, since they were made of his seed, which is at once the ground, the form, and the substance of the vital force of the world, from which derives the motion and the persistence of created beings. This force is water, and the pair are present in all waters: they are water, the water of the seas, of coasts, of torrents, of storms, and of the spoonfuls we drink."[6]

The Principles in the Development of Things

The rays of the sun (which are described by Ogotemmêli as excrements of the twin-pair *Nommo*), which are copper and light, are also water, because they sustain the humidity of the earth in its ascendance heavenwards. The pair give forth light because they are themselves light. From above, *Nommo* sees the impoverished mother earth and comes down, bringing with it fibers of some heavenly created plants. These fibers were spread out by *Nommo* in mat form so that mother earth could cover her nakedness. This, according to Ogotemmêli, is the first act of the universal order. The fibers, in fact, fell from heaven to earth in spirals, the symbol of tornadoes, of the meander of torrents, of the whirlwind, of water and wind (Word), and of the wave-like or zigzag movements of a snake. The fibers were also reminiscent of the eight round spirals of the sun (which were copper), the aspirator of humidity. The spirals were themselves a path of water because they were swollen with the coolness obtained from the celestial plants. They were full of the essence of *Nommo*; they were *Nommo* itself in movement, as indicated by the undular spring which prolongs itself to infinity.

Nommo, when it speaks, emits, as does every human, a lukewarm vapor or breath, carrier of the Word and the Word itself. Thus the coming of the Word to earth, which is the phenomenon at the beginning of each sector of human activity, was "a spiritual revelation that was penetrating the technical teaching." Thus the Word, in its simplicity, was adapted in the great works of the beginning. In each and every act of human life, in everything, the principle of *Nommo* is indispensable. Even in the creation of man and in the process of regeneration, the *Nommo* pair is always present. In the latter activity, it assumes the work of God, of whom it is also the essence; the Word gives to the womb of the woman its regenerative movement.

At the beginning of humanity, the Dogon people had been represented by a series of eight ancestors, the seventh of whom represented responsibility over the Word and the eighth the Word itself. At the beginning of each technique, such as basket weaving or cotton spinning, the seventh ancestor preaches the Word. According to Ogotemmêli, this is to prove the identity of material gestures and of spiritual forces or the necessity of their cooperation in all things. The Word (because the first weaver wove speaking) became the fabric woven, and the fabric was the Word. This fabric is called *soy*, which means in the Dogon language, "it is the Word." And this expression also means seven, the rank of him who speaks while weaving. But a termite stole this Word and took it to men in the neighborhood, who had assisted at the transformation of the sex of the earth. In this way the human race learned how to weave, thus acquiring access to the great wisdom brought to earth by the seventh ancestor.

For the subject treated from the fourth to the sixth day of the conversations, Ogotemmêli reverts to the use of quite complicated symbolic language detailing the geometrical forms of the world-system. These forms are materially represented by the Dogon in the shapes of the woven baskets and granaries. According to Ogotemmêli, the purpose of this symbolic extravaganza is "to make the lowly understand." But this is not of major concern for us here, as Ogotemmêli himself avoids the geometrical details which explain the structuring of the world-system into holy domain of religion, reserved for priests and other ritual leaders. It is, however, essential to note the persistent and dominating role of *Nommo* and the Word, and the constant play of numeric symbols in the progress and development of the cosmic system. Among all the numbers, the number eight was the most privileged. Seven is the rank of the Lord of the Word. But one plus seven gives eight. The eighth rank is that of the Word itself. The Word is on the outside of the seventh that preaches it. It (the Word) is the eighth ancestor. The eighth is the support of the Word that the other seven had and which was taught by the seventh.[7] So, belonging to the eighth family, the oldest of all living humans was the only earthly being that represented the Word most directly. He was called Lebe. The old man, however, had to die. It was said to simple men that he died, while in actual fact he did not. He could not die since death had not appeared on earth. For the same reason, neither did the seventh *Nommo*-ancestor die, though it was mutilated (while in the form of snake) and was consumed by the population. It too could not die, being immune to death by virtue of being *Nommo*.[8] When Lebe (fictitiously) died, he was buried in a tomb beneath the earth. But at this stage the seventh *Nommo*-ancestor comes back to life, still in the form of snake, and enters the tomb of Lebe and devours him, and then substitutes for his body eight stones to represent the eight ancestors.

[So] "The seventh *Nommo* ate Lebe, in order that men should believe that the stones were his bones digested and transformed . . . , in order that the affair should be an affair of men and not of heaven, so that something of heaven should become part of human nature; it was to make men believe that the aged Lebe, the oldest and most venerable of them all, and he alone, was present in the covenant stones. It was so that men might understand all the things he had done, that the *Nommo* came down onto the skeleton of a man. . . .

"Lebe was eaten because he was a descendant of the eighth ancestor, of the family of the Word. The Word is the most important thing in the world. By eating Lebe, the seventh *Nommo*, the Lord of the Word, took all that there was of good in the earlier Word and incorporated it in the stones. . . .

"The seventh ancestor, dead only in appearance, ate Lebe, also dead only in appearance. By eating the man, he took what was good in him but, for his own part, he gave his life force to the human flesh of the man, that is to say, to all humans: for in doing this for the oldest man he did it for all mankind. Thus because the seventh ancestor consumed Lebe, a descendant of his brother the eighth ancestor, their respective life forces were mingled."[9]

Nommo *and the Drums*

The exemplary drum, the armpit drum, was made by *Nommo*. He made it by tying thread around his fingers while his palms represented the tight skins on both tops of a drum. And while he wove or intertwined thread from side to side in his fingers, he often passed his tongue through the threads, thus giving them the humidity necessary for the existence of all things and, since the tongue is the propeller of the Word, *Nommo* made the drums with the Word, the indispensable element in all things. But *Nommo* never had any ears, only auditive holes. So his hands served him as ears. In order to hear, he used to put his hands on both sides of his head. To beat on the drum is like beating on the palms of *Nommo*'s hands, and is like beating on his ears. In this sense, even music is not merely for entertainment. The beat of the drums is an act of creation. The dance, which is a response to this act of creation, is the symbol of man's participation in the act of creation.

The big needle for making holes on the edges of the drum leathers today symbolizes the tongue of *Nommo*. The spiral of copper is for transmitting the sound and the Word. But this single drum was not enough to diffuse the Word to all peoples and to cater to the many necessities of diverse peoples. So *Nommo* permitted each of the eight families to construct a drum for itself. These were made in different sizes and therefore different tunes—and this is the origin of the different languages of the eight different families or clans that make up the Dogon people. But the eighth drum dominates the rest by its size, being that of the eighth family—descendants of the eighth ancestor, the Word itself.

The Word is integrated into every thing. It gives things their meaning, it penetrates all things. In the process of weaving,

"The Word is in the sound of the pulley and spool. The Dogon name for a pulley means 'the creaking of the Word.' All hear the Word. It enters between the threads and fills up the spaces of the material woven. It belongs to the eight ancestors. The first seven possess it, but the seventh is its master, while the eighth is the Word itself. The weaver sings while weaving, filling up the gaps of the material with the Word. He is the *Lebe*, that is, one who belongs to the eighth family and, therefore, himself the Word. . . . The Word, being water, follows the zigzag line of the woof."[10]

Even the working of the fields, which, in a symbolically analogous form represent the original celestial granary, is kept intact by the power of the Word, the power of *Nommo*.[11]

A woven dress is therefore full of *Nommo*, and to put on a dress (*soy*) means to cover oneself with the words of *Nommo*-ancestor, the *Nommo* of the seventh rank. For a woman, to carry ornaments and to dress means to cover oneself with the seventh *Nommo*.[12] A woman attracts men because of the Word that *Nommo* puts in the dress of the woman. It is this Word that attracts men. "To be naked," says Ogotemmêli, "is to be without the Word,"[13] and, however beautiful, a woman without ornaments will never attract men; a woman with ornaments attracts men, however much she may not be beautiful. Ornament is a call to love, it fulfills its function of attracting men as *Nommo* wanted.

The position of the smithy in the center of the village resembles a similar thing in the primordial field where the celestial granary landed on earth. The celestial granary was a hammer, and the hammer is the entire body of the water spirit, the great masculine *Nommo* in heaven.[14] The anvil is, on the other hand, the form of the feminine *Nommo*. The wood of the anvil is the bed of the two great water spirits. When the hammer strikes the anvil, the pair unites.

Symbolism and the use of analogy rule over Ogotemmêli's method of exposition, so as "to make the lowly understand." The structure of the living house, for example, is inseparable from the chain of symbols connected with the number of the first ancestors and their multiple descendants. That structure is reminiscent of the whole metaphorical structure of the earth, the structure of the first celestial granary, the physical structures of man and woman, etc. The very way of sleeping, with man and woman each with his or her immutable side of the bed, and even the conjugal act find their meaning in the unity of the universal order. Nothing is without the proper place or element it symbolizes in the original structure when the universe first took shape and order reigned upon it. The complex structure of the universe was symbolized in the material form of the first house built by man—the sanctuary of Binu.[15] The ground plan of the eight pillars in the house resembles a serpent coiled along a broken line and surrounding the symbols of the seventh ancestor, the master of the Word, and the eighth ancestor, who is the Word itself.[16]

As a symbol of the total world order, the sanctuary of Binu represents the process of metamorphism of the world, its order, regeneration, death, and resurrection, all within it. It is thus a symbolic combination of sanctuary, tomb (of

Lebe), and smithy functions, all of which represent the origin and reorganization of the cosmic system. But to the profane, to ordinary people, the sanctuary was nothing more than a structurally complicated and inexplicable edifice.

The instructed person, however, saw in it many symbols. On the front of the sanctuary were various drawings which symbolized the dispersion of natural objects in the order of the world; some, on the left-hand side of the door, stood for the metaphysical order. "The dispersion of objects," says Ogotemmêli, "serves to hide the symbolism from those who would like to understand it."[17] The metaphysics, however, is complicated. Ogotemmêli says, for example, that the symbols of the "urinating 'arietis'," *Nommo*, the copper and its younger brother gold, illustrate the functioning of the life of the universe, a life of endless movement. The rays of the sun, which are fire and excrements of *Nommo*, are responsible for the power of the sun. The rays of light and heat attract water. They make it climb, and later make it drop in the form of rain. It is a good thing. This go-and-come that creates movements is a good thing. By means of the rays, *Nommo* gives and takes again the vital force. It is this movement that makes life. It was not the forces that mattered in the making of life, but rather the movement of these forces. "To pull so as to make climb; to pull so as to make descend, this is the life of the world."[18]

The symbols of the terrestial order, on the other hand, represent the phenomenal world, which is, however, not separated from the metaphysical one. The solar system, the eight families, and the order of the fields are all symbolized on the terrestrial order.

The Cult of Lebe

One of the most significant objects in the cult of Lebe is copper, which has its origin in the primordial field, in the tomb of Lebe, who was defecated by the seventh *Nommo* after the latter swallowed him. The rings made out of the metal are the property of Lebe, and are successively passed on to the oldest man in the family. The Hogon, the priest of Lebe, preserves the metal rings while alive. He is impregnated with copper and must therefore avoid watery places. *Nommo*, who is copper by his celestial essence, takes all the copper found in the watery places reserved for him. The copper, symbolized by the rays of the sun, is the aspirator of humidity because it contains water as a result of evaporation due to the heat of the sun. To pass with this metal in the vicinity of certain waters, therefore, is to risk its return to the waters. In fact, if the copper is connected with *Nommo*, and *Nommo* is water, then liquid and metal have the same essence.[19]

In a way, *Nommo* resembles Anaximander's indeterminate ultimate stuff of all things in the pre-Socratic Greek cosmology. Like Anaximander's *apeiron*, *Nommo* is both externally unbounded and internally indefinite. It is externally unbounded because it is not contained in anything else. It has no boundaries. It is internally indefinite because it assumes all possible forms, including incompatible ones, such as water and fire. It has no definite form of its own.

All this indicates some eagerness in Griaule, not in Ogotemmêli, to characterize *Nommo* as a true universal essence to which all things can be reduced. The aim of this ambition could well have been to explain *Nommo* as a kind of universal force similar to Tempels's "vital force." Ultimately, however, there is a great difference between *Nommo* and Tempels's vital force. We have seen on the one hand that the vital force cannot be equated with being as Tempels indicated. Like Aristotle's *proprium*, the vital force is a necessary, but non-essential property. In our correction of Tempels, the property "being capable of influencing others" may belong to all things necessarily. In this case, if something exists, then it is capable of influencing others, and vice versa. But this capability is something different from the substance of the thing. *Nommo*, on the other hand, is explained by Griaule in such a manner that it indicates a substance, not a property. As unpredicated substance, *Nommo* is capable of taking many forms. It is only as predicated substance that *Nommo* possesses certain qualities, including the "ability to influence."

Binuism

The most interesting thing in the cult of Binu, the cult of those ancestors who returned to live with men condemned to mortality, is what Griaule, for convenience perhaps, calls *Binuism*, the relations of men with different families of animals. It interests us in that it ends in a hierarchical order of the universe. Every human family, according to Ogotemmêli, makes part of a long series of beings, and the whole set of human families together is connected with the entire animal realm. And, behind them, appears obscurely the vegetal series. When a person is born, says Ogotemmêli, all the animals of the series are born at the same time. This is because there is a human being at the head of every series as its leader. Every human birth sets in motion the births of all the animals and vegetables connected with his or her family.[20] The entire world system is held together by this law of parallelism.

Sacrifice

The act of sacrifice is a creation of the movement of forces in a circuit composed of the officiating personality, the sacrificial victim, the altar, and the invoked power. The very voice that invokes a power like *Nommo* is itself an emission of force that is mingled with the breath emerging from the mouth. On the one hand this force is a call for *Nommo*, and on the other it leads that which comes out of the open throat of the sacrificial victim and directs it onto the altar. Thus while in this way the altar gets fed and its power is reinvigorated by the new relationship, *Nommo*, called by the Word, comes to drink to purify itself, to nourish its life. The liver of the sacrificial animal, which is filled up with force to the brim, is eaten by the oldest of the "impure" (the officiators) and it makes him assimilate a part of the force of *Nommo*, in this way closing the circle opened by the Word emerging from his own liver.[21] By eating the liver, the "impure" also symbolizes the eating of the skull of Lebe, the skull of his ancient father. It is the force of Lebe's skull that passes into the animal.[22]

The "impure," the officiator of sacrifice, is like Lebe himself, because he carries the vital force of Lebe in his liver. It is as if he substituted for his own nature that of Lebe. So when he speaks, after sacrifice and for a long time after, it is as if Lebe himself spoke; and thus, by speaking, the "impure" communicates the good Word to all.[23]

Recapitulation on Griaule

These explanations are strikingly enlightening. But, as we have remarked above, there has been suspicion that the explanation of the world system in Ogotemmêli's narratives was a deliberate hoax on the part of Ogotemmêli, probably acting under instructions from the experts. Whatever the case, he fulfills his plan in a rigorous method, always beginning with the most basic principles, at the very formation of the world, and subsequently moving on to the cardinal factors that would slowly furnish the explanations of the more complicated progress. Each day the explanations began with an enigmatic phrase, which constituted the point of departure. With sharp imagination and infallible logic, Ogotemmêli tied up the content of the phrase with previous explanations as a form of summary. Only after this would he be ready for the analysis of a new subject matter. But this aspect too has been highly criticized as Griaule's own imposition. D. A. Lettens and F. Michel-Jones[24] have even pointed out internal contradictions in the system in which nothing is left out, nothing falls outside the circle of the cosmic system. Everything, every phenomenon, all reality, traces its meaning to the origin of creation, to the principle of duality, and to the principle of *Nommo*, the essence of all things, and to the principle of movement. These are the principles that have given order to the world. Everything has its meaning. Even beer-drinking and dancing have their part in the metaphysical network of the universe. "To play on the drum," says Ogotemmêli, "means to make the bellows, the symbol of the sun, to move,"[25] and the drum-sun, as the star, emanates heat and water vapor, warm and resonant, on the dancers. Dancing has diffused *Nommo*, the Word, on earth. The first dance, Ogotemmêli tells us, was a dance of divination which projected into the soil the very secret Word contained in the fibers worn by the dancer. Many movements in dancing are symbols for movements in the cosmic system. Trade and exchange of commodity also find their meanings as symbols of the cosmic system.

About this coherence of the cosmic system as viewed by the Dogon, Griaule himself says:

The recent researches of the team . . . have led to the certitude that no image, no spiritual approach, no technical or religious gesticulation, [is] absent from the total system of classification that itself tends to enclose the future world, though not as yet perceived. Furthermore, the classification is based on a binary system and does nothing but to establish the ranks of which each thing would constitute an autonomous category related to the next by a joint [*"charnière"* in French] of double reasoning: every component term is related to the other of the adjacent suit, such that the line finally forms a chain of symbols.²⁶

The Dogon universe is one in which the real world of things is only a reflection of the causal relations of metaphysical entities and categories. According to this view, language is a complex system of metaphorical representations of the invisible world of metaphysics. But because language has autonomous property of its own as a unifying power, it ties the different categories of the universe into one system.

The Word, *Nommo*, reigns over them all. Exchange of commodity in trade signifies exchange of the Word, of *Nommo*. In the complicated cosmic system explained by means of innumerable symbols and myths, we are thus able to point out some fundamental principles: of *Nommo*, of *duality*, and of *movement*. These three principles were related from the beginning of time. The pair of *Nommo*, the spirits of water, the first offspring of God, were molded in water. The sperm of God, made of water, after the first attempt, which failed and resulted in the birth of a single being, later impregnated the mother earth and occasioned the birth of the celestial pair that were to become the *"monitrice"* of the world. "Had it not been for the pair of *Nommo*," says Ogotemmêli, "nobody would have been able to reorganize the world."²⁷ Duality, on the other hand, inseparable from the very nature and legitimacy of the pair of *Nommo*, had also appeared in a wide variety of aspects of the system and played a key role in important institutions. Movement, we are told, "is the life of the world."²⁸ But more than a mere juxtaposition of symbols, the system displayed by Ogotemmêli presents "rather a continuity that marks without doubt, a stage of scientific knowledge."²⁹

This cosmogony, "metaphysic," and religion of the Dogon, as evident throughout the work of Griaule, is an expression of unity, harmony, and concentration of nature and, in a general sense, expresses the One; it is a philosophy of nature.³⁰ This "philosophy of nature" rests on the principle of movement. *Nommo* is, then, not only the essence of beings, but also the essence that connotes and points to the dynamic nature of beings. This dynamism or movement, which "is the life of the world," derives from one fundamental idea, that of harmony, which, in turn, is the manifestation of the One, the God Amma. And thus the Dogon complete their system of the world.

The Vital Force

A curious problem arises in the texts of Ogotemmêli, concerning the notion of human personality, the notion of the spiritual principles of human nature. The existence of these spiritual principles or the complex of personality in humans is already clear from the conversations with Ogotemmêli, though Griaule passes over them without mention nor does he ask his interlocutor to expound more on the subject. Griaule seems content that the question had been treated by him in the *Masques Dogons* and specially by Germaine Dieterlen in her *Les Âmes des Dogons*. As a result, Griaule takes no pain to use the native names for these principles. He leaves the text in pure translation, once more with the problematic term *force* or, as Mme. Dieterlen had earlier called it, *force vitale*.

Talking about the first incident of death on earth, about the death of the old man-serpent, Ogotemmêli said:

> "When the old man-serpent addressed the young men with invective, the fibers [worn by the young men] drank his Word; they drank the breath that came to them because of them, since they were the object of scolding. . . . Since there remained some little water of *Nommo*, it was him, *Nommo*, who drank the force of the old man. He drank the blood of the old man. This consumed force, this blood, went with the Word of the old man that went from his mouth to the fibers."[31]

Two pages later Griaule himself tells us that "the soul [*l'âme* in French] of the old man, together with the remaining force which had not been consumed by the fibers, had escaped from the body."[32] Thus began also the rite of *Sigui*, as these spiritual entities went about seeking support. Living humans have the obligation to provide all the dead with support for the souls and forces set loose by the virtue or power of death.

But what are the natures of and differences between soul and force? What is their role in relation to the life and death of an individual person? These are the questions with which Dieterlen deals and which we will soon consider in detail. Though published much earlier than was Griaule's *Dieu d'Eau*, Dieterlen's work deals with one single aspect of the system narrated to us by the old sage Ogotemmêli. Her work deals with the problem of the human soul and its relation to the appearance and problems of death. This allows us to consider the work of Dieterlen after Griaule's *Dieu d'Eau*, as forming a continuation of it.

The Notion of Nyama

Before the appearance of death in the human world, order reigned among the spirits; humans and things created by Amma were provided with a soul and a vital principle (*Nyama*). "Desiring to retain contact with his descendants, Binu gave to one of the members of his group a stone that would be the support for his soul and vital principle."[33] The cult of the Great Mask "addresses itself to the old ancestor who, having undergone death according to animal form, transmitted, by contagion, his *Nyama* to the entire human race."[34]

The aim of Dieterlen's work is to identify and comment on the different modalities of the cult of souls, which, like the cults of masks, has its origin in the appearance of death among humans. Dieterlen begins her work with an analysis of the notion of the individual soul. She shows how the personality of every person is related to the supernatural powers and to his or her ancesters. Having defined the soul, and explicated its state and role, Dieterlen treats the effects of death and the people's reactions to the reality of death in relation to the concept of soul. The soul, after the rites following death, is allowed to embark on the long journey that leads it to the God Amma. But despite this departure, the soul remains in contact with the living, signifying, among the descendants, a perpetuation of the vital force, *Nyama*, and enabling the departed to be the object of a personal cult that will aid the *Nyama* of the departed on its long journey. "Now the personality is expressed in a device that assumes the qualities and history of the being to which it refers and from which the declamation has a powerful effect over the *Nyama* with which every human is provided."[35]

After the God Amma had created everything, he provided each being with an individual soul. Moreover, "all living beings and some inanimate beings were equally provided with an imperishable force, *Nyama*, jointly responsible with the soul for their temporary support. In humans and animals, this force, blind and docile, is directed by the soul."[36] But with the appearance of death,[37] even man, by contagion, became subject to death and mortality, insofar as these two principles, the soul and the force *Nyama*, were able to "escape" from the body.

The human person, according to the Dogon, is therefore composed of two principles. In the notion of the person the Dogon conceive the existence of *kikinu say*, a double, immaterial shadow, an immortal spirit independent of the body and within which the spiritual faculties of morality and intelligence are inscribed. Its counterpart ("double") remains equally intangible but comes from and depends on divine will. This divine will is also said to be provided with an essence, *Nyama*, which is spiritual and material at the same time.[38] There is individual *Nyama* and group *Nyama*.

"The substance and life-force, *Nyama*, spread out in the universe, was divided, from the beginning of the world, to all animals and at times communicated also to certain inanimate beings. The part of *Nyama* accorded to man is considered as blindly submitted to the authority of *kikinu say*." The Dogon believe that all animals, including those of the human subcategory, as well as certain inanimate beings, are made of matter and *Nyama*. The *Nyama* in humans, however, is considered to be subordinately related to another principle, the *kikinu say*. The *Nyama* of every group—tribe, clan, family, or gender—is composed of the *Nyama* of all beings which participate as members of the group. "It is by his *Nyama* that each person is attached to the mythical or true groups and societies of which he or she makes part; it is by this group *Nyama* that he submits to the authority of his mortal and immortal ancestors."[39]

It is thanks to his *Nyama* that an individual lives and in turn gives life to his descendants. It is also through the intermediary of this force, directed daily by *kikinu say* that the individual continues, even after his death, to play an active role in the lives of his descendants. At death *kikinu say* separates itself from the body and continues to make the dead retain a role among the living. *Kikinu say* integrates itself to the group of immortal souls, which makes the dead pass over to the rank of ancestor while his *Nyama* continues its sojourn amongst the living.[40]

The *kikinu say* (literally, the intelligent shadow of man, as opposed to *kikinu bumone*, the foolish shadow) is the skillful soul (*l'âme savante*), intelligent and willful, the cognitive thought of man. It is not situated in any organ, being spiritual and independent of the body. *Nyama*, a principle spread in the blood of man, is the vital force transmitted from father to son and from generation to generation. It makes beings have life, have movement and the Word. It is the executor of the human will, his thought, and it acts "blindly."[41] Following Ogotemmêli's logic, we see that the *Nyama* cannot act without the direction of *kikinu say*, the intelligent shadow, the opaque shadow, which is double the size of the body (in quality or essence) and which is therefore greater than *Nyama* as well.

Nyama *and* Nommo

Considering the principles of reality as explained in *Dieu d'Eau*, it may be inferred that *Nyama* is deeper and more general than *kikinu say*. It is found in the blood of man. Its affinity to blood, "the rain that falls on the world," and to humidity, the symbol of life and reproduction, brings it near to the notion of *Nommo*, whose essence is humidity. And since humidity is found everywhere, being the essence of things, *Nyama* cannot be less in its extension than the humidity of the Word or *Nommo*, which "is for all," as Ogotemmêli told us. Griaule describes the flow of blood at sacrifice from the throat of the sacrificial victim as the flow of this force. And thus, "In all its different forms, whether of consecration, expiation, divination for oneself, sacrifice for the Dogon has one unchanging effect—the redistribution of life-force."[42] In a general fashion, therefore, "Nyama is energy in instance, impersonal, unconscious, and divided among all animals and vegetables, among supernatural beings, among the things of nature."[43] It is thus easier to understand the play of symbols in Ogotemmêli's narration of the death of the old man-serpent in front of the young men wearing the blood-stained fibers.[44]

The transmission of *Nyama* is therefore possible.

The *Nyama* of an individual, at the beginning of its existence, is composed of
a total of 'particles' of different *Nyama* which later amalgamate themselves to
form his personality. In the first place, the human person is endowed with a
'particle' of the *Nyama* of his father, received at the time of procreation and
which, during conception and the first movements of the foetus, would be the
one to be animated. This force increases from that of the dead relative whose
soul, in the course of pregnancy, touches the womb of the woman . . . [45]

which makes the dead person become the *nani* (ancestor) of the child to be born.
This transmission of *Nyama* is ritualized in the name-giving ceremonies which
take place during the first days of a child's life so that it may participate in the
Nyama or *Binu* of its clan.[46] Later, if the child assists in the *Sigui* rites, it becomes
Binu, the mythical ancestor who was the first to undergo death. "The composition of his *Nyama* having been given, an individual becomes an emanation of the
actual society through his father; of the recent society through his *nani*; of the
historical society through his ancestors; of the mythical society through his *Binu*
and, if he assists at the *Sigui*, through the Great Mask."[47]

The *kikinu say*, which quits its corporeal envelope three years before the
actual physical death of an individual, forms part of the flock of the God Amma,
whose decision is responsible for its separation from the body. *Kikinu say* then
continues to wander about, while the individual continues to live, still animated
by *Nyama*.[48] Thus it is God who "kills" man at his death. "He slaughters their
soul (*kikinu say*) as you slaughter chicken. . . . It is the God Amma who makes
us die."[49]

At the moment of the slaughter of the soul (*kikinu say*), man dies and the
Nyama follows up a determined and constant itinerary within the body. Placed
in the blood during life, at death it passes into the liver (*kinne*) and then into the
heart (*kinne dono*). At the last moments, it goes into the head and finally goes
out with the last breath to escape into the air, where it rejoins *kikinu say* which
is then back from its temporary sojourn in the bush. The symbolism about
Nyama's itinerary within the body is again indicative of its importance and its
role as general essence. With the departure of *Nyama* from the body, man ceases
to be a human being. He becomes a corpse. Ogotemmêli had pointed out the
importance of the liver when he dealt with sacrifice. It is the seat of *Nommo*, the
Word. The eating of the liver at sacrifice by the "impure" brings him near to
Lebe; it makes him like Lebe: "The impure is like Lebe; he carries the vital-force
of Lebe in the liver." It is as if he is deprived of his own proper nature so as to
redress himself in that of the ancestor. And since it is in the liver that the Word
is born, all that which the "impure says immediately after the sacrifice and for
a long time after, is as if said by Lebe himself. By speaking, the 'impure' communicates the good Word to all."[50]

We have already seen Ogotemmêli's account of the origin of the institution of the rite of *Sigui*.[51] The will of the *kikinu say* of the dead intervenes to choose, from among the living, a candidate to be in charge of watering it. This designation, in which *Nyama* plays an important role, "responds to a double need" of the Dogon: "On one side, to ensure the future life of the *kikinu say*; it is not in fact until the *nani* has been duly designated and has been able, be it directly or through intermediaries, to assume his ritual functions that the *kikinu say*, while abandoning the temporary sojourn of the South, takes the road to 'Manga'." On the other side, the selection of the *nani* ensures the continuity of the group by putting into circulation a part of the *Nyama* of the dead.[52] This makes it clear that *Nyama* is a more general principle than *kikinu say*, for only a "part" of *Nyama* assures the reestablishment of the *kikinu say*. The use of the word *part* (of *Nyama*) is doubtless to put stress on the importance of *Nyama* as essence and perhaps to safeguard the doctrine against that of the transmission or transmigration of souls. The word *nani* refers to the ancestor who has chosen from among the living a young child whose role will be that of rendering support to the ancestor through a cult (*Sigue*). *Nani* also refers to the chosen child itself.

4 | Language and Reality

Alexis Kagame

By 1953, THE WORKS of Tempels, Griaule, and Dieterlen had established a new trend in the study of African cultures which stressed the metaphysical dimension of the African concept of "Being." This was, however, not without the considerable debate to which Tempels's book had been subjected since its translation into French in 1945. When Alexis Kagame undertook his philosophical studies at the Gregorian University in Rome (between 1951 and 1955), Tempels's book was still very much under discussion. The debate created two camps: the pro-Tempelsians and the anti-Tempelsians, with the latter charging that Tempels had made a perverse use of the concept "philosophy."

Among African pro-Tempelsians there was a general feeling that Tempels's ideas about the existence of a Bantu philosophy were positive and defendable. Yet, at the same time, Tempels's book was regarded as essentially part of the colonial discourse on Africa. According to this view, Tempels's work was part of the West's self-definition, which included the attributes of science, rationality, logic, and philosophy, and the denial of the same as the characteristics of *others*. For this reason, the pro-Tempelsians thought, there was need for the new African intellectual elite, with solid preparation in philosophy and knowledge of the traditions, to give Tempels's hypotheses a better grounding. Kagame was the first African scholar to take up this task.

Apart from his preparations in philosophy, Kagame was also an established scholar of Bantu languages. With this background, Kagame decided to give Bantu philosophy a fresh approach: to uncover the concept of "Being" among the Bantu through the analysis of their language.

The Categories

Kagame began his analysis on the hypothesis that the philosophical elements in the linguistic structure of Rwanda reveal the manner in which the Bantu of that country have conceived the categories of Being in their "philosophy." Such conception of Being, he said, is opened up by their confrontation with the problem of existence as the whole general phenomenon in which the categorical or hierarchical structure of beings play a vital role. In his voluminous works,

84

Kagame analyzes, from the language of the Bantu of Rwanda, and Bantu in general, the concept and categorical structure of Being as conceived by these people.

Kagame's major philosophical works remain fundamentally two: *La Philosophie bantu-rwandaise de l'être* (1956), and *La Philosophie bantu comparée* (1976). While the ideas in these two works remain largely the same, the second one brings these notions to the level of Bantu peoples in general, beyond the Rwandaise limitations of the first work. The rationale for the second book was to show that it is meaningful to talk of a philosophy that belongs to the Bantu in general, based on concrete evidence rather than on unproved generalizations as Tempels had done. For this reason, *La Philosophie bantu comparée* had only one message: that other Bantu-speaking peoples of central and eastern Africa had linguistic structures similar to those of the Bantu of Rwanda which reveal the unique way in which all the Bantu-speaking peoples conceive Being. This information does not add anything of philosophical significance to the first work. For this reason, our analysis will be based on the first work.

In Kinyarwanda (the language of the Bantu of Rwanda), says Kagame, all terms are divided into groups or classes. There are eleven such classes of words in Kinyarwanda under which terms or words can be grouped. These classes[1] also control the grammatical syntax of Kinyarwanda. Each word, says Kagame, is composed of four elements, which have some "philosophical" role depending on the class to which the word belongs, from which are derived the four general categories of speech. For Kagame, it appears, language is primarily a taxonomic tool; and its effectiveness as a communicative tool depends on the precision of its taxonomic roles.

Kagame produces the four philosophical elements of words from the eleven general grammatical classes of Kinyarwanda as follows (p. 42):

1er cl.:	u-mŭ-ntu	(pl. a-bă-ntu)	= man (men)
2^e cl.:	u-mu-horo	(pl. i-mi-horo)	= pruning knife (knives)
3^e cl.:	u-ru-tügu	(pl. í-n-tügu)	= shoulder(s)
4^e cl.:	ï-n-ka	(pl. ï-n-ka)	= cow(s)
5^e cl.:	i-i-buye	(pl. a-ma-buye)	= pebble(s)
6^e cl.:	i-gï-ti	(pl. i-bï-ti)	= tree(s)
7^e cl.:	u-ku-guru	(pl. a-ma-guru)	= leg(s)
8^e cl.:	u-bü-shyo	(pl. u-bü-shyo)	= herd(s)
9^e cl.:	a-ka-buye	(pl. u-tu-buye)	= small stone(s)
10^e cl.:	u-ru-gabo	(pl. i-bi-gabo)	= a giant [of a man] (giants)
11^e cl.:	a-hă-ntu	(—)	= place(s)

As shown, the elements of the words are separated by hyphens.

According to Kagame, although the first vowel, which is the first element in every word above, usually translates into a sort of "article" (*le, la, les*) in French, its role in Kinyarwanda is more than just syntactical. Yet, at the same time, it does not appear to bear philosophical import on its own. Philosophical weight is borne by the second (mŭ, mu, ru, n, i, gï, ku, bü, ka, ru, hă) and third (ntu, horo, tügu, ka, buye, ti, guru, shyo, buye, gabo, ntu) elements. The second element is the "prefix" and the third the "radical." According to the argument (p. 45), the "radical" does not have a determinate meaning on its own unless it is preceded by and joined to the second element, the "prefix." But because it carries the generic and nondeterminate significance, the "radical" confers to the "prefix" the qualifications of specificity and determinacy. However, Kagame argues, the second element in Kinyarwanda does not serve the same role of "prefix" as do prefixes in European languages. This conventional role of the prefix in European languages is served by the first vowel(s) in Kinyarwanda, which had wrongly been identified with "article." This being the case, then, the second element could be rightly called the "determinative" or, in agreement with the grammarians' and linguists' possible wording, we could also call it the "classificative"; it puts the generic meanings of the third element into their specific classes. The fourth element is obscurely identified to exist in the ending of words.

All the words given below as examples of the eleven classes have one or the other of the letters A, I, or U, in singular or in plural form. As we shall see, the letters are key in signifying categorical differentiations in ordinary language description of the Rwandan world of experience. These letters may appear at the beginning of words, such as in *UMUntu* (human person), *IKIntu* (object), *UKUntu* (to be), and *AHAntu* (place), all in Kinyarwanda. In this case, the words are pronounced in two syllables with phonological emphasis placed on the first syllable (which we have indicated with capital letters). The other syllable is pronounced softly. In other Bantu variations, these letters are combined with their similars but appear in the middle of the words, such as in *MUntu*, *KIntu*, *KUntu*, and *HAntu*, in Kimeru (Kenya). These words are also divided into two syllables, and the phonological emphasis is again placed upon the first syllable, but in this case the first syllable is composed of only two letters. In Kiswahili, Kagame says, the following variations occur: *Mtu*, *KItu*, *KUwa*, *paHAli*. Even here, the words retain their duosyllabic structure. According to Kagame, the change of voice in the pronunciation of these words is not only to indicate their syllabic structure but also, and more important, to indicate the metaphysical categories—human being, thing or object, place or time, mode of being—to which the referents of the words belong. The first letters (U, I, U, and A) express, in Kinyarwanda, the abstract "state" or nature of the thing; for example, *Umuntu* expresses the category of (sayable also as "the act of being") a person.

Through this kind of linguistic analysis, Kagame arrives at the notion of the "predicables," the first three relations (genus, species, and specific difference) of which, according to Kagame, express the essence of Being.[2] The presence of these notions, explicit or implicit, is verifiable, according to Kagame, from the current Kinyarwanda and reveals the four general categories under which the Bantu of Rwanda conceive Being and express it in current (ordinary) language.

This established, Kagame goes on to apply these notions to the "philosophy" of the Bantu of Rwanda, that is, to list the categories which, "as regards their number, will have to respond to Being within the whole of its span and correspond exactly to the categories which the great metaphysicians of the European culture have already identified."[3] The second part of the definition of the four categories is based on the meaning given to the common radical in all the categories: NTU. "In considering the four terms under which the 'categories' are expressed, it is already evident that the radical NTU has the generic meaning of 'some-thing' [Fr. *un quelque-chose*], a being [Fr. *un être*]."[4] But, as Kagame himself says in a famous Italian phrase, "se non è vero, è ben trovato" (if not true, then well invented), that is, even if the Bantu of Rwanda do not *in fact* think and talk of "being" as Kagame has portrayed and claimed,[5] still his theory is well constructed and has the semblance of truth. The Italian saying indicates that Kagame is not so much concerned about the significance of the presence of this radical in this language as he is about giving it a philosophical meaning.

But "among the Bantu of Rwanda," he says, "substance is envisaged inasmuch as its nature is concerned. That is to say: in function of its operation, of its mode of acting."[6] The categories, in their complete form, are then listed:

1. UMUNTU   the category of 'human being' or force with intelligence. It includes spirits, the human dead, and living humans.
2. IKINTU   the category of 'thing'. It includes all the forces which do not act on their own but only through agency, that is, under the command of a force with intelligence. This category includes such things as animals, plants, minerals, and any inanimate thing.
3. AHANTU   the category of 'place' and 'time'.
4. UKUNTU   the category of 'mode'.

We will here anticipate the thesis that Kagame clarifies on pages 288–298 of the book, that is, that the "property" common to all things or beings is their activity and that divination and magic are based on the metaphysics of these "properties." These "properties," translated into Tempels's language, assert that "all beings influence one another" or that all beings manifest a variety of "occult powers" that put them into relation with other beings. Every being is furnished with only some of these "properties." The calculation and use of these "properties," however, require intelligence or some sort of knowledge. Thus only humans can use the "properties" of inferior beings by calculating for them some determined effect to produce. The effect is then attributed not to the means but to the intelligent being who is the true agent and therefore responsible for the act. With intelligence, humans dominate nature; "the beings-things belong to humans."[7]

Thus the four categories into which, according to Kagame, the Bantu of Rwanda classify Being, are: being with intelligence *Umuntu* (Fr. *l'être qui a l'intelligence*), being without intelligence *Ikintu* (Fr. *l'être qui n'a pas l'intelligence*), localizing being *Ahantu* (Fr. *l'être localisateur*), and the modal being *Ukuntu* (Fr. *l'être modal*). According to Kagame, the first two Bantu categories (*Umuntu* and *Ikintu*) correspond to the Aristotelian category of Substance, the third (*Ahantu*) corresponds to the Aristotelian categories of Place and Time, while the fourth (*Ukuntu*) is shared among the remaining seven Aristotelian categories of Quality, Quantity, Relation, Action, Passion, Position, and Possession.[8]

Being and Nothingness

Like the Bambara, the Bantu of Rwanda also have a concept of "nothingness" in relation to Being. This "nothingness" is not "absolute nothingness" because the Bantu of Rwanda, in Kagame's view, cannot conceive nonexistence as a negation of Being. On the contrary, to these people "nothingness" is conceived as existing on its own. It is the element of separation between beings. "Nothingness" exists (habitually), for if it did not exist, all bodies would touch and intertwine among themselves—something contrary to the Bantu table of classes and categories of Being which presuppose identity among beings. In between things there is "nothingness."[9] "Nothingness" is primarily opposed to substance in general and to material substance in particular. It is opposed to anything that can be qualified as "some-thing" (*Ikintu*). "It results that in our [Bantu] philosophy," Kagame says, "nothingness is the negation of determined being which is realized in nature. It [nothingness] means neither non-essence nor nonexistence, but rather the nondetermined-substance and the nonconcrete-existent."[10] In this way, Kagame adopts Dieterlen's interpretation of the Bambara notion of nothingness, but makes his own interpretation closer to the scholastic notion of nothingness as a prelude to the concept of creation.

Bantu Metaphysics of Different Beings

The study of "Bantu metaphysics of different beings" is based on their conception of the predicables and their relations of genus, species, and specific difference. The difference between beings is based on degrees of forces and principles. Inorganic nature is considered by the Bantu as "fixed" and is separated from the vegetal level by a substantial form which Kagame calls, in French, *viridité* (in Kinyarwanda *ububisi*). The latter is separated from the animal sphere by the animal "soul"—*igicūcū*, a spiritual principle responsible for some animal powers similar to those of humans, such as knowledge, love, desire, etc.[11] These are some of the "faculties" that the animal shares with man. Humans are different from the animal only in their ability to reflect, compare, and invent, all of which are attributes of intelligence. The knowledge attributable to the animal can be said to mean only perspicacity or nonintellectual knowledge.[12]

The Problem of the "Vital Principle" in the Being with Intelligence

From the animals our analysis of the categories leads us upward to the level of *Umuntu*, being with intelligence. Among other things, the terms *birth* and *death* are used only in reference to animals and humans. These two terms describe a reality which is dependent on a principle attributed only to animals and humans—the principle of *igicūcū* (shadow). "Birth" or "death" are talked of with regard to this principle's union with or separation from the body. And it is this principle that is responsible for the "faculties" of the animal as described above. It is clear, then, that in order to be different from the animals, humans must have two vital principles. Humans share the same properties with the animal on the level of *igicūcū*. But human and animal are separated by the human's further possession of *Amagara*, the principle of intelligence. Human nature is therefore the vital union of body (already living in union with *igicūcū*) with the principle of intelligence.[13]

Amagara means "life," but definitely not on the same level with the other two types (*Ubuzima* and *Ubugingo*), since these two, pertaining to the sensitive beings as such, are already possessed by man as a sensitive being. Man thus has two vital principles: (a) *igicūcū* (shadow); and (b) the "unnamed principle with intelligence."

At the time of death or dissolution, the principle of *igicūcū* comes to an end but liberates the other principle which "henceforth acquires a determined nomenclature and continues just to-be-there [Fr. *être là*] but without hereafter having to be given the attribute of 'life.' " The Bantu of Rwanda, therefore, "establish in their philosophy, a clearly marked difference between 'sensitive' being in general and the 'sensitive-that-has-intelligence'. The two beings have certain 'faculties' and 'operations' characterizing the 'sensitive'. But these 'faculties' and 'operations' carry, in man, some particularities in relation with his intelligence,"[14] the power to reflect, compare, and invent. The term *ubwenge* means intelligence as it is attributed to man, and cannot mean the same thing when attributed to the animal. It can be attributed to the latter only in an analogical sense. That is why the Bantu talk of man having (possessing) intelligence, but of an animal only "knowing" intelligence; the animal is able to exercise some of the properties of *ubwenge* but only on the level of sensations, while man, apart from being able to get sensations like the animal, is also able to get to the explanations: he has a coordinating principle.

Human Immortality

Kagame calls this problem of human immortality "the problem of the 'disincarnated' soul." This other principle (with intelligence) in man, when liberated, is called *Umuzimu* (pl. *Abazimu*), spirit(s) of the dead. The term *Umuzimu*, as analyzed by Kagame, applies only to beings with intelligence and never to animals. We saw that one of the terms for "life" is *Ubizima*, from which *Umuzima*, the living, comes. The "u" at the end of the word *Umuzimu* carries the weight of its opposition to *Umuzima*. *Umuzimu* thus means a nonliving being with intelligence. The knowledge of these beings, says Kagame, is mostly abstract; though the Bantu also know the concrete, they are more interested in the *Abazimu* only insofar as they are symbols and appear in many practices of reverence to ancestors.

The *Abazimu* are immortal, they cannot die. But *Abazimu* are not eternal, since they have their coming-into-existence when man thus became. The *Abazimu* have a beginning but no end (immortal); they are "eviternal."[15] But the term *Abazimu* is not classifiable according to Kagame's standard classes, so he pushes it aside as an effect of missionary influence, because all known and possible words are classified by the Bantu into the eleven classes and therefore into the four categories of Being, except for God whose essence goes beyond the categories of finite beings, of NTU. Kagame's account for the exclusion of this word from the classes appears to be that although it makes grammatical sense in Kinyarwanda, the concept which it designates is not distinctly separated from that of personality in concrete terms. The Bantu never talk of "the dead" as belonging to a separate conceptual category distinct from that of persons. In Kiswahili the word *Uzima* means life, biological life. But *mtu mzima* may sometimes mean something more than or different from just a "live person." It may mean a mature person or one who is judged capable of exercising correct mental activities expected of adulthood. The opposite of this is rendered by the word *wazimu*, which means "out of right mind," "incapable of good reasoning," "mad," etc. It does not mean "dead." For death Kiswahili uses the word *kifo*, from the verb *kufa* (to die). The dead are called *wafu* (sing. *mfu*).

Kagame appears to argue that even in Kinyarwanda, the coinage of the word *Umuzimu* (pl. *Abazimu*) to designate the opposite of *Umuzima* is inappropriate. He attributes the origin of the term and concept to the reconstruction of Kinyarwanda by missionaries. From our explanation, however, it appears that *uzima*, at least in its Kiswahili use, is a polysemic term. Apart from the biological and psychological meanings mentioned above, the word also has a physical meaning in the sense of size and is in this sense properly used as an adjective of words signifying objects, such as *nyumba nzima* (whole house) or *mkate mzima* (whole loaf of bread), *mwili mzima* (whole body), *mji mzima* (whole city), and so on. In another respect, when used in the form *mtu mzima* (literally "whole person"), the word *uzima* is used to render the sense of "full growth" or maturity; and the idea of wholeness in this respect acquires a metaphysical connotation of (physical) maturity and attainment of the ideal state of personhood. It is this metaphysical idea of ideal state or perfection which is the referent when the same phrase *mtu mzima* is used to signify good health.

Being and Movement

Kagame had told us of the active nature of beings when he talked of the metaphysics of the vegetables. Drawing upon Tempels's *La Philosophie bantoue* and its vitalist conception of the universe, Kagame talks of beings as possessing a certain principle or force that makes them act upon each other. This general activity of beings on one another (at different levels or degrees, according to the categories) enters into the general concept of movement as an essential element of beings or nature as we have seen in the foregoing authors. In Kagame, this metaphysical aspect is attributed to the category of Ahantu, which he calls in French *"l'être individualisateur du mouvement (lieu-temps)."* Kagame distinguishes three types of "place." The first is the "physical place," which we often mean when we refer to the "locality" or "space" susceptible of being occupied by an object. The second type is the "localization" insofar as it is a position in space, or "internal place." Then there is the third, the "external place." For example, the hairs of the body certainly delimit the "internal place," but they are not in nothing. They are themselves delimited by space exterior to the body. This is the "external place." It is what is called in Latin *ubi*. "That is to say: if it is me that a corporal being metaphysically exiges, being spatial in its internal constitution, then it is totally necessary that this same being be clothed by a 'place'. In other words, the notion of 'there where' signifies 'the actual application' of bodies to the space where they are situated."[16] The "internal" and "external" places are metaphysical places and are different in this aspect from the "physical place."[17]

The category of Ahantu as the category of localization includes also the category of time, for the two concepts are interchangeable in Bantu ordinary language.[18] The essence of time, however, is becoming, which means passage and transition from any one state to another. Within the categories of Being, time falls under the category of Ahantu. It converges with the category of space to individualize movement of Being, which means individualizing Being even as its activity and internal perfection proceed. Movement is attributed to Being insofar as it is Being, as invisible passages and transitions that characterize all beings of all categories.

Bantu Theodicy

The Bantu believe in a Supreme Being who is the first cause of all things or beings —NTU, as Kagame prefers to call them. These concepts which imply the transcendence of God are implicit in His two names, *Iya-mbere* and *Iya-kare*, which mean "he who is before everything" and "he who is at the very beginning." The eternity of God is expressed in Kinyarwanda by *Haba*, which implies "permanent habit"—always. The attributes of God are multiple and, as is the case with many other African groups, the attributes serve also as names for God, usually in praise form.

God is *Iya-mbere* (he who is before everything else); *Iya-kare* (he who is at the very beginning, the Initial); *Rurema* (Creator); *Rugira* (he who acts [par excellence]); *Rugabo* (the powerful); *Rugaba* (distributor of goods); *Rwagisha* (he who gives benedictions); *Nyamurunga* (he who puts together). The name *Immana*, though problematic as to its exact meaning or etymology, is the official and popular Rwanda-Bantu name for God.

Kagame summarizes the most important metaphysical characteristics of the concept of God as follows:

(i) God as the external existent: God does not form part of the four metaphysical categories and therefore is on the outside of created or qualified beings –NTU; He is eternal.

(ii) God as the Creator: God is considered as the Existent which puts the existence [Fr. *l'exister*] of beings –NTU—there, and confers to them the property of reproduction and activity.

(iii) God as the Conserver [*Conservateur*]: The actual existence of beings is thought to be regulated [begin and end] by his decision.[19]

God is also the "final cause" of all things. "God is, in some way, the destiny of men and of all the goods that He puts to their disposition. Man can never lose his existence as a living being, nor can he be deprived of his temporal goods if not [only] at the instance and in the fashion determined by God."[20] Thus God, though also an Existent, exists in a mode different from that of beings –NTU. We saw that movement (to act and to be acted upon) is the essential characteristic of beings –NTU.[21] It is their mode of being. Now this type of movement does concern God. He is the "habitual" source of activity in beings –NTU, though God himself does not belong to this sphere of NTU categories, for He transcends them. The concepts of the absolute power of God and of his "masterdom" over everything logically lead the Bantu of Rwanda to believe that all human activities are to be attributed to them only in an analogical way. It is God who actually knows, sees, acts, etc. Although we talk of man as knowing, seeing, acting, it is God who knows, sees, acts in a perfect way because He is the author of all activities.[22] On this Kagame draws upon neo-Thomistic philosophy.

Immana thus created everything; and He created them either to act or to be acted upon, each according to its proper nature. Since this activity requires intelligence, and having intelligence means *de facto* acting, man needs to act and all the beings-things were created for his use in exercising this activity. This is the foundation of the "final cause" in Rwanda-Bantu philosophy and undergirds their ethics, for all acts which conform with the preservation of one's force are allowed by *Immana*. A moral act is thus judged or qualified as "good" or "bad" according to whether it conforms or not to an already prescribed law (prohibition). These prohibitions or laws, some of which might have been determined and profoundly refined as a result of social experience, are all directed toward the well-being of man and all move under the ultimate decision of *Immana*, the powerful God.

Influence of Kagame

Kagame has been rightly criticized for being too Aristotelian in his elaboration of what he calls the "Bantu philosophy of being." This defect is partly because of the wrong basis for Kagame's thesis. He rests his exposition rather exceedingly on the assumption of similarities in thinking between the ancient Greek philosophers and the ordinary Bantu. The basis for this comparison is his erroneous belief that philosophical problems are common or similar to all peoples without distinction.[23]

What Kagame does then, as suggested by the titles of his works, is to examine the cultural differences in the application of categories to the concept of Being. To do this, Kagame, as Lyndon Harries said in his review of the book in question, "chooses Aristotelian metaphysical categories as 'un instrument de contrôle, un point de repere déjà connu' for his treatment of what he terms 'les catégories bantu-rwandaises'."[24] This method is carried out throughout the whole work. Though there could easily be a similarity between certain aspects of specialized Greek thought and Bantu worldviews or concepts as Kagame assumed, these similarities need not produce the same results, and the two systems need to be treated, at least initially, independently. Kagame wants to prove that the unity of a metaphysical principle—a characteristic of Aristotelian-Cartesian philosophies—is as much Hellenic as it is Bantu. He does so by, first, portraying the ordinary person among the Bantu as being primarily a sort of "res cogitans" whose primary attribute is the contemplation of essences. Second, Kagame attempts to prove the universality of the principle of unity through his rather forceful formulation of the category of NTU as a sign of the unity in beings. Harries is therefore perhaps right when he says that "Kagame is principally concerned with establishing philosophic categories, not linguistic ones."[25] It is this interest which pushes Kagame into construing linguistic evidence for what he believes is the central philosophical interest of all human experiences.

This ingenious linguistic analysis is also due to the fact that Kagame seeks to explain too much and consequently also formulates too many concepts that are unknown to the Bantu, not because they cannot formulate them, but rather because such notions as unity, causality, categories of being, etc., lie outside the focus and interests of ordinary experience. The result of Kagame's work is therefore simply "a scholarly exercise in Aristotelian philosophy." It is, however, wrong to think that "the Aristotelian system is being used by Kagame . . . as the parent philosophy from which the Ruanda [Rwanda] philosophy must be shown to have its birth."[26]

Although Kagame followed in the footsteps of Tempels, he also differed from him in many ways. If Tempels had methodically erred in his ambitious generalization on the Bantu and on primitive peoples in general, Kagame confined his subject matter to a limited linguistic and geographical group—the Bantu of Rwanda. Second, Tempels had developed a particular stand for the Bantu. His theory of philosophy projected the Bantu as a people possessing a particular type of intellect from which emanates the being-force theory. In other words, Tempels's conception of the Bantu is similar to that of Horton (1967), which represents Africans as the exemplary negation of rationality. This view claims that African traditional thought bases its explanation of reality on spiritual and personal elements as contrasted to the nonpersonal, objective, and experimental elements of Western science. From this conception emerged the notion that the African conception of reality in terms of vital forces was radically opposed to its Western variant which focuses on the objective condition of reality as made up of "things." Kagame, on the other hand, made this particularity into a universalism with the rest of world cultures and thought systems. For Kagame, the problems of Being, as we saw, are problems that face all peoples regardless of their culture or continent. So also is formal logic, which guards ideas and guides reasoning and judgment in the process of identifying and formulating the universal categories. These elements, says Kagame, have no Bantu particularity, they belong to a universal philosophy.[27]

For a generalized Bantu philosophy, however, Kagame had to wait until he had done a meticulous comparative analysis of the different Bantu languages of the region. The result of this study was his *La Philosophie bantu comparée* (1976), that is, a set of overall generalizations based on evidence.

Another important point that separates Kagame from Tempels is his interpretation of the content of this "philosophy." The essential factor in "Bantu philosophy" according to Tempels, was the force theory, with force being interpreted as the Bantu parallel for being or object. Kagame critizes this theory. In fact he avoids the mention of it for a long time in his work. When he talks of it at all, he mentions it in relation to the dynamic consideration of Being among the Bantu, as opposed to the static orientation in Aristotelian-scholastic philosophy. But even here, Kagame holds that there are no significant differences in the concepts of Being as they are found in Greek and Bantu systems of thought. Although the Bantu emphasize the dynamic nature of Being in their theoretical and practical endeavors, there are several ways in which the static and objective characteristics of beings play a central role in their everyday lives. Similarly, among Western peoples, the philosophical emphasis on static Being blends well with the dynamic characteristics of things and events in everyday experience. In real experiences, the dynamic and static characteristics of reality are always complementary. Kagame's theory of Being is therefore that which designates "force" as a substantial quality in some beings, as opposed to Tempels's theory which made "force" the African parallel or equivalent of substance. However, both concur that the concept of "force" is primarily important in Bantu thinking; and Kagame affirms that the Bantu, at least in Rwanda, conceive Being in terms of its operations, its modes of acting. But this does not mean that the Bantu are incapable of conceiving beings in their static aspect, for this latter is always presupposed by the concept of movement as a property. So, "if the philosophy of the Bantu has been denominated as dynamic," says Kagame, "it must be recalled that it is primarily static. [And] If that of European culture has been qualified as static, it must not be forgotten that it is secondarily dynamic," because, continues Kagame,

> (i) The operational predisposition supposes essence
>
> and
>
> (ii) The structure of essence is in function of its finality.[28]

For him, then, the notions of force and substance are different, and the Bantu, like the famous Greek philosophers, recognize as much. Force is a predicate of substance and can therefore not be identical with it. It denotes the dynamism of Being. Conversely, concrete substance is predicated substance, whether we focus our attention on the predicate or on the substance itself.

Ordinary Language, or Philosophy?

It must be stated that the point which Kagame raises on the relationship between language and concept is of great theoretical interest, and must not be dismissed as simplistic.[29] That this is his primary interest is suggested by his disinterest in the objective truth of the affirmations he makes about the conceptual referents in his analyses. This is evidenced by his contention that "se non è vero, è ben trovato" (p.87 above), which removes emphasis from the objective presence of metaphysical notions, such as substance, unity, causality, etc., in Bantu thought and places it on the theoretical constructions of the author. In other words, the whole analysis is Kagame's own invention, his theoretical assumption. This theoretical assumption is about the conceptual referents of words in ordinary language or the theoretical content in ordinary language. His works, then, may not be so much analyses of conceptual issues in defense of African ethnophilosophy as they are a practice in universal philosophy with a foundation on an African experience. And in this case, his point might be pushed to another level: that he makes a claim to the effect that all philosophical systems bear some ethnocentrism despite the universal character of the problems they treat.

The basic point Kagame expresses is that concepts, and indeed whole world-views, precede language. The structure and grammatical rules of language are modeled in agreement with the cosmological ordering of the universe. The modeling of linguistic structure in accordance with philosophy, according to Kagame, was done by the great ancestors—philosophers who were also the sages of the tribe. It is what was formulated by these forefathers that constitutes both the language and the philosophy of the Bantu. It is this premise that drives Kagame into making the comparative study of Bantu philosophy based on the analysis of linguistic variations back to the original roots or anything approximate thereto. In this sense, it can be said that Kagame accepts and applauds Tempels's presentation of African philosophy as a static phenomenon that is impervious to change.

Linguistic analysis, on the other hand, is useful, according to Kagame, only insofar as it is also true that philosophy precedes language. The implications of this view carry some unacceptable conclusions that Kagame himself infers. Grammar, Kagame contends, is structured in complete compliance with our conceptualizations and classifications of the world. Is this true? Numerous examples of exceptions from other languages—including Kiswahili, which is built upon strong Bantu structures—suggest that this cannot be accepted as a general theoretical premise.

Human languages have great importance for the intersubjective function that they perform. Although it is the means by which we convey our ideas about the world, language cannot be reduced to a subordinate or secondary position in relation to thought. Experience shows that there are many ideas for which we have no words, as well as words that do not correspond exactly with our perceptions of reality in their general grammatical structure and classifications. The laws that determine grammatical structures must therefore be separated from their theoretical content. Otherwise, how would we understand single words whose different meanings, which sometimes span different metaphysical categories, depend only on tonality? The value and significance of ordinary language lie in its communicative role. Our world of perception has differences. Effective communication about the world of experience requires that ordinary language indicate such differences.

Ordinary language is also highly taxonomic. However, there is no evidence from empirical study of language that such taxonomy is based on philosophy or metaphysics. Prominent theorists of language and philosophy, such as Gilbert Ryle, Stanley Cavell, and Zeno Vendler, have argued that the results of linguistics cannot possibly support philosophical conclusions. Their contention is that since linguistics is primarily an objective science, that is, a science whose results are of the nature of empirical generalizations and which merely express contingent facts resulting from the structural analysis of language, it cannot give support to philosophical statements, which are themselves not empirical generalizations. "Ergo, no linguistic result can amount to a philosophical assertion, nor can it support one," writes Vendler.[30] For these theorists, at least for Cavell, the interest of philosophy lies in the *a priori*, based upon the categorical declaratives. Wittgenstein himself had earlier sustained a similar argument when he talked of the "possibilities of phenomena" as the area to which the philosopher is (always) directed rather than to the phenomena themselves.[31]

Both Vendler and Cavell were influenced by the second Wittgenstein. Thus Vendler argues that philosophers who want to trace the *a priori* in linguistic structure are forcing arguments which do not conform with the functions of language. Undeniably, structure plays a central role in determining the function of a word within a given proposition, and structural complexes differ not only from one language to another but also in regard to whether the word is written or spoken. In the words of the structuralists, as expressed by Martinet, "it is a question of the way in which these materials (seen as either phonic symbols or graphic transcriptions of these) are assembled and combined to obtain an object created for specific purposes and capable of satisfying well-defined functions."[32] Vendler's argument is that function is primarily (or solely?) communication, and is properly performed according to the degree of practical efficiency, which is judgeable upon an objective observation of the *use* of the object. Adherence to strict observation of the demands of structure or of rules renders the practical efficiency of a function most reliable.

The same applies to language. In order that communication may be possible, and this means that in order for information so passed to remain the same for all the interlocutors in a given context, linguistic details must be equally adhered to by all those concerned. But, in all such instances, meanings of words are kept strictly tied to their referents, even where the referents are varied or altered. Thus, for example, to keep each other within the same speech "wavelength," Luo-speaking people talking about feelings (of pain) would need to use the Luo word *Rem* the same way to keep information or communication related to that referent possible for all concerned. And anywhere else where the same letter combination is used, as in the verb *rem* (to fail) or as a noun derived from this, change of use must be expressly indicated to reduce the amount of strain required to switch the reference of the word to another referent or object.

Let us take another example: common sense, and perhaps logic, would instruct us that a round rectangular object is not only unusual or unlikely, it is in fact inconceivable. Now one could contend that it is possible, and go on to add that the word *round* is a property of size to him and not of shape. Then the other person might say, "No. Properties of size are designated as either 'small', 'big', or 'medium', etc." And at this point the objector says: "Use whatever word you wish, it wouldn't matter to me so long as you accept that whenever you or I use the word 'round' it must be taken—or at least I will take it—to mean 'big'." Communication becomes awesome. To make conceptual pictures and to communicate them effectively, words must be used in the same way by all speakers of any language. So to make that conversation possible at all, one of the speakers must abandon his "usual" meaning of the word *round*. So too, the inconceivability of a round rectangular table would not be attainable as a universal logical rule unless the words mean exactly the same "thing" to all speakers of English. This implies that, as far as structural significances are concerned, words are all contingent facts. Now, whoever uses those concepts only in a sentence like "some tables were round while others were rectangular" is, according to Vendler, not concerned about giving "rules constituting the conceptual framework of the language but, talking in that very framework, expresses a truth necessitated by it." Rules of language definitely do always reflect this "presupposed" or assumed conceptual framework, within which a language "banks" the correctness of the application of its words in daily use. But, the question now is: Is this conceptual framework, or what Vendler variably calls the *a priori*, always the object of our speech?

We can now come back to Kagame. In his analysis, Kagame contends that the structure of Bantu languages can be analyzed to reveal that the Bantu divide their "reality" into four categories or classes expressible by the combination of a *specific* classificative to a unique genus, NTU, which reflects the most abstract concept in Bantu languages. The four categories of reality can be summarized as follows:

MUntu = existent with intelligence (man);
KIntu = existent without intelligence (thing);
HAntu = existent that determines space-time;
KUntu = existent that determines manner or mode of existing.[33]

By saying that these categories manifest or prove the manner in which "the Bantu have both posed and solved the problem [of Being] in another way"[34] different from the European way, Kagame appears to be suggesting that all Bantu are always *aware* of the categorizational (*a priori*) roles of those words, and that when used in speech, the grammatical categories are primarily destined to convey those analytic meanings. If this premise is accepted as Kagame argues it should be, then the first two letters (MU, KI, HA, and KU) of the words Muntu, Kintu, Hantu, and Kuntu are the classificative variables which determine the class for the abstract superordinate NTU, which Kagame also calls the "ultimate unifying notion." They predicate NTU, and therefore indicate the families or categories of Being. In other words, their role is to express the "specific difference" of NTU.

Undeniably, Kinyarwanda, like many other Bantu languages analyzed by Kagame in his *La Philosophie bantu comparée*, is a highly classificative language. It is a declinative language in which most words are grouped in accordance to certain declinative families to which their referents belong. For example, the M class not only includes man (*Mtu*), but also dog (*Mbwa*), cow (*Ngombe*), snake (*Nyoka*), etc., which can be classified together as "sensitives." And all of them are indicatively referred to as *huyu* (this), so that one says of man "*mtu huyu*" (this man) as he says of a dog "*mbwa huyu*" (this dog). Equally there is the K class to which all words beginning with "ki" belong, and in most cases these denote "things" as inanimate entities. Its plural is formed by changing "k" to "v"; thus *kijana* (young man) becomes *vijana* (young people). And, indicatively, they should, by grammatical rule, be referred to as *hiki* (this), hence "*kitu hiki*" (this thing). Yet all Swahili-speaking people know that in order to speak correct Kiswahili one does not say "*kijana hiki*." That is, that although *kijana* begins with the inanimate classificative "ki," its referent is actually a man and therefore ought to be referred to as *huyu*. The possessive pronoun used for nouns in the M class is generally of the "wa" type, such as in "*mtu wangu*" (my man), "*mke wangu*" (my wife), etc. But we say "*baba yangu*" (my father), "*kipusa changu*" (my pretty girl), thus using pronouns that fall generally in the "inanimate" class. In making propositions with the last two examples one would say "Huyu ni baba yangu" (this is my father) and "Huyu ni kipusa changu" (this is my pretty girl) and not "*Hii* ni baba yangu" nor "*Hiki* ni kipusa changu." These examples show that classification is frequently a binary exercise, and that sometimes words belong to different classes from those of their referents without violating the established grammar or structural syntax of a language.

Now, anybody learning to use Kiswahili *correctly*, including Swahili children themselves, merely learns these grammatical structures as they are *in fact* employed in speaking correct Kiswahili. And at no time is the grammar taught as a reflection of the Swahili understanding of the world. It is true that grammar and vocabulary of many languages often reflect a taxonomic achievement in grouping objects into classes, but there is nothing to suggest that such taxonomy is carried out purely on the basis of metaphysical differences between things. Those who speak German know that words in that language are grammatically classified into either masculine or feminine or neuter groupings. One would assume that in this language all objects that are obviously masculine or male would fall under the masculine gender, while all "inanimates" would go under the neuter gender and likewise all female objects under the feminine gender. But this is not a general rule in German at all. For example, *Mädchen* (girl), a word that obviously refers to a female, falls under neuter so that one says "*das Mädchen*" instead of "*die Mädchen*" for "that girl." Yet all German speakers know that when they say "*das Mädchen*" they do not mean a "thing" in the sense of "inanimate," but indeed a human being. A table, on the other hand, which in our understanding belongs to the class of "things" as an "inanimate," does not belong to this class in the German grammar. It belongs to the masculine gender, so that one refers to it as "*der Tisch*" rather than "*das Tisch*." Yet we know of no German philosopher who explained why girls are "things" and tables "men" to Germans.

From the above argument we are bound to accept that gender and other declination types are major linguistic classification factors. There are two types of gender. The first type refers to a natural characteristic which classifies many living organisms into male and female. This is sexual gender, and mainly describes the roles of such living organisms in the reproductive process. The second type of gender, which also includes the first type, is a purely grammatical one and has the function of determining grammatical structure in languages. Some structurally complex languages, such as Latin and German, have the neuter class in addition to the standard masculine (male) and feminine (female) genders.

There is not however, as far as we know, any logical basis or metalinguistic ground on which the determination of grammatical gender is made. As a result, there is no uniformity among and within languages about exactly what must belong to which grammatical gender class. At times, words denoting things which belong to a specific sexual gender are shifted to a different gender at the grammatical level, like the German *Mädchen*, or are sometimes retained in two different grammatical gender classes at the same time, like the Italian *un tavolo* (m.) and *una tavola* (f.), both meaning "table." In German, table is only masculine *(der Tisch)*. Sometimes too, meticulous sexual gender classifications are totally ignored at the grammatical level. A good example of this is the fact that although many communities recognize sexual gender classifications of plants and snakes, for example, their names are generally classified together under one grammatical class. In Italian, German, and French, for example, all trees are considered to be masculine, like rivers, lakes, seas, etc. The English language is indifferent about all of them. The Luo of Kenya have a detailed list of things, including plants and fish, classified according to gender, although the Luo talk of all of them as if they were only inanimate things. Thus, although linguists recognize gender systems in languages, they are also quite clear that such grammatical systems correlate in no decisive way with sex.

Every language, therefore, seems to have its own regulations and practical purposes independent of the worldview that the people who speak it may have. Language changes; it loses many of its components and acquires new ones without subtracting or adding any new element of the people's worldview. Or, too, people may be aware of values or of metaphysical concepts about the world without necessarily having corresponding words in their language in which such values or metaphysical concepts are reflected. For example, there are no pronouns in Dholuo that indicate gender classification into masculine, feminine, and neuter, as there are in the German language or in Latin. But this does not constitute proof that the Luo are not conscious of gender differences between male and female or that a certain group of existents have life and others do not. Nor is it proof, as would be argued in certain feminist circles today, that because the Luo have no structure in their language by which one easily recognizes when they are talking of women and when they are talking of men, they are less oppressors of women than the Indo-Germanic speaking peoples whose languages have sharp structural distinctions between the two. Also, the Luo lack the kind of linguistic classifications that Kagame describes for the Bantu languages. But that does not mean that the Luo are incapable of abstracting or that they do not distinguish between substances or nouns and other forms of language such as adverbs, verbs, adjectives, etc. They simply have other ways of indicating such grammatical relations in their language. Differences in complexity of language cannot, therefore, be used as examples to prove corresponding differences in the complexity of worldviews.

These and many other examples show that the grammatical rules of any language do not always reflect a definite worldview. Every language has its own structure which indicates the manner in which its speakers must handle it in order to communicate in it correctly and efficiently. Admittedly, some languages are structurally more complex and present more difficulties to learn than others, but they certainly cannot be used as proofs that certain minds are more "complex" than others.

It is true that language is a good store of people's ideas about their own environment and that by learning another people's language we are better able to understand that people's worldview. But the question one raises quickly here is: How much is the language of a people a denoter of the *a priori* and not only of the referent which is the object of communication? In other words, with what exactitude do we know that when a Bantu-speaking native says *"muntu"* he or she actually means "being with intelligence" and not merely "a person" irrespective of what may be his or her "definition"? Of course, one does not deny that eventually or analytically the word *muntu* refers to that which philosophers have defined as "being with intelligence." But just how many native speakers have this analytic *a priori* at the back of their minds when they use the word?

Hence, while it is true that language is built upon our perception of reality in its diversity, and that therefore one is able to arrive at the structure of reality of a particular people beginning from their language, language is not made dependent upon the reality of experience on the basis of an analytical knowledge of the world. Some of the many possible reasons for this are, first, that in order to carry out this exercise we would need a language (of whatever kind) which in turn would need other primitive concepts, and so on. But we cannot go backwards *ad absurdum*. Second, concepts about reality are limitless, and all of us, even from the same speech communities, have various concepts about reality while our language seems to be quite uniform. If concepts controlled language, each individual would have his own language. But this is not the case. And third, as John Lyons says, it would clearly be wrong to assume that *"Muntu,"* for example, "is two words for those who know the history of the language and one word for the rest of us—unless it were in fact discovered that those who know the history of the language use words [like *muntu*] differently from those who do not know the history of the language."[35] If that were so, then those who know more than one meaning of words, that is, knowing their "meanings" as well as the uses we make of them, would need to construct afresh such words on each occasion on which they are used.

Naming and classifying are thus mere taxonomic exercises, and we do them because things are different anyway. The question here, then, is whether the exercise of naming and classifying does not, in fact, *per se* make up a philosophical exercise.

Whatever the case, meanings of words in ordinary language are fixed with regard to their communicative function, and this is all language is meant to serve in its ordinary use. Thus when through some rigorous analysis we are able to trace word formation to the word's conceptual significances, we are actually doing an exercise that is essentially out of the context of the original function of the word. In other words, at this level we would be doing our own private abstractions and ploughing into fields completely unintended and possibly even unknown to the common native speaker of that language. It would be naive to assume that language was made for the philosophical mind only, or that stupid people who nevertheless can talk and who speak grammatically are also philosophers. Whatever other meanings a word or group of words may have other than the one intended as the object of communication is not the subject matter of the linguist, and can therefore not be proved on the basis of linguistic facts alone. The philosopher's interests in meaning go beyond the limits of the linguist. His "meaning" searches for or denotes "essential" properties by which we identify things as belonging to a specific class. But this is beyond the communicative meaning that words denote in common language. While an "essentialist" analyzes his objects before classifying (and naming) them, the native speaker of the language merely needs to know rules of application regulating the use of the language, whatever may be the underlying "essential" or common properties in the referents of the words. So people learning new languages hardly undergo philosophical training to learn or master first the "reasons" of classification of realities and the conceptual determination of terms used for them.

So while it is true that linguistic data cannot be denied philosophical interest merely on the ground that they are empirical, it must also be said that such philosophical significances traceable in the empirical data of linguistics are on a different level and are the interest of a few experts imposing new roles on an already existing and functional complex. From the ordinary common language they build another language, a language of experts. The meaning of a specific word in ordinary language, on the other hand, must be sought in "what it stands for" for the majority of its speakers, who never have to qualify first as metaphysicians before they qualify as speakers of their own language, whether it is their native language or a new one.

5 | Cultures Without Time?
Mbiti's Religious Ethnology

ONE OF THE most widely known scholars of traditional African religious thought is John S. Mbiti. Although the writings of such scholars as Vincent Mulago (gwa Cikala), François Lufuluabo, Bolaji Idowu, and others on subjects relating to African Christian theology date much earlier than Mbiti's works, the study of African theology in English-speaking institutions has become so much identified with his name that he is considered by many as the father of African Christian theology and, until recently, perhaps its most popular exponent. This popularity, however, stands in contrast to the weakness of many of Mbiti's assumptions and arguments concerning what he believes are the primary principles and premises of African traditional religions. His descriptions of African traditional religions do not compare well, for example, with Bolaji Idowu's *African Traditional Religion: A Definition* (1973). Although Mbiti's single concern has been to unveil the "philosophy" beneath African traditional religious concepts, practices, and languages, he does not indicate his own theoretical justification and definition of religion or of religious experience. Mbiti has written numerous books and articles on this subject, but his most important works are *African Religions and Philosophy* (1969), *African Concepts of God* (1970), and *New Testament Eschatology in an African Background: A Study of the Encounter Between New Testament Theology and African Traditional Concepts* (1971). This, however, does not mean that we wish to belittle the other books and numerous scholarly articles that Mbiti has contributed to international journals and scholarly volumes. Although all the books cited above reveal Mbiti's deep concern with the basic "philosophy of African religions," the first volume remains, in my opinion, the backbone of Mbiti's ideas and is the one responsible for the great and undisputed popularity that he enjoyed following its publication, among both his admirers and his critics.

African Religions and Philosophy is concerned with the description or analysis of religious concepts in black Africa (which means Africa south of the Sahara) and, together with *African Concepts of God*, provides a systematic theology of African traditional religions. Mbiti's aim in these two works is "to put emphasis on the philosophical content of African religions" by treating religion as an ontological phenomenon. Other than the concept of time, it is not clear, as far as the book itself is concerned, what else forms the separating lines between the religious concepts already formulated and cited in various rituals or applied in other religious practices and the "philosophical" principles and premises on which they are based. Here one thinks of such systems as we have seen for the Dogon and Bambara, where a neat explanation of the "general philosophy" is presented, followed by its religious derivations; such a system provides a detailed knowledge of the religious beliefs or cults, based on and derived from some "philosophical" pillar that gives this knowledge strength and inserts it within the whole system of thought to make part of the coherent chain. In this respect Mbiti differs strikingly from either Mulago or Jean-Calvin Bahoken. He makes no attempt, as the latter two do, to provide the philosophical analysis of the ontology upon which African traditional religious systems are based.

Perhaps Mbiti is writing for a particular audience—those already acquainted with "African philosophy"—so that he leaves the discernment of these "philosophical" contents from religion to the alert mind and sensitive imagination of the expert. But in order not to assume too much, one can only say that Mbiti's work is not very clear as far as its aims are concerned. And this obscurity in a way partly justifies the criticisms which claim that Mbiti merely parades African traditional beliefs (which, to these critics, are nothing but mythology) as "philosophy."

This lack of separation between "African philosophy" and African religious concepts can only be assumed to be intentional in Mbiti's works, so that when he describes a religious belief or ritual, he there talks of "African religions and philosophy" at the same time. To Mbiti, "religion is part and parcel of the African heritage which goes back many thousands of years." African religion, he says, "is the product of the thinking and experiences of our [Africans'] forefathers. They formed religious ideas, they formulated religious beliefs, they observed religious ceremonies and rituals, they told proverbs and myths which carried religious meanings, and they evolved laws and customs which safeguarded the life of the individual and his community."[1] In other words, as Mbiti himself likes to say, African religions or "philosophy" are not found neatly formulated in library books, but rather in the very life of the people, in their daily practices and language. "It is integrated so much into different areas of life that in fact most of the African languages do not have a word for religion as such,"[2] for African religions "evolved slowly through many centuries, as people responded to the situations of their life and reflected upon their experiences."[3]

African religion, then, is a dynamic phenomenon—it is found in all aspects of Africans' lives, in their activities, which "include occasions like the birth of a child, the giving of names, circumcision and other initiation ceremonies, marriage, funerals, harvesting festivals, praying for rain, and many others."[4] Shrines, sacred places, religious objects, art, symbols, music and dance, proverbs, riddles, and wise sayings are all forms of religious expression. And, writes Mbiti, because traditional religions permeate all the departments of life, there is no formal distinction between the sacred and the secular, between the religious and the non-religious, between the spiritual and the material areas of life. Wherever the African is, there is his religion: he carries it to the field where he is sowing seeds or harvesting a new crop; he takes it with him to the beer party or to attend a funeral ceremony. . . . [5]

This is the general frame of mind within which the African conceives God:

Expressed ontologically, God is the origin and sustenance of all things. He is "older" than the *Zamani* [Swahili word for "past"] period; He is outside and beyond His creation. On the other hand, He is personally involved in His creation, so that it is not outside of Him or His reach. God is thus simultaneously transcendent and immanent; and a balanced understanding of these two extremes is necessary in our [Africans'] discussion of African conceptions of God. [6]

Most African peoples, says Mbiti, believe in God's transcendence and supremacy. He (God) is the One transcendent and supreme Being. But given that African thought forms are more concrete than they are abstract, and though we find "considerable examples of how African peoples conceive of the eternal (abstract) nature of God," the expression of these concepts remains in a large part connected to reality and everyday experiences of it. Mbiti says that these attributes of transcendence and immanence are "paradoxically complementary" in African conceptions of God. "This means that He is so 'far' [transcendent] that men cannot reach Him; yet, He is also so 'near' [immanent] that He comes close to men." [7] His presence is thus realized and recognized in many events and phenomena (things) surrounding man. But this, Mbiti says, "is not pantheism, and there is no evidence that people consider God to be everything and everything to be God." [8] The conceptions of a number of African peoples of God as self-existent and preeminent, expressed in "logico-philosophical" or biological terms, are signs of His transcendence. The Zulu, for example, speak of God as "He who throws Himself into being" and the Luo say that God is *Kumu* (He of no normal conception). Yet the manners of offering sacrifice, prayers, and invocations are evidence of His "nearness" and immanence. In worship, these two attributes are connected through symbolism. God is there, a spiritual, transcendent, and supreme Being. These abstract and eternal attributes justify man's inability to know God, for, as the Bantu say, how can man know God who is spiritual, transcendent, and "far off" when he, man, cannot even master the knowledge of his own "near" environment? But God's activities are "near" and they reveal Him. According to Mbiti, belief in the immanence of God explains the careful choice of places of worship and the symbolic language adopted by most African peoples in the description and practice of their religious beliefs. [9] God is the Most Powerful, and most phenomena in nature reveal this attribute of God—they mirror His great power.

One of the most common conceptions among African peoples of God's power is the attribution of the work of creation to Him. Most African peoples have different names for God by means of which they describe His creative work.[10] Apart from creating the world and everything in it, God also provides for and sustains His creation—He provides people and all things with life. Hence the description of God in symbolic language reflecting His great works. Sometimes people talk of things and fellow humans calling them their "God" because such things or people have at one time or another been their protector. Edwin W. Smith, for example, records a Bena talking to his charm: "This medicine is my life, it is my *Mulungu* (God)" or "The evil power of the wizard is *Mulungu*," etc.[11] Then Smith himself, not understanding the symbolic equation of medicine or wizard with God, comments:

> What A. T. and G. M. Culwich say of the Bena is true also of other tribes: The belief in Mulungu is exceedingly complicated and the ideas held about him or it are both *contradictory and confused....* [12] [emphasis mine]

The symbolism is the same when Africans attribute to the sun the usually reserved name for God and vice versa, or when in the morning they throw small objects of sacrifice in the direction of the rising sun while claiming they are meant for God. Witchcraft and magic in African religion, or the significance of the attributes of God in relation to natural objects and phenomena, are based on the simple criterion of analogical symbolism. Thus God is called the sun because He, like the celestial body, is powerful despite the great distance between Him and humans on earth. In this way, believes Mbiti, Africans try to explain the nature of the invisible spiritual world by means of ordinary language and with reference to objects and phenomena of ordinary experience. According to Mbiti, magic, witchcraft, and worship have the same ontological significance. Their aim is to procure and maintain the ontological balance between God and man, the spirits and man, the departed and the living, or, in other words, between the spiritual and the physical worlds.[13] They are rational deliberations by people in the process of their explanation of the environment.

African Religion and the Spiritual World

Among African peoples, there is a wide variety of concepts about the world of spiritual beings or divinities, ancestral or otherwise. These spirits, which vary in number from one community to another, are believed to have been created by God and to belong to the ontological mode of existence, occupying some spiritual "space" between God and humans. Mbiti differentiates between divinities and spirits. The former are associated with God "and often stand for His activities or manifestations either as personifications or as the spiritual beings in charge of these major objects or phenomena of nature."[14] This constant personification of God and spirits, holds Mbiti, is due to the strong anthropocentric characteristic in African thinking. According to him, Africans always see the spiritual world in relation to the physical world, in which man stands at the center. Everything is in relation to man. There are a number of African peoples who have these spirits in their thought systems, but perhaps the most noteworthy are the Yoruba.[15]

Then there are the major objects of nature, such as the sun, mountains, earth, etc., which are said to have or to be spiritual beings or divinities. Sometimes offerings are made to them. According to Mbiti, such objects of nature are not divinities *per se*. They are, however, significant for two reasons. First, they are the media of God's self-revelation to man. Africans recognize them as created objects. But, they appear to have reasoned, if such created objects are of such magnitude and power, then he who created them must possess such qualities in their perfection. Second, people use them for analogical reference to God's qualities. So when they address the sun in prayers, it is not the sun as a physical object which they intend to communicate to. The role of the sun in worship becomes merely symbolic: it bridges the atemporal with the temporal, the spiritual with the physical. As religious symbols, the great phenomena of nature enter the same category as that of mythological figures. "These mythological figures of a spiritual nature," Mbiti says,

> are on the whole men's attempts to historicize what is otherwise "timeless," and what man experiences in another context as divinities. They explain customs, ideas, or institutions whose origin is otherwise lost to historical sight, in the oblivion of the *Zamani* [Swahili for "past"] period. The explanation is an unconscious attempt to bring into the *Sasa* [Swahili for "present"] a phenomenon which is either difficult to grasp or is shrouded with the mystery which covers it as it sinks deeper into the *Zamani* reality.[16]
>
> The spirits fill up the ontological region of the *Zamani* between God and man's *Sasa*. The ontological transcendence of God is bridged by the spiritual mode of existence. Individual spirits may or may not remain forever, but the class of the spirits is an essential and integral part of African ontology.[17]

In dealing with other issues of philosophical importance, such as death, the hereafter, evil, ethics, and justice, Mbiti adopts a method that is more ethnological than "philosophical." But we do not wish to say that for this reason these issues are deprived of all "philosophical" significance or that they are mere myths. All these aspects of thought and life are clothed, in one way or another, by the general ontology from which they derive. This ontology comprises all possible existence and, within it, a balance must be maintained so that these [different] modes [of existence] neither drift too far apart from one another nor get too close to one another. In addition to the five categories [of African ontology], there seems to be a force, power or energy permeating the whole universe. God is the Source and ultimate controller of this force: but the spirits have access to some of it. A few human beings have the knowledge and ability to tap, manipulate and use it, such as the medicine-men, witches, priests and rainmakers, some for the good and others for the ill of their communities.[18]

African Concept of Time in Mbiti and Its Relation to Christian (NT) Eschatology

Mbiti's analysis of the concept of time in African thought is very important and interesting. As he claims, this concept of time is the key to reaching some understanding of "African religions and philosophy." According to him, time, for Africans, is simply a composition of those events which have occurred, those which are taking place now, and those which are immediately to occur. From this Mbiti infers that, according to African traditional concepts, time is only a two-dimensional phenomenon, with a long past, or *zamani*, a present, or *sasa*, and, in his own words, virtually NO FUTURE.[19] According to this view, the *sasa* has the sense of immediacy, nearness and nowness, and is the period of immediate concern for the people, since that is where and when they exist. *Sasa* is in itself a complete or full time dimension, with its own short future, a dynamic present, and an experienced past. It is the "Micro-Time." In other words, the *sasa* period has its own miniature tridimensional structure.

Zamani, on the other hand, is not limited to what in English is called past. It also has its own past, present, and future, but on a larger scale. The *zamani* overlaps with the *sasa* and the two are not separable. The *sasa* feeds and disappears into the *zamani*.

Mbiti, I think, is caught up within his primary objective, viz., to demonstrate the irrelevance and meaninglessness of the Christian eschatology as taught to African peoples by some missionaries (Mbiti himself is a Protestant pastor and so limits his examples to a Protestant missionary church). He carries out this task more completely in his third work, *New Testament Eschatology in an African Background: A Study of the Encounter Between New Testament Theology and African Traditional Concepts.*[20]

> The Christian faith [says Mbiti] is intensely eschatological, and wherever the church expands it brings and displays its eschatological presence, manifested in activities and experiences like the kerygma, repentance, conversion, salvation, sacraments, mission and Christian hope. . . . Wherever the Church is conquering new fields in individual or community lives, it is making a deeply eschatological progress.[21]

And, as other authors of African theodicy and theology have tried to build up a fertile ground on which the Church would successfully sow its teaching, so also Mbiti goes on to examine the meaningfulness of the eschatological mission of the Church in relation to the African traditional concept of time.

The important element in African conceptions of time is the past, or *tene*, according to the Wakamba; and this importance of *tene* is opposed to the importance fixed on the "future" in the eschatological thinking and hopes expressed in some Christian teachings.

> *Tene* becomes the final storehouse, the point beyond which a phenomenon cannot go, the ultimate destiny of all things that may be caught up in the rhythm of motion.
>
> Because *tene* (past) is the dimension into which all phenomena sink, history, according to Akamba conceptions, is a movement from the *mituki* (temporal dimension signifying present, very near past, or the future just about to be realized) dimension to the *tene* period. History moves backwards from the now moment to that period in the past beyond which nothing can go. So the *tene* period is the centre of gravity in the Akamba conception of history: people's thinking and understanding of the world are orientated towards this finality—not in the future but in the past, in the *tene* dimension of time.[22]

This, together with the fact that "Human life follows also another rhythm which knows neither end nor radical alteration (the rhythm of birth, initiation, marriage, procreation, old age, death and entry into the company of the departed)," is placed against the Christian concept of time and eschatology in the New Testament teaching.[23] The teaching of Christian eschatology by the African Inland Mission (A.I.M.), Mbiti observes, was basically futuristic, based on biblical or metaphysical exaggerations about the "next" world, the world "to come," and the events that lead thereto.[24] Mbiti's point, then, is that A.I.M.'s teachings about salvation and the life to come were based purely on one dimension of time, and particularly the one that the Wakamba (and perhaps many other African peoples) *do not have* in their conception. The A.I.M.'s emphasis on salvation as a "future" event, Mbiti argues, was a wrong interpretation of the central theological point of Christic intervention in history. Furthermore, the idea of "future" is only a minor point in New Testament theology. With such arguments Mbiti identifies and separates missionary politics from what he believes to be correct theological teaching of the New Testament. The A.I.M, therefore, by stressing what amounts to a minor part of the New Testament teaching on eschatology, came into serious conflict with the linguistic and conceptual understanding of the Akamba.[25]

The concept of time is closely related to the concept of the hereafter, of the "life" after physical life and death, and to the concept of the personality of man, in which the name plays an essential role, for the name describes the personality of an individual. These concepts are all integrated into the Akamba ontological classification of existence into five modes or levels: at the top level is God; the second level has two substrata, the upper substratum which is populated by the Aimu, who are the real dead, and the lower one which makes the abode of the living dead, those who have just recently died and are still remembered by their living relatives; the third level is that of living humans; animals and plants occupy the fourth level; finally, on the fifth level are objects without the capacity to have life.[26] The third level is significant in that it is the one directly related to the concept of time.

The living-dead are the departed of the society whose names are still retained and transmitted to descendants, that is, their personalities are still living with the people. They make part of the *sasa* or the nearest *zamani*. "After three to five generations," however, "when ordinary people can no longer recognise a living-dead by name, he becomes a spirit, *Iimu* (pl. *Aimu*)."[27] And, as Mbiti says, the spiritual world—the world of those who *have gone*—is the center toward which existence is directed. Time and history are equally directed toward this *tene*, the period when the ancestors cease to be human beings, in which they become truly dead and can be said to deteriorate. "In terms of Time," says Mbiti, "death ultimately deprives the individual of his participation in the *mituki* [Kikamba for "present"] period, it removes him from the moment of intense living, from a dual-dimensional time to a monodimensional time—the *tene*, the past, even beyond the point of his start—and hence to the point of his non-being, complete disappearance, depersonification, and non-presence."[28]

Mbiti's rendition and discussion of African concepts of time is a critique of the New Testament message in its Hellenized representation. In the Hellenized world, from which the missionary practice draws its epistemic frame, history is the development of reason in time, just as nature is the development of the idea in space. The idea is the nature of God's will, and since this idea becomes truly itself only in and through history, history is the autobiography of God. History, then, is the actualization, the unfolding of the divine plan in time. Salvation, as the process or the unfolding of the divine plan instantiated in the concrete life of every individual person, takes place in history. Its summation occurs in the last judgment. The missionary enterprise in Africa, Mbiti contends, came to set this process in motion, not only by preaching salvation but also by introducing the new Hellenized timeframe within which this process occurs. In his view, however, the linear and tridimensional timeframe of the missionaries was incompatible with both the true eschatology of the New Testament and African representations of time.

According to Mbiti, then, history, including the history of salvation as preached by the missionaries, is a creature of the modern Western nations; as such, it oppresses peoples of other cultures and excludes them from the rightful experience of Christ's presence in the *sasa* which merges the physically and anthropocentrically conceived spirit world of the Akamba with the "spiritual" and Christocentric view of the New Testament.[29]

The conception of time is also seen as a means of abstraction, for anything that transcends the *sasa* period goes over and beyond the present concrete existence because it falls into the dimension of *zamani*; and whatever transcends all the minidimensions of the *zamani* period is of absolute transcendence. This, according to Mbiti, is how Africans conceive, at least partly, the transcendence of God, for God "stretches over and beyond the whole period of *Zamani*, so that not even human imagination can get at Him. He [God] not only fills up the *Zamani* period, He also transcends it."[30]

Time and Language

Of all the things Mbiti says about African religions and philosophy, he is by comparison most vividly remembered and associated with what he says about the African concept of time. But few, apart from Kwame Gyekye,[31] have discussed Mbiti from the linguistic premises which his claims seem to assume. We will try to discuss Mbiti's contentions only on the basis of what he says of them, that is, first, that "it [time] is an ontological phenomenon; [that] it pertains to the question of existence or being";[32] and second, that his claims on the concept of time are based on linguistic evidence.

For Mbiti, time is an extra-mental category into which the order of things fits. Man's physical and mental aspects of existence too are ordered in accordance with this ontological structure of time. According to Mbiti, therefore, this structure is to be found only in the domain of being, of events and existences already accomplished, never in mere projections; that is, time does not exist beyond the up-to-now or just-about-to-happen events and facts. If this is correct, then Mbiti's point raises a problem about the definition and concept of being—but this is not the object of discussion at this point. Whatever the case, the concept of being is a doctrine about reality whose main characteristics are, in fact, omnicomprehensivity and omniextensivity, which, to our understanding, go beyond any temporal limitation.

The comprehensivity of being includes not only actual but also possible being. Thus, to say at the same time of the same people that their concept of time is necessarily related to that of being and that their concept of time extends only backwards is in itself contradictory. Now portraying the African conception of God as one which includes the atemporality or infinitude of God is in itself to suggest that such a conception implied also a conception of infinitude as part of the philosophico-theological conceptualization of reality. In other words, the concept of the infinitude of God must of necessity include a concept of the infinite time within which God executes His acts and plans. To say that someone conceives God as infinite but at the same time has no concept of future is self-contradictory. This is the point expressed by Gyekye when he says of the Akans:

> The Akans of Ghana conceive of God as an Infinite Being . . . , a fact known to Mbiti. Although infinity is here ascribed to a being and not to time, it must be assumed, of course, that a concept of an infinite time is already involved in that of an infinite being, for the infinite being necessarily (logically) exists in an infinite time. In Akan, then, the future exists as an actual time.[33]

According to Gyekye, the belief in and practice of divination depend on the very definition of the concept as an attempt to discover future events. And the future of diviners cannot by any logic be said to be limited to a maximum of two years. Gyekye therefore suggests that perhaps Mbiti merely (wrongfully) generalized what is otherwise a characteristic of only Eastern African peoples. But even the truth of this suggestion is itself unacceptable. Gyekye says:

> For if "the African concept of time" were in fact the key to the understanding of African religions and philosophical ideas, then the Akans and Eastern African peoples, holding different conceptions of time, must logically differ in most, if not all, of their religious and philosophical doctrines; and yet this most probably is not so.[34]

Mbiti's central point is that "according to [African] traditional concepts, time is dual-dimensional with a long *past*, a *present*, and virtually *no future*,"[35] and he claims to have come to this through linguistic evidence taken from verb tenses in the Kikamba and Gikuyu languages. He says that "In the East African languages in which I have carried out research and tested my findings, there are no concrete words or expressions to convey the idea of a distant future."[36] And that "People have little or no active interest in events that lie in the future beyond, at most, two years from now; and the languages concerned lack words by which such events can be conceived or expressed."[37] Again, that "When Africans reckon time, it is for a concrete and specific purpose, in connection with events but not just for the sake of mathematics. Since time is a composition of events, people cannot and do not reckon it in a vacuum."[38] It is obvious from these that Mbiti bases his claims on the African concept of time mainly on language, and we take the verb "to reckon" in the last quotation to mean a mental-linguistic exercise.

For his purposes Mbiti chooses the verb "to come" as used in both languages (Kikamba and Gikuyu). Now, whatever their tense structure to indicate the relationship of the time of speech and the time of event (being communicated), Mbiti observes that for the remote past both languages add in a qualificative "*tene*," such that "I came" without specification of time in the past is expressed as "Tene ninookie" or "Nookie tene" in Kikamba and as "Nindookire tene" in Gikuyu.[39] No similar qualification is given to the remote future tense, which simply appears as "Ningauka" and "Ningoka," in Kikamba and Gikuyu, respectively.

For some reason Mbiti concludes that the future meant by these two tenses stretches ahead of us only by about six months, and at most by two years. They are both translated into English as "I will come." The problem is, however, that unless we mention the exact or approximate time in future, also the English "I will come" remains vague and can mean anything in the period following the time of speech up to infinity. In order to make it precise, an Englishman, or any other person used to the mechanical aids of reckoning time, will qualify it by relating it to some event of everyday experience when the arms of the clock rest on some definite points on the face of the clock. This machine has enabled modern man, as heir to Western technological and industrial inventions, to break down a day's duration into calculable units. Its mechanical standardization has further made it possible for many people worldwide to communicate uniformly in regard to time. Together with the calendar, the clock has revolutionized man's life in communication and planning. Other methods of expressing moments or periods of duration such as "Opon," "Chwiri," "Winter," "Spring," etc. have remained related to the climatic contrasts of the world and to local activities associated with them and are thus not easy to communicate with universally.

It appears that traditional Africans did not designate chronological periods or moments of duration by names or words such as "hours," "days," "weeks," "months," and "years." Moments of time were kept in memory by relating occurrences to some other, maybe more commonly known and greater events. Logically, however, this is possible only in regard to the past, as that is the aspect of duration that has already left us with records of big events with which we can relate other, lesser occurrences that we may find ourselves talking about. The periods to come have not yet been experienced, and therefore have not given us any events which could help us to relate moments of our reference in language other than those that are known to be likely to happen. Because of this, it becomes linguistically easier to talk of the future by making reference to events that are more or less already commonly anticipated by people within a particular environment, speaking the same language, and sharing in the same pattern of life.

Here again, language is used for communication, and what matters is that one succeeds in communicating what one means, that is, the approximate point of occurrence in the period to come that he or she is talking about. Such people may therefore find it very difficult to talk of a thousand years from now, as there would be no event that could be reasonably foreseen for that time to help in the precision or approximation of the actual time in question. But this would not in any way mean or suggest that they cannot conceive or imagine this kind of "long time to come." Time reckoning is always event-related, regardless of the language it is expressed in, and indeed it is in this sense that we use such event-related qualifiers as "tomorrow," "next week," "next year," etc. Where such event-related qualifiers are not used, even in English something like "I will come" does not suggest any frame within which that "coming" would ever be done. It is merely indefinite, in the proper sense of the word, as it includes even the remotest and most unimaginable time possible. Why "Ningauka" and "Ningoka" ("I will come," in Kikamba and Gikuyu respectively) are limited, according to Mbiti, to a maximum of "six months" is difficult to understand, unless these two languages are indeed a unique species in the world. But this is not the case. The absence of a tense structure through which the notion of the future is linguistically expressible cannot be taken as proof that the Akamba and Agikuyu have no concept of the future or, for that matter—and this is a logical point which is not our concern here—that Africans in general have no concept of the future. Time reckoning may be equally difficult for the past where the people concerned lack common elements of reference to facilitate precision and communication. While a particular moment of time may be clear in one's mind as a mental fact and act of identification, it may not always be easy to communicate such precise time unless the structure of the language of the person attempting such communication provides the expressive "manner" of doing so. And this assumes that the person to whom the precise time is being communicated is within that same linguistic world, in order to make that act of communication complete. One wonders how, if Mbiti's conclusion is conceded, the pre-clock European, or any other person to whom clocks and other modern time reckoning methods are unknown, could possibly "precise" a remote future.

In the true sense, then, the problem of precision or imprecision is not so much the issue as the communicative utility of the event-reference. If precision means something like saying "twenty minutes and thirty-seven seconds past four in the afternoon," then one who simply says "when it was raining" is definitely vague, and there is no reason for us to assume that the person who uses the latter qualifier is himself unaware of being vague. If he were aware of other events more closely related to or contemporaneous with the occurrence in question, and also known by the recipient of the information, he could probably be more "exact" about the time by relating his referent to them; for example, "when that lightning flashed" narrows the time reference to a much more definite point than "when it was raining." Precision is thus always there as a mental fixation, and although its communication becomes difficult in the absence of mechanical aids, it is this mental fixation which we not only intend to communicate when talking about time, but also to create for the person to whom we talk.

Perhaps inadvertently, Mbiti's notion of African time coincides with that of Lévy-Bruhl, who also believed that (a) primitive languages were deficient in methods of reckoning time and rendering the relations of time, and that (b) primitive people had no concept of the future because they cannot abstract from the series of events of experience in order to conceive a lineal order of succession in which such events occur. They cannot abstract from occurrences to order.[40]

Although Mbiti's notion, like that of Lévy-Bruhl, compares an assumed African mentality with Western thought, Mbiti intends by it to achieve something essentially different from the intentions of Lévy-Bruhl. By juxtaposing "primitive mentality" and Western thought, Lévy-Bruhl had wanted to demonstrate, as did Hegel before him and Horton after him, that Western conceptualizations of the nature of time, space, experience, and belief were self-evidently "rational" and "scientific," representing the logical unity of the thinking subject, which the primitives had no notions of. Mbiti, on the other hand, aims by his comparison to demonstrate that African conceptualizations of time, space, and being are closer to the original biblical teachings than are some modern Western interpretations of the Bible. For him, then, Africans have a primitive or preindustrial concept of time in contrast to the mechanical and industrial concept of time prevalent in the Western mode of thought.

Peter Rigby[41] calls the Lévy-Bruhlian approach to the study of time reckoning methods in other cultures the abstract-mentalist approach. About it he says:

> . . . by recognizing 'differences', the 'abstract-mentalist' approach (a form of philosophical idealism) does not positively impose the constructs of one culture upon another, but 'negatively' destroys the basis for understanding by an idealistic 'comparison' which ignores the social and historical origins and social production of both sets of concepts.[42]

According to Rigby, concepts of time are products of social and historical determinants of people's perception, particularly their mode of production. He agrees with Evans-Pritchard's, Beidelman's, and Bohannan's[43] acceptance of this premise in their analyses of, respectively, Nuer, Kaguru, and Tiv time reckoning systems. According to Rigby, these three studies belong to another approach in the study of time-reckoning methods. He calls it the abstract-empiricist approach. For Rigby, both Evans-Pritchard and Beidelman appear to accept that the notions of time which they analyze in comparison to "their own" time concepts of Western philosophical and scientific investigations are determined by the different "preoccupations" or political economies of the Nuer and Kaguru respectively. Rigby regrets, however, that the works are lacking in the exploration of the implications of such comparisons. In other words, Evans-Pritchard and Beidelman should have gone ahead to demonstrate how African concepts of time and time reckoning methods differ from the Western ones not on the basis of the Lévy-Bruhlian ratiocinations, but on account of the different social structures and economies.

Rigby states that Bohannan's additional point beyond Evans-Pritchard and Beidelman is that the Tiv place incidents in time, both future and past, by "a direct association of two events," or a "conjuncture." This method is in agreement with what we argued above in relation to the combination of language use on the one hand with event-association on the other as a method of time reckoning. In other words, the ability to express time linguistically, whether past or future, assumes the availability of some event(s) to which the specific moment being expressed may be related. Rigby's contribution to this argument is that the events used in the association are those which make part of the prevalent means of production. Although this point is largely valid, it is perhaps more useful where the specific time to be expressed is relatively distant from the time of speech, and for which other associative events (such as "when it was raining," "the lightning in the night," "the leopard roar," etc.) may not be effectively useful. More important, Bohannan says that the Tiv use this method to indicate periods of future time which exceed four or five years, either by specific seasonal or cyclical events, or by life-expectancy events of a particular person.[44] They may be the equivalents of the Western "one thousand years." The problem with this observation is that it does not sufficiently disprove Lévy-Bruhl's and Mbiti's points that "Frequently a future event, if considered certain to happen, and if provocative of great emotion, is felt to be already present."[45]

In agreement with Lenin[46] and Leach,[47] Rigby argues that there is no such thing as actual time which can be actually experienced. According to them, the concept of actual time is wrong because concepts of time differ dialectically in accordance with changing perceptions which themselves emerge from changing and diverse modes of production. On this account, Rigby accuses the Lévy-Bruhlian approach of not realizing that "[his] own [Western] assumed, scientific" time reckoning method was itself a historically and socially determined (bourgeois) notion of time which could not be compared with similar notions merging out of precapitalist conditions. But, strangely, he agrees with Horton on face value when the latter states that "In traditional Africa, methods of time reckoning vary greatly from culture to culture."[48] Although Horton here states something in keeping with Rigby's own beliefs, I suppose he says so for a completely different reason—to point out that in Africa, regulation of life, including time reckoning, is not based on generally accepted "scientific" laws as is done in the more objective Western world.

Rigby classifies Mbiti's notions on the African concept of time into what he characterizes as the "philosophical-theological" approach. In a familiar Marxist fashion, Rigby accuses this approach of neglecting the historical context of the concepts discussed and defended by its exponents, such as Mbiti and Benjamin C. Ray.[49] According to Rigby, both Mbiti and Ray attribute to Africans what is essentially a bourgeois futurology when they say that African concepts of time are relatively ahistorical, and that they do not encompass an indefinite future. Rigby, unfortunately, does not confront either on the veracity of their claims, satisfying himself with stating that such a claim (about indefinite future) "exhibits a specific form commensurate with the nature of their social formations, and is not a mere replication of the (also specific) notions of the future embodied in capitalist ideology, bolstered by Christian dogma and eschatology."[50]

In Rigby's own approach to the study of time reckoning methods—he calls it the approach of structuralist totality—time reckoning methods are part of a total and specific historicity arising from the nature of the specific social formation under consideration, which in turn is itself a product of that specific historical development. According to this view, time is not a fixed ontological entity. In other words, time is not an *a priori* structure of existence or an *a priori* conceptual scheme into which the data of perception fall. This ontological notion of time was first postulated by Kant. According to Kant, we experience ourselves as perceiving other entities and ourselves together in a world which has a certain structure. So we experience the objects of (outer) perception as being all in space and all in time, as spatially and temporally related to each other. We perceive events, and events are ordered in time. Since we cannot perceive time itself, the mind needs certain rules whereby it reconstructs this order. Kant further attempted to show that the basic principles of modern science correspond to basic features of our conceptual scheme, which determines the structure of any possible experience. He believed that with his notion of time he had uncovered the sole conditions under which coherent, objective experience is possible.

According to Rigby, however, there can be no objective general time or history. With quotes from Louis Althusser,[51] he argues that because the concept of time is a product of social formations arising from specific modes of production, there cannot be history in general, as there is no production in general. There can only be specific structures of historicity in the form of existence of determinate social formations. History, therefore, is part of social consciousness, an element of discourse about the world in which man is the principal actor *in social relations* with others in society. What Rigby does not address himself to is the eschatological nature of his own approach, that is, the deterministic nature of historical time.

The Marxist approach to the analysis of reality is one which does not admit of a futile existentialist struggle. In other words, it does not envisage the dialectical nature of social formation in relation to the ownership of the means of production as being the existential permanent feature of human life. It envisages an end in a deterministic manner. For it too, history is moving toward some sort of "end."

We wish, however, to agree with Rigby that modes of production may be important in temporal location because they provide the definite associative events in relation to which definite time is expressed. But they are not important because they determine our concept of time. The *concept* of time is distinct from *expressions* of time. But neither, in answer to Mbiti and Ray, does the absence of definite expressions such as "two years to come," "ten years to come," etc., in temporal location indicate the absence of the concept. Terms such as "ten years," "five months," etc. are only numerical differences between temporal coordinates (dates of events); they have nearly nothing to do with the concept of order. What Mbiti fails to recognize is that there may be other semantic categories which Africans use to express the notion of indefinite future. The Luo, for example have at least two expressions which indicate their knowledge of indefinite future. These expressions are:

Oru wuod aming'a; and
Aming'a piny nene ochiego apindi e thim.

The first saying is difficult to translate into English. The word *Oru* itself means "day and night are the father and son of each other." It signifies the endless dialectical alternation between day and night. This alternation is regarded as a single phenomenon. It is one reality, *Oru*. This *Oru* is "the son of duration (*wuod aming'a*)." This saying is usually used to refer to the impact of time on certain diehard behavior and circumstances. The meaning of the saying is that duration, the endless alternation between day and night, often brings about change even to the most stubborn situations. This notion indicates a conception of time as a category of order which outlasts the events which take place within it.

In this saying, the Luo conceive of time and space as two interrelated categories. *Oru*, which means the persistent alternation of day and night, is thought of in connection with the world, *piny*. It is *piny* which endures time. They coexist. No one competes with *piny*. The Luo believe that it is due to this power of *piny* that it absorbs and swallows all. *Lowo* (soil), which is the material aspect of *piny*, does not perish. It endures the cruelty of time. *Ru piny* (the endurance of the world or soil) is the spatiotemporal category within which all other events take place. So, it is the world which in fact endures through time. All other things and events occur within the endurance of the world without affecting it. They come and go, however stubborn they may be.

The second saying is closely related to the first. It is a proverb which literally translates into English as "the [endless] endurance of the world forces even the stubborn *apindi* (*Vangueria acutiloba*) to ripen." The meaning of the saying is that there is no thing or event whose endurance can be greater than the endurance of the world itself. *Apindi* is used in this proverb because of its long life. It takes long (about ten years) to mature and bear fruits. And once it does, the fruits also take long to ripen. The important point here is that the Luo make a fairly abstract notion of time as an endless duration in which many things happen. It goes beyond mere events and things. Events occur within it.

The two proverbs are used by the Luo to warn people against pride and complacency. We must not be proud and complacent about anything, and especially about our achievements. Pride would be justifiable only if we were in control of time and therefore capable of determining the content of the future. This idea resembles what Jean-Jacques Rousseau called the veil of ignorance about the future. For the Luo, justifiable pride is based on confidence in the face of change in the future. But humans have no assurance that the future will not change adversely, since they have no control over time, within which changes occur. In the idea of time conveyed in the saying quoted above, the future is not limited by the events of any particular moment. Events can take place at specific moments, but time itself has no limits. For this reason, the ordinary Luo is characteristically quite reluctant to accept distant or long-term appointments, because they are for *"ji ma oru"* (people who will endure). For them, the future is indeterminable. Hence the famous Luo saying, "Gino ma ichamo e mari, gi'modong' kik igen" (Count on what you have, not on what is to come).

It is obvious from the above that the Luo have a concept of infinite future, even though they have no single word which is equivalent to the English word *future.*[52]

Man and the Cosmos

Mbiti portrays African ontology as highly anthropocentric. Everything is centered around man:

> it is an extremely anthropocentric ontology in the sense that everything is seen in terms of its relation to man . . . [and deducing from the five categories], God is the Originator and Sustainer of man; the Spirits explain the destiny of man; Man is at the centre of this ontological hierarchy; the Animals, Plants and natural phenomena and objects constitute the environment in which man lives, provide a means of existence and if need be, man establishes a mystical relationship with them.[53]

Mbiti thus expresses an ontological hierarchy similar to the ones built by Kagame, Mulago, and Bahoken. But in contrast to Bahoken, Mbiti stresses the importance of life as we know and live it. He is less concerned with the abstract ontological relationship between existents. According to Mbiti, man is primarily concerned with the problems of practical happiness in this life as well as in the life to come. It is this concern, he says, which influences man to establish a constant relationship with the spirits and with God as a way of guaranteeing the continuity of happiness from this life into the next.

For Mbiti, it would seem, Africans need no conversion to Christianity. They already live the Christian message. They need no teachings on the "life to come" because they already participate in that life as part of the present. African theology is therefore the systematic formulation of African thought to describe their ideas or conceptions of God and their religious experience in general. But some critics, mostly of the anti-negritude trend of thinking, have nursed little taste for "African theology." For some critics, such as Byang Kato, "African Theology seeks for the identity of the African. In order to do this, the advocates exalt African culture, religion, and philosophy beyond proportion."[54] The practice of African theology is an attempt to "purify" Christianity from its Western association. By this "beyond proportion," no doubt, Kato means that "the interest in traditional religion associated with it [African theology] calls up in the minds of many a return to paganism. . . . "[55] Kato therefore criticizes Mbiti not because he does not accept the subject with which Mbiti is primarily concerned, i.e., the basic "African philosophy" on which the Christian theology must be grounded, but because, to him (Kato), the outcome of such intellectual venture is a mere return to what he terms "paganism."

But that is not all. Though Kato esteems Mbiti's intellectual acumen, he holds that Mbiti's works involve many contradictions. This criticism is, unfortunately, based on lack of adequate understanding of Mbiti's position. Kato quotes two cases in Mbiti's book *African Religions and Philosophy*, however, which can not be said to be contradictory. First, he quotes from Mbiti's discussion of Placide Tempels's theory of the vital force: "It is open to a great deal of criticism, and the theory of 'vital force' cannot be applied to other African peoples with whose life and ideas I am familiar."[56] Kato compares this to what Mbiti says a few pages later, that "in addition to the five categories there seems to be a force, power or energy permeating the whole universe."[57] At first sight these two quotations seem to be contradictory, especially when they happen to be said by the same author in the same work. But that is only an apparent contradiction. We saw that in Tempels's analysis "force" means merely substance. In the original French edition of *La philosophie bantoue* of 1945, of which Mbiti himself takes note, Tempels indicated two different distinctions in the concept of "force." "Force" signifies "Being" in the sense of thing or matter as "that which is," an individual "force." But also "among visible beings," says Tempels, "the Bantu distinguish that which is perceived by the senses from the 'thing in itself'; by the 'thing in itself' they designate its very intimate nature, the very being of the thing or, more precisely, the force of this thing."[58] This is "force" as form, and Tempels calls it the "true force" (Fr. *force vraie*). Now I do not see how Tempels's concept of "force" in the second sense could be contradictory to Mbiti's concept of force since it implies a universal and indifferent entity like *mana*, meaning indeterminable substance. Indeed, Mbiti himself indicates this in a footnote on the same page from which Kato quotes. Mbiti says that "this [permeating force] is approximately what the anthropologists call mana, but it has nothing to do with Tempels' 'vital force'."[59] Surprisingly, Kato overlooks this.

Second, Kato observes that according to Mbiti, Africans "set their minds not on future things, but chiefly on what has taken place,"[60] a saying which, according to Kato, is contradicted by another one appearing later on in the book, that the African concept of the family "includes the unborn members who are still in the loins of the living. They are the buds of hope and expectation, and each family makes sure that its own existence is not extinguished."[61] That these two sayings are contradictory is something to be highly doubted, especially when one looks more closely at the very book Kato quotes from, and also at *New*

Testament Eschatology. Kato's criticisms against Mbiti are a fruit of inadequate examination of the matter *as Mbiti treats it*. The criticisms are based on two observations: first, that Mbiti asserts that the African concept of time has "virtually no future" dimension while at the same time claiming that "African concept of the family also includes the unborn members who are still in the loins of the living . . . "; and second, that the Akamba circumcision rite which takes place when an individual is fifteen years old is actually anticipated at birth. These assertions, however, do not in themselves constitute a contradiction, especially if they are viewed within the general context of Mbiti's work. Such events as circumcision and marriage, in the texts in question, cannot be divorced from the significance they share with the "dynamic present" dimension of time as Mbiti explains it. Perhaps a valid criticism and rejection of Mbiti's position could be derived by citing contradictory or invalid examples as the text of Dr. Lugira, quoted by Kato,[62] suggests, or as Gyekye does, or as we have done above. But even here, one would call for a keen examination. Kato himself just makes another mistake similar to one of which he accuses Mbiti, i.e., the mistake of generalization, when he says that, "From *the African point of view*, a belief in the future is an attested fact."[63] Such an unwarranted generalization contradicts the very position Kato wishes to hold.

Is the Idea of Monotheism Liberating Enough?

African traditional religions have been the most affected aspects of African life since Africa became victim of the processes of modernization, Europeanization, and colonization. Since the beginning of these processes, African gods have gradually and systematically been obliterated from the scene of African discourse. And the biggest blows dealt to African gods have come from those very Africans who call themselves the custodians of African religious heritage.

The works of Mulago, Bahoken, and Mbiti are just three examples of the modern African study of African traditional religions. The aim of such works has been to prove that Africans have a belief in one supreme being. The concept of the supreme being is a scholastic concept developed in medieval times as part of the endeavor to rationalize Christian beliefs and doctrines when the leading philosophical thought of the time posed a danger to them. It is closely related to and, at the time of its formulation, represented a modern way of expressing the old Greek paradox of the one and the many. In its philosophical formulation, it was first expressed by the ancient Greek philosopher Xenophane with his idea of the "one and All." Xenophane developed this idea through his elaboration of polytheism according to the genealogy and hierarchy of the gods of ancient Greek traditional religion. This idea of "All" was later expressed as an absolute and homogeneous unity by Parmenides. Later, Hellenic religious thought of the fifth century B.C. attempted to liberate philosophy from the limitations of immanentism in its elaboration of monotheism and gave the concept a new connotation in the doctrine of transcendental unity. This notion of a unified and transcendent power is what Anaxagoras called the Intellect, and Socrates God; the idea of God acquired the characteristic of being one over and above the multiplicity of things and events toward which it has a providential relationship.

This idea found its way, through the Neoplatonism of Plotinus, into medieval philosophy, where it was used to explain the idea of the one God, and particularly in relation to the doctrine of the Trinity. It is during this period that the theories of participation and analogy were developed as a means of toning down human expressions of power and its attribution to both human and other natural phenomena. According to these theories, perfection, of essence and of properties, belongs only and truly to God—and to created nature only by analogy and derivation.

In the evolutionist anthropology of Edward Burnett Tylor and Lewis Henry Morgan, monotheism was presented as the most developed religious idea, which appears contemporaneously with the highest levels of evolution in science, social organization, philosophy, and physiology.

The African scholars we have discussed above have been eager to demonstrate that African religious concepts could be explained in terms of Greek metaphysics. This demonstration, however, has not been convincing. There is nothing, for example, which proves that the idea of unity is superior to that of multiplicity or pluralism, or that monotheism is superior to or develops from polytheism. Even in the evolutionist anthropology, the assertions to the effect that unity and monotheism were more advanced conceptual stages than those of pluralism and polytheism did not make much sense at all. Yet, African scholars of African religions were convinced of the relative superiority of monotheism, and have since been eager to squeeze many African religious concepts into monotheistic conceptual frameworks.

Thus, the disappearance of African religions from the present scene was accelerated by our own African scholars. Like the study of most other aspects of African cultures, the study of African traditional religions is now, for all practical purposes, a study of an irrecoverable past, and its importance is thus reduced to its historicity. Today, many Africans become adults without hearing a single statement about African traditional religion.

The disappearance of African religions from the conceptual and practical frameworks of contemporary Africa is perhaps due also to a number of other factors. First, the practice and management of African traditional religions were not strongly organized and controlled. Although it is frequently stated that Africans are notoriously religious, in their traditional setup this religion was loosely intertwined with nearly all aspects of their lives. Widespreadness is frequently a sign of strength just as much as it is of weakness and lack of proper grounding. Mbiti argues that the omnipresence of religious explanations in all departments of life was the strength of African religions. The danger, however, is that in such circumstances there may be attempts to drag religion unnecessarily into situations requiring simple practical approaches. And this may gradually paint even the strong aspects of religious belief with the appearance of superstition. Wiredu contends that the superstitious dimension of African traditional beliefs is a vice which leads to stagnation of knowledge in general. In the traditional society religion was not learned as a complete or distinct unit, but in bits with the other aspects of life. This left African religions vaguely defined, even to Africans themselves, except, perhaps, in rituals and other more outstanding events and performances. Combined with the suppressive measures taken against African religious beliefs and practices by the colonial and missionary forces, the vagueness of African traditional religions has contributed significantly to their rapid collapse and disappearance.

6 | Mysticism, Science, Philosophy, and Rationality

The Analytic Point of View

W HAT GRIAULE SAYS of the Dogon system of thought in general and of the theory of *Nommo* in particular has raised much debate among members of another school of those engaged in the analysis and understanding of African systems of thought. In its present form, this debate begins in the mid-sixties with the publication in 1964 of Peter Winch's article "Understanding a Primitive Society" and in 1967 of Robin Horton's now famous paper "African Traditional Religion and Western Science."[1] Since then, there has been a protracted debate on the definition and nature of rationality, exposing and contrasting long lists of what are considered to be the characteristics not only of African traditional thought, but of traditional thought in general, with the characteristics of Western scientific thinking.

This debate has attracted scholars from as far afield as social anthropology, sociology, epistemology, and the philosophy of science, thus extending backwards in time through reference to the works of people like Lévy-Bruhl, Lévi-Strauss, Godfrey Lienhardt, Evans-Pritchard, and others, as well as to the influential works of Karl Popper, Thomas Kuhn, Richard Rorty, Hilary Putnam, Michael Polanyi, Ernest Gellner, and other philosophers of science and related theories of knowledge, among them Kwasi Wiredu and Peter Bodunrin, who have been extensively cited and referred to in the debate. Either as a result of the influence of anthropology or as a result of a crisis within the institution of philosophy itself, the discussion on rationality has turned philosophers into anthropologists or sociologists of alien cultures, and anthropologists and sociologists into philosophers.

In its precise form, the current debate owes its origin to the debate between the two philosophers Peter Winch and Alasdair MacIntyre involving the definition and differentiation of three important notions which have become major concepts in the study of knowledge and its various manifestations. The three notions are: rationality, translation, and commensurability. Because it made use of Evans-Pritchard's famous work *Witchcraft, Oracles, and Magic among the Azande*, first published in 1937, this debate soon not only engaged social anthropologists and sociologists as well, but has recently also moved into a central position in the discussion of African philosophy. The major contending positions in this debate are Rationalism and Relativism.

In *Witchcraft, Oracles, and Magic*, Evans-Pritchard describes and compares the practice of and the notions within the poison oracle *benge* to scientific notions and experiments which are carried out essentially to ascertain hidden things of the present and to corroborate hypothetical explanatory statements. Evans-Pritchard's argument is that although the Zande method and process of corroboration by means of the poison oracle are rational from the point of view of consistency, they are, however, mistaken from the point of view of the scientific (context-independent) notion of reality. In contrast, "Winch held that there is no reality independent of the language games and forms of life of a given language community."[2] In *Personal Knowledge: Towards a Post-Critical Philosophy* Michael Polanyi argues that the reason for the parallels between the attitudes which guide scientific practice and those which the Azande use in the administration of *benge* is that, universally, "our most deeply ingrained convictions are determined by the idiom in which we interpret our experience and in terms of which we erect our articulate systems."[3] Both Polanyi and Winch therefore challenge Evans-Pritchard's claim that Azande beliefs about witchcraft, magic, and oracles are logical but mistaken. Evans-Pritchard bases his evaluation of Zande rationality on a notion of reality in which scientific objectivity (truth value and power over the physical world) plays a major part. But according to Polanyi and Winch, science is itself no less a form of idiom or social reality than is a religious worldview on the basis of which we are capable of making many inferences. "Our formally declared beliefs," says Polanyi, "can be held to be true in the last resort only because of our logically anterior acceptance of a particular set of terms, from which all our references to reality are constructed."[4]

In 1970 Bryan Wilson edited a volume of essays by philosophers, anthropologists, and sociologists, entitled *Rationality*, which reprinted and focused on Winch's article. The consensus of these essays, against Winch and in agreement with Evans-Pritchard, is that the cognitive skills of Western science are superior to traditional skills of knowledge. Other works in this debate include *The Idea of a Social Science and Its Relation to Philosophy* by Winch himself in 1958; *Modes of Thought*, edited by Robin Horton and Ruth Finnegan in 1973; *Symbol and Theory* by John Skorupski in 1976; *Theories of Primitive Religion* by Evans-Pritchard in 1965; *The Domestication of the Savage Mind* by Jack Goody in 1977; *Models of Man* by Martin Hollis in 1977; *Philosophical Disputes in the Social Sciences*, edited by S. C. Brown in 1979; *Rationality and Relativism*, edited by Martin Hollis and Steven Lukes in 1982; *Reason and Morality*, edited by Joanna Overing in 1985; and *Magic, Science, Religion and the Scope of Rationality* by Stanley J. Tambiah in 1990. Together, these works delineate and either affirm or challenge the conviction so widespread in the 1970s "that the West was a highly rational place, while traditional societies lived a more poetic, mystical, less rational and more restricted world of thought."[5]

Horton's "African Traditional Religion and Western Science," the essays collected in his *Modes of Thought*, and those in Hollis and Lukes's *Rationality and Relativism* and Hollis's *Models of Man* strongly defend the above conviction, which is itself based on a specific and super-realist notion of humankind, science, and rationality. The theme they defend is that man is a natural creature in a rational world of cause and effect; that we are rational creators in a natural world of cause and effect; and that with the aid of reason we can master nature, manipulate society, change culture, and, indeed, shape our selves. This position holds a conception of rationality that identifies logical consistency and coherence in the explanation of reality as its minimal characteristic. The truth of this "reality," they believe, is established by science. According to this school of thought, there can be only one rationality based on universally valid rules of logic and inference. These rules, according to Hollis, can be stated as follows:

(1) The law of identity (If P, then P)
(2) The law of noncontradiction (Not–(P and not–P))
(3) *Modus Ponens* (If (P and (if P, then Q)) then Q)[6]

Arguing against the relativism held by Winch and Polanyi, Hollis states that these rules render it possible to make transcultural and comparative judgments as to the degree of rationality and irrationality manifest in a belief or action system.

Hollis and his cohorts therefore do not accept the theory of relativism of truth or knowledge. They hold that there is only one reality, whose relations are objectively discernible by science. Because of this, propositions about this reality must be guided by the universal rules stated above. It was on the basis of this realist position that even Evans-Pritchard held the notion that there was a context-independent notion of reality against which the rationality of Zande notions of witchcraft, magic, and oracles could be judged and be found wanting.

> In imputing consistency [says Hollis], the Enquirer is also imputing the intuition needed to grasp logical relation. For knowing that P implies Q is not solely a matter of being able to follow a rigmarole which starts with P and ends with Q. The point of the rigmarole is to lead the mind's eye to see that (if P, then Q) is a necessary truth. . . . But in general necessary truths are not true because they are provable, but provable because they are true.[7]

In this view, a rational explanation is defined in the analytic fashion as a body of verifiable propositions relating cause to effects. This position consequently views the notions of consistency and reason as functions of scientific evidence. "This kind of 'rationality'," writes Tambiah, "has been, everyone will assent, most self-consciously formalized and systematized in the West, and the comparative question relates to the grounds and contexts in which, and the social and religious phenomena to which, this conception of rationality can be used as a universal yardstick."[8] But Hollis, Lukes, Horton, and their cohorts, particularly the arch-rationalist Ian Hacking, believe there is no other form of rationality. According to Hacking, "Arch-rationalism is convinced that there are good and bad reasons. . . . There are good and bad reasons for propositions about nature. They are not relative to anything. They do not depend on context."[9] Any form of life which is not based on the arch-rationalist's conceptual scheme is described by Hacking as romantic, simpler, and less reason-impregnated.

The rationalists therefore reject any form of relativism of reason. In particular they side with Evans-Pritchard and challenge Winch's declaration that "the criteria of logic are not a direct gift from God but arise out of and are only intelligible in the context of ways of living and modes of social life."[10] Like Polanyi, Winch believes that the logicality of inference (the laws of consistency and coherence) is itself guided by such modes of social life, of which science and religion are two. "It follows," he says,

> that one cannot apply criteria of logic to modes of social life as such. For instance, science is one such mode and religion is another; and each has criteria of intelligibility peculiar to itself. So within science or religion actions can be logical or illogical; in science, for example, it would be illogical to refuse to be bound by the results of a properly carried out experiment; in religion it would be illogical to suppose that one could pit one's own strength against God's; and so on.[11]

This position, insist Hollis and Lukes, sees only differences (pluralism) in the standards for rating reasons as good whereas they insist on ranking the standards themselves. In this view, there are the three categories of answers they give in evaluation of non-Western beliefs and actions. These answers reflect the positions held by the authors of the essays in Hollis and Lukes's *Rationality and Relativism*. They state that

either   (1)   apparently irrational beliefs really are irrational beliefs, backed by mistaken beliefs about what is really reasonable (Hollis and Newton-Smith);

or   (2)   they are not really irrational, given the (technical or social or cultural or psychological) context (Horton and Lukes);

or   (3)   they are not really beliefs, at least in the propositional sense meriting rational appraisal (Sperber).

All three positions affirm the unity and superiority of science-based rationality and reject the theory of relativism of reason emerging from evidence, provided by, among others, social anthropologists, out of non-Western beliefs and practices. Challenges to this Western-type definition of rationality or to the analytic establishment generally by the proponents of pluralism have engulfed both anthropology and philosophy, bringing both into the postmodernist movement. The historical merit of the postmodernist critique arises out of its questioning of the validity of taking the Western model of rationality as the yardstick for judging others. It argues that judgments of what counts as good philosophy or good reason are ultimately conventional. These pluralists further contend that Western social science gained ground through its critical function, which is to use knowledge of other cultures to examine the unconscious assumptions of Western rationality. Other cultures emerged therefore as "creations" or representations of Western social science. In this sense, then, the present debate marks an important era as a period of self-critique in the social sciences and the humanities. Sometimes this conflict tends to take on political features, as suggested by A. J. Mandt[12] or as analyzed by V. Y. Mudimbe.[13] But the underlying issue, as we have seen—although this could be made an overrider for ideological interests—is the legitimacy of the currently employed criteria of philosophical evaluation.[14] Let us now examine some of the arguments leveled directly at African philosophy, beliefs, and practices within this stream of debate.

Language, Truth, and Reason

According to Kwasi Wiredu, an ardent positivist African philosopher,[15] there is no meaning of language other than in terms of what it signifies and refers to. In themselves, he says, words are sheer physical existences exactly like chairs, tables, and trees. They are simple conventional signs made into a system to impart information. Their significance, then, derives from the ideas which are connected to that which they signify or to which they refer. There is no magical connection between the word and the sort of thing that it refers to. A philosopher, Wiredu believes, must of necessity direct his search for the meaning of words only to their relationship with the objects or situations they stand for.

If we apply this statement to the evaluation of Griaule's description of *Nommo* as both word and force, as both an utterance and a primordial principle of unity, Wiredu would certainly dismiss the theory as belonging not to a philosophical analysis, but to mysticism. And the latter, according to him, is frequently contradictory and defies the rules of meaning and the laws of logic.

A contrast to this theory of *Nommo* is to be found in the famous work of Robin Horton, "African Traditional Thought and Western Science."[16] Horton observes in this essay that one central characteristic difference between traditional African worldviews and scientific theories is that the former treats words as if they are able to produce the things for which they stand. In other words, "the words of men are granted a certain measure of control over the situations they refer to."[17] This, he thinks, is due to the recourse made by African traditional religious thought to formulating a theory of reality based on the concept of human agency. In this way, Horton thought, Africans personalize the causal forces in nature in contrast to the impersonal forces operational in scientific explanations. Traditional people therefore believe in the power of words in the sense that words, when uttered in appropriate circumstances, are capable of bringing into being the events or states they stand for. Horton calls this a common magical belief of closed cultures. He argues that because they lack alternative theories and are unaware that ideas can be expressed in different languages without affecting them, peoples of primitive (nonscientific) societies tend to think that the words of the language they speak must have an inextricable relationship with the reality they stand for: "There is no way at all in which they [words] can be seen as varying independently of the segments of reality they stand for. So they appear so integrally involved with their referents that any manipulation of the one self-evidently affects the other."[18]

This traditional attitude to words, says Horton, is radically different from that of the scientist. The scientist, he says, believes the power of words to rest only in their explanatory and predictional functions in relation to reality. Horton's scientist is compelled to reject the magician's view of words; why? Note the following reason that Horton gives: "he has come to know better: magical behaviour has been found not to produce the results it claims to. . . . "[19] Because of this, says Horton, the scientist does not even bother to test the magical causal claims. He finds it futile to test these claims because the magical world depends, in Horton's words, on human whim. That is, the world of magic is not an objective world of natural laws which operate independently of the human will. In a system of thought where the objectivity of reality is posited as being independent not only of human will but also of the ideas which describe such objectivity, the trend will be one of constantly testing ideas by contrasting them to the reality they represent. In this analytic tradition, ideas may be rejected when they are disproved as worthless and new ones are developed to replace them. So ideas generate ideas. And this leads to the establishment of a theory. And because ideas are related only to ideas, they compare with each other regardless of origin.

In the magical world, on the other hand, claims Horton, ideas are not discussed or talked of as ideas. They are offered piecemeal according to the occasions to which they are bound and which give birth to them. They lack a theoretical grounding and cannot give rise to any. In this sense, ideas and words are inextricably related to the realities they describe or stand for; they are identical. Because of this, the world of magical beliefs is resistant to change—at least to change of ideas without change in the reality to which they are pegged. Traditional thought systems, then, claims Horton, are conditioned by a single scheme of thought. The traditional thinker (the diviner, the sorcerer, the "clever," etc.) operates within a closed culture.

To sum it all up, Horton argues that in the explanation of reality, that is, in an attempt to give a theoretical grounding for why things happen the way they do, Africans revert to spirits as Westerners revert to science. Spirits are to African traditional thought what material particles are to Western scientific thought. And because traditional thought, Horton observes, invariably makes recourse to personal spiritual explanations to account for practical or empirical events, such explanations become comparable to Western science, which serves the same purpose. He rejects the symbolist arguments of John Beattie which claim that the personal spiritual explanations become symbolic upon their failure to cope with empirical issues on the basis of available empirically grounded techniques. If this were so, Horton argues, then scientific theory would also turn symbolic whenever it fails to account for facts. He argues that there is little evidence to prove that African traditional thought deliberately displays symbolism and figurative language in its explanations. In lack of such evidence, there is no reason not to believe that traditional thought uses literally and seriously the notion of spiritual agency rather than natural processes in its causal explanations of reality. In this, Kwame Appiah agrees with Horton.[20]

Scientific theory, on the other hand, tries and tests any other available empirical explanation. But, Horton insists, in order to understand the role of spirits in traditional thought it is essential to treat them as theoretical entities whose characteristics can then be explained in terms of the model-building process familiar from Western scientific theory.

Thus Horton starts his contrast of traditional thought with scientific thought by identifying their distinctive characteristics as closedness and openness respectively. These characteristics fail, however, on realization that traditional thought remains fairly intact despite new experiences—which, for Horton, are essentially alternative explanations—offered by the twentieth century. A good example in this respect is the persistence of magic (divination) despite the experiences of modern medicine (diagnosis). Because of this, Appiah reports, "[In a later work] Horton speaks of traditional belief systems not as closed but . . . of their being 'accommodative'."[21] Horton is apparently forced into this change of terminology by the ability of Africans to absorb new scientific implements into their thought pattern rather than abandon the latter for the former. But even this accommodative style is contrasted with the "adversary" style of scientific theory.

Lastly, one is tempted to preempt the discussion on Wiredu here by questioning the plausibility of the wholesale comparison of traditional thought—African or any other—with scientific thought, which essentially belongs to a small community of scientists. We believe that traditional thought is not formulated along theoretical lines, nor is it founded on accepted theoretical frameworks. Horton himself accepts as much when he criticizes anthropologists for searching for theories or systematic beliefs in traditional worldviews. He criticizes this search on the grounds that such theories or systematic beliefs do not belong to the traditional cognitive experience. What is unacceptable about Horton's view is his conclusion from this that no proper philosophy can be drawn from the traditional experience.

Horton is an ardent positivist who believes that no meaningful discourse can come from empirically meaningless experiences—in the sense of a body of utterances meant to control people's lives—as are found in the traditional domain. To him, then, one cannot take ethnophilosophy seriously. He likens African traditional thought to idealism and solipsism in the West. The latter, to him, are the Western versions of magical conceptions of reality. He says:

> Both in traditional African cosmologies and in European cosmologies before Descartes, the modern distinction between "mind" and "matter" does not appear. Although everything in the universe is underpinned by spiritual forces, what moderns would call "mental activities" and "material things" are both part of a single reality, neither material nor immaterial. Thinking, conceiving, saying, etc. are described in terms of organs like heart and brain and actions like the uttering of words.[22]

As we have said earlier, and Horton would indeed be in agreement, traditional thought is not specialized knowledge. It cares neither for the theoretical plausibility nor for the logical consistency of its many claims because its production does not take place under the awareness of or need for theoretical plausibility or logical consistency as guidelines for its internal structure. Often traditional thought is not consistent at all. Even the concept of causality which is ascribed to the power of the word is not consistently held. The "theory" of words *only sometimes* exhibits causal claims. Thus, to reduce the only occasional causal claims about words entirely to the domain of causal explanations would therefore amount to failure to distinguish the different ways in which Africans use the concept "cause" in different contexts. Consider the following examples from the Luo of Kenya:

1. The Luo believe that the *ochwinjo* bird burns your house if you take back what you have already given out as a gift. They talk of the bird as capable of burning down a house if anyone who lives in it partakes in anything given out from the same household as a gift to others.

2. The Luo also make claims to the effect that when a person bites another and the bitten person smears brown chicken feces (*osirogoho*) on the wound, the teeth of the aggressor will rot and turn brown like the *osirogoho* and eventually fall out.

3. "Dhok e juok" is a Luo saying which translates into something like "it is the word which is witchcraft." It is used in claims that to talk of a possible event in a certain way may actually cause the event to happen.

Now each of these examples depicts a statement of causal relationship between various elements: the eating of something already gifted out by your household *causes* the *ochwinjo* to burn your house; smearing chicken feces on a wound from a human bite *causes* the teeth which did the biting to rot; and talk-ing about a possible event *causes* it to happen.

In all three examples, the claim of causal relationship is rendered apparent only by linguistic expression. For each it is considered a matter of common sense that the apparent claim made therein would never be real in the sense of material causal relations. On a rational note, it is assumed that there is no material causal relationship between the antecedents and the consequent events which appear to be causally related in the expressions. In this respect, the personal and spiritual characteristics observed by Horton do not give any weight to the claims. Their explanatory relevance is simply beside the point. But they serve a purpose none-theless. In the contexts in which they are made, the expressions—in whole, not in the relation of their parts—are themselves directed at creating specific results. They are meant to cause change in social behavior just as is expected of moral or legal rules and admonitions.

Second, the expressions are aimed at a specific audience in specific contexts. Thus, example one is usually said to children whose parents have given out gifts in the form of food to another household. The expression in such contexts is meant to restrain the children from partaking in gifts given out from their own households to other people. The expression has nothing to do with either the material relationship between the partaking of one's own gifts to others and the burning of houses, or with the *ochwinjo's* physical capability to burn houses. Like example one, example two is also not to be taken literally. Both are the type of discourse usually classified as "children's language" which adults are not ex-pected to accept in their literal form.

The third example is interesting, but differs slightly from the first two. It expresses belief in the magical power of the word. It expresses a claim to the effect that by words alone, people can cause harm to happen to other people or to their property. In another sense, the expression also implies that the stereotype forms of magic and witchcraft are not actually true; that what is often referred to as *juok* is nothing more than a mere evil *feeling* about other people and their property.

Let us illustrate this second meaning further. "Dhok e juok" ("the word can be evil [witchcraft]") is an expression which describes the relationship between will and evil. The expression is made in situations of threat to others, such as on occasions of warning of possible danger—if, for example, A says to B: "I have warned you not to go to the lake but you do not heed; I wish something hap-pened to you there," or, "I wish you drowned there." Now if, in this situation, B indeed proceeds to the lake, and if something bad happens to him there, A will certainly be suspected and charged with *juok*. His words of warning to B are held to have caused whatever happened to B to happen. In this context, the ex-pression "dhok e juok" is a suggestion that, one, there may indeed not be any provable action of A that led to the misfortune of B, and two, that the attribution of *juok* to the words of A may not entail causal claims connecting A's warning and B's misfortune. Rather, the evilness of A is held to consist in A's attitude—the evil attitude of wishing other people bad things. The condemnation is therefore not of the utterance *per se*, but of the attitude which the utterance reveals. The expression "dhok e juok" therefore does not mean that words have the power to create situations. Rather, it means that the significance of events is tied to the wills and intentions of people. "Dhok e juok" is also an expression of an ideal, that is, that human discourse must be aimed at creating good order for all.

Admittedly, Horton is right that sometimes traditional utterances exhibit beliefs in causal claims which contrast sharply with scientific claims. The consistency of these traditional utterances, however, does show one important thing: that at the level of ordinary life, traditional people have not been interested in theory in any form, whether scientific or symbolic. To look at and judge African traditional thought only in terms of either of these two forms of explanation is therefore to commit the reductionist fallacy. The argument that African traditional thought is only either scientific or symbolic is too restrictive and belongs to the same epistemic framework. What is important to consider in Horton's analysis is the strength of reductionism. It is difficult to see how Horton claims that science is still an "open" activity in the face of the recent reductionist tendencies not only in scientific practice but also in the positivist school of philosophy. These tendencies run through Horton's own work under discussion here. In this respect, Horton's analysis is fundamentally similar to the anthropologists retreat to symbolism which he criticizes. In other words, the strength of Horton's paper relies significantly on his attempt to reduce the anthropologists' reduction (to symbolism) to his own reduction of the fundamental questions of explanation to scientific explanations. Whatever does not fit into this conceptual framework and scheme of explanation, such as idealism or African traditional religion, is vehemently discredited.

But another merit of the pluralist critique lies right here: that it rejects reductionism of any form. While the pluralists defend the theory of commensurability of or "bridgeheads" between worldviews or ontologies, such as the scientific and the "traditional," they regard such worldviews as perspectives rather than as typologies of "modes of thought" or "cognitive styles." They are wary of postulations of the absolute authority of hierarchical oppositions, such as reason over emotions, and *langue* over *parole*.

Let us return to the fallacy of reductionism which leads to mistaken comparison. If, indeed, Western science deals only with theory as such, it would appear that the theoretical premises from Western science used by Horton as his grounds of argument are invalidly used, as they are applied to assess what Appiah calls "straightforward beliefs" of ordinary African peoples. This fallacy applies not only to those people like Horton who use theoretical premises developed by Western specialists to discredit principles of simple beliefs, it applies equally to those like John Skorupski who use Western theoretical premises in an attempt to identify the similarity of premises supposedly underlying African beliefs. Wiredu criticizes this type of comparison.[23] In agreement with Wiredu, Appiah makes the following observation about the comparison:

> The difficulty with Skorupski's approach is that it compares the Christianity of the theologians—theorists who use Aristotelian-Thomist conceptions of 'substance' to defend a view of the Eucharist, for example—with the straight-forward beliefs of ordinary Nuer. . . . This is not to say that religion in the West necessarily provides a poor model of traditional religion, only that in comparing formal, literate tradition of theology with informal, preliterate traditions of belief, we are not comparing like with like. And, as Kwasi Wiredu has suggested, we may understand African traditional belief better if we take as our model not the religion of the theologians, not the theories of the scientist, but the unformalised beliefs of Western folk traditions of thought.[24]

Another prominent writer who agrees with Horton's thesis that scientific thought is characteristically different from traditional thought is Jack Goody, notably through his now popular work *The Domestication of the Savage Mind* (1977). He disagrees with Horton, however, about what constitutes the essential difference between the two systems. According to Horton, it is above all his essential skepticism toward established beliefs that distinguishes the scientist from the traditional thinker. Because of this attitude, scientific ideas deal with other ideas or with abstract programs rather than with the specific occasions out of which they arise, while traditional thought remains bound to occasions. In Goody's view, Horton himself offers explanations which seem to contradict his own thesis:

> If traditional cultures see ideas as bound to occasions—if, for example, general statements arise in the context of healing rather than as abstract programmes about what we believe—then, when the contexts change (because of famine, invasion, or disease) or when individual attitudes change (because of the recognition that the remedy has not worked), the ideas and practices will themselves change. They seem more likely to do so here than in societies where ideas, religious or scientific, are written down in scholarly treatises or in Holy Writ.[25]

According to Goody, Africans are skeptical, especially about witchcraft, divination, and similar matters. In a manner that may contrast with the positions of John Sodipo, Barry Hallen, and Henry Odera Oruka, Goody argues that

> what seems to be the essential difference, however, is not so much the skeptical attitude in itself but the accumulation (or reproduction) of skepticism. Members of oral (i.e. 'traditional') societies find it difficult to develop a line of skep-

tical thinking about, say, the nature of matter or man's relationship to God simply because a continuing critical tradition can hardly exist when skeptical thoughts are *not* written down, *not* communicated across time and space, *not* made available for men to contemplate in privacy as well as to hear in performance.[26]

The significant contrast, according to Goody, is not so much between the traditional and the scientific or modern as between the oral and the literate. But, Sodipo, Hallen, and Odera Oruka disagree, albeit from different angles. Sodipo and Hallen argue, with reference to and through a subtle analysis of the oral usages of the concepts *mo* (knowledge) and *gbagbo* (belief—or, better, agreeing to accept what someone else says) among the Yoruba *onisegun*, that oral tradition has produced much more critical thinking than has been generally assumed. Odera Oruka, on his part, quotes the example of Socrates as well as traditional sage philosophers to argue that literacy is not a *sine qua non* for critical thinking. Although some of Odera Oruka's examples play into the territory of Goody's argument, his position differs from that of Goody in an important way.

According to Odera Oruka, much of the knowledge that informs everyday cultural practice is the result of theoretical deliberations and negotiations between the producers of traditional knowledge whom he calls sages and sage philosophers. These persons, Odera Oruka contends, are constantly engaged in behind-the-scenes discussions about what is good for society. Because their objective is usually to produce what is good for society, these persons often have to suppress, but do not abandon, their personal critical perspectives. According to Odera Oruka, then, while the sages, like Ogotemmêli of the Dogon, preserve the public knowledge thus produced and pass it on to the people, the role of sage philosophers remains that of shedding light where contradictions, obscurities, and other difficulties may occur or hinder practice. The thoughts of sage philosophers remain thus consistently critical, and frequently depart from the general knowledge shared by the majority.

Kuhn, of course, argues that neither skepticism in itself nor the accumulated skepticism which writing makes possible is sufficient to result in critical thinking. And science itself is not an essential condition for critical thinking. For critical thinking to emerge, Kuhn argues, there needs to be crisis in the fundamental bases of whatever form of knowledge is in question. For Kuhn, the scientific spirit pervading the practice of science is a result of that discipline's basic purpose—puzzle solving. It is this fundamental purpose or goal that distinguishes science from all other disciplines. Scientific thinking grows not just because of the presence of critical thinking as such, but because of science's fundamental purpose of solving puzzles. The contrast Kuhn makes between astronomy and astrology remarkably resembles the kind of contrast that Horton would have more reasonably made between science and traditional thought (made up of religion and magic). Kuhn says:

If an astronomer's prediction failed and his calculations checked, he could hope to set the situation right. Perhaps the data were at fault: old observations could be reexamined and new measurements made, tasks which posed a host of calculational and instrumental puzzles. . . . The astrologer, by contrast, had no such puzzles. The occurrence of failures could be explained, but particular failures did not give rise to research puzzles, for no man, however skilled, could make use of them in a constructive attempt to revise the astrological tradition. . . . And without puzzles, able first to challenge and then to attest the ingenuity of the individual practitioner, astrology could not have become a science even if the stars had, in fact, controlled human destiny.[27]

For Kuhn, Popper's test criterion for scientific revolutions is only a function of the more fundamental puzzle solving goal:

One of the reasons why normal science seems to progress so rapidly is that its practitioners concentrate on problems that only their own lack of ingenuity should keep them from solving—[and to ensure solution] there must also be rules that limit both the nature of acceptable solutions and the steps by which they are to be obtained.[28]

Michael Polanyi, in support of Kuhn's thesis about the role of skepticism in the growth of knowledge, argues that the kind of skepticism referred to in scientific theory is only apparent. Even in the natural sciences and in legal court proceedings, he says, "We often refuse to accept an alleged scientific proof largely because on general grounds we are reluctant to believe what it tries to prove."[29] For Polanyi, both laboratory scientific practice and the Zande practice of the poison oracle reported by Evans-Pritchard are guided by the same principle of self-preservation: commitment to an underlying general belief. "A scientist," says Polanyi, "must commit himself in respect to any important claim put forward within his field of knowledge. . . . Only if a claim lies totally outside his range of responsible interests can the scientist assume an attitude of completely impartial doubt towards it. He can be strictly agnostic only on subjects of which he knows little and cares nothing."[30] And he narrates an interesting example to illustrate his point:

In an earlier book (*The Logic of Liberty*, p.12), I have mentioned a paper published by Lord Rayleigh in June, 1947, in the *Proceedings of the Royal Society*, describing a simple experiment which demonstrated that a hydrogen atom impinging on a metal wire released energies ranging up to a hundred electron volts. This conclusion, if correct, would have been of immense importance. Physicists whom I consulted could find no fault with the experiment, yet they ignored its results, and did not even think it worth while to repeat it.[31]

Polanyi compares this attitude of scientists toward alternative experiments and theories which challenge their fundamental commitments to similar Zande indifference to questions which suggest alteration of procedures and their results. In the case of such alterations (alternatives), writes Evans-Pritchard,

> The Zande does not know what would happen and is not interested in what would happen; no one has been fool enough to waste good oracle-poison in making such pointless experiments which only a European (i.e. a person who knows little and cares nothing about the whole practice) could imagine. . . . If the fowl died they would simply say that it was not good *benge*. The very fact of the fowl dying proves to them its badness.[32]

It is therefore wrong not only to compare traditional thought with scientific practice but also to suggest that the former must learn from and adopt or develop the distinctive characteristics of the latter in order to constitute proper knowledge. Perhaps Wiredu's suggestion is more appropriate, taking into account the Kuhnian argument that science cannot be developed out of what is primarily non-science. Astrology cannot, in Kuhn's sense, develop into astronomy on the basis of its internal proceedings. In noting the distinctive characteristics of traditional thought and science, Wiredu recommends the abandonment of the former in favor of the modern (theories and puzzle-solving equations) purely on pragmatic grounds.

Evans-Pritchard holds that the comparison between traditional thought and science results in one major problem which in turn becomes responsible for the *imaginary* problems which traditional thought is assumed to have. His argument is the anthropological parallel to that of Kuhn, although it predates the latter by six years. His point is that some of the problems discussed by Western scholars about traditional thought are the result of the invalid application of the principles, characteristics, and concepts developed within the practice of and reflection on Western science to the evaluation or judgment of the characteristics and content of traditional thought. He examines, as an example, the question of identity and contradiction in Nuer belief.

Evans-Pritchard holds that the problem of identity as expressed in Nuer belief or, for that matter, in Dogon belief (between *Nommo* and the eighth ancestor) is only a problem to an outsider who applies to the beliefs foreign logical principles of judgment (of the meaning of identity). For sacrificial purposes, the Nuer assert that cucumbers are oxen, "and they act accordingly by performing the sacrificial rites as closely as possible to what happens when the [sacrificial] victim is an Ox."[33] And, in a rather different example, Evans-Pritchard records that the Nuer assert that twins are one person and that they are birds. According to Evans-Pritchard, to call such assertions of identity illogical—as Lévy-Bruhl did—is a misinterpretation which emerges out of the outsider's wrong application of the identity factor "is," which, in the syntactical laws of the outsider's own linguistic structure, conjuncts only two or more arguments of the same nature. About this problem, Evans-Pritchard has the following to say:

What appear to be hopeless contradictions when translated into English may not appear so in the native language. When, for instance, a native statement is translated that a man of such-and-such a clan is a leopard, it appears to us to be absurd, but the word he uses which we translate by 'is' may not have the same meaning for him that the word 'is' has for us.[34]

In this respect, then, says Evans-Pritchard in *Nuer Religion*:

When they say "twins are not two persons, they are one person" they are not saying that they are one individual but that they have a single personality. It is significant that in speaking of the unity of twins they only use the word *ran*, which, like our word 'person', leaves sex, age, and other distinguishing qualities of individuals undefined. They would not say that twins of the same sex were one *dhol*, boy, or one *nyal*, girl, but they do say, whether they are of the same sex or not, that they are one *ran*, person.[35]

The above passage is only part of Evans-Pritchard's answer to Lévy-Bruhl's comparative criticisms of traditional African religions. In another fashion, it equally offers answers to Robin Horton. Both Lévy-Bruhl and Horton made their analyses of the (supposedly) theoretical content of African religious beliefs taking Western science as the model of reference. Evans-Pritchard's point, as reiterated even more strongly by Okot p'Bitek in his *African Religions in Western Scholarship*, is that much of the controversy raised by Western scholars about African religions is all part and parcel of some *controversy* or *debate* in the Western world, which is only unduly extended to traditional African assertions and beliefs. According to this view, ordinary Africans, like many ordinary people everywhere else, do not make such abstract notions as nuptial causality, causal potency of words, or even the problems of identity part of their worry.

In *Witchcraft, Oracles, and Magic among the Azande* Evans-Pritchard says the following:

... the desire to assimilate primitive notions to kindred notions of our own tempts us, in the first place, to read into their beliefs concepts peculiar to our own, and, in the second place, to interpret their beliefs by introspection or in terms of our own sentiments.[36]

In general, therefore, Evans-Pritchard argues that the nature of predication in African religious expressions must not be taken literally. These expressions must be taken in context. Literal translations of African statements about reality, he argues, are responsible for the false arguments and conclusions held by Lévy-Bruhl and, by implication, also by Horton. This argument runs through Evans-Pritchard's major works, but notably in *Witchcraft, Oracles, and Magic among the Azande, Nuer Religion*, and *Theories of Primitive Religion*.

In another instance Evans-Pritchard argues, against Lévy-Bruhl, that objective (scientific) causal explanation can be held together with a nuptial one, "the one supplementing the other; and they are not therefore exclusive." According to Evans-Pritchard, it is not the case that traditional thought develops mystical explanations as correlates or in total ignorance of objective ones. Ordinary African people, however, place greater emphasis on the social representation, where the empirical event may be directly relevant in emphasizing a social value, as in the case of *juok* which we explained above. The empirical events, in themselves, are recognized as facts and are acknowledged as such. They are not denied. Thus, for example, Evans-Pritchard says, in *Theories of Primitive Religion*, that

> A representation which asserts that fire does not burn the hand thrust into it would not long survive. A representation which asserts that it will not burn you if you have sufficient faith may survive.[37]

According to Evans-Pritchard, then, traditional thought acknowledges natural causation of events, but regards these events as socially incomplete unless they are related to the corresponding (relevant) social representation. This necessitates the nuptial explanation as a supplementary explanation in traditional thought.

There are two epistemological domains which can be discerned from Evans-Pritchard's thesis: there is the domain of knowledge as well as the domain of belief in the African worldview. In *Theories of Primitive Religion* he says the following about this distinction:

> Lévy-Bruhl is also wrong in supposing that there is necessarily a contradiction between an objective causal explanation and a mystical one. It is not so. The two kinds of explanation can be, as indeed they are, held together, the one supplementing the other; and they are not therefore exclusive. For example, the dogma that death is due to witchcraft does not exclude the observation that the man was killed by a buffalo. For Lévy-Bruhl there is here a contradiction, to which natives are indifferent. But no contradiction is involved. On the contrary, the natives are making a very acute analysis of the situation. They are perfectly well aware that a buffalo killed the man, but they hold that he would not have been killed by it if he had not been bewitched.[38]

Against Lévy-Bruhl and Horton, then, Evans-Pritchard is arguing that statements which assert magical causality are not substitutes, correlates, parallels, or analogies of scientific explanation statements.

Other prominent defenders of Evans-Pritchard's argument are Barry Hallen and J. O. Sodipo in their book *Knowledge, Belief, and Witchcraft* (1986). Basing themselves on Willard Quine's distinction between observation and standing sentences, Hallen and Sodipo argue that even in the case of witchcraft there are two kinds of statement categories which ought to be made: those that belong to assertions about the material event, and those which assert witchcraft accusation. For Hallen and Sodipo, if we may take Evans-Pritchard's example as point of reference, statements which assert the material cause of death, such as "the buffalo killed him," belong to Quine's category of observation sentences. Those which attribute the death to witchcraft, such as "the buffalo killed him because

X bewitched him," belong to Quine's category of standing sentences. Now sentences of the former category describe events which are readily observable or are verifiable by evidence, while the latter category contains statements which are abstracted from immediate experience and may therefore be described as theoretical. Such sentences are open to modification or even falsification without modifying the facts of experience from which they are abstracted.

It would appear, then, that for Hallen and Sodipo the level of theory is an attempt by man to close or complete the circle of meaning by providing explanations which throw light on observable experiences by providing them with a social stratum. This argument resembles Evans-Pritchard's own explanation of the necessity of social representation in explanatory accounts of observable events. But Hallen and Sodipo seem to be saying more than that; they imply that the nature of the standing sentences is not important so long as they provide explanations which are culturally meaningful to members of the cultural (or language) system within which such an account occurs. They say: "it is when one attempts to be more specific about the connections between *observation* and *standing* [or theoretical] sentences that one discerns how arbitrary the latter are".[39]

In this respect, *theories* about facts may vary both intraculturally as well as interculturally. An example of the former is, for example, the explanation of the condition of an AIDS victim as being the consequence of either *chira* or *tung'* among the Kenya Luo. While the two are different circumstances which are believed to result in a condition of gradual body wastage, the provision of either or both to account for a specific body wastage does not change the observable facts in question. An example of intercultural theories, on the other hand, can be given from the popular contrast between the so-called scientific and traditional explanations.

According to Hallen and Sodipo, the variety of theoretical levels determines the kind of language system each uses to account for the relationship between the *event* and its *theory*. Thus one language system will usually vary from others on account of the nature of explanations it focuses on. Each system develops notions and truth-determinant principles and consequently fixes the use or role of certain words to convey these on the basis of their theoretical variables. If this is so, then standing (theoretical) sentences of any language system become so rife with the element of indeterminacy that, for Hallen and Sodipo,

> Translating the statements of a people who appear not to honour the principle of contradiction into the statements of a people who do would be a worthless exercise. If he cannot identify truth functional equivalents, is the linguist entitled to conclude that the aliens are prelogical, illogical or that they subscribe to one of the so-called 'deviant' logics? Only as a last resort—when certain that the apparent alien absurdity or silliness is not being caused by 'hidden differences of language' or 'bad translations'.[40]

Hallen and Sodipo proceed from this position to state that such indeterminacy leads to a plurality of systems of explanation, "all purportedly true, 'that are equally satisfactory from the stand point of explanation'."[41] The outcome, then, is a plurality of incommensurable systems (of truths) having a maximum of explanatory coherence.

The aim of Hallen and Sodipo's long analytic debate is to explain that the *onisegun* make a very clear distinction between *knowledge* and *belief*, a distinction which shows that the Yoruba *onisegun* are more sophisticated epistemologically, and are more critically and indeed empirically minded, than has been generally supposed. The former, knowledge, known in Yoruba as *mo*, refers to first-hand experience. It is knowledge acquired through sensory experience, particularly visual perception. The statements made of this kind of knowledge are *observation sentences*. They are empirical statements which are subject to verification.[42] Statements of *mo* belong to first-order knowledge.

Belief, on the other hand, is known in Yoruba as *gbagbo*. It refers to second-order knowledge, which an individual may or may not accept, depending on the degree of the reasonableness of the "syllogism" used to result in *gbagbo* in the form of a proposition such as "I believe that P." Statements of *gbagbo* are not empirical statements, nor do they, as was wrongly claimed by Horton, pretend or aim to be objective. *Gbagbo* statements are, according to Hallen and Sodipo, standing statements. They are statements about statement. But what is presented as *gbagbo* can become *mo* after verification or testing. On their own, according to Hallen and Sodipo, *gbagbo* statements form

> a theoretical *system* as well as its component elements. Testing does not occur in isolation. It occurs as one possibility when there is a controversial information claim. . . . The system that this paper presents in outline form is radically different from the model assumed appropriate to traditional cultures. If that difference is not a consequence of our faulty methodology, then it represents what the *onisegun* really do think. If so, it is extremely important to pay careful attention to how they apply this system in practice (p. 76) . . . without immediately importing alien notions of meaningful behaviour, scientific method, functional relevance, or even of 'common' sense.[43]

Hallen and Sodipo's debate therefore is a corroboration of Evans-Pritchard's thesis on witchcraft against the thesis of Lévy-Bruhl. But it also embraces the latter's and Godfrey Lienhardt's arguments on identity.

The rationalization of the paradox of identity has not been without challenge. One such challenge to the paradox is Raymond Firth's paper "Twins, Birds and Vegetables: Problems of Identification in Primitive Religious Thought,"[44] which discusses the paradox of identity between humans and nonhuman realities as presented in the works of Godfrey Lienhardt and E. E. Evans-Pritchard. According to Firth, the problem which the paradox of identity presents to the Western mind is whether such a creature is "really" a man or "really" a lion. "For the people concerned, however, he [Lienhardt][45] argues that it would seem that an animal's nature and a man's nature can be co-present in the same being."[46]

Like Martin Hollis, Firth holds that the principles which guide reasoning processes are universal, and he therefore (by implication) rejects Evans-Pritchard's thesis that the principle of noncontradiction is alien to African modes of thought. He rejects also Sodipo and Hallen's theory of independently true incommensurable systems. What might be different, Firth thinks, are the basic first premises or assumptions of various thought systems. "We demonstrate where possible that the thought processes involved in drawing inferences from, or in acting upon, such assumptions are not unintelligible to us. The assumptions may be non-rational, but the thinking from them is not illogical."[47]

Identity and separation in such cases are matters of specified particulars, of level of abstraction and of context. For example, Firth says, "when it is said 'that man has the heart of a lion', or 'he was a lion in battle', no anatomical identity is understood, but an identity with that bravery, that courage, which is traditionally [and probably incorrectly] attributed to lions. The two items, man and lion, are joined by an abstract quality, hence [only] metaphorically."[48]

With reference to Lévi-Strauss's theory of binary categorization, Firth suggests that the Dinka's fusion of man and lion is an attempt, in the manner of biblical creation myths, to strike concord between contraries. The concept of men-lions, he says, "can thus be a resolution of opposites and a fusion of characteristics. It provides a category of beings who combine the behaviour of both lions and men, epitomise both the dichotomy and the bridge between nature and culture."[49] But Firth picks the wrong metaphorical point when he says, "They are lions who are men; as such they are men who eat other men, destroy cattle instead of preserving them, and so on."[50] The point, I believe, is that men are comparable to lions in the contexts where they exhibit admired lion qualities in parallel contexts—aggressiveness toward the enemy, power and bravery in attack, confidence and humility at times of peace, etc. Configurative likening of men to animals in specific contexts plays a central role in many forms of discourse on behavioral qualities. The Luo saying that "*dhano winyo*," which poorly translates into English as "humans are birds," and the more common saying that "so and so is a snake" or "so and so is a hare" are good examples which illustrate the point.

Firth therefore agrees with Evans-Pritchard that the Nuer may very well make the analogy twins-spirits or air-birds. But for an explanation Firth says:

> My own guess at an interpretation is the following: Twins to the Nuer are physiologically and socially abnormal—they are duplicate personalities, as Schapera has pointed out, or 'one person' as Nuer state. So, initially, they are regarded as dangerous and they are equated with birds, perhaps because of multi-birth, and with spirit.[51]

For Firth, the identification of spirits with social realities is a mystical identification based on attitudes. Firth's argument, however, does not resolve the issue of the paradoxicality of identity claims. Evans-Pritchard himself explains, as we have seen, that the attribution of paradoxicality to the Nuer claims about the identity of twins to birds, or the Dinka's claims to the effect that some people are lions, is, as Peter Bodunrin also argues in his " 'Theoretical Identities' and Scientific Explanation: The Horton-Skorupski Debate,"[52] based on the intellectualist confusion of ontological and metaphysical issues with logical ones.

Bodunrin bases his argument on the Principle of Indiscernibility of Identicals, according to which two entities are identical if, and only if, the one has all and only those properties which the other has. Now it is quite clear, at least from the explanation given by Evans-Pritchard, that the Nuer recognize that twins, as humans, have certain properties which birds do not have. The problem, as we have noted above, arises from the use of the English verb "to be" (are/is) in translation, which the intellectuals have tended to assume is indicative of an ontological identity claim. We have indicated above, for example, that it is wrong to translate the Luo saying "*dhano winyo*" as "humans are birds." It is wrong because, despite the verb *are*, the statement has no commitment to the existential (ontological) characteristics or constitutions of either humans or birds. Certainly ontological identity could be one possible meaning of the statement "*dhano winyo*," but not the only one. It is our task to identify the most rational meaning from among all the possible ones. And this would require an analysis of the statement in the different contexts in which it is used so as to draw a table to show the degrees of the constancy or variance of its signification and reference. Such a table would lead to the determination of the meaning of the statement.

Following Hallen-Sodipo's scale of rationality of meanings, we can list such possible meanings of the statement "*dhano winyo*" as follows:

1. The entities we call humans are the same entities we call birds.
2. Humans sing like birds.
3. Humans have hairs like birds have feathers.
4. Humans are unreliable in character like birds of the air are unreliable in flight.

Now both Horton and Skorupski assume that Africans make identity statements such as the ones observed above only in the nature of the first possible meaning. And they both derive their view of the paradox of identity from that reductive assumption. Horton argues that the kind of identity is a "paradoxical identity," or what Lévy-Bruhl called "mystical participation." Lévy-Bruhl called mystical any statement which he thought was incapable of being intelligible to *ordinary* reason. To this, Evans-Pritchard, Hallen, Sodipo, and Bodunrin—and perhaps others—object that the concept of the *ordinariness* of reason referred to by Lévy-Bruhl has, as its content, principles of justification which are particular to only one epistemological tradition, of which the attitudes of Lévy-Bruhl, Horton, Skorupski, Firth, et al. are only a function. Such principles are deeply rooted in their "thought parameters" because they constitute the epistemological and linguistic systems of the people who grow up in them. They are alien to all other systems.

One such principle is the Principle of Identity, which operates on the basis of the definition given above from Bodunrin. It states that two things can be identical only if all the qualities or properties of the compared things are indiscernible. Therefore, where two or more things are compared and asserted to be identical, as in the expression "X is Y," that copula "*is*" is taken to indicate indiscernibility of all the properties constituting X and Y. If X and Y are objects, "*is*" will be taken to indicate ontological identity of X to Y; and where X and Y are different statements, "*is*" is taken to indicate a logical identity between the statements, that is, that X, as a statement, expresses exactly what is expressed by statement Y. And because the statements described above ("twins *are* birds"; "some men *are* lions"; and "humans *are* birds") can only be sensibly translated into English by using the copula "*is/are*," it was assumed by some that Africans make statements which claim ontological identity between objects whose properties are in fact very discernible, such as twins-birds, men-lions, humans-birds, etc. For this view, the statement in example one above could be the only meaning of "*dhano winyo*" in its English translation as "humans are birds." And this would constitute a paradox or mysticism, because, on the basis of the Principle of Indiscernibles, it is not rational to assert identity between two or more ontologically different objects such as humans and birds.

Skorupski, on his part, thought, also on the basis of assumed ontological identity, that the claims (twins are birds; some men are lions; humans are birds) could still be accepted as *rational* on the same grounds as those used by Westerners when they accept the mysteries of Christian faith. In the relationship between the physical and historical body and blood of Christ and the physical bread and wine of the Eucharist, Christians claim a certain degree of ontological identity. They claim a relation holding between objects.

It is worth noting at this point that even Tempels's theory of vital forces confuses ontological and theoretical identities. Although he did not make direct references to the relationship between the theory of forces and Christian mysticism, T. pels too misconstrued the concept of the vital force as the African analogy of the Hellenic "thing" or object. These views are wrong. They are wrong because they unjustifiably reduce all statements of identity to only ontological identity. According to Bodunrin, both Horton and Skorupski—and we can add Tempels—wrongly equated perceptual (ontological) objects with theoretical objects.

In his rejoinder to Bodunrin, R. J. M. Lithown[53] argues that Bodunrin's argument against Horton and Skorupski was essentially semantic, that is, that it discussed mainly how sentences asserting theoretical identity are to be interpreted. This is correct. But the concern with meanings of propositions arises out of another concern: the need to distinguish and elucidate the nature of realities described in language.

Bodunrin's concern must therefore be seen in the context of the more basic concern about the nature of the theoretical content of *real definitions* of perceptual objects or phenomena. Real definitions, in agreement with Aristotle, express the properties that are essential to a thing's being what it is. Such definitions are not contingent definitions. They are not empirical statements, because, as Bodunrin says, they give the essential properties which, together, connote the nature of the perceptual object or phenomena for which the definition stands. Real definitions are analytic statements. They are tautological. It is in this sense that the copula *"is"* uniting a perceptual object or phenomenon (*definiendum*) with its *definiens* adopts the mathematical equative role, such as in "a man is a rational animal (man = rational animal)." In this sense, it means that if it did not impede speech, we could as well use the phrase to the right side of the equation sign instead of the single word *man* without gaining or losing anything.

Now Bodunrin's argument is, I believe, that first, science often makes definitions which are not contingent but analytical because, in them, as in the examples he gives of the temperature of gas, lightning flashes, and a crystal of salt, the *definiens* is purely theoretical just as "rational animal" in the definition of man is. Second, Bodunrin argues that some people think that such scientific definitional equations are also usually operational in ordinary experiences and speech, such that, for example, when people talk of "systems of forces" they mean physical relations obtaining between objects (as Tempels claims), or that when they talk of "person" they actually mean its theoretical identity (*definiens*) "being with intelligence" (as Kagame argues), just as scientists do in their analytic theoretical identities. I have argued against this pretention in my "Alexis Kagame and African Socio-linguistics."[54]

Conclusion

We have been discussing the meaning of reason and the nature of rational statements. Models have been drawn, comparing paradigms of scientific principles and notions with those assumed to characterize religious beliefs and other forms of traditional beliefs and utterances. The discussion has further revealed the continued pairing of views in close relation to the Hegelian dichotomy with which we started. But the anglophone debate on the issue has certainly been much more spirited and interesting than we have probably been able to present here. Through it the dichotomization of reason (or the rational) versus nonreason (or the nonrational) has been much more clearly presented than ever before. But what is even more interesting is the contrast between the anglophone and the francophone approaches to the study of African philosophy, or to thought systems in general. One emphasizes knowledge, and the other discourse. Each is rooted in deeper philosophical traditions, themselves quite distinct in many ways. This distinctive nature of the two (analytic and phenomenological) approaches to the study of African culture has largely been responsible for rendering the development of African philosophy in the last two decades into two camps which are rarely accessible to each other.

It is perhaps futile to weigh the qualities of the two approaches, as neither is superior. Also futile is the merely descriptive analysis of the nature and characteristic features of the two. Science and ordinary experience are by far more important and superior in certain respects of our practical lives. But it is also certainly not enough to have only the knowledge which the sciences and ordinary experience provide. It is not enough to have only knowledge. The limitations of science and analytical philosophy are enduring in the sorts of questions which people keep on asking about human nature. These sorts of questions are answered neither by science nor by analytical philosophy. But it is also not enough to have only an orderly and complex system of communication which does not sufficiently convey knowledge for practical life as well. Without proper knowledge and analysis, discourse alone cannot lead to practice.

7 | Excavating Africa in Western Discourse

A NEW SCHOOL HAS come to the fore recently in the study of African systems of thought in general and African philosophy in particular. Initiated by Franz Crahay's now famous paper "Le 'décollage' conceptuel: conditions d'une philosophie bantoue" (1965), this school examines the nature and forms of African intellectual practice in its historical emergence and conditioning. Philosophy is regarded by this school as only one type or form of the wider sense of discourse. According to Crahay, for Africans to produce a system of philosophy they need to reconstruct African discourse at the speculative (*décollage*) level by first identifying and then employing conceptual schemes or basic principles of reasoning indigenous to Africa. Ardent followers of Crahay in this orientation include Fabien Eboussi-Boulaga, Marcien Towa, Meinrad Hebga, and V. Y. Mudimbe among others.

Although it is difficult to represent such a school under a common nomenclature, its members are at least thinly connected by their common critique of ethnophilosophy, which they all regard as a product of Western power/knowledge. In their different ways, they concur that the production of ethnophilosophy expresses the epistemological roots of: the deep social, political, and cultural crisis of *muntu*, the African person (Eboussi-Boulaga); Africans' continued servitude to Western domination (Towa); Africa's dependence on Western tutelage (Hebga); the invention of Africa at the margins of Western knowledge (Mudimbe). Common to these characterizations of ethnophilosophy is also the concern, first, to expose the politics that produces ethnophilosophy as its inferior margin, its negative reflection awaiting assimilation, and, second, to describe for African *gnosis* the course for a deliverance from the politics of marginalization and assimilation, which produce the passive image represented not only in ethnophilosophy but, according to Mudimbe, in the entire present philosophical discourse in Africa.

Departing from the premise that contemporary African intellectual practice takes place within the format and formulas dictated by Western epistemological categories and principles, this school of thought ostensibly argues that African intellectual practice must break away from its Western conditionings to be able to make any sense to Africans themselves. As a step toward the realization of this separation, they have concentrated on the deconstruction of the links tying

African intellectual practice to Western conceptual schemes or *episteme* and historical plots. This deconstructive project gets close to the position of the anglophone school discussed in chapter six above and particularly as represented by Evans-Pritchard and Godfrey Lienhardt. This position states a methodological strategy for the study of African systems of thought. The strategy states that whoever desires to study African systems of thought must not employ the method of analytic study of specific or special aspects of thought (such as concepts) in isolation, but rather must examine thought as people use it in relation to practices of everyday life. Only this method will help to establish a sharp break with Western categories.

Fabien Eboussi-Boulaga: Ethnophilosophy as a Philosophy of the Dominated

For Eboussi-Boulaga, ethnology is the putting together of facts in relations and correlations without profundity or substance; and this, to Eboussi-Boulaga, is what Tempels seems to have done with the Bantu. Furthermore, the precision of Tempels's factual accounts is to be highly doubted. To take account of the particularity of the Bantu, Tempels hurried a little too ambitiously to construct a system of formal logic for them and, as a result, parted company with precision and immediacy of his ethnographical facts. Yet he dared present this "construction" of the Bantu as what they actually are in reality.[1]

In a fateful paragraph in *La Philosophie bantoue*, Tempels wrote:

> We will certainly not pretend that the Bantu are in a position to present to us a philosophical treatise exposed in an adequate vocabulary. It is here that it falls on us to make a systematic development of it. It is we who are able to tell them in a precise manner what their intimate conception of beings is.[2]

In a commentary on this passage, Eboussi-Boulaga writes: "Such is the paradox: this ontological system is entirely unconscious and is expressed in an inadequate vocabulary without coherence. . . . "[3] We here only wish to point out one weakness among others of that group of African critics of the ethnophilosophical literature ("African philosophy"). Most of these people base their criticisms principally on Tempels's work. In going through most of these criticisms, however, it must be said that they are frequently bound up with some degree of exaggeration which renders them unfair to some extent. In comparing the two passages (of Tempels and Eboussi-Boulaga) quoted above, one sees nothing in Tempels's passage that talks of the lack of coherence which Eboussi-Boulaga criticizes in his comment. This sort of exaggeration has its roots in the anger against Tempels's position and has led many African critics of ethnophilosophy to make sweeping statements about or to invent criticisms about things that just don't exist in Tempels's work. They may even be right in some aspects of their criticism, but one often sees an exaggerated attention drawn only to the supposed historico-political implications of Tempels's work and position. This is what, for example, Aimé Césaire addresses in his *Discours sur le colonialisme*.[4]

The coherence of which Tempels himself talks so much, and which is the pivot in his hypothetical exposition, is an internal coherence of the conceptual elements in Bantu worldview and, to our view, has nothing to do with their not having been expressed in an adequate vocabulary. In any case, Eboussi-Boulaga refutes both the method and the object of Tempels's work:

> Tempels wished to apply to the ethnological facts a causal type of explanation that leads to principles in order to realize becoming and contingency. Unfortunately, instead of resorting to a topology or to structural models, he made of this principle a substance which is capable of realizing diversity and attitudes of behavior at the same time. This done, Tempels makes an appeal to a thing, a substance (vital force), as the principle of some general explanation.[5]

Like many other African critics of Tempels's work, Eboussi-Boulaga is also referring, in this passage, to the interpretation of Tempels's equation of the concept of Being in Western philosophy with the concept of Force in Bantu thought. The following is my interpretation of the thematic procedural scheme of Eboussi-Boulaga's critique.

The Logical Analysis

Eboussi-Boulaga holds that Tempels treats of elements that lack logical coherence and hence makes these sporadic testimonies lose their persuasive force. Indeed, recourse to certain facts for establishing a hypothesis that would be proved by the same facts is at least begging the question. Second, some of these elements, such as force, are not as important or frequent in the daily life of the Bantu as Tempels seems to have believed. Eboussi-Boulaga denies any significant recurrence of words signifying force in the ordinary languages of the Bantu, except for some allusions in greetings and formulas expressing condolences.[6] Yet Tempels establishes his theory on these banal facts of language and makes a hasty generalization in three directions: for the entire linguistic structure, for all the Bantu, and for all "primitives."

Tempels's interpretation of force is at times contrary to the social values of the Bantu. Tempels explained force as the highest value in Bantu life, and supreme felicity as the possession of the greatest vital power (*puissance vitale*), as opposed to conditions of sickness, plague, suffering, depression, fatigue, injustice, etc., which designate, for the Bantu, the loss or diminution of the vital force.[7]

But, Eboussi-Boulaga asks:

> What, then, would one say about the rites of passage, of initiations and circumcision, which, according to Tempels's logic, result in the diminution of force, and yet, for the Bantu themselves, it is by going through the same cere-

monies, by going through fasting, pain, and suffering, that one becomes more fully a man? The loss of that which is socially valued is at times valued to the point of being the necessary condition for access to certain highly valued roles in society. The rites of aggregation or separation and purification do not have, as their unique key, a capital of force which they have to preserve or increase. The principle of many observances and practices is quite different: it is within the symbolic activity that one takes possession of the world, discovers the order of the world, and tells that which is from that which ought to be. The Bantu speak what they live by means of fables, proverbs, and by their myths and institutions. And the word that composes and divides does not content itself by reducing all phenomena to one common element.

The reduction of all things to a common denominator leads to the evacuation of that which makes the originality of man. The *muntu* of Tempels is a utilitarian, greedy to assimilate the vital force: reality for him is only "good to eat" [Lévi-Strauss] and not to think and describe; he is nothing but an instinct of conservation and biological procreation. Now this "putting of natural forces to work" of which Tempels speaks, we call culture. And this is not a simple play or equilibration of forces, be it among the Bantu or among magicians.[8]

We saw that Tempels distinguishes two levels in the concept of force. First, he defines force as that which signifies being, in the sense of thing or matter, as "that which is." He calls this individual force. But then he also says that "Among visible beings the Bantu distinguish that which is perceived by the senses from the 'thing in itself'; by the 'thing in itself' they designate its very intimate nature, the very being of the thing or more precisely, the force of this thing."[9] This latter distinction or level defines force in the sense of form in scholastic terms. But Eboussi-Boulaga observes that this doubling of the concept of force presents a contradiction in the attempt to substitute being with force. The formula "being is force," in order to have one sense, must signify a dialectic identity supposing a process of identification—which is not supposed here. According to Eboussi-Boulaga, the result is that

> the Bantu of Tempels, as bad Platonists, reject the sensible aspect of being. Hence Tempels is at pains throughout his work to account for the Bantu ordinary knowledge of nature. And by the force of this logic, Tempels denies that the Bantu are capable of the science of the concrete which is recognized of them today. For him, the knowledge of the world, including simple technology, belongs to the domain of approximations and suppositions in the domain of art and fingering. And the science of essences, failing to take support on sensible data, is literally reduced to divination and to a play of imagination.[10]

"The ambiguity lies," writes Eboussi-Boulaga, "not only in this duplication of force, in this division of a thing into exterior and interior essence that lifts the concrete man to the play of appearances, but also in the attempt to hierarchize force. Force, in contrast to the being for which it is made the dynamic substitute, is ambivalent: it can be good or bad. . . . "

There exist, therefore, superior evil forces. [And] the contradiction becomes superlative, if we follow the principles of hierarchization and of "interaction" according to Tempels: on the ontological ladder beings are placed high or low in accordance with the degree of their strength and ability to exercise power on the inferior ones. This is to say that man reinforces himself with things in order to be able to resist the power of beings above him; this is equivalent to saying that the evil forces that torment man are enthroned above him on the "ontological ladder."[11]

Eboussi-Boulaga does not say how this presents a contradiction in Tempels's pages, but the point is clear. If, according to Tempels's "ontological ladder," forces are arranged in the order of their power and ability to influence inferior ones, then it follows that there are evil forces superior to man which torment him. But if so, then why does man use things (which are supposed to be forces inferior to him and therefore at least two steps inferior to the evil forces above man) to reinforce himself so as to resist the torments of the evil superior forces? According to ethnographical data, Africans use charms for protection, a practice which implies that the things (forces inferior to man) are superior to the evil forces above man himself because they influence (resist) them and are therefore superior to man as well, for they are able to do what those above man cannot do. All this shows, Eboussi-Boulaga concludes, that "force is equivocal and ambiguous."[12]

Eboussi-Boulaga also observes that such a contradiction is reproduced in the discussion of man, of the living as opposed to the dead. Tempels writes that, "for the Blacks, life is a question of intensity." Yet he also writes that "The elder [dead] force dominates the younger [living] force on which it continues to exercise its influence."[13] In view of this, Eboussi-Boulaga asks the following question: "Are the forces of the one and the other of the same nature?, and is the criterion of classification still that of intensity? . . . Must force be distinguished from life?" Here we seemingly fall back on the two (exterior-interior) concepts of being-force. But Tempels says again that "for the Bantu the dead equally live a diminished life, they are the reduced vital energies."[14] And Eboussi-Boulaga concludes that, in the face of such logical complications, the only conclusion that Tempels must inevitably draw is that "there exists a worldview of an anthropological type different from the ontology of forces."[15] These logical flaws changed the outcome of Tempels's project substantially. They made the Bantu appear to be more primitive than they actually are: people who are unaware of the concrete (material) reality which they are and which surrounds them; people who hold contradictory statements about themselves and about the world in which they live; people who are chained to the shackles of ontology without salvation. Such are the Bantu of Tempels; they are the Monsieur Jourdain of philosophy. Tempels had evidently intended well with his work, Eboussi-Boulaga proclaims—that is, to rehabilitate the Bantu and all the "primitives" from the scorns of Lévy-Bruhl.

Tempels had set out to prove that, contrary to their classification in Western discourse as "prelogical," the Bantu had a logically coherent system of thought about man, the universe, things, life, etc., and that they also had a "philosophy." But unfortunately the work that translated these good intentions came out in contrast to the intentions themselves.

However, according to Eboussi-Boulaga, Tempels's ontology of forces not only is contradictory in terms, but is simply impossible and cannot be the immediate base of morality or law.[16] Serving himself with a quotation from Bergson's *La Pensée et le mouvant*, he asks Tempels:

> When in the end the world comes to mean all that exists, it does not mean more than existence. What, then, do you earn by saying that the world is will, instead of establishing well what it is?[17]

Tempels's ontology of forces, holds Eboussi-Boulaga, is not original. His axiom "Being is force" is a mere attribution of essence and the dynamic character becomes harmonized to this essence. "Now the paradoxical coexistence of being and becoming is precisely the theme of Greek philosophy [also]."[18] All early Greek philosophers, with the "scandalous" exception of Parmenides, had pondered on and affirmed this position of the dynamicity of being. What Tempels writes is therefore nothing but Greek philosophy, concludes Eboussi-Boulaga.

> "The [only] error of Tempels is having affirmed the convertibility of being and acting, of having ignored the logical priority of existence that it [activity] presupposes, since he affirms that "Force is being" [Fr. *La force, c'est l'être*]. The mystery of being is that of being able to dissociate itself [from itself] on the level of existence, to become other than what it is. The illusion of force is that of not being able to become its other: it ignores negativity.[19] Force is the refusal of discourse, it is dumb and brutal, it does not articulate anything. And the proposition [of Tempels] "being is force, force is being" deserves the sarcasm of Hegel: "It degrades itself into a silly representation when its content is not taken as a concept, but as a representation."[20]

The concept of force cannot be understood, in terms of substance, in the same way as we understand the concept of being. But to whom do we attribute this "silly representation"? What Eboussi-Boulaga calls a silly imagination is of course the "concept" of force as it is exposed by Tempels. But Eboussi-Boulaga himself believes that African thought has not passed the preconceptual stage.[21]

In his examination of Tempels's definition of Bantu ethics, Eboussi-Boulaga states that ontology is oppressive and does not give room for freedom of action. Ethics can therefore not be based on ontology as Tempels claims for the Bantu. Ontology, Eboussi-Boulaga says, "suppresses human action, not only in culture, but also in the ethical domain. The primitives will never know moral obligation: they will never abstain except in order to conform themselves to the hierarchy of beings, searching for what is, but not what ought to be."[22] Acceptance of an ontological explanation of social order is an acceptance of a given order of nature which the social order itself participates in and reflects. And this order, to which conformity is the goal of behavior, denies every individual among the Bantu his human responsibility. He only knows an abstract morality which is identical with ontological knowledge of the general laws of causality and includes criteria for distinguishing good forces from the evil ones.

> But so far as it is a question of making a practical syllogism, of answering to the 'quid faciendum' in view of a good, the *Muntu* is freed to hazard. An act of liberty is not required of him because he has nothing to choose, but only to recognize. His morality is therefore defined as recognition of benevolent forces. He therefore gets involved in divination, not in order to prevent misfortune, but in order to practice virtue![23]

But, Eboussi-Boulaga holds, Tempels can hardly provide proof for the assertion that " 'objective morality' among the Blacks is an ontological, immanent, and intrinsical morality."[24] On the contrary, Eboussi-Boulaga agrees with Mauss that "Morality is wisdom, because it is the diction from human experience, because it is the praise of the knowledge of man in his relations with the other in society. It [morality] is not only a simple echo of an impersonal cosmic life that the Bantu [of Tempels's book] live."[25]

Eboussi-Boulaga is quite right in trying to distinguish and liberate ethics from metaphysics. However, one might object that sometimes metaphysical explanations of ethics serve to clarify or account for the common good or ideal on account of which human action itself is regulated and subjected to judgment. Those disciplines which aim at providing regulative or prescriptive statements, including ethics and axiology in philosophy, tend to presuppose some metaphysical explanation. Those who oppose various aspects of modern medical engineering on ethical grounds cannot sufficiently account, for example, for their condemnation of surrogate motherhood or birth control or abortion or trade in human organs for medical transplants without recourse to metaphysical justifications. In such condemnations they expound propositions which state that ideal human *nature* does not allow for such practices. In other words, the practices derive their moral quality from their conformity or nonconformity to what is expected of the *nature* of man. The definition of a moral practice could therefore be expressed in the following manner: a practice is moral if the proposition asserting it is derivable as part of a more basic proposition asserting the *nature* of man.

Philosophy is not only a series of statements whose sole significance is based on truth value and/or logical coherence. This may be true of philosophy as a speculative activity. But can the same be said of philosophy in terms of the specific ends of some of its practical branches? Is the Bantu moral system improper simply because it calls for conformity to the ideal? By nature, moral judgments call for conformity with a specific ideal or good. The significance of morality is not to be found in the *process* through which individual judgments are made, but in the realization of the ideal toward which the process moves. As practical knowledge, ethics cannot be consummated in the judgments alone but in the actual living which the art—and good judgment for that matter—is meant to facilitate.

The shift of the moral focus from the end to the means, as Eboussi-Boulaga does in his critique of Tempels, goes back to Aristotle's individualistic outlook, which in turn owes its strength to the experiences of a philosopher who lived at the time of the disintegration of the older Greek social values. Aristotle's time was marked by the emergent triumph of the individual as a moral agent as opposed to the traditional class collectivisms. In ethical terms, this separation led to the distinction between what *is* and what *ought* to be. Ever since then, ethics concentrated more and more on the analysis of *what ought* an individual to do as opposed to the collective *ought*. But nowhere does this imply that the *ought* as the ideal of morality lost its significance. The whole game of moral judgments is an appraisal of our approximation to the ideal. But are these judgments for fun or for real? We believe that, whether in their theoretical elucidation or in their normative presentations, moral judgments tend to have, as their essential dimension, practical ends in the domain of human relations. It would be a futile exercise to engage in writing texts of ethics if, at least at the back of the writer's mind, there was no strong desire and objective that the valuative statements in such a text should be applied to practical behavior. The pertinence of valuative statments lies in the fact that they usually pretend to have a universalistic character which calls for conformism as opposed to subjective relativism.

There are two senses of the word *ethics* which appear to be at the center of the differences between Eboussi-Boulaga and Tempels. The first sense of the word *ethics* is the ordinary or layman's sense according to which it suggests a set of standards by which a society or community regulates its behavior. In this sense, ethics is just part of the general worldview or system of thought. In the second sense, ethics is defined purely as a philosophical practice, a theoretical investigation into the fundamental principles and basic concepts that underlie both human behavior and common ideas about such behavior. As such, it differs from ethics in the first sense.

In this second sense ethics differs from morals or moral behavior. The latter are usually a set of statements which regulate social behavior by stating what people ought and ought not do. And neither the knowledge of such statements nor their application to the guidance and control of practical life constitutes ethics by itself or in combination with the other. According to Eboussi-Boulaga, then, what Tempels presents as Bantu ethics is only their morality. But even in this, Eboussi-Boulaga objects that the Bantu are not as primitive in their morality as Tempels presents them to be. In Tempels's analysis, Bantu "ethics" expressed their traditional settled agreements regarding the right ways of doing things. In this system, "right" signifies both "indubitably effective" and "mysteriously sanctioned." The latter firm conviction permitted no hesitation regarding the former. Overwhelmed by mysteries which they could not probe, the Bantu dared not question the practical effectiveness of their customary ways or depart from them one whit. So we may adapt the poet's lines:

Theirs not to make reply,
Theirs not to reason why,
Theirs but to do and die.

Such conformism, argues Eboussi-Boulaga, does not constitute ethics in the second sense above. This objection arises out of Eboussi-Boulaga's suspicion that Tempels had used the term "Bantu ethics" in the second sense. And this, in turn, is also based on another but not wholly justified suspicion that Tempels had used the term "philosophy"—of which ethics is part—in the title "Bantu philosophy" in the academic sense.

This chain of suspicions is not peculiar to Eboussi-Boulaga. It underlies the entire anti-ethnophilosophy debate. As we said in chapter two above, this suspicion arises out of a myth created by Tempels's commentators rather than out of what Tempels states in his works.

The Sociohistorical Significance of La Philosophie bantoue

According to Eboussi-Boulaga, Tempels's work hides many degrading European perceptions of the Bantu and of Africans in general. These perceptions, argues Eboussi-Boulaga, have not only lowered the social status of the Bantu, but have also made them ahistorical. Because the Bantu are portrayed as incapable of forming concepts and knowledge about the world of experience, they are also thought of as incapable of transforming their environment and influencing history. Likewise, history and environmental changes have no transformational effects on the way the Bantu perceive themselves, their relations, and the environment around them. In this view, Tempels's theory (ontology) of forces as the center of the Bantu worldview is a modernized perpetuation of the old Hegelian view of Africans in history.

First, *La Philosophie bantoue* was written for the rehabilitation of the Bantu and the "primitives" in general from their declared "pre-logical" state, and hence was addressed to a public other than the Bantu themselves. It was addressed to the "colonials of good will" and particularly to the missionaries, that through it they may be able to adopt a more fruitful approach in their missionary task of "raising" the "primitives." And this task was to be accomplished by recognizing them as men, men who have their own way of life, their own system of thought furnished by logically coherent (though scientifically unacceptable) ideas. "The time has come for making a general confession and, in all cases, to open the eyes. . . . "

Second, Tempels's work defines the Bantu as a mass of "primitives" who are called to judgment by the supercivilized Europeans. Epistemologically, they are not subjects but simple objects of European knowledge who can be known in detail.[26] According to Eboussi-Boulaga, this is the social background of Tempels's work. "It was written primarily as a guide to action and to justify exploitation, since it aspires to understand so as to possess the Bantu; to correct, to sort out that which is valid from that which is false so that the valid may immediately serve in the education and civilization of the primitives."[27]

"Bantu philosophy," in contrast to that of the Western world, which is "thorough, objective, scientific, and based on Christian concepts," is unacceptable from the points of view of reasonableness, objectivity, and science. It is a product of a vain imagination of these "primitives." It does not correspond to reality. Western civilization thus finds itself as "everything" in front of "nothing."[28]

Eboussi-Boulaga holds that Tempels endeavored to prove three things: the difference, the particularity, and the alterity of the mentality of the primitives. Furthermore, Tempels wanted to demonstrate that African mentality is divorced from technological civilization, which it considers as inessential to man. Last, Tempels used his wrong conception of the Bantu as proof that Christianity was the original and absolute religion. And to do this,

> two possible solutions presented themselves [to Tempels]: either to consider the primitives as [mentally] retarded people, or to hold them as degenerated people who have fallen back on the outside of the original point. [And] it is this second hypothesis that Father Tempels adopts and transforms into a certitude in his dogmatic system. According to this hypothesis, the evolution of the primitives is regressing, and time is only drawing them farther from the primordial revelation. In order to civilize them, people must take account of these distortions rather than treat them as if they were a 'tabula rasa'. This is the re-education of which Tempels talks.[29]

His work, therefore, has the primary aim of bringing back the Bantu to the mental point where Christianity can be of salvific use. And, according to Eboussi-Boulaga, the fundamental question to be asked about Tempels's project is whether the Bantu state of mind can still be saved. And in response Tempels writes: "Yes, through Grace." Through the process of assimilation, the irrational can still be absorbed into the supernatural. "That is precisely what the Christian doctrine of Grace teaches, founded on the certitude of Revelation."[30] Christianity or Christian civilization is thus to be the only savior of the Bantu, because, according to Tempels, "their health cannot come from anywhere else." It will raise them from the level of irrationality to that of rationality. Eboussi-Boulaga calls this "the error latent in most of missionary attitudes [that] expresses itself here [in Tempels] with brutality: though unworthy of being admitted within the ranks of reason, the blacks are nevertheless called to enter the kingdom of heaven that was promised to the poor in spirit."[31] This missionary approach to the study of African peoples is also adopted by some African followers of Tempels, as in "*Dialectique existentielle des Bantous et sacramentalisme*"[32] of Vincent Mulago, and in many of those works on African wisdom and cultural elements evaluated and interpreted as a "pierre d'attente" for the Christian teaching! In adopting this approach, eminent African theologians have made Christianity "behave as though it had been sent by the Being hidden to the Bantu, by the being of the Bantu themselves, as if it were a pure transparency. In the end, the Bantu will not be able to understand themselves nor will they be able to understand their world unless they look into the eyes of the missionaries."[33]

But "Alas," writes Eboussi-Boulaga,

> it is too late! ... Too late, the *Muntu* is dead! Ontology is making the vain effort to stop the course of time, to fix forever the rules of becoming. The irony of history has already mixed up the cards and changed the facts. Because it [ontology] has denied all temporality to the primitive or slave, the theorizer or master always informs himself too late.[34]

According to Eboussi-Boulaga, the *muntu* of the new savior-civilization is a *muntu* who is dead to history. He has been lured into this money-vital-force, the new symbol of desire and satisfaction both at the same time, the new force. He is therefore trodden underfoot by the new superior force, the white man, who, by virtue of his dominating role through mercantile power, is drawn into the ontological ladder of the Bantu. This is the sad situation of the *évolué* who, by force, becomes the provocative agent of disorder.[35]

Tempels's analysis divides Bantu society into those who have been disillusioned (mentally purified) through evolution, that is, the "*évolués*" and the "*basenji*," the savages among the brave peoples of the interior in whom the nostalgia to participate in the ontology of force is still evident. This is the representation of a colonized society. In this representation, Bantu society appears cracked, it has lost its image of unity; its typology has lost its image of the proverbial simplicity. According to Eboussi-Boulaga, such a society is profoundly Manichean, divided between, on the one hand, those who no longer believe in the mysterious power of the white man—to them the biological and magical secrets of the white man have been laid bare, his whiteness made transparent, without depth, a mere accident—and, on the other hand, the *muntu*, who has been fondly qualified as "brave," the perfect antithesis of the "*évolué*." This "brave" *muntu* still aspires for "vital reinforcement," for participation in the superior force of the white man. The "*évolué*" on his part seeks contentment in the satisfaction of his needs, which are artificially heightened thanks to such (colonial) commodities as money and pleasure. But instead of being grateful for his "privileged" social condition, the "*évolué*" becomes a rebel; he realizes that his new social condition tends to impose on him a loan of a new personality which must be rejected because it is only a sign of foreign conquest. This, Eboussi-Boulaga declares, is the kind of brief account of the Congolese drama to which the author (of Bantu ontology) remained totally blind; it never occurred to him as a sign of Bantu destiny which could be discovered by historical analysis. Instead, for Tempels, says Eboussi-Boulaga,

> Ontology is [made to look] not only a refusal of [ordinary] human language [which reflects relevant practical moments and concerns of life], but also a rejection of the historical reality in which man lives; it is presented as essentially consisting of a nostalgia for the [linguistically and historically] lost paradise. At the end, Bantu destiny appears [only] as a history of vicissitudes, its evolution nothing more than a series of successive degradations.[36]

Tempels thus represents the Bantu and other colonized peoples as people who are insensitive to the ordinariness of life, to the changes that history brings to language and knowledge. They live in the dead past, where "the original and more sane thought [as opposed to later polluted philosophy] is found precisely among the most conservative tribes,"[37] meaning, in Eboussi-Boulaga's critique, "the most archaic"[38] Africans.

"African Philosophy" and Its African Exponents

According to Tempels, the Bantu must therefore be assimilated into a superior and more human (by being constituted on rationality) Christian civilization so as to save their own humanity. "The desire of philosophy is one of the efforts for access to the humanity of the master" and is one of the differentiating elements that constitute civilization in its transcendence. He who introduces "philosophy" or attributes it to himself abolishes and nullifies the separations between those who are "true men" and those who are not.

This is the situation in which the African claims the possession of philosophy. For him philosophy makes part of the definition of man. It is proper to man and part of his essence. It is the manifestation of rationality. Through his or her claims for the possession of a "philosophy," therefore, the African only expresses his or her claims for an entry to this humanity; "he only asks that it be admitted that his capacity to conform is real, that the metamorphoses that he undergoes be recognized, that he be granted, by 'matriculation,' the 'citizenship' "[39] of the superior master-civilization. The African philosopher in Tempels's conception thus becomes an intermediary between the master and the people whom he represents. He speaks for them to the master, who is the standard of their measurement. He becomes a secondary master by delegation. His contributions thus only take the form of a novel of customs, of an ethnographical monograph, or of a study of mentality. And he does not address himself to the local people but to the administrators and missionaries, to the foreign experts, to the ethnological institutes, or to the schools for colonial administrators. He is an ethnophilosopher.

This role of ethnophilosopher, says Eboussi-Boulaga, forms the negation of the negation of the self. It is a return to affirm what had been negated of him by the master. But what is accomplished by this dialectic, says Eboussi-Boulaga, is the interiorization of dependence.[40]

> Despite his relationship to the people and their values, despite the nostalgia for the lost typology of unity, the rupture is effectual. And, logically, the negation of the self gives place to the empty self-affirmation by a subject in search of his lost attributes; and he finds them, he thinks, in the attributes of man in general by reference to liberty, to the ideology of development, to the state, and to political power.[41]

The invented ethnophilosophy has one major objective or aspiration: to improve existing human relations between Europeans and "primitive peoples" by portraying the latter as more "human" than they were once thought by Europeans to be. "But because it is still addressed to the good will, or better, to the kindness of the other, ethnophilosophy transforms itself into a persuasive apology, a rhetoric that only places it on the conjectural and not intrinsical value of its arguments, that sees not the true but the seemingly-true."[42]

According to Eboussi-Boulaga, the African ethnophilosopher thus detaches himself from the masses of the people. His language is the abstract language of the master. It becomes abstract in his mouth. The masses of the people whom he claims to represent become for him subjects without historical content, without place. He affirms one (the master) and negates the other (the people) in their being, having, and doing. This is the violent movement that has separated the world into two groups—the dominant and the dominated, the master and the slave. But can we expect less of a philosopher anywhere?

The writers of ethnophilosophy, says Boulaga, seem to have ignored the conditions of time, place, mode, relation, and object within which they began to produce these texts under the pretention of "philosophy." This refusal to recognize those conditions has transformed itself into a constituent or determinant principle which introduces those very conditions into a conceptual structure, that is, as mere descriptions or repetitions of the already given data without depth or originality. The practice of ethnophilosophy is an illusion. Says Eboussi-Boulaga:

> It is not enough for *Muntu* to decree that he is doing philosophy, that he has the intention of looking only for the "reasonable and the true".... *Muntu* will never be able, in silence or in a verbal "coup d'état," to take his right place within the "philosophical tradition" without first questioning himself about the significance, the why of his entering philosophy, and without making the interrogation of his historical situation his start in philosophy or the beginning of his own philosophy.[43]

It does not suffice to make such formal distinctions as implicit and explicit philosophies, lived and reflected philosophies, etc. These do not exhibit the reflection which imposes the true status of philosophy. They only bring us back to the undeveloped "preambles" which, in fact, should form the basis of an original thinking of *Muntu*—"concealed in the vow of philosophy to know, to be, by and for himself, by the articulation of having and doing according to an order that excludes violence."

What the ethnophilosophers have depicted as "African philosophy" is nothing but detached and objectified descriptions of a cultural experience as lived by a people whom they no longer make part of themselves. They are able to objectify and describe it because they no longer are part of it. According to Eboussi-Boulaga, "By experience is meant a connaturality with a certain thing, such a mutual belonging that becomes the object only of intuition and feeling. It is a putting into the present that excludes the taking of distance, mediation of 'discourse.' Presence is never proved; it is (only) affirmed or it is testified to."⁴⁴ In order to confirm these "preambles," the writers of "African philosophy" have taken a generally simple entry into philosophy through applied phenomenology. The philosophical vocabulary of phenomenology is adopted, often with some sort of lexical alterations. "The result is a translation or an equivalence" with chains of notions (where it is convenient) heaped under one conceptual vocabulary drawn from classical manuals.

The texts (of "African philosophy") are in the first place descriptions of mentalities and beliefs; they are monographs of ethnographical material, but treated in a philosophical form. Philosophy is drawn in and related to ethnography—often without even minimal modification. "The specific share is a mere substitution of such terms as 'moral', 'religious', 'conception of life, and of the world', 'representation of the human structure', etc., with the synthetic term 'philosophy'."⁴⁵ By doing this, the philosopher's role turns into that of being a mere revealer, in the physical sense of the term; he renders visible that which already is, he calls with a new name that which has always been. But the true subject of philosophy, he who makes it, remains the anonymous and eternal ethnic group. His product is ethnophilosophy.⁴⁶

Ontology (which constitutes the main subject matter of these texts) is here reduced to human nature. It makes part of man, whose new nature is *Homo ontologicus*, in the sense that, by his very nature, he thinks ontologically. To contemplate the ontological structure of the universe is *per se* a human attribute. It is rooted in all men, in their language, in their customs and behavior. It is found in the ethnic group, making part of the substance of the community; it is its inseparable property. What matters is to demonstrate or prove that Africans are also men, that they too have an ontology which, since the origins of times, has been recorded in their languages and other forms of cultural expression. "Language is the language of being. It expresses being in the articulation of being written, in its simple unit, in its hierarchy and liaisons. . . . Language in its whole is an ontology and a metaphysics. Such is man and such is his nature."[47]

But this cannot go without comment, says Eboussi-Boulaga, "since it is the beginning of his [*Muntu's*] defeat, from which his humanity was put in cause and derouted. Nothing remains except the persuasive word, eloquence; since he cannot conquer, he will try to convince and persuade."[48] The texts of "African philosophy" are therefore characterized by a rhetorical style—descriptions and illustrations with the objective to convince and persuade, a characteristic which risks, in the long run, turning into a philosophy of its own. And this is violence. The language is born out of a violent situation and philosophy is thus viewed as the instrument of salvation, the instrument of the weak, of the conquered. To what purpose? That he (*Muntu* or Africans in general) may achieve his legitimate belonging to this equality of all men. That he may regain his violated humanity. And *Muntu* ends up alienating himself, negating his own being, for his own tendencies reduce him to the opposed subject with whom he aspires to be equal by comparing himself by imitation.

> We are on the course [terrain] of ambiguity where the starting point, the beginning, relates itself to the metaphysical prestiges of the origin, to the principle and to the base, where history transforms itself into nature, moral qualities into "virtues" and not specific properties without allotment, without any possible migration outside the species. The incommunicability or nontransmissibility is the enclosure of the whole particularity that changes itself in particularism, it is the resort of the polemic parallelism. It is present in all those views that blaze the itinerary which goes from self-affirmation accompanied by the total negation of the other to the total negation of the self, accompanied by the affirmation of the other.[49]

For Eboussi-Boulaga, therefore, the greatest evil of ethnophilosophy lies in the historical circumstances of its origin. "It appears that the claim of philosophy perceives the latter [philosophy] as a sign of the organization of the relationships between men in a situation of domination. It acquires meaning within a structure of communication or noncommunication. That is where the truth of ethnophilosophies and the global systems has been and still is."[50] And it cannot be overcome by merely giving philosophy a mode of existence which does not correspond at all to the structures of communication of those who give themselves up to it. No philosophical system can be envisaged outside the form of organization of human relations where it is usually integrated. When this abstraction is done by the African ethnophilosopher, it means that he admits, as a universal requirement, the organization of the communication of a particular group, that he confirms the point of view of those whose authority he has inherited (by being the spokesman and mediator between the ethnic group and the master), and that he does it faithfully. Not taking explicitly the conditions of the production of philosophical discourses into consideration leads to introducing them into the discourse as determinant factors, to making those factors the ideological legitimation of the existing force in the relationships, to putting oneself to the service of the powers of the day.[51]

But how has the institutionalization of "philosophy" come about? Eboussi-Boulaga answers that it has necessarily come in as part and parcel of the newly institutionalized social structure brought in by the colonial master. "The claim [of philosophy] becomes that of being in positions of command of the system of institutions necessary for the imposition of colonial domination. Instruction, that of philosophy included, is one of the principal instances of the legitimation (since it is identified with the mode of life of the master) and effective exercise of power and domination."[52] Philosophy can therefore not be situated beside the traditional structures. But in his role as the interpreter of the people, their spokesman, the African ethnophilosopher will be able to proclaim the existence of "world visions" or "philosophies" common to all people. Yet philosophy conceived in this sense only becomes part of a certain human relationship of domination, an organization of interhuman relationship, of subordination. It is the master who confers the teaching powers and organizes the programs, while the teacher of philosophy becomes a mere administrator or administrative agent.[53] For the teacher, philosophy is therefore presented as an authoritative tradition that transforms itself into a commodified and luxurious type of knowledge, but which has the advantage of giving access to the arbitrary power of a dominant class. For Eboussi-Boulaga, African teachers of philosophy form a dominant class within the dominated masses.

This rather exaggerated statement resembles the notion held by Henri Maurier in his *Philosophie de l'Afrique noire* that the traditional African society was a capitalist-oriented structure based on the intentionally unequal distribution of rights, privileges, and possession of exotic knowledge and the domination of these by the male elders of the tribes in contrast to the women and youth. Maurier's thesis reproduces Gramsci's position in cultural Marxism, which takes as its starting point the notion that all actors are intellectuals, that the concern with meaning is an inseparable dimension of every human action and every historical form of social order. Maurier views culture as being primarily the servant of power. In the traditional African social context, he argues, culture served to hold in place a power structure based on gender and gerontological factors. Gender and age thus became important means of production in a system of relations where knowledge acquired a commodified value and a basis of class stratification of society. This is a reading which we do not intend to pursue further here.

According to Eboussi-Boulaga, Western philosophy has been imposed as a negative exteriority. And the crisis of *Muntu* is connected with this evil view of philosophy as identical with the human nature of Western man, as a necessity of their biological mechanism and order,[54] and therefore "one among the symbols and institutions which the Western world has exported as a means of assimilating the other."[55] And what has been *Muntu*'s reaction? He has fallen victim, alienated and derouted from his own ages-old historicocultural experience. Philosophy is for him

> a strange language that speaks of an unknown world without any analogy with his own familiar universe. It is not only by fooling oneself but also by reducing oneself to nothingness that one becomes born to philosophy. It is by self-substraction that one rejoins philosophy as a non-lived and unlivable reality.
>
> To rejoin a reality that one does not live, that cannot be lived, is to deceive oneself; it is the discovery of one's own possibility as negativity, the capacity to deny oneself which is, at the same time, the capacity to be under the mode of not being. It is the discovery of oneself as a joke, as a play. To begin with, *Muntu* is the virtuous man capable of reciting that which he does not comprehend, of affirming that to which he actually does not give his intimate assent. He can play all roles, give pleasant answers, reason in an already determined fashion [provided] he observes the rules of the game.[56]

Philosophy is presented to *Muntu* as an ideal image to which one only needs to conform oneself. "In short, it remains for *Muntu* to realize for himself that which is already in him; to realize for himself, for his own advantage, by putting himself at the feet of the good teachers; by making himself be helped or by learning to reproduce [and] to imitate according to the measure of his own capacity."[57] He participates in and helps worsen his own situation of servitude. He is truly exploited, in the strong sense of the word. And this is no philosophy, Eboussi-Boulaga concludes. "There is no 'African philosophy' enclosed in African languages which would be or would give the actual meaning of our existence."[58]

> The structure of language does not necessarily conform to the subjective organization of meanings. It can produce an "undoing" between words and their referents. Words change their meanings, and their use is not always motivated by their adequation to an analysis of the real. Perhaps the words, or generally the linguistic structures, impose the manner of apprehending the real. But as soon as their apprehension becomes history, that is to say, when it develops or undergoes unforeseen accidental modifications, it imposes a manner of speaking as well, or it brings in different contents in the words of a tribe. Also, language as a system follows a logic of its modifications by assimilation, analogy without relation to the referents or historical experience.[59]

Language is neutral to truth. The philosophy of Tempels thus turns out to be a philosophy of imperialism, and its African exponents have accepted it in an underdeveloped manner. *La Philosophie bantoue* was, for Eboussi-Boulaga, a perfect economic theory of philosophical attribution from the imperialist point of view. In a crucial and deeply critical sense, Eboussi-Boulaga believes that the urgent question for African philosophers is to interrogate why Africans need philosophy at all, and what it is that will make them better off with it than they are without it.

To sum up, Eboussi-Boulaga places Tempels's project within the practice of Western imperialism. Many critics of Tempels, among them Aimé Césaire, have persistently attacked Tempels on these grounds. To say the least about this point, it is very difficult to infer implications of political and economic nature from Tempels's definition of African philosophy. There is sense in arguing, however, that Tempels's definition portrays African thought as one that does not seriously consider the objective and utilitarian aspects of reality. And such a philosophy, however elegant, cannot contribute to the development of the people. Those who hold this view argue further that to accept the definition of African philosophy as an implicit enterprise based on emotion rather than reason also means accepting that the mentality of African people is subordinate to that of European people. Any African who defines African philosophy in line with Senghor's epistemology argues in favor of European superiority and accepts the lower position of servitude under neocolonialism and imperialism.

Of the exponents of the latter argument, Marcien Towa is perhaps the best known and most articulate. He joins Hountondji and Eboussi-Boulaga as one of the sharpest critics of ethnophilosophy.

Marcien Towa: Ethnophilosophy and the Negritude of Senghor as Ideologies of Servitude

For Marcien Towa, African ethnophilosophy cannot avoid being seen as a logical consequence and legitimation of Western imperialism. Even in such a system where the nature of this discipline is so eminently defined, as in Hegel, still on one side one finds it stuffed with imperialist attitudes toward the colonized peoples. Reason and liberty, which are believed to characterize philosophical activity, are, according to Hegel, to be found only in the Western world. Towa writes: "Historically, philosophy, according to Hegel, is found only where political liberty flourishes—liberty in the state; and the latter begins where an individual subject feels himself as such, as an individual within the generality, where the consciousness of personality appears as having an infinite value in itself, and where the thought that thinks the general is a manifested being."[60] And such a view of reason and liberty is categorically reduced to the Western world;[61] it is therefore only in the Western world that philosophy can exist or flourish.

When Franz Crahay wrote of the "Conditions for a Bantu Philosophy," he never realized the profound dialectic of which the project of a "Bantu (or African) philosophy" was only but a moment. "This project," writes Towa, "is born precisely of the revolt against the categorical affirmation of the *essential and exclusive*[62] occidentality of philosophy. . . . [And] if it is true that the thesis of the exclusive occidentality of philosophy is directed toward the legitimation of Western imperialism, is it not normal that the negation of imperialism involves the negation of this thesis as well?"[63]

Thus, against such an absolute exclusion, *Muntu* is reduced to constituting for himself a world of his own, founded on his own values, and this became the time of the return to the sources, to the exaltation of originality and difference— the time of negritude, the time of recession into a general submissive particularism (Senghor). According to this project, the notion of philosophy is enlarged to embrace that of culture, a natural element of humanity as opposed to animals. Cultural facts are here recognized as having, in their phenomenon or daily practicality, philosophical significance. The problem is only to know the bonds that connect them one to the other and assure the cohesion therein and their structure as a whole (Basil Fouda).[64] And it is this general bond or the structure of the whole of African cultural facts that becomes "African philosophy" in its specificity.[65]

These ethnological interpretations do not have, as their aim, the production of a specifically African "philosophy"; they result rather from a revised notion of philosophy to include collective cultural wisdom. In this way the notion of philosophy is reduced to the sense of being-in-the-world of all cultures (cf. Sartre in "Orphée noir"). For Towa, "African philosophy" does not radically differ from European philosophy. Just as in the assertion that " 'Negro-African philosophy' exists," "African philosophy" is already implied by necessity in the extension of the notion of philosophy to include all cultural forms without distinction.[66] Philosophy is made inseparable from any culture and is manifested, albeit in varying forms, in the different overt as well as covert cultural phenomena. And in all these cultural facts or phenomena, philosophy is transmitted through the ages as a heritage to be received (Mbiti), defended, and incarnated, so as to attain an authentic existence (Fouda). Thus, as we saw in the analysis of Eboussi-Boulaga, in the rhetorical literature that constitutes what is called "African philosophy" the authors are mainly concerned, in their reaction against the thesis of the occidentality of philosophy, to demonstrate that they (Africans or Bantu) too have a culture and therefore a philosophy that unites and assures the cohesion between the various elements of this culture. *Africans too have a philosophy!* goes the ecstatic exclamation. The demonstration of this antithesis as a new thesis becomes the main concern of this literature where the affirmation (of "African philosophy") has been rendered necessary by the negation. Without knowledge of the negation, the structure of the affirmation that connects philosophy to the unchangeable essence of man would be incomprehensible.

According to the ethnophilosophical project, later generations receive and conform themselves to the plans of their ancestors. Philosophy, in this way, reduced to the dogmatism of culture, has been determined by the sacred ancestors for all generations. Philosophy is wisdom to be learned and lived, defended, and, in turn, incarnated. Now this simple conformity to tradition, maintains Towa, is no philosophy, and can in no way give birth to it. "Philosophy does not begin if not with the decision to submit the philosophical and cultural heritage to a critical examination (and evaluation) without complacency,"[67] he says.

For any philosopher, no idea, however venerable it may be, is receivable before it passes through the screen of critical thought. Thus the opposition that has long been established between African cultural products and philosophy still exists and remains intact even after the (exhaustive) efforts to demonstrate the existence of an original "Negro-African philosophy."[68] The philosophical exposition in ethnophilosophical texts is reduced to argumentation, demonstration, or refutation of what is or of what is not African. The method adopted draws from ethnology and philosophy at the same time, but without proper integration of the two. It is ethnophilosophical. "The ethnologist describes, exposes, and explains, but does not separate at all" (at least not openly) as far as the basic foundation of that which is described and explained is concerned (Mbiti). The ethnologist uses philosophy only arbitrarily, since the vital criterion he uses for choosing between ideas is not their rational quality but rather whether or not such ideas belong to the African tradition in question. On the contrary, "what a philosopher retains and proposes is always, at least by the rule, the conclusion of an (often) contradictory debate, that is to say, of a critical and absolutely free examination."[69]

Ethnophilosophy, says Towa, is a backward dimension of the original and revolutionary negritude (of Aimé Césaire, Leon Damas, and David Diop) as the ideological and spiritual dimension of the anticolonial liberation movements; like negritude and together with it, ethnophilosophy must be superseded with the achievement of political independence (Ezekiel Mphahlele). If the main objective of negritude—which engendered ethnophilosophy—was the achievement of political independence (Césaire and Senghor), then its time has expired.

> The desire to be ourselves, to assume our destiny, [says Towa] finally drives us back to the necessity to transform ourselves in depth, to deny our very intimate being so as to become other. And this necessity brings us back to the point of departure, of our confrontation with the Western world, to the epoch when we tried with much effort to reestablish the balance of forces by securing ourselves from the secrets of the Western world's victory over us. The movement of negritude, which ethnophilosophy would artificially like to prolong, has diverted us from this search.[70]

Rather, if liberation (from Western domination) is the goal, the last thing to engage would certainly be the restoration of the ancient world, the conservation of specificity—the cult of difference and originality. What is required, says Towa, is to know the Western civilization in depth, to discover the secret of its power and success, and to introduce this "secret" element into our own culture: "it implies that the indigenous culture be revolutionized from bottom to top; it implies rupture with this culture, with our past, that is to say, with ourselves,"[71] because the cause of our defeat and of our actual state of effective dependence consists in this search into the past, which, after all, already proved vulnerable to European power. We must evaluate this past, make it dynamic and progressive, take charge of it, for "the essence of being oneself is not other than the result of the past of the self."[72]

In other words, continues Towa, "in order to affirm and assume oneself, the self must deny itself, it must deny its essence and therefore its past, it must expressly aim at becoming like the other, similar to him and hence uncolonizable by him. That is the necessary mediation that leads to the real affirmation of ourselves in the present world."[73] This is the type of event that took place in China (the May Fourth Movement). In order to become modern, in order to adopt modern science and preserve democracy, China had to dismantle the old tradition, Confucianism, old art, and traditional morality. That movement stands as the point of departure for contemporary China. "The option," says Towa, "is without ambiguity: to deny oneself, to put the very being of the self in question, and to Europeanize oneself fundamentally."[74] That is the only way. It is only a similar revolution that will lead to the emergence of a robust and rejuvenated African humanity and authenticity. And such a change of perspectives involves the abandoning of the ethnophilosophical method.

But what is this European secret that guaranteed their victory over us Africans? This, Towa holds, must be the very thing that Europe itself holds to as its distinctive mark, that is, philosophy and science.[75] In Europe in the first decade of the seventeenth century, both science and philosophy were amalgamated under the common name "philosophy"; and this proved positive for the betterment of knowledge of the world, and through this knowledge, man's power over it. "Knowledge is power" (Francis Bacon). It is this that Africa must investigate as the secret of European power. Philosophy, Towa maintains, must be interrogated in the very sense in which Europeans conceive it, that is, as to what they mean by it. Such inquiry, according to Towa, will lead to philosophy *in the strict sense.*[76] But does this not constitute a vicious circle back to what he had earlier called the imperialistic Hegelian notion of philosophy?

We saw that according to Hegel, whom Towa takes again as the eminent representative of the analysis of the European notion of philosophy, that philosophy (as well as science) has the characteristic of not presupposing anything, of not accepting anything as true merely on the ground of external authority without submitting it under the screen of critical thought, which does not accept anything outside itself.[77] Now this position is diametrically opposed to that of religion; and Hegel, says Towa, "conceived the history of philosophy as the study of the evolution of free thought in its opposition to the authority of religion,"[78] and any reconciliation between the two is possible only after the triumph of philosophy over religion. In other words, it is only in philosophy that religious and mythological representations are interpreted and their true contents determined.

This philosophy as understood by Hegel is opposed to "popular philosophy" as based, not on critical reason, but on intuition or internal sentiment. Such philosophy can be found in the writings of as Cicero, Jacobi, and Schleiermacher, among others, as well as in the philosophy of common sense. "Popular philosophy," writes Towa, "may seem to repose on conviction and on personal comprehension and to exclude all external authority and the arbitrary. But the immediate representations, the interior sentiments, being accepted from their revelation without examination, still constitute a sort of authority, the interior authority of conscience and the heart."[79]

For Towa, European philosophy reached its highest points in modern times. He thinks of Enlightenment thought in general and particularly of philosophy conceived in the manner of Hegel or in the manner of Descartes, Bacon, Galileo, Hobbes, and others in earlier modern times, that is, philosophy which has a close relationship with science, as lying at the origin of European power. It is the secret of their vast victory over other peoples. It helps, as in China, in the urgency and necessity to revolutionize culture from bottom to top so as, by avoiding the simple and pure disappearance of local traditions, to render their renaissance and rejuvenation possible. In other words, a revolution takes account of the past and reevaluates it in the perspective of the present and future.

"It is in the perspective of this possibility of ourselves, of this anticipation of ourselves," writes Towa, "that the interest that the European philosophy offers us is situated, and it is in relation to the same end that other cultures, including our own, must be judged and appreciated."[80] With such philosophy, Africa will be able to build up its own power and will become "a free Africa in a free world." It is the European philosophy that takes part in a project that is completely African, rather than Africa submitting itself to European philosophy and power. Africa must turn European philosophy to the dialectic of Africa's needs. But what could be more Senghorian or submissive than this?

According to Towa, however, his thesis is opposed to the type of Senghorian negritude which denies the black man any reason or rationality and reduces him to a being dominated by emotion and instinct. Towa's thesis necessarily refutes all the positions or views and methods of ethnophilosophy which, to him, are mere prolongations of the Senghorian negritude. They reduced the black man to the servitude of European imperialism.[81] For Towa, therefore, in sharp contrast to Crahay and Maurier,[82] African philosophy begins with the publication of Kwame Nkrumah's *Consciencism*. Towa's point is that philosophy plays and must be made to play a revolutionary role in social history.

For Towa, however, the essential finality of philosophy is the promotion of science and socioeconomic development for a more equal society for people of all races. The role of philosophy, for him, is to advance critical reason and liberty. Therefore, for the African, the pursuit of cultural (political, economic, social, and scientifico-technological) development is to be based on philosophy. With philosophy, Africa must pursue the high levels of scientifico-technological development that the Western world has attained. Philosophy becomes the instrument of equality as well as of domination. Those who have it remain equal and dominate those deprived of it. The present inequality between the Western world and Africa, Towa believes, lies in the fact that the Western world has established a scientific philosophy upon which its advancement in science and technology are based while Africa has no tradition of scientific philosophy. To attain similar levels of scientifico-technological development as in the Western world, Africa needs to adopt a scientific attitude toward philosophy as the Western people have done.

For Towa, then, Western philosophy is the paradigmatic model of the proper kind of philosophy which must be adopted by all peoples. Like science, philosophy is for Towa an activity whose effectiveness is objectively measurable in terms of its practical effects in the transformation of the world. For him, the scientific and technological inferiority of Africa or China in comparison with Europe is historical evidence that neither Africans nor the Chinese have had the proper kind of philosophy in their traditional past. It is this lack of proper philosophy that is responsible, in Towa's view, for their scientific and technological inferiority. If they wish to attain levels of scientific and technological development as Europeans have done, they must abandon their past and acquire the scientific techniques and methods of European philosophy. Only this will pull them out of the inertia of their traditional past, of their ethnophilosophies. For Towa, then, philosophy has two major roles: social critique and the analysis and evaluation of science.

Towa's thesis contains a controversial premise: that Western philosophy has developed, throughout its history, with the deliberate objective to—at least — produce theories of experimental science. It is true that Western philosophy and science have influenced each other significantly, especially since the seventeenth century. There is no evidence, however, that it is philosophy which has always dictated to science its procedural methods and premises. Philosophy, I believe, is a body of human knowledge that has, in history, formulated itself into an autonomous discipline capable of internal developments regardless of its external effects on other branches of knowledge. According to Fillippo Selvaggi, philosophy may study "the nature and value of scientific knowledge, and therefore also its methods for teaching them" as in the philosophy of science, which has, as its object, "science as such, or rather, science in its formal aspect, insofar as it is a process of knowledge, and not in its material aspect, or rather in its content of affirmations about material reality."[83] The philosophy of nature comes nearer to science in this respect, and forms a basis for a mutual and constructive dialogue between philosophy and science, a point of collaboration between the two. But even here, this is only possible insofar as the two operate on two different levels and as two different forms (though) of the same human knowledge. We are not speaking here of opposing philosophy to science, but rather we want to point out that between philosophy and science, two disciplines which work on different levels of abstraction, "there is diversity in formal object, diversity in mode of definition, diversity in the criterion of judgment; in other words, diversity in content and method."[84] One can therefore not be reduced to the other or extend itself unnecessarily without going over its limits and thus ceasing to be what it should be.

Towa, however, reduces philosophy to science for a different reason. He views the seventeenth century as the period in which philosophical thinking and ambitions gave birth to what has turned out to be one of the greatest transformations of the world by means of science and technology. And it is on the basis of this science and technology (based on the seventeenth-century philosophy that gave birth to it) that the structure of world social classes as affirmed by Hegel has arisen. It is for this reason that Towa views European modern philosophy as the one which must be adopted again for another transformation of the world, for the restoration of equality.

For Towa, who was once himself a Marxist, philosophy must be practical to the point of being able to transform society. According to him, "Theory and practice, in every form of human activity, are only two aspects of the same and unique process of struggle for the transformation of human society through the proletariat revolution."[85] This is where, according to Towa, the negritude of Senghor as well as "African philosophy" (ethnophilosophy) movements lacked significance. Not only did these two movements remain pure theories, but they also submitted to Western philosophy as being superior to them on the ground of reason. They never tried to change the state of relations that existed between Africa and the West as a result of reason and science.

Africa, like China or Russia, must make a revolution, according to Towa. It must take from the Western world the philosophical tradition appropriate to its situation, and apply it to the analysis of its specific condition. Philosophy, for Towa, has two vital functions: it provides the self-critiquing space for the sciences; it is also a criterion for hierarchizing relations between nations. "Rather than the exhumation of an original African philosophy according to ways which don't pay heed to the exigencies of science nor to those of philosophy, our principal intention should be that of attaining a . . . philosophical expression of our 'being-in-the-world' of today and a determination of a mode of taking charge of it and directing it in a definite direction."[86]

Instead of looking for or concentrating our analysis on those elements which differentiate us from Europe, we should take after them (Europeans) and learn the secret of the power with which they have dominated and still are dominating us and the rest of the world. This power is Western science and technology. It is our material inferiority which has placed our culture at the mercy of the powers of our time.

Towa's thought cannot, however, be described only in empiricist terms. It also embraces traits of a revolutionary materialism in the Marxist sense. His admiration of the Chinese revolution against Confucianism and the old Chinese traditional philosophy in general clearly indicates this. "The movement of May 4," he says, "denounces these principles [of Confucius's philosophy] as constituting the pillars of the ancient Chinese despotism. The new society which the movement intends to install will be based on democracy and science."[87]

Revolution is therefore essential in his view, as the examples of China and the Soviet Union show us, for a true renaissance and self-affirmation, for "that is when radical praxis becomes imagination, audacity and courage, energy in action, and leads thus to the zenith of human liberty; it is the highest form of human creativity . . . , (for) it is in and through radicalism that man affirms his humanity with most glamour."[88]

This Towaian revolution involves a historical dialectic. The African must negate his past, that is, his essence, himself, in order to affirm himself in a better and more effective manner. He must die to himself in order to be born in the other, from or through whom he attains a more meaningful and liberating self-expression. For when he identifies himself with the other in the form of equality, he kills the differences in power which made him a victim of the other. By becoming like and equal to the other, he makes himself uncolonizable by the other. Quoting from Marx, Towa says:

> The class which is the dominating power in the society is also the spiritually dominating power. The class which disposes of the means of material production also disposes, with the same voice, the means of intellectual production so well that, one in the other, the thoughts of those who are refused the means of intellectual production are also dominated by the dominant class. The dominant thoughts are nothing else other than the ideal expression of dominant material relations.[89]

Philosophy must be seen not as a mere abstract contemplation of human problems, but as a fruitful means of reaching equality of all races by providing for the secret of their material progress. This difference in races, which Senghor's negritude and "African philosophy" (ethnophilosophy) movements have submitted themselves to and which represents the difference of class in global society, must be eliminated—by a cultural revolution. Africans, who represent the proletariat, must revolutionize the present state of relations and restore the original equality. When he, the African, also takes possession and control (by knowledge) of European philosophy, the Western intellectual means of production, he will have taken the secret of European power; it is by Western philosophy that the European, according to Towa, has been able to advance so much in science and technology, with which he has dominated and still dominates the others. It is therefore by the possession of this Western philosophy that the African will also reach the secret of European scientific and technological achievements. And when all have this secret of production and power, the concept and existence of classes in racial terms will vanish. One will become the same and equal to the other. One will be uncolonizable by the other.

For this reason Towa denies individuality and particularity, which, according to him, are only destructive, never philosophically constructive. In the present neocolonial situation, such particularisms as exalted by ethnophilosophy can only be discounted as forms of alienation. They are submissive to neocolonialism and imperialism. In this regard Towa comes nearer to Frantz Fanon in his attacks on negritude as a disabling ideology.

Recapitulation on Towa

The revolution proposed by Towa, however, is valuable and relevant to the problems of international political economy of our day. It is necessary to say, and to repeat, that this is a crucial point that no serious African student can afford to ignore. The basic problem for us is to find our own way of reconsidering the structures of the past, and of reconsidering the colonial structures we have had imposed upon us. It is enough to consider the structure and nature of events between the rich nations of the Western block and the "poverty nations" of the Third World block. Anyone having a sense of responsibility and of justice and human dignity can draw his or her own conclusions.

But this does not mean Towa is right. If anything, Towa's work has a noble project, but a rather complex method for achieving it. If he differs from Senghor or any other ethnophilosopher in any significant way, it is because he replaces the ancestors in African ethnophilosophy, as Hountondji says, with new ones— Marx, Lenin, Mao, and Fanon. One must appreciate, however, his *"passionate faith* in the effective significance of philosophy within the context of real life," as Abiola Irele puts it.[90]

As far as philosophy is concerned, however, the method proposed by Towa doesn't seem to us to be the only or the most adequate solution. The dogmatic retention of Marx's stress on the mode of production as a key to understanding historical development creates a barrier through which it is difficult to see some of these authors' creative work. And there seems to be an illegitimate extension and application of Marx's social theory to cover all aspects of human life. To change the type of relations in existence within the economic structure of the world, it is true, certain radical actions need to be mapped out in one way or another. A revision in production relations would be needed, and with it control over capital would necessarily be revised. He who does not have the necessary material force required for production would need to borrow. And there would be little or no contradiction, since the question is merely on the material means of production. Even where the practice of technological and economic borrowing from the West—as in the current world economic "order"—would lead to theories, the latter would not necessarily be those of the giver, unless offered with theoretico-ideological strings attached as political contradictions all too often reveal. Otherwise the borrowed scientific knowledge and technological know-how would, by way of modifications and development, give continuity to the pre-existing theories. There would be concordance, for scientific truth is universal. There can be no African or American, European or Asian empirical sciences reflecting divergent empirical truths.

But in philosophy the same does not apply. This sort of concordance is often lacking in philosophy. Why? Because "philosophy is necessarily the taking of the total position of man, of oneself and of reality. It is taking of a position before the universe, of which the essential part is man himself."[91] Not only does philosophy imply the human liberty that easily gives way to such common discordances that are so characteristic of it, but it also indicates the variety of cultural experience that often strongly builds the background of the differences and oppositions in many philosophical beliefs and doctrines. This is because "we refer, from time to time, to different systems of reference, to schemes of thought that are often almost irreconcilable" to our own. And, above all, Meinrad Hebga says, there is no canon-logic. There is no single, common, and standard intuitionistic logic in the sense of a set of principles which depend on the consideration of an object.[92] There is no canon of a universal system of human thought. Karp and Bird maintain a similar view.[93] What there are are different thought models operating side by side, but which ought not be confused.

Even if we applied the scholastic principle of contradiction, which does not admit of the middle way between the true and the false, "such a principle, metaphysical and absolute, does not prevent two diametrically opposed systems from being [both] true at the same time, if their basic postulates are different."[94] Two systems may be opposed to one another in their general conclusions (extrinsic truth), but their respective procedures, given their different basic postulates, together with their propositions and conclusions, are controlled by a legitimate and rigorous logic (intrinsic truth) which alone assures the coherency between the many single assertions and the general and total system. There is a need, therefore, writes Hebga, "to distinguish, but not to separate intrinsic truth from extrinsic truth; because a logical system equipped with internal coherency is not built in the air. It is founded on experience, thanks to its axioms and primary principles, and therefore already tried by the empirical data right from the beginning and in the whole of the procedure. . . . "[95]

It is therefore possible to meet two contradictory assertions, both of which will be true, each in its respective case, as in:

1. Metaphysical statements are meaningless.
2. Metaphysical statements are meaningful.

In such cases, Hebga holds, "one can only say that each of them reflects only a part of the truth." Hebga, however, maintains that such a position should not lead to absolute relativism or to agnosticism. In this respect, every system is completely independent of any other, and any dialectic conception of human evolutions which tries to line African systems of thought with the great systems of the ancient world (Griaule) must be absolutely rejected. "It is therefore right to reject, in logic as well as in aesthetics, every pretentious imperialism."[96]

> Why could not African peoples have their own way of seeing the world, and man, and the problems raised by our human existence? . . . The so called pure and universal mankind's philosophy is a mythical being or, at best, an ideal never to be reached; it is an asymptote of some sort, to use a mathematical concept.
> Even putting aside Plato, and other philosophers' recourse to myths in their philosophical reflection, their respective philosophical systems cannot be understood if not replaced in their, say, Greek or German birthplace and atmosphere: they are therefore ethnically marked, and yet they have a claim to universality. Kant's system owes very much to Newton's physics and Leibnitz's mathematical works, not to mention the political, moral, and religious situation of late eighteenth century Europe. Hegel's philosophy too would be unthinkable outside the frame of Napoleonic Europe and Germany.
> In short, any philosophy is ethnical more or less. The thinker is expected to transcend his personal, familial, national, ethnic, political, or religious creeds and 'conditionments', to place himself at a universal level, but his effort of impurification is indefinite."[97]

In the same way, the negritude which African critics have so unquestioningly rejected is therefore, according to Hebga, a deeply indispensable document of our own thoughts as Africans. According to him, "It represents the whole of truths which is our system of reference and is therefore of capital importance in the understanding of the mechanism of our thought: it is the traditional lore made of history, legends, social, moral, and religious laws, of more or less developed techniques and of customs, with the whole based on a metaphysics that guarantees it its unity."[98] This metaphysics entails the conception of being and of the vital force and its consequent logic of reasoning. It can therefore not be cast overboard as easily as is suggested by Towa's new philosophical method of a complete intellectual as well as material revolution in Africa. Hebga writes: "As regards the fact that our system of reference has not been a factor of progress, especially technological, we admit it humbly, but noting, however, that a minor cultural efficiency does not prove, by itself, the incoherency or the absence of the critical value in a philosophy, but rather that it [the philosophy] was perhaps not exploited to depth or with sufficient method."[99] "It is necessary that human civilizations penetrate one another without alienating or losing themselves one into the other. This variety is a richness that we will one day regret having sacrificed for a cultural imperialism,"[100] as, according to Hebga's argument, Towa tends to do.

Not only does Hebga introduce a new sense of ethnophilosophy in a way that does not address the focus of the critiques against the texts of Tempels, Griaule, Kagame, and Mbiti, for example, but also his defense of African logic and of the relativity of modes of thinking invokes an unavoidable objection. The defense is based on the claim that non-Euclidean geometries form coherent and consistent systems, like the Euclidean, in which an indefinite number of propositions might be shown to follow from their initial definitions. That they are, that is to say, thoroughly *thinkable* and free from contradiction, and intellectually on a level with the Euclidean conception of space. Strong objections to the theory of non-Euclidean geometries state that claims of the plausibility of non-Euclidean geometries are hard to accept beyond the single claim that they are indeed *thinkable*, but hardly anything more; that although the theory of non-Euclidean geometries gives a good account of itself, this only accentuates its practical failure.

The objection against non-Euclidean geometries makes a distinction between *intrinsic certainty* and *real validity* of a theory. It argues that the plausibility of a theory consists not only in its intrinsic certainty with which conclusions may follow from the definitions of its basic noncontradictory premises, but also in whether or not such a theory can be successfully applied to the organization of experiences in real life. It is in regard to this second criterion of theoretical plausibility that the theory of non-Euclidean geometries fails. Hebga's defense of African logic and of the relativity of modes of thinking ignores this criterion. It suggests that the certainty of geometry is nothing more than the certainty with which conclusions follow from noncontradictory premises; that in each (Euclidean and non-Euclidean) geometry it flows from the definitions. Thus, for him as for the defenders of non-Euclidean geometries, the certainty with which the sum of the angles of a triangle may be asserted as equal to two right angles in Euclidean geometry is precisely the same as that with which it may be shown to be greater or less in non-Euclidean systems. Experience shows, however, that because we apply such principles (as of geometry) to the systematization and organization of real life—that is, of perceptual spaces—certainty, in the sense of intrinsic (conceptual) consistency, is, on its own, neither a sufficient nor a useful criterion of any theory, in geometry or in logical apparatus.

Towa's position reflects his own personal view about African history. He tries to cure present wounds in relation to past remedies already evident elsewhere, thus proposing a way that would lead to a sort of universal good health in the form of egalitarianism. Those who are still sick must obtain the diagnosis and the remedies of those who have managed to heal themselves. However, for us, this view, even in the field of political economy where we have tried to dump it, or in social philosophy, seems to underrate the complex nature of events that have contributed to Africa's present situation in terms of scientifico-technological development. That Africa has been halted at a level of technological stagnation and turned into a mere consumer society (and often of its own goods at an exorbitant price!), some scholars maintain, is at least partially the responsibility of Europe's economic exploitation and distortion in this continent (and elsewhere) from as far back as the fifteenth and sixteenth centuries. Europe had come to Africa as the conqueror and master and, therefore, had to keep this superiority at all costs. Not only was the slave trade used by Europe for the promotion of its economy with free, forced, and inhumane African labor, but it also served, even if secondarily, but consciously to the traders, as a means of distracting the attention of the African population from internal development of skills and techniques. It served as an excellent tool in hampering the improvement and innovation of these factors. But, as W. Rodney writes,

> another remarkable fact that is seldom brought to light is that several African rulers in different parts of the continent saw the situation clearly, and sought European technology for internal development, which was meant to replace the trade in slaves.
>
> Europeans deliberately ignored those African requests that Europe should place certain skills and techniques at their disposal. This was an element in the Kongo situation of the early sixteenth century. . . . It happened in Ethiopia also. . . . Correspondence exists between the Emperor and European rulers such as kings Manuel I and John III of Portugal and Pope Leo X, in which requests were made for European assistance to Ethiopian industry. Until late in the nineteenth century, Ethiopian petitions to that effect were being repeated with little or no success.[101]

Many more examples can be given to show that Africa's present situation in industrial development has been and is still being kept at the foot of the scale, at least partially, by European or Western power strategies. As many radical political economists and historians have argued, a Third World block of nations must be kept in existence so that the industrial nations may thrive. Others must be kept in a condition of perpetual need so that some may sell at gain. According to Rodney, " . . . [C]apitalism introduced into Africa only such limited aspects of its material culture as were essential to more efficient exploitation, but the general tendency has been for capitalism to underdevelop Africa in technology."[102]

Another point is that Towa wants all African problems to be concentrated on Africa's material needs. This view also seems to us to be insufficiently critical in relation to what Towa himself expects of philosophy. Humans need science and technology and their products; they also need spiritual values and well-being. It is only in the light of the equal integration of these human aspects that Africans will be able to claim development not only in the economic, scientific, and material senses, but in the true and integral cultural sense as well. A philosophical understanding of man must take the whole of man into consideration. It is only in this respect that philosophy will embark on a more constructive dialogue with the vitally important and indispensable scientific world. Thus it is not the question which Towa raises that we refer to as irrelevant. It is rather the answer he gives to it that we oppose and the proposal that he offers for a solution that we hold to be irrelevant.[103]

Although his tone is uniquely sharper in comparison to that of many of his French-speaking counterparts, Towa's strong attacks on ethnophilosophy still remain quite typical of the professional philosophical current in French-speaking Africa. Whether this is in any way an indication of a special reaction toward the French colonial system is of course a matter of conjecture. It contrasts sharply, however, with the more serene yet equally articulate kind of thinking typical of African professional philosophers from former British colonies. The French method of assimilation was aimed at making the educated colonized people repudiate their traditional past in order to take on the "more civilized" French cultural values and mannerisms. The thesis advanced by Towa, and which strongly rejects ethnophilosophy as an empty, nostalgic return to the past, does in a way reflect one type of reaction in the fight against assimilation. For Hountondji and Towa particularly, the traditional past is a liability that needs to be transcended. But they all express this transcendence differently.

This attitude is, of course, not common to all French-speaking professional African philosophers. There are those like Ntumba Tshiamalenga who take a position somewhere between the extremisms of Towa and Hountondji on the one hand, and of Tempels, Kagame, and Mulago on the other. In the views of Towa and Hountondji, ethnophilosophy and philosophy in the Western sense are two irreconcilable poles of mental productions. These views, as least those of Hountondji, have been recently modified somewhat and so no longer sharply regard the two systems in oppositional contrast. Hountondji's paper "Occidentalism, Elitism: Answer to Two Critiques" (1989) attests to such change, thus marking a division between his earlier, more dogmatic views and the more recent reconciliatory ones.

The British, on the other hand, used a method of colonization quite different from the French assimilation. Their "indirect rule" had left the native largely free to live and practice his traditions provided he was peaceful and paid his taxes. This experience has left many English-speaking African elites still attached to their traditional past. Although they accept the values of modern living and knowledge and defend the methods that go with them, they do not reject the past. The relevance of traditional methods of knowledge in the context of modern patterns of living is to be dictated by the empirical needs and the living patterns of contemporary society. It is this attitude toward the traditional past that underlines the philosophical thoughts of such people as Peter Bodunrin, Kwasi Wiredu, and Henry Odera Oruka, among others, in their versions of anti-ethno-philosophy.

V. Y. Mudimbe: An Archaeology of African Knowledge

The significance of V. Y. Mudimbe's work can be cited from various points of view. First, it makes part of the growing literature in recent years which critically reviews some of the epistemological claims underlying the history of the construction of the image of otherness in Western scholarship. Mudimbe's *The Invention of Africa*[104] is a brilliant general survey of how Western construction of "primitive" and "savage" images of Africa, particularly in historical and anthropological studies, has influenced the rise of alienated discourse and self-identity among Africans themselves. Modern African intellectual history is part of a consistent escape from the harshly negated African past. In the humanities and social sciences in general, and in philosophy and religion in particular, African intellectuals continue to define their world on the basis of Western epistemological standards.

Second, we can say Mudimbe's work is also a brilliant intellectual description of the historical dilemmas which many educated African "elites" face daily in regard to how best to adapt what Bogumil Jewsiewicki[105] calls the "usable past" to the construction of their present. Haunted by their denigrated past, Mudimbe argues, African "elites" are constantly eager to abandon their past in order to adopt what is foreign (Western) because they think that it is "modern" and "civilized." Every day, the battle against the past is fought, and the past, frequently called the "traditional" in the constructed discourse, is suppressed in legal suits, political rhetoric, and in economic and social planning and policy-making. In this respect, Mudimbe implicitly raises significant questions about the contrast and complementarity of past and present as distinct periodizations of history and identity. We can summarize those questions under the following three main points:

(1) how is "tradition" defined and what is its role in African representational discourse?

(2) the contrast between "traditionalism" and "Westernism": must they be contrasted, and what makes each of them acceptable or unacceptable?

(3) what are the instruments for judging the acceptability or unacceptability of either "traditionalism" or "Westernism," and who sets and standardizes those instruments?

The Invention of Africa does not answer all these questions, but they set, I believe, the intellectual and social dilemmas and contexts which Mudimbe's work basically deals with and which are brilliantly portrayed also in his novels:

the polygamous African husband married to two wives, one African, the other white; or the contrast between the church as a Western institution and Christianity as a set of deinstitutionalized values universally open to all. The contemporary African intellectual in the humanities and social sciences is torn between two intellectual directions and does not quite know how to strike a compromise between the two in a way that will make him/her a fruitful user of the correct processes of knowledge for the improvement of his/her values and "traditions."

Although Mudimbe's work makes an important contribution to the debate on the creation of knowledge, he lamentably fails to emancipate himself from the vicious circle inherent in the deconstructionist stance. In other words, he fails, in *The Invention of Africa* and elsewhere, to show clearly how the "usable past" should be used by "experts" to construct an "authentic" African *episteme*. Mudimbe's estrangement of intellectuals as people who rise above their own "traditions" by their cognitive practice places him in the center of another Western value, that is, the view that experts are isolated producers and owners of the knowledge which their communities consume. And this seems to bring Mudimbe back to the center of the old debate on rationality. Western literature which constructs the other identifies individuality as a major characteristic of Western rationality. In contrast to this, it identifies anonymity and collectiveness to be the distinctive characteristics of the other. According to this Western view, only the individual thinks and constructs knowledge (Socratic dialogues). It is this same view which has been widely used in the creation of the distinction between "ethnophilosophy" and "philosophy proper" (Hountondji, Odera Oruka, Hallen and Sodipo, Crahay). So, while the individual creates what can be properly defined as knowledge, the rest of society, removed from the ivory tower of intellectuals, constructs *mythos* (Odera Oruka). This position makes Mudimbe's definitions and uses of the concepts of "knowledge" and "tradition" highly ambiguous and controversial throughout his work.

Mudimbe's evaluation and appraisal of modern European philosophy contrasts sharply with that of Marcien Towa. Towa affirms the superiority of European *episteme*, with all its pragmatic conclusions, over African modes of thought. For him, philosophy is an instrument of material change. For this reason, he defines a meaningful philosophical system as one which postulates the premises from which desirable practical consequences can be drawn for the transformation of both reality and society. In contrast to this view, Mudimbe conceives philosophy as being primarily a form of discourse, a system of making representations and explanations of history. What is important in philosophy for Mudimbe are the epistemological values on the basis of which the representations and history have their foundation, usefulness, and relevance. Philosophy, in other words, is the means through which "the world" is constructed and structured. In this sense, for Mudimbe, no philosophical system can validly judge others. No one enjoys the privilege of being at the center while others remain peripheralized.

But philosophy, he contends, can sometimes be drawn into and made part of a wider historical program of the people to whom it belongs. It can be used, for example, to justify ideological programs, such as the alienation of others and justification of one's own assumed superiority. For Mudimbe, then, the notion of the superiority of Western philosophy over African modes of thought is part of a wider Western ideological plot rather than a fact.

The theme of the historical plot by the West against Africa is perhaps best depicted today by Mudimbe. In *The Invention of Africa*, Mudimbe argues that the present debate on African philosophy is only part of a wider and more complex discourse invented and maintained by Europe as an aspect of the epistemological order through which it (Europe) has aimed at affirming itself in opposition to "others." This ideological campaign is set around the Western intellectual configuration of knowledge as the epitome of European power against which all other peoples would be compared and judged. Rationality, based upon and defined by Western epistemological codes, was used as the yardstick of judgment against others.

In order to maintain and justify this hegemony and power, the West invented the image of "primitive" Africa. Out of this project, new branches of knowledge such as anthropology—the study of primitive societies—became historical necessities to confirm and maintain the image of the primitive under the guise of science.

The purpose of all this, argues Mudimbe, was to create a sharp dichotomy between "the Same" and "the Other" in which the former, Europe, is viewed as superior to the latter. According to Mudimbe, many African scholars were beaten into this mental framework. "The fact of the matter," he says, "is that, until now, Western interpreters as well as African analysts have been using categories and conceptual systems which depend on a Western epistemological order."[106]

According to Mudimbe, then, it is the aggressive Western aspiration to establish its epistemological power and hegemony as a means to social and political power which resulted in the politics and discourses of otherness and ideologies of alterity as depicted in such movements as negritude, black personality, and African philosophy. *The Invention of Africa* contributes tremendously to the deconstruction of this politics of otherness by compiling some minute and rarely cited examples in analyzing the dialectical discourse on and causation between Same and Other—that is, the dialectical discourse about and struggles for the control of identity.

This view largely agrees with our own thesis that the contestation over the definition of and claim over reason is an important center of the discourse on African philosophy. But Mudimbe builds his structuralist phenomenology of African knowledge on a meticulous combination of the position of Michel Foucault and Claude Lévi-Strauss. What Mudimbe says of the invention of Africa as a product of Western discourse is an illustration of the power of knowledge. In *The*

Order of Things Foucault states that the emergence of the modern world and modern man, in terms of who and what they are understood to be, are events in the order of knowledge. That emergence is the result of man's own self-constitution "in Western culture as both that which must be conceived and that which is to be known."[107] Foucault therefore describes power/knowledge partly in terms quite close to those of Thomas Kuhn—that knowledge arises out of a determined set of circumstances and in answer to a specific and precise question. For Foucault, these pragmatic and empirical undertakings are only part of *episteme*, an order of representation, a small part of a socially constructed reality. Man's domination of nature through the various sciences is therefore, for Foucault, his biggest ideological achievement, but one which nevertheless embodies many imbalances and contradictions. Nevertheless, he says, "all knowledge, of whatever kind, proceeded to the offering of its material by the establishment of differences and defined those differences by the establishment of order. . . . "[108]

Mudimbe's *Invention of Africa* is almost a rewriting of Foucault's neostructuralism (as in *Power/Knowledge* and *The Order of Things*) in an African perspective. A brief comparison will confirm this: While Foucault's essential concern is with the culture of the West, Mudimbe's pain is with modern African cultural dependence on the West. While Foucault does not accept the categories which are customarily used to describe Western culture, Mudimbe's major theme is that the various Western discourses on Africa and Africans have conditioned the establishment of the conceptual categories in which Africans today conceive and express their own identity.

What Foucault is really writing about is all human thinking and the institutions that both perpetuate and inhibit this thinking; Mudimbe's concern, on the other hand, is with the phenomenology of the discourses which have shaped the modern meaning of Africa and of being African. Foucault's subject is all history, but history as seen in terms of the shaping of modern Western culture, in terms that is, of the dominant forces of power and knowledge. The power of Mudimbe's work, on the other hand, is the illustration of the ways in which Western anthropological and missionary interpretations of African life and thought have induced distortions, not only for Westerners, but also for Africans who try to understand themselves by means of Western epistemological models. Mudimbe has in mind not only ethnophilosophers such as Tempels, Kagame, and Mbiti, but also those who attempt to critique them, such as Hountondji, Wiredu, Towa, Bodunrin, Eboussi-Boulaga, and others of their school. Like Foucault, therefore, Mudimbe too proceeds from the assumption that reality is socially constructed.

Mudimbe admits this conspicuous presence of Foucault in his work. He admits that his task in *The Invention of Africa* is to account for the possibility of anthropological knowledge and its meaning for the foundation of both Africanist discourses and African *gnosis* partly through a critical synthesis of Foucault's thesis on the last archaeological rupture in Western epistemology.

Nevertheless, despite this dependence on Foucault, Mudimbe's work still contributes significantly to the understanding of modern African intellectual development. Mudimbe's contribution is the introvertive moment in the order of knowledge which he examines. It is a historical deconstruction of the bits and pieces of the power/knowledge that have determined the representation of Africa and Africans in contemporary social sciences as well as in contemporary sociopolitical thought and practice. And he laments thus:

> Even in the most explicitly "Afrocentric" descriptions, models of analysis, explicitly or implicitly, knowingly or unknowingly, refer to the same order. Does this mean that African *Weltanschauungen* and African traditional systems of thought are unthinkable and cannot be made explicit within the framework of their own rationality?[109]

For Mudimbe, then, the most important questions in the debate on African philosophy are those about the epistemological groundings which define African rationality. Doesn't Africa have its own order of knowledge or *episteme* on the basis of which to define its rules and parameters of rational discourse away from the epistemological locus in the West? he asks.

The epistemological hiatus in Africans' discourse about Africa, says Mudimbe, is the logical result of the power/knowledge which was wielded by Europe against Africa—a process to create the identity of the Same through the discrimination of the Other. In art, anthropology, and history, Africa is sharply contrasted to Europe, creating a process of dichotomization and polarization in which Africa occupies the bottom and Europe the top positions on the scale. In art and painting, Africans are depicted in the state of nature, exposing their nudity and proximity to savagery. Where Africa scores points, such as in the statecraft of empires and states (Bornu Kanem, Ghana, Songai, Buganda, Nyoro, etc.) or in architectural marvels such as in old Zimbabwe, or in plant domestication as happened during the dawn of agriculture, all such achievements are theorized as results of cultural diffusion from outside Africa or as direct achievements of some non-African technicians and other foreign experts present in Africa. Everything expressing valid and acceptable knowledge in Africa must, by power of Western epistemological ethnocentrism, have started or come directly from some Western origin.

According to Mudimbe, the concurrence of both imperialism and anthropology in the latter part of the nineteenth century allowed for the crystallization of the "primitive" image of Africa. Central to Mudimbe's work is a focus on discourse. From it flows many insights derived from the relations between different discourses, between theory and practice, between history and anthropology, and between the desire for knowledge and the power and profit accruing to the ones who have and control knowledge. Even the definition of primitivity, argues Mudimbe, always depends upon the Western intellectual elite, as well as upon its need for "primitive" outcasts. Thus, primitivity is a judgment, an ideological concept, rather than a fact.

The discipline of anthropology helped to crystallize this ideology of the "primitives," so that, at the end of the nineteenth century and at the beginning of the twentieth, everyone was fascinated by primitivity, by its ambiguity, and by its "exotic" existence at the edge of experience. Hence, Mudimbe connects the conditions of horror to which the so-called primitives were condemned to their domination by colonists, whose power of authority and direction, administration and commerce, police and jurisdiction, correction and punishment, allowed them to use chains, prisons, and dungeons to tame Africans. The association here is with Foucault's description of madness as contrasted to and controlled by civilization or by medical experts as the agents of sanity.

Concurrently, the anthropologist bore the task of "account[ing] for the normality, creative dynamism, and achievements of the 'civilized world' against the abnormality, deviance, and primitiveness of 'non-literate societies.' "[110]

Mudimbe gives many minute examples of such inventive or ideological discourses developed in the West, tying them to coherences that are said to indicate similarities between chronological discourse and lateral discourse. But he does not try to reconstruct a total rival picture, he tells us; he only wants to "reveal" the relation between various well-determined sets of discursive formations about Africa.

Through and through, then, Africa as we *know* it (through its Western representation) is a social construct. To produce this construct, the African intellectual has been successfully used. Pulled away from the masses, he has been made both a victim and an agent of his own alienation. Foucault writes —and Mudimbe also believes—that the African and Africanist intellectuals who have participated in this game

> discovered that the masses no longer need to gain knowledge: They know perfectly well, without illusion; they know far better than he and they are certainly capable of expressing themselves. But there exists a system of power which blocks, prohibits, and invalidates this discourse and this knowledge, a power not only found in the manifest authority of censorship, but one that profoundly and subtly penetrates an entire social network. Intellectuals are themselves agents of this system of power—the idea of their responsibility for "consciousness" and discourse forms part of the system.[111]

Like Foucault, Mudimbe appears to hold that even an author is no more than an expression of the relationship between his work, his era, and his own talent, and that deviance, for the most part, depends upon its social definition rather than upon individual performance. Both these notions suggest an intellectual filiation, perhaps through Foucualt himself, that can be traced to Marx's concept of *false consciousness* and to Durkheim's concept of *anomie*. History, for Foucault, is a creature of the modern Western nations in which knowledge functions as a form of power. As such, it is said to "oppress" others; it is an instrument of control. Mudimbe's account of anthropologists' and missionaries' enterprise in Africa represents them as agents of this history and the knowledge which it embodies.

> Since the end of the eighteenth century anthropological discourses represent [this history]. They are constrained discourses and develop within the general system of knowledge which is in an interdependent relationship with systems of power and social control. Durkheim's prescriptions on the pathology of civilizations, Lévy-Bruhl's theses on prelogical systems of thought, as well as Frazer's hypothesis on primitive societies, bear witness, from a functional viewpoint, to the same epistemological space in which stories about Others, as well as commentaries on their differences, are but elements in the history of the Same and its knowledge.[112]

According to this position, the entire discourse on African philosophy has taken place within and forms part of the discursive separation of the Same from the Other, an exercise which conjoins knowledge and power. The self-revindications of the Other in black personality movements, in negritude, in ethnophilosophy, and in the critique of the latter are all moments in and aspects of the same alienating epistemological order which is created, set, and controlled by the West. They are part, to use Edward Blyden's terminology, of the "Negro myth." Mudimbe's own work is an attempt to counter this anthropology—as it was practiced in France at the turn of the century—with another one in a manner that is both oppositional and postmodern.

Of the philosophical critique of ethnophilosophy Mudimbe writes as follows:

> The philosophical critique of ethnophilosophy is not the reverse of Tempels and Kagame's school. It is a policy discourse on philosophy aimed at examining methods and requirements for practicing philosophy in Africa. As a trend, it derives its conviction from its status as a discourse which is firmly linked to both the Western tradition of philosophy as a discipline and the academic structures which guarantee institutionally accepted philosophical practices. As such, the critique of ethnophilosophy can be understood as subsuming two main genres: on the one hand, a reflection on the methodological limits of Tempels and Kagame's school and, on the other hand, . . . African practices and works bearing on Western subjects and topics in the most classical tradition of philosophy.[113]

This point is important, and the suggestion which it implicitly makes is a word of hope for an independent African thought system to be founded on authentic epistemological structures of African thought and practices. A good and insightful student of philosophy at Kenyatta University, Kimani Kiiru, suggests that this independence can be attained if African philosophers care to articulate the rules of inference in certain African beliefs. He takes as example the Gikuyu beliefs regarding a hyena's laughter in a homestead or a persistent owl's cry around a home as indicators of misfortune. Kiiru's concern is not just with the statements as expressions of beliefs. His concern is that the statements posit relations of events which need to be thoroughly investigated. Among the Gikuyu, he says, a hyena's laughter or an owl's cry around a home has *always* been followed by the death of a member of the families concerned. Although reluctant to infer a causal relationship between the two sets of events (the laughter of the hyena and the cry of the owl with death), Kiiru suggests that the expression of the belief concerning the causal conjunction of the two events is a pointer to some epistemological model and a logical operation worth investigating. I believe he does not claim that hyenas or owls are causal agents in themselves but only symbols within a long causal chain which is frequently obscured by the elimination of the first part of the explanation. His remark is, however, important because it points to an explanation embodied in idioms and representations of everyday life. It also fits well into the rationality debate which we discussed above.

Mudimbe does not go this far in suggesting specific directions of the search for the authentic African epistemological locus. Nonetheless, he indicates an alternative general direction in stating that there is still hope for authentic African systems of thought which can be revealed through another anthropology of knowledge. Mudimbe's new anthropology draws prominently from Lévi-Strauss's structuralism, which proposes not opposition but complementarity between history and anthropology, between the Same and the Other. Anthropology is the science of the concrete and it is illustrated in magic and mythical thought; it is the *bricolage*, as opposed to history, which is the engineered, the abstract, the invented, the construed or the constructed, the scientific. In other words, Mudimbe surpasses Horton, who contrasts history and anthropology irreconcilably in the models of science and traditional thought by falling back on Lévi-Strauss, for whom the two are only aspects of the structure of knowing. According to Lévi-Strauss, "It is important not to make the mistake of thinking that these two are stages or phases of evolution of knowledge. Both approaches are equally valid."[114]

The Lévi-Straussian combination of the scientific and the "*bricoleur*" suggests for Mudimbe the exit from the epistemological impasse gripping Africa today. Salvation lies in the marriage between anthropology and intellectualist philosophical practice. The future of African philosophy, for Mudimbe, lies within the need to analyze African cultural dynamics as portrayed in their languages. "This orientation," he says, "is revealed most explicitly in Bird and Karp's [sic] collection of specialized studies, *Explorations in African Systems of Thought* (1980), and in Beidelman's study on Kaguru modes of thought [*Moral Imagination in Kaguru Modes of Thought*] (1986)"[115] and, one might add, in Peter Rigby's *Persistent Pastoralists* (1985). Mudimbe is, however, very critical of Rigby's Marxist reading of Ilparakuyo pastoralism and alleged resistance to change as a resistance against capitalist economy in preference for their economy of "sharing." A detailed discussion of Rigby's work is contained in Mudimbe's more recent work, *Parables and Fables: Exegesis, Textuality, and Politics in Central Africa* (1991).

Although with some differences, this recommendation brings Mudimbe close to both Vansina on the one hand and Odera Oruka and Hallen and Sodipo on the other: (a) to Vansina[116] because through the analysis of everyday language, or oral expression and discourse, the scholar constructs objective knowledge in the form of history, his own science;—(b) to Odera Oruka[117] and Hallen and Sodipo[118] because the *"bricoleur"* is best portrayed in the philosophies of the wise, the sage philosophers and the *onisegun* (traditional experts in medicine and divination among the Yoruba), not because they are specialists or a sort of mirage of the scientist—although Odera Oruka compares his sage philosophers to Socrates while Hallen and Sodipo compare their *onisegun* with Willard Quine—but because of their concern for the concrete dynamics of everyday life.

But the positions of Vansina and Odera Oruka lead to another issue which has triggered off an interesting debate among students of hermeneutics in social anthropology and philosophy. In his treatment of oral tradition as a source of history, Vansina regards narrative as a body of discourse in which an objective body of knowledge, especially "historical knowledge," can be discerned by the scholar. He therefore treats the storyteller as a mere resource from whom the scholar extracts and constructs his mute knowledge. Odera Oruka's position, on the other hand, draws significantly from the Socratic dialogues, which set up the expert scholar—in this case the philosopher—as the systematic thinker (lover of wisdom, the scientist) who wades through the ignorance of his interlocutors in order to sift out *episteme* from *doxa*. In both these positions (of Vansina and Odera Oruka), knowledge is defined as an objective product of the expert. This position runs clearly counter to the current debate which defines knowledge as a common product of the dialogue between the scholar, the cultural practitioners or experts, and the social actors of everyday life. Although Hallen and Sodipo tried to extricate themselves from this problem by stating that they treated the *onisegun* as their equals in the course of their research, they still significantly omitted the ordinary people from any role in the construction of knowledge.

Thus, although Mudimbe eloquently recommends a return, to use Jewsiewicki's expression again, to the "usable past," he does not even slightly indicate what he envisages as the relationship between the stylish, scholarly, and elegant deconstructionist method and the idioms of everyday life which embody the mental (epistemological?) schemes of "traditional" discourse. The basis of this project is the now familiar postmodernist or superstructuralist belief that science is only one discursive formation among many others and its ideological function is open for examination. Its filiation is Foucault's idea of the limitation of systems of thought. In the preface to *The Order of Things*, Foucault makes reference to

Jorge Luis Borges where the latter too makes reference to "a certain Chinese encyclopedia" in which it is written that animals are divided into fourteen categories. "In the wonderment of this taxonomy," says Foucault, "the thing we apprehend in one great leap, the thing that, by means of the fable, is demonstrated as the exotic charm of another system of thought, is the limitation of our own, the stark impossibility of thinking *that*. But what is it impossible to think, and what kind of impossibility are we faced with here?"[119]

Put simply, Foucualt is telling us that cultural factors limit our thinking, that even the most imaginative individual functions within his or her own language, that the individual's imagination itself is sparked by the age in which he or she lives, and that each age has its own codes of knowledge. Time (i.e., history) and space (i.e., anthropology) thus predetermine the individual's scope of thought and action and therefore figure prominently in Mudimbe's project—the geography of African *gnosis*.

Like Foucault, Mudimbe directs attention toward the marginalized who must be recognized by expanding the horizon of the Same. "Foucault's horizon is, one might say, a relativization of the truth of the Same in the dispersion of history; in other words, 'a decentralizing that leaves no privilege to any center.' "[120] At the World Congress of Philosophy in Dusseldorf in 1978, Odera Oruka was widely quoted in European dailies as having shouted that, "philosophy is not a monopoly of the West."

By recognizing marginality, Foucault opens up a new horizon which engulfs non-Western systems of thought. Similarly, Mudimbe, in modification of Janheinz Jahn's intellectualist paradigm, states that the production of knowledge within the geography of African *gnosis* must cover a wider horizon than the intellectuals' restricted world, and must transcend the world of political power. Mudimbe says:

> Jahn's decision seems exaggerated. I would prefer a wider authority [on what is truly African]: intellectuals' discourses as a critical library and, if I could, the experience of rejected forms of wisdom which are not part of the structures of political power and scientific knowledge.[121]

Mudimbe's project is doubtlessly a noble one—to recapture *authenticity*. But this desire is not without contradictions. The other must regain himself or herself in "the freedom of thinking of himself or herself as the starting point of an absolute discourse,"[122] free from the epistemological codes of Western philosophy. Yet in this same project Mudimbe invests heavily in the positions of Lévi-Strauss and Foucault[123] as the openings that lead to the *bricolage*, the framework of authentic African rationality. This said, pertinent questions remain in Mudimbe's project: which and where is the African epistemological locus? and how does one reach it without recourse to some established method(s), like Mudimbe himself uses, to state its necessity? Mudimbe's reference to Karp and

Bird, Beidelman, and others as important reference points in African philosophy is certainly very important. But this is not sufficient. What is required in this combination of philosophy with anthropology must be a greater effort to bring together anthropologists with philosophical insight and philosophers with anthropological empiricism. But what is even more crucial is the need to define African discourse together with its rules of inference, in everyday life as well as in specialized circumstances.

The claim by Meinrad Hebga that spirits, magic, oracles, and witchcraft are real is a claim which suggests that those who believe in spirits, magic, oracles, and witchcraft operate in a thought pattern or use basic epistemological principles which are quite distinct from the pattern or principles which form the basis of claims which deny the reality of spirits, oracles, and witchcraft. In other words, the former claim is based on a specific "mode of thought," on patterns of proof and judging, of making inference, and of defining the real which are opposed to the characteristics and "modus operandi" of the models which deny them. This is an example of what Kuhn meant when he argued that any defense of a particular paradigm must possess a certain circularity in that whoever rejects the paradigm is also committed to a rejection of the standards by which it is defended.

The claims of Hebga are not new. They form the basic or primary premises of "*juogi*" possession or spirit busting in the Legio Maria sect among the Luo of Kenya and, I believe, in many other religious or quasi-religious beliefs and practices in other societies of Africa. Their importance for us now, however, is that we are being called upon to regard them as leads in our archaeological search for the basic epistemological assumptions in African *episteme* and discourse. In other words, the call by Mudimbe is that we go slightly ahead of Hebga's "Plaidoyer pour les logiques d'Afrique noire,"[124] perhaps by doing the kind of analysis done by Evans-Pritchard about the Nuer concepts of identity, symbolism, and contradiction, or about the logical forms in the Azande beliefs regarding oracle powers.

Assuming that the project of identifying epistemological assumptions within which authentically African knowledge can reside is possible, there will still be the problem of making such fundamental principles operative in the thinking modes of young Africans today rather than merely listing them as antiquarian products of a postmodern engagement in the politics of knowledge. I do not want to assume that any perceived practical difficulty with Mudimbe's new anthropology undermines the significance of his project in any vital way. Yet there is a way in which it is legitimate to regard Mudimbe's project as directed beyond its mere subversive (postmodern) role. At least many of Mudimbe's African readers will, and many already do, look up to him with this expectation: that his work is not only diagnostic of a (gnostic) malady, but also prognostic of its cure. Mudimbe is, despite his own modesty, fast gaining a prophetic role in the project of reordering African knowledge in a manner that will make a demand—whether or not justifiably—for a translation of his observations and proposals into practice, into an effectual new order. Because Mudimbe's engagement of Western anthropology is not only postmodern but also oppositional, a demand that will be made of him can be framed in the form of the following question: How can basic African epistemological principles be integrated into already alienated modes of thinking? This demand will place Mudimbe in a position similar to that once occupied by Kwame Nkrumah and Julius Nyerere in regard to their proposals for a new political and economic order in postcolonial Africa. What Mudimbe does with *gnosis*, that is, with the creation of a new order of knowledge, cannot be fully isolated from the ideology of empowerment on which Africa has focused over the past three decades.

There is already an indication of Mudimbe's difference from Foucault. Despite his respect for and dependence on Foucault's work, in *L'Odeur du père* Mudimbe recognizes his mentor as "a noteworthy symbol of the sovereignty of the European thought from which we wish to disentangle ourselves." Through this disentanglement Mudimbe wishes to reestablish the subject in African discourse. The creation of the new epistemic order is the empowerment of the African subject. Mudimbe borrows from Foucault the premises which empower the subject, but identifies at the same time the premises of Western discourse which African subjects must reverse by turning to their own discursive space. Thus, by prognosing a new discursive formation centered on African social-cultural space, Mudimbe erects the African subject, and hopes to give deliverance to those already captivated within Western epistemic canon. It is easy, in this sense, to understand why Mudimbe is opposed to those like Senghor—and in that sense also to Towa—who propose that Africans master the values and literary styles of the West as a way of universalizing themselves.

According to Mudimbe, the perceptual and conceptual spaces of Africa already provide the African subject with enough means for constructing an alternative discursive formation, but in a way that is free of the essentialist claims produced by, for example, Senghor's negritude or Meinrad Hebga's "Plaidoyer pour les logiques d'Afrique noire" (Defense of African Logic). The rejection of the essentialist position allows Mudimbe to apply Foucault to his (Mudimbe's) own project of subverting, not only the Western discursive canon through which the negative images of Africa have been invented, but also Foucault himself as part of that canon. It is only through this double subversion that it is possible to erect the African subject.

But of course it is still significant that we go beyond Hebga by producing the logical formulas and epistemological premises or laws which guide African discourse formations. Let me call the suggested project an archaeological deconstruction of African discourse. Such a project, I believe, could produce good debate and fruitful discourse among African philosophers—and would perhaps extend its invitation to Odera Oruka's sages in the periphery.

This debate, however, is possible only if there is a realization that even Mudimbe's idea of an invented Africa is itself also a construct, an ideology which in turn requires deconstruction. If we realize this then we are indeed in the process of creating a discourse on African ideas—that is, writing the history of African thought through a series of discourses about meaning and interpretation. But this is perhaps not exactly what Mudimbe has in mind.

The impression which *The Invention of Africa* gives is that there is a distinction between facts representing African reality on the one hand, and a construct or an invention as the colonial discourse on the other. But how does one distinguish between "facts" and constructs in regard to conceptual representations? According to Mudimbe, it would appear, the difference between the two is similar to the difference between ethnography and ethnophilosophy. Mudimbe discredits ethnophilosophy in its present form, and suggests that there is a need to return to ethnography in order to carry out a new process of deconstruction using the epistemological categories of African rationality as opposed to what has been done so far in the present ethnophilosophy. But what are these categories of African rationality? How do we identify them? And how do we annotate them?

Perhaps another understanding of Mudimbe's project lies in the suggestion that his biggest worry is about the annihilistic tendency of colonial scholarship to negate African values and discourses through Western logic. This concern would point particularly at Lévy-Bruhl and Robin Horton, for example. But Mudimbe's concern is different from that of Wiredu, because he criticizes the latter as well. Wiredu's suggestion is that comparison operates only between similars and not between dissimilars. So traditional thought cannot be compared with Western scientific thought. However, he believes that rationality is universal in the sense of that which controls judgment on the validity of the theoretical in light of the practical inferences derivable from theoretical models. In this respect, Wiredu follows Horton's path by concluding that certain propositions as expressions of African traditional belief systems and discourse ought to be rejected on the basis of the rules of universal rationality.

Mudimbe does not appear to want to walk this analytical path of Wiredu's eclecticism. His orientation appears to be more in the direction of phenomenological or synthetic exposition and explanation. But are there methods of explanation which are intrinsic to African *episteme*? Let me perhaps paraphrase the questions Sybil Wolfram asks about defining assumed "basic differences of thought":

1. What differences in societies' thought or thinking could qualify as the "basic" ones?

2. What makes a difference basic?
3. Which items of thought are supposed to be different?
4. What is the nature of the difference between them supposed to be?[125]

The main contender in the search for the assumed differences has been the distinction between the scientific and the nonscientific. According to Wolfram, there are different ways of making that distinction. The first is to mark off scientific from, say, practical or artistic thought within Western society as a whole. This is to distinguish the scientific from the nonscientific by the nature of the path sought, such as marking off the mathematical differences between scientific propositions and historical or mathematical propositions.

In the second way, "scientific" is ascribed to a mode of thinking assumed to be generally characteristic of "Western society" as a whole, and is marked off from the magical or the religious. "In other words," says Wolfram, "the comparison is between that portion of our [Western] thinking which concerns generalization about the world and a similar portion in other societies." Wolfram seems to suggest that magic and religion in nonscientific societies seek to establish truths similar to those that science in the strict sense seeks to establish in the West. She shares this assumption with Horton. "In our society," she goes on, "observation of the world would be regarded as the only good foundation of a general belief about it and the possession of well-founded general beliefs as in turn the only sound basis for beliefs about particular things when we lack the evidence for direct observation of them, as we do for instance in the case of events which have not yet occurred."[126] So, for Wolfram as for Horton, observation and formulation of general laws are the characteristics of scientific discourse as opposed to magical and religious discourse.

Wolfram's argument is made even more poignantly by the contributors to *Reason and Morality*, a collection of essays dedicated to the discussion of rationality and factors revitalizing its general definition. In *Reason and Morality* one of the contributors, Joanna Overing, strongly argues that

> It would be self-defeating to compare 'models of thought' in the conviction that the intellectual capacities of humankind are already known absolutely and that the forms of correct reasoning are definitely exemplified in the thoughts of the anthropologist and the Western scientist. The contributors [to her anthology] are therefore uneasy about the idea that our own [Western] notion of humankind in its enthronement of reason can provide a firm basis from which to judge the capacities either of ourselves or [of] other human beings.[127]

In this quotation, Overing is referring to an attitude which critiques the position of the school of philosophy of science which strongly defends Western control of reality construction based on reason as a bedrock of reality.

The neostructuralism of Foucault which Mudimbe endorses has been a milestone in giving a counterposition to this "Westernization" by offering a softer version of relativism which encourages contact rather than estrangement between diverse rationalities or cultural perspectives. And one important way in which this contact can be established is by eliminating the gap between the "rational" and the "irrational" through the definition of knowledge as paradigms of discourses and representations. This perspectivist position, however, has its own problems, particularly those of commensurability and translation between the various paradigms.

The major reason for this difficulty is what Mudimbe himself has written about—that claims within the beliefs of spirits, magic, witchcraft, and oracles are not statements of physics or chemistry. But how does one explain the differences between nonscientific discourse and scientific discourse without using linguistic and conceptual categories, also called universals of mind, which are accessible to both?

These observations and questions do point to the ambiguous nature of the project suggested by Mudimbe. This ambiguity is also demonstrated by Kwame Gyekye, another Ghanaian philosopher like Wiredu. Like Mudimbe, Gyekye claims that looking at African traditional philosophy through foreign eyes is one of the major problems besetting the study of African traditional philosophy.[128] This difficulty, he says, occurs especially in the use of foreign languages to analyze concepts in African traditional philosophy—an exercise which involves applying foreign conceptual schemes hidden in the language to analyze and interpret African traditional concepts. He therefore lists what he regards as the content of African conceptual schemata in an attempt to protect them from misreading. Among the items listed are

— God and other categories of being;
— the principle of causality;
— the mind-body problem;
— the concept of a person or body-spirit-soul relationship;
— propositional categories of subject and rules of predication.[129]

However, one sees little that is fundamentally Akan or African in the listed items beyond linguistic variances of conceptual expression. So long as these concepts continue to be expressed in terms of categories of relation (cause-effect), ontological hierarchies of being, and dualism (mind-body, contingency and necessity), "basic" epistemological premises become highly elusive and difficult to define. We, however, believe that some fundamental conceptual differences can be found within and between cultural systems.

Ocholla-Ayayo, a Kenyan ethnographer, in reference to the Luo, suggests that there are basic premises which control or guide his society's thinking. He lists his examples as follows:

1. "Piny agonda; piny ochwere; piny k'nyal"
— The universe is order and infinite.
2. "Ok timore nono; ginmoro ema nitie, pok noneye"
— All events are caused and interrelated; nothing happens by chance.
3. "nosekor; ochopone; e kaka nene osendikne"
— What happens now is what was predicted.
4. "Luor lwar' ok inyal ng'eyo pod itin; ang'o ma iseneno"
— Old age is the basis of wisdom as well as the source of respect.
5. "Cham gi wadu"
— Share with your brother.
6. "Chan ma kowadu ok moni nindo"
— Your brother's poverty does not prevent you from sleeping.[130]

Most of the above examples are proverbs quite frequently used in Dholuo. The problem, however, is that Ocholla-Ayayo does not tell us when and why, by and to whom they are usually used, thus giving the impression that they are general principles assumed to condition the acquisition and processing of knowledge. He does not even care to explain that some of them are contradictory. But what is important is that, except for the first, they are not exactly categories within which the process of knowing or reasoning takes place. Rather, they are situational or contextual dicta used to express social control or social rebellion. So perhaps what we need to do, then, is situational analysis of how people use different aspects of everyday discourse.

8 | "Tradition" and "Modernity"
The Role of Reason

As AFRICAN CIVILIZATIONS entered the twentieth century a number of forces combined to produce a revolution in many Africans' conception of the universe. This new view of the universe has led to the complete repudiation of traditional belief systems in some cases and to a sharp modification of them in others. Some African thinkers now claim that traditional reasoning was often inexact; that its physics was moral rather than scientific, that is, that it was divided into good motions and bad motions, good causes and bad causes; that its classifications were static and were based on supposedly unchanging forms and essences; and finally, that its formulations were useless, for they gave to people no control over natural forces.

The above passage captures the spirit of the works of the people discussed in this chapter: Hountondji, Wiredu, Odera Oruka. They would see the current revolution in African thinking as a parallel of the great intellectual revolution in Western civilization in the seventeenth century. Their view is that African cultural history, like all others, must be brought into the linear spectrum of time, in which it must constantly renovate itself. Wiredu identifies three evils (he calls them complaints) which can frustrate cultural regeneration: anachronism, authoritarianism, and supernaturalism. They are the weapons of resistance to change and modernization. Traditions tend to incorporate all three as shields for the protection of purity and stability. These two values of culture are contradictory to the very nature of man and to man's relationship with reality, according to Hountondji and Wiredu. Their point of departure is dialectical theory. Knowledge is dialectically related to reality and history, which themselves are always in dialectical movement. Truth itself is dialectical, continually changing, and as elusive as it is real. As Wiredu describes it, it is a sort of opinion. Marx's dialectical philosophy calls for reality to be viewed as the reflective and actively redirective existence of human beings in relation to a continually changing and relational world. Knowledge is the inseparable joint creation of subjective activity and external reality moving through history. The basic concern for Hountondji and Wiredu in appealing to dialectical Marxism is to make a case for the unity of theory and practice in African culture. The epistemological (practical) quest for a union of theory and practice focuses particularly upon an understanding and changing of one of the most basic facts of our current existence: double alienation—alienation from history, alienation into cultural staticism and anachronism, alienation into underdevelopment.

The foregoing remarks only indicate generally some of the essential elements of the thoughts of the people discussed in this chapter and provide background to their definitions of reason and knowledge as propaedeutic therapy for African cultural alienation and backwardness. These people focus strongly therefore on appraisal or critique of tradition and on analysis of the factors which transform it into modernity. These positions bring Hountondji and Wiredu—but perhaps Wiredu more than Hountondji—close to the position held by Horton, which we discussed in chapter 6 above, that the inability of traditional thought systems to distinguish material causality from human agency has largely been responsible for their exclusion from the history of scientific thought.

Paulin Hountondji: African Ethnophilosophy and Its Public

Paulin Hountondji is, in my opinion, perhaps the best known, until recently the most unrelenting, and still the clearest critic of ethnophilosophy. Although Hountondji is a very prolific writer and one of Africa's best philosophers, his philosophy became known to the English-speaking world only after the English translation of his first full book, *Sur la "philosophie africaine": critique de l'ethnophilosophie* (1977), in 1983 as *African Philosophy: Myth and Reality*. Since that translation, Hountondji became one of the most popular and most widely read of African philosophers. Recently Mudimbe joined him in this status, particularly in North America, as a result of the English publication of *The Invention of Africa* (1988).

For Hountondji, the texts written by Africans and designated by them as philosophical are what constitute "African philosophy." This is what the definition of "African philosophy" therefore is—all texts, or the body of literature, written by Africans and designated by them as philosophical. Hountondji holds that it is essential that "African philosophy" be written exclusively by Africans; thus, under any consideration of "African philosophy" must be included also all those works that have been carried out by Africans on Western philosophy and philosophers. They all have elements of a possible and true African philosophy. The existing texts answering to the name of "African philosophy" at the moment are, however, little more than mere analyses of cultural elements (stories, proverbs, poems, language structures, and institutions) that constitute *Weltanschauungen* or worldviews, wrongly supposed by these authors to be common to all Africans. Hountondji, however, recognizes that the designation of these texts as "philosophical" has been deliberate and therefore constitutes a definite view of what philosophy is. This is what he wishes to challenge.

Hountondji holds that such analyses of cultural elements as done by Tempels and his followers contain nothing but a mysterious recess of our supposedly immobile soul, a collective and unconscious worldview. This is what these texts want to restore.

But this exercise, Hountondji says, is not philosophy. Tempels's *La philosophie bantoue* and all those works for which it opened the way are nothing but works of ethnology with a philosophical pretention. They are works of *ethnophilosophy*. For Hountondji, these works are concerned, "thanks to the interpretation of custom and tradition, proverbs, institutions, or, in brief, of the cultural data of the African peoples, with reconstructing a particular *weltanschauung*, a specific worldview supposed to be common to all Africans, removed from history and change and, in addition, considered to be philosophical."[1]

According to Hountondji, the authors have tried to confuse this "hypothetical worldview of collective wisdom with philosophy rightly so-called. And from there the whole of our philosophical literature has limited itself in its object to this sterile myth of a *philosophie-déjà-là*; that it would only have to narrate, in an exhaustive search for a specific mark, for an originality that will mark, at all costs, the difference between our thought and that of the West."[2]

And the history of "African philosophy," as we already remarked, has not been other than to repeat this set-up tradition, to analyze the elements of different given cultures in order to show the "philosophy" therein; that is, to show the coherence between the true or supposed ideas that sustain these cultures.

This ethnocentricity of Tempels's "philosophical" work is highly refuted by Hountondji. At first sight, says Hountondji, *La Philosophie bantoue* seems sympathetic in having rehabilitated the black man and his culture from the scorn of which they had till then been victims. But looked at more closely, it becomes clear that ethnophilosophy does not avoid the radical vice of ethnology in general. Tempels's book is not addressed to Africans at all, but to Europeans—the colonists and the missionaries. In it the author recognizes that Africans are not worthy of this title (philosophy), but, all the same, he asserts this under the pretext of offering a point of discussion about the African (Bantu) to European circles. Writes Hountondji: "The black continues, from this fact, to be the contrary of an interlocutor: he is the one about whom others speak, a face without a voice that other people try to decipher among themselves, an object to be defined, and not a subject of a possible discourse."[3]

African authors of this literature, in an attempt to define themselves and their people, have tried to revolt against being defined and petrified by a non-African. In other words, ethnophilosophy, like other forms of colonial discourse, is an exercise whose primary aim is to justify European superiority. Hountondji therefore sees ethnophilosophy as a new version of the Hegelian analysis of history. For him, Tempels tried to accomplish with philosophy what Hegel had attempted to accomplish with history. But, on the other hand, if this will to self-definition has produced among our authors any fiction of a collective philosophy, they have nevertheless proved their incontestable philosophical abilities by the manner in which they have tried to justify this fiction. The rigor of certain deductions, the precision of certain analyses, the skill with which they in certain cases handle the dialogue, leave no doubt as to this ability. Although they are incontestably philosophers, their single weakness has been to realize mythically, under a sort of collective philosophy, the philosophical form of their very discourse.[4]

Like Crahay,[5] Hountondji thus believes that an acceptable "African philosophy" could have come from these very African writers and teachers of philosophy. But instead, all of them (Kagame, Mulago, Mbiti, Bahoken, et al.) have believed in reproducing the preexistent *philosophèmes* which have made their writings essentially no less than mere ethnophilosophy: an imaginary search for a collective and unchangeable philosophy common to all Africans, even though only in an unconscious form.[6]

This "philosophy" was considered by Tempels as eternally unchangeable, and by Kagame as changeable at most only within the permanent essence of the Bantu culture. Thus Kagame recognizes such new concepts as that of *Immana* as having been brought by missionaries and now forming part of Bantu concepts of the Supreme Being. He recognizes dynamicity in the evolution of thought. But who of the two is right? asks Hountondji. To answer this question, as in any scientifically carried out research, one would need to go back to the original sources to check where the error lies in the case of a conflict of interpretations. But in African thought this is not possible.

Unfortunately, [writes Hountondji] in the case of "African philosophy" the independent sources are lacking; and if they exist, they are neither texts nor philosophical discourses. The "institutionalized documents" of which Kagame speaks, or which Tempels submitted in the ethnophilosophical manner before him, are radically heterogeneous to philosophy, they are not to be compared to "sources" that would constitute, for an interpreter of Hegelianism for example . . . explicit texts of Hegel . . . in their discussive purport as a perpetually available language.[7]

Africa is rich in its products of language (proverbs, stories, dynastic poems, and the whole of oral literature); but this language, Hountondji tells us, is not philosophical. "Scientific rigor" requires that no philosophical meaning be read into such linguistic forms beyond what they express or are meant to serve. Although they are important, many such proverbs, stories, epics, and dynastic poems do not necessarily have a philosophical agenda.

A philosophical practice, in its theoretical implications, supposes, above all, and by all evidence, a responsible thought, a theoretical effort of an individual subject, and excludes, by this fact, any reduction of philosophy to a *system* of *collective* thought. In this way Hountondji agrees with Crahay, whose work, for

Hountondji, remained the most sound European reaction to Tempels's work to that day. In this way Hountondji also criticizes the writers of the "Témoignages," who endorsed *La philosophie bantoue*, as having contradicted the theoretical implications of their own philosophical practice.[8] Kagame's philosophical projection into Bantu thought, as Tempels did before him, was simply a confusion of philosophy. Despite his strong linguistic analysis and deductive inferences, Kagame, according to Hountondji, still remained on the whole a prisoner of an ideological myth: that of a collective "philosophy" of Africans. To Hountondji, this ideological myth is simply another reevaluated version of the "primitive mentality" theory of Lévy-Bruhl, an imaginary object of the scholarly discourse of ethnology. "It would have been better," says Hountondji, "if Kagame had provided philosophical texts of Africans, or transcribed their words. In this way his interpretation would have been founded on an effective philosophical discourse, universally accessible and controllable."[9] Such a work would not be there simply for the eventual admiration of its non-African public but, above all, it would thus be submitted to the appreciation and criticisms of all Africans. In other words, it would be a philosophical text and would open the way for a philosophical discourse. In this manner Hountondji recognizes and appreciates the work of Marcel Griaule which reported the narrations of Ogotemmêli about the Dogon cosmological system.

Hountondji's position is that the transcribed thoughts of traditional sages would form the "philosophical texts" on which African philosophers could base their philosophical discourse. But he adds that the work of Griaule must be surpassed. He believes that such a work builds the ground for making a philosophy, for it gives room for interpretations and eventual examination of that philosophy, based on an available text—and that is doing philosophy. According to Hountondji, the insufficiency of Crahay's article consists in its unscientific degradation of myths and (according to Crahay's own standards) of the works or texts which answer to the designation "African philosophy."

In reply to Crahay, Hountondji writes as follows:

> The "décollage conceptuel," to say the truth, has always been realized. All men think by concepts, under all the heavens, in all civilizations, even if they integrate mythological sequences in their discourses (like Parmenides, Plato, Confucius, Hegel, Nietzsche, Kagame, et al.) or even if the discourse rests, in its totality, on fragile ideological foundations from which the scientific vigilance must liberate it at every instance. African civilizations, from this point of view, are not exceptions to the rule.
>
> On the contrary, the true problem [of "African philosophy" as defined by Hountondji], which F. Crahay fails to see, is the choice of the interlocutor, of the destination of the discourse. Mythical or ideological, language is always directed, in the social trail of the discourse, toward self-perfection and to clear, by successive bonds, all the degrees of the rigor of precision. It remains therefore [for African philosophers] to throw it first into Africa, within her social

trail, and allow it to develop in its own history, thanks to the written tradition and, as a necessary addition, to political democracy.[10]

It is only in this way that we shall be able to promote a scientific movement in Africa and put an end to this dreadful theoretical void that does not cease to enlarge itself each day amongst a weary population that is indifferent to theoretical problems for which it does not see any more interest.[11]

Hountondji sees philosophy more as an activity than as a system. As an activity, philosophy grounds itself as a process that expresses and transcends itself in *history*. In this way, it transcends *systems*. The latter are often defined by a characteristic of "dumb acceptance, a contented purring, [or] the catechistic repetition of intangible dogmas."[12] As the contemporary Italian philosopher of history Arturo Massolo says in his *Storia della filosofia come problema*, the strength of philosophy lies in the peculiar relationship between its exteriority and its interiority, in the peculiar synthesis of continuity and opposition—according to Hountondji, "in a *dialectical* relation in the strict sense."[13]

Hountondji compares the duty of the contemporary African philosopher vis-à-vis dogmatic traditions on the one hand with the historical pertinence of Kant's *Critique of Pure Reason* vis-à-vis all Western philosophy thereto on the other hand. Hountondji writes:

> One can find in the last pages of the *Critique of Pure Reason*, in that 'Transcendental Doctrine of Method' which is supposed to constitute the second part of the book but is very much shorter than the first, the Transcendental Doctrine of Elements, an outline of what Kant calls a 'History of Pure Reason'.
>
> This history may present us with nothing but 'structure in ruins', rotting systems stripped of all credibility and powers of persuasion, but these ruins are nevertheless instructive, and they have a history that is not purely negative, since it was to nurture the idea, the project of a critique of pure reason.[14]

Thus, for Hountondji, philosophy has always been punctuated by a series of revolutions which, in the words of his teacher and mentor Louis Althusser, are functions of scientific revolutions.[15] So, Hountondji says,

> if the development of philosophy is in some way a function of the development of the sciences, then African philosophy cannot be separated from African science and we shall never have, in Africa, a philosophy in the strict sense, a philosophy articulated as an endless search, until we have produced, in Africa, a history of science, a history of the sciences. Philosophical practice, that peculiar form of theoretical practice that is called philosophy, is inseparable from that other form of theoretical practice called science.[16]

The important point in Hountondji's position is that he sees the strength of science to lie in one point: its hypothetical nature. Because of this hypothetical characteristic of scientific statements, there is no absolute truth in scientific theory. All truths of scientific statements remain so only for as long as there is no alternative theory to disprove them. In this sense, emphasis shifts in all scientific theories from the truth of any moment to the search for it.

It is this characteristic of scientific knowledge which Hountondji applies to philosophy. In other words, philosophy is for him the *love* of wisdom rather than the accomplished wisdom *per se*. Hountondji thus goes back to the original Socratic meaning of philosophy, which, according to him, has been clouded by the creation of systems in the course of history.

According to Althusser,

> Philosophy functions by intervening not in matter (the mechanic), or on a living body (the surgeon), or in the class struggle (the politician), but *in theory*: not with tools or a scalpel or through the organization and leadership of the masses, but simply by stating *theoretical* propositions (theses), rationally adjusted and justified. This intervention in theory provokes *theoretical* effects: the positions of new philosophical interventions, etc., and *practical* effects on the balance of power between the "ideas" in question.[17]

According to Althusser, knowledge is to be thought of as the outcome of a process of production structurally analogous to economic production. Althusser therefore compares the elements involved in the production of knowledge to those elements or factors in the productive process: the "raw materials" (ideas), the "means" (theory, method, and technique) and the "relations" (theoretical, ideological, and social). "This definite system of conditions of theoretical practice," Althusser declares, "is what assigns any given thinking subject (individual) its place and function in the production of knowledge."[18] This is Althusser's conceptualization of scientific knowledge and its growth or production. What is important in this theory is its variance from the Kuhnian explanation of the growth of knowledge by superimposing "universal" or "scientific" characteristics of the production of knowledge.

This view has led to the charge that according to Hountondji, in his discipleship to Althusser, philosophy is nothing but an account of the progress of science; that true philosophy is philosophy of science in the positivistic sense of analysis of the propositions of the experimental sciences. This charge stems especially from the English translation of the original *Sur la "philosophie africaine"* in regard to the translation of the French adjective "scientifique." The English word "science" sometimes differs slightly from the way the word "science" is used in French and generally in recent continental European philosophical circles. In the latter, the word has been frequently used in recent times to mean a rigorous methodological spirit in reasoning or attitude of conduct in any scholarly endeavor. In this respect it becomes acceptable and it is in fact usual to hear reference made to such things as history or even ethics as sciences (in Latin, *scientia historiae* or *scientia moralis*, respectively) in the old-fashioned classical manner.

In positivistic terms, one admits, it would be heretical to talk of *scientia moralis*, because, according to the demand of neopositivism, nothing lies within the domain of moral propositions that satisfies the verificative requirements in the analytic notion of science. The Cartesian method is a paradigmatic model of the continental use of "esprit scientifique" *as a rigorous and disciplined theoretical discourse* which alone is the authority upon which to base any proposition. In this sense "science" equates "reason," and must be understood "as an organized material practice reflected in discourse."[19]

Of course, admittedly, there is some affinity between the positivistic "esprit scientifique" and the continental "esprit scientifique," as much as there was between their respective fathers, Francis Bacon and René Descartes. But one still contends that Hountondji is mainly concerned about Cartesian "science" rather than with Baconian empiricism. However, he does not deny the pertinence and importance of empiricism as representing the attitude of basing theoretical discourse upon facts of life as opposed to empty dreams. Otherwise, how would Hountondji account for using the phrase "African science" if what he means by "science" is only where we would put physics, chemistry, biology, and other experimental disciplines? Proper philosophy must belong to the tradition of scientific discourse as a *recorded, systematized*, and *integrated* form of knowledge.[20] It is this form of knowledge which Hountondji defines as "a scientific practice" or as "science as an organized material practice reflected in discourse." In this regard, however, Hountondji puts philosophy and science (physics, chemistry, biology, etc.) on the same level.[21] Even Althusser explains this difference when he says:

> The expression *the scientific* is not identical to the expression *the sciences*; the expression *the ideological* is not identical to the expression *theoretical ideologies*. The new expressions do not reproduce the older ones: they bring to light a contradictory couple, a *philosophical* couple. The sciences are sciences: they are not philosophy. Theoretical ideologies are theoretical ideologies: they are not reducible to philosophy. But 'the scientific' and 'the ideological' are *philosophical* categories and the contradictory couple they form is brought to light by philosophy: it is philosophical.[22]

It is worth noting, therefore, that there is a difference between Hountondji and Horton in their respective prescriptive definitions of philosophy.

As is evident, it becomes difficult for Hountondji to accept any claim of a traditional African philosophy. Why? Because, in the traditional African society, there was no recorded, systematized, and integrated form of knowledge. There was no science. If mere *systems* do not constitute philosophy, then it is not even worth dreaming of those traditions which, apart from establishing perennial and insoluble metaphysical problems, also depend on *oral* transmission as belonging to philosophy. Thus ethnophilosophy, or what was hitherto regarded as *African philosophy*, defined as supposedly collective, spontaneous, unreflective, and implicit worldviews, is a double negation of philosophy.

The Limits of Hountondji

In the end, therefore, Hountondji defines philosophy in two ways: first, philosophy is a discourse, a scientific discourse, a methodical inquiry with universal aims; second, as history, philosophy is metaphilosophy, a philosophical reflection on philosophical discourse. For, as Althusser states, "philosophy intervenes in reality only by producing results *within itself*. It acts *outside of itself* through the result that it produces *within itself*."[23] Hountondji will not accept any other view of philosophy.

But a dialectical orientation to inquiry cannot require an absolute non- or antiabsoluteness, for then it falls prey to its own antiabsolutist critique. Thus in being necessarily self-critical, a dialectical Marxist orientation can only be continually nonabsolutely nonabsolutist. In contemporary philosophy, there have been two types of this development of dialectical Marxism. Some have been able to maintain an open, nonabsolutist antiabsolutism (such as Merleau-Ponty) while others have fallen prey to their own critique by adopting an absolutist antiabsolutism. The first group, to which belong Marx, Gramsci, and Merleau-Ponty, maintains what may be called a truly dialectical dialectic. But the second group, to which belong Engels, Lenin, Bukharin, and Althusser, maintains what can be called the absolutist antiabsolutism, a closed dialectic. Such normativity cannot itself avoid creating the image of a system, of a dogma or even a myth about what philosophy ought to be.

Can Hountondji be saved from this dogmatic slumber by his own quest for philosophy as history, as a dialectical progression? What Hountondji does not realize is that dialectical progression in philosophy does not always mean a vertical movement to progressively new points without return, what Crahay called taking-off (*décollage*) as total separation from the material runway. In some way history is a process of reconsideration, of return to the past for reevaluation and integration of the old into the new. Every system has its own limitations, and every reflection upon a system leads itself into a new system. In this sense, then, either the whole history of philosophy is nothing but the history of myths, or there is no myth at all in philosophy. Hountondji might reject both these arguments, or might even accept only the first one with a modification. What is at stake, however, is the objective status of the very basis of a scientific discourse.

According to the Kuhnian theory, there are no superparadigmatic standards of explanation. In this sense, Kuhn argues, any defense of a particular paradigm must possess a certain circularity, in that whoever rejects the paradigm is also committed to a rejection of the standards by which it is defended. Kuhn concurs with Polanyi on the commitment theory of the bases of explanatory paradigms. The problem which Hountondji's contention elicits has in fact been in philosophical debate for some time. It states that philosophy is to begin with the empirically given and move in general accordance with the procedures of scientific inquiry. But whether just in the world or in texts, how does one justify empiricism empirically? It is indeed true that the *development* of philosophy depends essentially on an open debate which generates and eventually requires some material points of reference. But it is also true that the foundations of a philosophical orientation, and thus the creativity of the philosopher, are often laid in the assumptions, presuppositions, initial posits, affirmations, trusts, with which one approaches the world. We submit that, in the final analysis, these posits cannot be justified but are the initial affirmations in terms of which one is prepared to interpret who and where one is. In this respect, we would be tempted to go further to say that the three thousand year effort of experiments in either the scientific establishment of philosophical positions or rational self-examination and self-justification must be declared a failure—interesting and imaginative experiments, but nevertheless a failure.

Thus, both ethnophilosophy and Hountondji's critique have their limitations. The former because it tries to perpetuate, by translating into an ontological constitution (beyond temporality and change), what was in fact a product of a historical conjunct. And Hountondji because, in trying to shatter this ontological mythologization, he creates another myth in its place: the scientific establishment of philosophical activity, the restoration of philosophy as a rigorous science. Hountondji's position must, however, be seen to be deeper than this. Under the influence of what Althusser calls "real humanism," Hountondji's dialectical philosophy is a formulation of the relation between consciousness and reality understood in terms of the reciprocally active creation by each one of the other. For dialectical Marxism, the questions of epistemology lead to the realm of ontology, and the relation between the two forms the basis for our understanding of the relation of knowledge and reality, and for an understanding of how we change reality. For Hountondji, philosophical discourse is essentially discourse on this dialectical relationship between knowledge and reality. Philosophy can therefore not be a reified body of beliefs.

For Hountondji, then, philosophy must attempt to make a union with politics. For him, the task of philosophy lies in Marx's formulation of the nature of political philosophy, which is to say, the correlative political realization of philosophy and the philosophical realization of politics. In this sense, a vision of the good society is an indispensable aspect of the movement of those who must change the destiny of African peoples. In contrast to Nkrumah and Towa, Hountondji states that philosophy cannot be reduced to a mere metaphysical commentary on politics. It is not just an ideological discourse. Philosophy must not be absorbed into politics.

Again like Althusser, Hountondji appears to demand the replacement of "theoretical humanism" by "real humanism," for freedom and progress are not achieved on the basis of what people should be, or on the basis of the ethno-philosophical cult of difference; it lies rather in the concept of dialectical and mutual creation as mediated through labor and accessible through active humanism. We neither create *ex nihilo* nor are we simply and completely acted upon by the overwhelming ratification of the *en soi*. Philosophy, says Hountondji, "must place itself on the terrain of science itself, as the ultimate source of power that we seek, and it must contribute in some way to its progress"[24] and involvement in the dialectical progress of reality. What Africa needs is therefore neither metaphysics nor ideology, but material power.

In view of this stand, V. Y. Mudimbe makes a correct observation when he states that Hountondji represents the neo-Marxist ideology in regard to the role of philosophy in the context of social and human studies in Africa.[25] The call that African philosophers need to turn their attention to more persistent and practical problems is a pragmatic flavor that is shared by many African philosophers who are difficult to classify as propounding any kind of Marxism. Peter Bodunrin[26] and Lansana Keita,[27] for example, make this vigorous call in their arguments against Odera Oruka's "Sagacity in African Philosophy." Before them, Mana Ka,[28] in his analysis of the thoughts of Nyerere and Nkrumah, had made a similar call for African philosophers to face the fundamental problem of development. Eventually, this is the kind of thing that Odera Oruka does in his *Punishment and Terrorism in Africa*, a philosophical analysis and evaluation of two of Africa's deadliest modern practices within state apparatus.

Not everyone who makes a call for the pragmatic approach to African philosophy is classifiable, like Hountondji, as a neo-Marxist. Admittedly, however, in order to draw attention to such serious problems as injustice, exploitation (by which is often meant low salaries), and imbalanced international trade relations, the Marxist theory of society is often suggested as a point of contrast with the *status quo*, not necessarily as adherence to Marxism, but sometimes more as philosophical openness to diverse theories that can help identify the nature of Africa's problems. In this regard philosophy is presented as a forum for diverse views, as a forum for a true democratic dialogue.

Kwasi Wiredu: Truth and the Question of African Philosophy

Wiredu's view on ethnophilosophy is moderate in comparison with the views of Towa and Hountondji on the same issue. Although he is a strong believer in the Western foundationalist model of rationality, and although he recognizes significant differences between the forms of knowledge prevalent in the traditional society and the modern scientific forms of knowledge, Wiredu does not consider the two historical cultural contexts as entirely irreconcilable. For him, ethnophilosophy is essentially a system of prescientific or preindustrial folk philosophies that have no direct relevance for the modern African who has adopted modern patterns of living. By "modern patterns of living" is to be understood living by integrating not only the use of modern machinery into one's life, but also the methods and techniques of acquiring knowledge so characteristic of modern disciplines of study, including philosophy. Both are important ways of living in the modern world.

In the practice of philosophy, however, modern African philosophers can fruitfully "integrate [their] individual reflections upon African material, upon themes contained in traditional African systems of thought, into a comprehensive philosophical enterprise informed in its spirit and methods by the canons of Western philosophy."[29]

This position, as presented above by Abiola Irele, leads to the question: What is the relationship between the modern African philosopher and his enterprise on the one hand and the traditional thought system on the other? This question solicits an answer that will be a valuation of ethnophilosophy or of traditional African thought in general and makes part of the long philosophical debate on rationality. In his book *Philosophy and an African Culture* Wiredu makes various points which can be taken together as forming an answer to the above question and so as forming a valuation of the nature and status of traditional thought and ethnophilosophy in the light of the demands and predications of modernity.

Although Wiredu's book is basically a collection of articles previously written and/or published independently of each other, their selection and publication together in book form is not without a certain uniform pattern of reasoning that binds them together, however loosely. The book is divided into three parts. Part I is dedicated to discussing African philosophy and philosophy in Africa. It is a direct critique of ethnophilosophy. Part II is a reworking of dialectical epistemological theory and a redefinition of philosophy from the point of view of Marxist dialecticism. Part III is dedicated to a general discussion of issues in epistemology and logic. Wiredu therefore uses a retrograde style by first discussing specific issues concerning the status and historical significance of ethnophilosophy in contemporary Africa, and then moving progressively into general theoretical issues the discussion of which, in fact, significantly enlightens the positions held in the first two parts. On the question of ethnophilosophy, the papers of Part I of Wiredu's book state his position in a direct manner. The papers of Part III deal with general issues of philosophy, yet give a wider theoretical support to the position held in Part I. The two papers of Part II, standing between the positions of the other two parts, are not oddly placed either, for what Wiredu says of the characteristics of ideology and utopianism runs well with what we believe is the central point that the book tries to defend; they give the notion of functional relativism in philosophy its historical grounding in the thoughts of Marx and Engels.

In the following presentation we have tried first to reconstruct Wiredu's general theoretical framework. Then we have gone on to apply this theoretical framework to his valuation of ethnophilosophy. In so doing, we have had to start with an analysis of the papers of Part III and then move on to tie their central argument with the positions of Parts I and II. The significance of this method, Wiredu says, is that we give the impression that the book has one central theme that runs through it, which was neither his original intention nor a consequent he has himself noticed. Our point is, however, that there are indeed at least two different arguments in the book: one on knowledge and valuation, and the other on the status of ethnophilosophy. What we say further is that the first argument, which is the last in the book, has something to give in support of the second argument, which is the first in the book. Without minimizing the value of the papers on Marxism and utopianism in Part II of Wiredu's the book, it is our view that the appearance of these two papers between the other two groups of papers reduces their role to that of historical illustration of the argument in Part III of the book.

Knowledge, Action, and Evaluation

In *Philosophy and an African Culture*, Wiredu adopts the position that although traditional African thought does not contain much that is, in its traditional form (as a stock of originally unwritten proverbs, maxims, usages, etc.), philosophically significant for us today, nevertheless it *was* a philosophy in its own right and context. Between the traditional society and the modern one, there are significant contrasts that must be taken into consideration. These contrasts are about living styles. In traditional times, the societies were simpler and organized science was as yet unknown. But traditional societies established their own values, including techniques and methods of reasoning and acquiring knowledge which solved some of the problems that arose out of that particular lifestyle. "For good or ill," Wiredu says, "that milieu is no more."[30] In contrast, the contemporary society reveals the inescapable influence of science or its industrial and technological consequences in the lives of a large and rapidly increasing proportion of mankind. This contrast between traditional and contemporary societies is true of Africa as it is of other parts of the world.

The contrasts in living styles reflect another contrast that exists in the areas of the kind of knowledge, morality, and social ties prevalent in the two historical scientific contexts. Numerous studies of the tensions that exist in the various aspects of life as a result of the meeting of the traditional and modern sets of values have been done in such areas as political practice, ideology, and the religious, moral, and social values of a changing culture. We are not concerned with all those areas of inquiry. What interests us here is the specific area of rationality, for Wiredu's argument is about the errors quite often made in applying a set of techniques of knowledge or of reasoning developed in the context of a particular system of rationality or life-style to the solution of problems inherent in another, radically different, system of rationality or life-style.

The argument which Wiredu advances in Part III of his book may be put as follows: knowledge, action, and evaluation are essentially connected. The primary significance of knowledge, for him, lies in its guidance of action, for knowing is for the sake of doing. The verification of knowledge, it would appear for Wiredu, depends on whether or not we are able to derive action from it, since to verify is to submit what is in question to the test of some experience. To know is to apprehend the future as qualified by values which action may realize; and empirical knowledge is essentially utilitarian and pragmatic. The utility of knowledge, Wiredu seems to argue, lies in the control it gives us, through appropriate action, over the quality of our future experience. These considerations do emphasize the essential relations between the knowledge we seek of objective facts, the values we hope to realize in experience, and the actions which, guided by the one, move toward the other. In this respect, Wiredu appears to hold the opinion that whoever knows or claims to know must always indicate the facts or state of affairs he refers to, because all knowledge involves an epistemological determination by circumstances. And he defines the epistemologically determinant circumstances as "such things as the nature of the evidence available to the most determined research, the existing background of accepted knowledge and the degree of development of experimental and logical techniques."[31] Such circumstances together form the *epistemological point of view*, or, simply, just the *point of view* on which truth value predications are usually based. For Wiredu, as it was for John Dewey, truth is rationally warranted assertibility. Note, however, Wiredu's own account of the difference between him and Dewey:

> For Dewey the relation between truth and rationally warranted assertibility is one of analytic kind. For me it is a synthetic relation, since not all points of view are rational. In my view the claim that truth is rationally warranted assertibility holds only in the case of normal belief. This relation between truth and rationality arises not from the formal significance of truth but from the substantive nature of belief . . . [from] an account of the vital importance of truth. [Access to the vital importance of truth] can only be done by a substantive exposition of the concepts in terms of which the formal definition of truth is fashioned. By a substantive exposition of a concept I mean an account that is not principally concerned with disclosing its conceptual relations but with its very possibility.[32]

According to Wiredu, then, a formal definition of truth as a rationally warranted assertibility is not sufficient unless we also give account of the circumstances under which the definition itself obtains. Such an account can be given by way of answering such questions as: "What are its canons? What is the fundamental basis of those canons and what role do they play in the interactions and transactions of human beings with their environment and with their own kind?"[33] For Wiredu, these questions are much more important than the formal analytic issues that are often raised about truth. The problem of truth begins with the concrete life of the people, with problems to be solved. Wiredu's position regarding the grounding of truth, that is, regarding the interrelations between knowledge, action, truth, and interests, is a fairly eclectic one. It brings him under the orbit of a number of social philosophers other than just Dewey. For example, his ideas regarding truth resemble Jürgen Habermas's ideas on truth. In the words of Habermas, "knowledge-constitutive interests take form in the medium of work, language and power."[34] But even more precisely, this contention brings Wiredu into agreement with Engels where the latter, he says, "asserts that a consciousness of limitation is a necessary element in all acquired knowledge; which limitation consists in 'the fact that it is conditioned by the circumstances in which it was acquired.' "[35] Truth is and cannot be anything more than opinion in the sense of a point of view.

Thus, the definition of knowledge and truth must include also the human or existential dimension. What humans know they know according to given circumstances within which the knowing process takes place and actualizes itself. These circumstances "define" the "res" according to the dispositions of the tamed "intellectus." This attempt to place the traditional theories of truth under a more general and humanistic consideration of truth is essentially the position that was advanced by Edmund Husserl in his re-proposition of the Kantian transcendental consciousness in the theory of *epoche*. In this sense, truths and meanings must be seen as *relative* "intentionalities," opinions or points of view, so that every originally offering (available) view is a legitimate source of knowledge. Even science is itself dependent on the existential situation of the people and therefore on a general metaphysical conception of a world order which alone explains its origins and validity, as the English philosopher John Locke remarked:

> Had you or I been born at the Bay of Soldania, possibly our thoughts and notions had not exceeded those brutish ones of the Hottentots that inhabit there. And had the Virginia king Apochancana been educated in England, he had been perhaps as knowing a divine, and as good a mathematician as any in it; the difference between him and more improved Englishman lying barely in this, that the exercise of his faculties was bounded within the ways, modes, and notions of his own country, and never directed to any other or further inquiries.[36]

Thus, despite the racist tone of his language, Locke still affirmed the relativity of knowledge, and seemed to be saying that we cannot separate the subject from the object in the discussion of knowledge, that knowledge is significant only within the inseparable relationship between the "intellectus" and the "res."

Truth as Opinion

At first sight, the saying that "there is nothing called truth as distinct from opinion" seems to be the most perplexing philosophical statement a man of Wiredu's stature could ever make. It is both paradoxical and confusing and, according to Wiredu himself, it has also been greatly misunderstood. The greatest misunderstanding, perhaps, is apt to be about the apparent relativism which the title of the essay "Truth as Opinion" quickly suggests.

While the subjective view tries to separate the object of knowledge ("res" as it is in itself) from the knowing subject ("intellectus"), Wiredu endeavors to reinstate the indispensable role of the subject (in his cognitive act) in the knowledge of *reality*. In this way, he hopes to defend George Berkeley's paradox "esse est percipi." His own paradox, that "to be true is to be opined," is only a special case of this principle, which he has expressed even more generally as "For anything whatever, to be is to be apprehended."[37]

The central notion of this paradox is not the denial of objective truth as such, but that even objective truth does not have much sense when separated from the cognitive relation which, according to the view in question, actually does determine what is true and what is not at any given time and place. Hence, Wiredu says, "in the case of truth . . . we must recognize the cognitive element of *point of view* as intrinsic to the concept of truth. Truth, then, is necessarily joined to point of view, or better, *truth is a view* from some point; and there are as many truths as there are points of view."[38]

Note that we have put emphasis on the phrase "truth is a view." We have done so because we feel that the phrase is vital in distinguishing Wiredu's use of the term *opinion* from its popular use, which is normally meant to give the sense of uncertainty, probability, and disputability. In the sense in which he uses it, Wiredu takes the word *view* to mean a judgment or set of judgments made up of specific concepts about reality. This differs from the kind of truths and errors we sometimes talk about in perceptual situations, such as illusions. The latter, it is to be understood, are determinable in their correct forms; that is, we are able to know physiological and psychological conditions that may lead to certain "appearances" which are in fact erroneous, and, by elimination of these conditions, and with the aid of some scientific methods, we are able to arrive at the knowledge of things as they really are. Such kinds of "appearances" or "opinions" are therefore corrigible and do not fall under what Wiredu means here as "opinion."

At this point Wiredu needs to explain how his view does not embody relativism. Indeed, in his most recent essays[39] Wiredu sharply criticizes relativism in a manner that we shall return to shortly. It is true that people have common basic ways of perceiving reality. It is equally true that with the advancement of science many areas that were once left as (intersubjectively) unknowable worlds of secondary qualities are becoming more easily determinable as areas of objective knowledge. But even science itself is regulated by a principle of relativism of sorts —its hypothetical nature—which has lived with it since ancient times. Clearly, Wiredu is not admitting individualistic relativism. But he cannot refute fully the type of relativism held by pragmatists whose thought has largely been a development of scientific relativism. One of these, Ferdinand Schiller, is known for his celebration of the ancient saying of Protagoras that "man is the measure of all things, of what is that it is, and of what is not that it is not."[40] But the "man" of these pragmatists is not the individual, but the human species. And even in Protagoras himself, the saying arose out of circumstances that were largely socio-cultural rather than individualistic. For John Dewey, thought has only an instrumental value, that is, insofar as it serves to reorganize an experience whose elements are in conflict and to reestablish a balance in the system. A certain system of thought is true according to this view, therefore, only in relation to a particular situation but not definitively, because conflict reappears with the needs of new situations and adaptations.

Wiredu, however, claims not to believe in relativism of any kind, and considers our interpretation of his "Truth as Opinion" as exaggeratedly leaning on the side of relativism. In this connection, it is appropriate to state here that there is no doubt that Wiredu endorses the thesis of the instrumentalist or participial theory of knowledge and truth as developed by John Dewey and C. I. Lewis, which, in our view, embodies relativism. This relativism is certainly not subjective relativism, which lays emphasis on the personal and transitory physiological and psychological states of the individual as the basis of truth value predication. Rather, it is one which ascribes to reason a historical and empirical method and vocation. It is a relativism of systems of rationality. For Dewey, as for Wiredu,[41] the justification of the procedures by which knowledge is attained and responsible moral conduct is practiced is to be found in the continued application of those procedures in effecting successful results. A method that regularly (even if not always) leads to satisfactory consequences with respect to specific problems is to that extent justified; that is, it is justified by its fruits. Obviously for Wiredu, as for Dewey, the method which has attained the greatest number of successes—and is by far most likely to continue to do so—is the experimental method of modern science. In this respect, people who live in the modern scientific situation have no business in *exhuming* or *defending* the procedures of knowledge obtaining in the traditional systems. The all-important point that needs to be noted is that problems of contemporary society must be dealt with in accordance with contemporary procedures of knowledge. In our view, this kind of reasoning embodies relativism. Furthermore, there is nothing incompatible about holding a relativist thesis in regard to the instrumentalist role of reason while also holding a rigid objectivist or realist thesis in the areas of science. The combination of the two, in any case, makes the world of experience.

But even at its best explanation, "truth as opinion" does not escape hints of some kind and extent of relativism, unless by this phrase Wiredu would understand only absolute subjectivism. If Wiredu holds—as he seems to do, judging from our personal discussions with him—that his saying "truth is opinion" has nothing to do with relativism, it will be upon him to dispel this otherwise ambiguous contention looming over the essay.

He further says that his main objective in the essay was not, as is seemingly being understood by some of his critics, to furnish a theory of truth. His main concern has been with judgment of rather than with reality. In other words, he is concerned with analyzing bases of rationality. In this respect, the problem shifts from truth as referring to the objective reality to another sense of truth as referring to the possible judgments we are able to draw from this reality. V. G. Childe, in his *Society and Knowledge*, defines "truth" in this second sense as "the correspondence of the conceptual reproduction of reality with the external reality it should reproduce."[42] To Childe, this conceptual model of reality exists in systems of propositions (that is, language patterns in which symbols, as the expressions of the concepts of which the "reproduction" is made up, have meanings), so that truth becomes a property of propositions. It becomes a correspondence between the meanings conveyed by propositions and the external world. Knowledge would then be a system of propositions which would be true insofar as they correspond with the external world. Childe writes: "But knowledge is not a prerogative of my head or yours; only the many heads of society comprehend it, and it is Society that expresses it in a system of propositions."[43]

It is clear, therefore, that Wiredu talks of truth in Childe's sense, that is, of truth as the propositions in which a society believes, and as contradistinct from truth in the sense of trueness.

If we posit that these lines express the central thesis of the essay, we can further bring him closer to the sociologists of knowledge by saying that even to him the function of knowledge is practical, at least in the attempt to achieve some measure of cohesion in human behavior. This being so, it follows that truth as defined above can be tested only by the degree of action it is supposed to solicit. By way of example, we are able to judge the truths of traditional African "philosophy" by indicating whether or not by them Africans of the time in question were able to achieve the ends reflected in their "philosophy" or "philosophies." If they did, then they were true regardless of whether or not the same "philosophies" would still be meaningful to the modern African of the industrialized world. "From the propositions that express it, can be deduced practically serviceable rules for behaviour. The success of action, guided by the rules thus deduced, is the decisive test of the truth of the proposition from which they are derived."[44] In this sense we have many truths according to different generations of even a single society as well as according to different societies. It is these "truths," it appears, that Wiredu says can be talked of as opinions, for always a new set of true propositions replaces the old.

Another reference to Childe might help us make this point clearer. Childe, to clarify this somewhat shocking and confusing assertion further, gives as example the contrast between the Ptolemaic or geocentric system of astronomy (according to which the sun, the planets, and the stars, like the moon, revolve round the earth) and Copernicus' heliocentric system (according to which it is the earth which rotates round the sun). According to Childe, these two positions, however different, do not point to any "error" in the former system, even if the latter, having more empirical data, asserted the contrary and achieved more accurate predictions (of eclipses). And Childe says: "Yet, I repeat, the Ptolemaic system was true as long as it enjoyed unchallenged social endorsement. Beliefs, now dismissed as errors or mistakes, were once truths,"[45] and "Error like truth is relative, or rather both are correlative. What once were truths are recognizable as errors only when contrasted with superior [later?] truths. Still the latter's superiority can only be vindicated operationally."[46] In other words, for Childe as for Wiredu, commensurability between different rationalities or forms of rationality is a historical and dialectical fact. Its rationale is the historical or dialectical nature of the growth of knowledge. The inference from this, for Wiredu, is that the indubitable superiority of Western rationality over traditional thought or rationality is a historical and dialectical truth.

These positions lead logically—even though Wiredu may claim derivation is irrelevant here since it was never his intention but to develop all the essays of the book as different and independent of each other—to the pragmatic (anthropological) defense and historical rejection of traditional African philosophy all at the same time.

The Question of Relativism

Those who are acquainted with Wiredu's later essays on the questions of "truth" and "relativism" will be hesitant to accept the impression that he is a relativist in any of the senses we construe here, or that he is necessarily pessimistic about cross-cultural dialogue between different modes of thinking or canons of rationality. In fact Wiredu thinks that relativism has received undue sympathy from recent philosophical thought. On the other hand, he believes that opining, representing, reasoning, conceiving—all have their place and function. According to Wiredu, they are more useful and necessary in most respects than they are usually thought to be. The accustomed ways of grasping thinking, according to him, are so stubborn because they have their own truth. Thus there is always a struggle to advance a new way of seeing things because customary ways and preconceptions about it stand in the way. The situation is similar to learning a foreign language: forgetting our mother tongue is the chief difficulty.

Wiredu makes no claim that traditional thinking can produce knowledge as do the sciences, nor that it can promote usable practical wisdom, solve any medical or mechanical problems. Yet, at the same time, traditional knowledge, for him, is part and parcel of the universal cognitive characteristics embodied in the sciences. Wiredu's project works toward a theory of the independent role of a kind of thinking that belongs to the sciences and which is at once pragmatic and universal.

For Wiredu as for George Berkeley, whose dictum that *esse est percipi*

Wiredu uses in a most original way, humans relate to their world by knowing it. For Berkeley, what *is* cannot be distinguished from what *is known*. To say that there is a world completely separate from the self is to sidestep the question of the nature of the world. If the reasoning self is established as a privileged substance in the world, the whole question of consciousness and knowledge becomes absurd. The mind that knows, the world that is known, and the relationship between them, cannot be separate issues.

This position illustrates Wiredu's advance in his recent work[47] to a radical reductionist materialism or physicalism which purports an order of invariance in the constitution of persons, of the physical world, and of the way persons relate epistemically to the physical world. This advance is compatible with the strong thesis of materialism that all mental and psychological attributes are reducible to physical or material attributes, explainable or analyzable without remainder in terms of such attributes. His insistence first that cultural universals—which he identifies as "the fact of language," logical reasoning (which includes the capacity of reflective perception, abstraction, and inference), knowledge of the objective world, and morality—are the only valid criteria for validating the universality of concepts, and second that conceptual communication, translatability, and commensurability within and across cultures are possible, without remainder, only through their reduction to physical reality, implies a reductionism which conjoins to materialism and physicalism. He says:

> [I]t is tautologically obvious that for any two persons to communicate at all they must share some common medium of communication. In turn this implies that at some level they must share a conceptual scheme, however minimal its dimensions. Any such scheme of concepts is a universal for the given participants in the communication, at least. The question now is "Is there any scheme of concepts which is shared by all the cultures of humankind?"
>
> This last question is equivalent to asking whether there is anything about which all different cultures of the world *can* communicate. The answer, in fact, is "Everything."[48]

For him, then, mental and psychological attributes must be universal because they are based on the invariant universality of the physical and material attributes—of humans and the physical world—to which they are reducible. Wiredu further provides a semantic rule in terms of which all mental and psychological predicates may be shown to be interculturally translatable by physical predicates. His example is the translatability of the concept rendered in English as "chairness" into Akan as "the circumstance of something being a chair."

This rule differs from W. V. Quine's view regarding the radical indeterminacy of translation on the basis of which it is possible to construct two incompatible ontologies each fitting a native speaker's utterance under simulation conditions without being able to decide conclusively which ontology is the correct one. According to Quine, the view about such translatability as defended by Wiredu is due to

a stubborn feeling that a true bilingual surely is in a position to make uniquely right correlations of sentences [or words] generally between his languages. This feeling is fostered by an uncritical mentalistic theory of ideas: each sentence [or word] and its admissible translations express an identical idea in the bilingual's mind . . . ; for my point is then that another bilingual could have a semantic correlation incompatible with the first bilingual's without deviating from the first bilingual in his speech dispositions within either language, except in his dispositions to translate.[49]

Because of his materialist reductionist theory, Wiredu cannot admit such indeterminacy of translation as implied by Quine except in weak noncognitive cases. According to him, the reductibility of mental and psychological predicates to physical and material ones allows not only for intercultural conceptual translatability but also for the possibility to determine which of the ontologies is correct and which one wrong, which one rational and which other irrational. He says:

And because a fundamental law governing this interaction is the drive for self-preservation and equilibrium, the essential discriminations of items of the environment, which the possession of the concept of object in general makes possible, will be of the same basic kind in fact, though not in name, among all humankind. These essential discriminations will obviously be of the objects or events of direct perception. . . . But at this level there is a basic similarity of conceptualization among humans by dint of semi-instinctual constraints.[50]

Wiredu appears to differ from Quine in one fundamental sense common to most adherents of reductive materialism or physicalism. For him, persons are essentially sentient beings, although they are also intelligent, with the capacity to communicate linguistically. I do not know Quine's definition of person, but he is at least not a reductionist in this sense. Wiredu's reductionism assumes what we have already refuted about Kagame on the question of linguistic universals, that is, the claim that the human mind is by nature so constructed that all so-called languages are determinate articulations of an innate or native set of invariant rules.

This theory has had its opponents. Noam Chomsky, who is himself credited with originating the theory of linguistic universals, reviewed it later toward the position held by Quine. In this review he says:

I have been using mentalistic terminology quite freely, but entirely without prejudice as to the question of what may be the physical realization of the abstract mechanisms postulated to account for the phenomena of behavior or the acquisition of knowledge. . . . It is an interesting question whether the functioning and evolution of human mentality can be accommodated within the framework of physical explanation, as presently conceived, or whether there are new principles, now unknown, that must be invoked, perhaps principles that emerge only at higher levels of organization than can now be submitted to physical investigation.[51]

The point here is that Chomsky realizes that linguistic universals are rules and not laws of nature as they are for Wiredu. Although Chomsky still held the view that there is correlation between structures of grammar and mental structures, the above revised statement made the fundamental point that because linguistic universals are rules rather than laws of nature, "they may be violated and conformed to—and therefore behave intentionally."[52]

Commenting on Chomsky's own self-revision, Joseph Margolis, a nonreductive materialist and relativist, concludes that "*if* intentionality and, in particular, the intensionality [*sic*] of language and of rules are irreducible, *then there can be no purely physical explanation of the psychological capacity of human beings to behave linguistically.*"[53] And I am almost tempted to concede with Margolis the next point, that "It looks very much as if, *if* language is irreducible in the manner conceded, then linguistic ability (which is a property of persons) is similarly irreducible."[54]

Chomsky's passage above argues against Wiredu and, by extension, also against Kagame on the subject of learning one's own and another language. While Wiredu and Kagame hold that learning one's own or another language and communicating in them are possible on account of a naturalist relationship between mentalist capacity, invariance of the physical reality and conceptual universality, Chomsky maintains that "the person who has acquired knowledge of a language has [only?] internalized a system of rules that relate sound and meaning in a particular way" without necessarily enlarging the concept of "physical explanation." For example, a statement such as "*X* is *Y*" may be considered to have different meanings and different deductive consequences for members of separate conceptual schemes. It may mean, in one such conceptual context, the *identity* of *X* and *Y* such that to say "*X* is *Y*" is assumed to mean that *X* is equal or identical in some fundamental or essential way to at least part of *Y* in a manner that is in accordance with the rational requirements assumed within that specific context such as what of *X* and of *Y* warrant their conjunctibility. Such assumptions clearly guide the uses—and the judgments thereof—of the conjunctive copula "is" as well as other linguistic forms with logical-cognitive consequences. The outcome is an image of epistemological and linguistic uniformity among people who share such a context. Let us say that such kind of sharing constitutes a community defined by a common system of rationality.

Wiredu's argument draws a close relation to the debate on Nuer sayings which we discussed above in chapter six. The debate on the meanings of the Nuer sayings that "Oxen are cucumbers" and "Twins are birds" focused on the rationality of the Nuer in the context of the logical-cognitive implications of the sayings in their English translations. As is known from its history, the debate focused on the "questionable" conceptual implication of the conjunctions the Nuer made of cows and cucumbers and of (human) twins and birds. Obviously the departure of the questioning was the application, to the English translations of the sayings, of the rule of syntax which states that conjunctive copulas such as "is" (or "are" in plural) can be used only to conjunct things which belong, first, to the same category or which have "identity" between them.

The significance of Wiredu's theory to the Nuer debate is that, first, the controversy could not have been about the Nuer's defective perception of the objective world. He would therefore argue that if the sayings could not be properly translated, then this probably meant that they could not be reduced to cognitive properties of the physical world. And so they must have been just some of the many irrational aspects of our traditions. According to Wiredu, the mental activities of reflective perception, abstraction, and inference are the same for all human persons irrespective of whether they inhabit Europe, Asia, or Africa. In particular, he says, the concept of object in general is the same for all beings capable of "reflective perception, for to recognize something as an X is to perceive it as an X rather than a non-X, which implies that it is not both X and non-X."[55] This is the foundation of the Principle of Noncontradiction. According to Wiredu, there are, apart from these universal mental activities or processes, also many common facts of the physical human habitat which make communication possible intra- and interculturally.

The significance of the Nuer examples to Wiredu's argument, on the other hand, is that they reveal the limitations of the physicalist reductionist theory of language in a significant way. The ability to construe a physical concept such as "chairness" in one word and differently in another cultural-linguistic context is in itself a significant pointer: that although the capacity to acquire language is universal, the actual acquisition of language is a cultural process. And the argument could be extended to the other "cultural universals" of Wiredu. Thus persons, as we know them, are culturally emergent rather than only subjects of natural laws.

Wiredu might however argue, like Margolis, that the admission of persons as culturally emergent does not in the least entail the admission of a substance other than matter out of which, dualistically, persons are composed.[56] Margolis still declares his position as hospitable to materialism of a nonreductive strand. However, Margolis's position that linguistic competence is culturally acquired regardless of whatever *innate lawlike* regularities may facilitate such acquisition is already a big step in the outward direction from reductionism. His position is particularly clear in regard to language. He says:

> But it is very clear, admitting the irreducibility of the intentional, that poems for instance exhibit certain inherent intentional properties as of the significance

of the words of which they are composed, their historically qualified style, and their inherent purposiveness. [Thus] No purely physical account of language can be supported; and words and sentences themselves cannot be reduced to mere physical marks or sounds. It seems reasonable to consider, therefore, that words and sentences are embodied in physical sounds and physical marks and are culturally emergent items of some sort; . . . [57]

"The embodiment relation is, therefore," Margolis concludes, "*sui generis*: [it] signifies a use of "is" distinct from that of identity and composition." Other opponents of the reductive physicalist theory include Herbert Feigl and Wilfrid Sellars,[58] who admit that intentional discourse cannot be reduced to discourse about purely physical phenomena. Supporting the theory of intentionality, Margolis argues that such cultural entities are to be treated as both culturally emergent and materially embodied. In their material embodiment, persons, for example, may be considered, like Wiredu does, as physically embodied in the sense of being sentient but also intelligent beings capable of the use of language and of self-reference. But apart from this, there are also cultural qualifications which explain persons as more complex compositions in senses that cannot be reduced to physical-instinctual levels. Similarly, words and sentences may be considered as both physical signs and complexes of culturally emergent meanings. Thus words and sentences do not perform the same functions for everybody. Apart from their physical embodiment and their reference to physical phenomena, words also play a vital role in communicating intentional or culturally emergent entitities and meanings.

Thus Chomsky, Feigl, Sellars, and Margolis establish a midway position which accepts the universality of the physical reality, but also variances in ways of representing this reality including the presence of physically irreducible cultural entities. They reject the mentalistic theory which relates language and knowledge in universal and invariant terms. They focus particularly on the diverse ways of articulating thought, as we have seen in reference to the Nuer, which reveal differences in ways people articulate concepts operative within their specific systems constituted by a combination of epistemological and linguistic elements. It is this combination which makes certain propositions sensible for some speakers and not for others. Drawing on linguistic characteristics similar to the ones we pointed out in our discussion of Kagame, namely that different people have different linguistic forms for expressing or suggesting various concepts, Wiredu argues in defense of intra- and intercultural translatability of concepts. This much granted. But his position is radically different in that he introduces the theory of reductive physicalism as the justification for intertranslatability in his sense.

The problem, however, is that such intertranslatability is hard to generalize. Kagame's *a priori* conviction in favor of the generality of such intertranslatability led him to invent many linguistic forms for expressing concepts which are not known to many Bantu-speaking peoples. His ambition was to show not just such conceptual intertranslatability between various Bantu languages, but also between them on the one hand and Western philosophical language on the other. We have shown that Kagame had significant problems trying to prove this thesis. We pointed out then that one of Kagame's basic errors was the attempt to establish intertranslatability between the specialized philosophical language of the West and the natural language(s) of the Bantu. A more useful option for Kagame would have been to establish a rule of abstraction for Bantu languages which could be used for specialized purposes like philosophical abstraction. In fact, his own description of his project in the traitorous phrase "se non è vero, è ben trovato (if not true, then cleverly invented)" had the power of suggesting just this better option. But instead, he pushed his theory, erroneously, I believe, to prove the general structural "verità" of Bantu languages' ability to translate Western philosophical concepts. There would have been more weight if he had presented his thesis as a new or invented ("trovato") rule of abstraction for Bantu languages in respect of some key philosophical concepts and discourse.

Wiredu on the other hand argues, however, that problems of intertranslatability obtain also in intracultural situations involving people who differ in their basic conceptual beliefs or orientations despite their belonging to a similar cultural milieu, such as between idealists and empiricists.

In this view, intercultural and even intracultural communication are possible on account of the existence of conceptual universals. From this point Wiredu's argument is similar to the argument usually advanced against the theory of non-Euclidean geometry to prove that it would be inconsistent, on the basis of what it means to understand a concept, to uphold the existence of conceptual universals and deny that of epistemological universals. We already pointed out the argument against non-Euclidean geometry on the occasion of discussing Meinrad Hebga, above. But let us state it again to clarify its significance to Wiredu's argument. It is pointed out in the non-Euclidean geometry debate that there are no limitations to levels of abstraction and concept formation, such as the formation of the concept of spherical surfaces considered possible under the theory of non-Euclidean geometries. Theoretically, such concepts are thinkable; we can *conceive* the peculiar properties of a spherical surface. But the viability of a concept is not just that it is *conceivable*, but that it must also be serviceable. It must be applicable to the systematization of spatial experience; the properties of conceptual space must be transferable to and consistent with those of perceptual space. And there has been no hope that non-Euclidean formulas can be found to be so serviceable.

Similarly, Wiredu argues—against those who believe in the incommensurability between disparate conceptual schemes—that the theory of conceptual relativism would be hard to defend on similar grounds as those developed against non-Euclidean geometry. At best conceptual relativism is, like non-Euclidean geometry, fanciful. Thus, for him, granting the existence of conceptual universals must include granting epistemological universals in order to be both consistent and viable, for, he says, "[t]o understand a concept is to grasp its possibility of application, that is, the conditions under which *it is true* to say that the concept holds."

This view is hard to refute, particularly in relation to theories which abstract from common realities of experience such as physical reality and some aspects of social reality, particularly in ethics. The problem with it, however, is that it does not seem to be generalizable to all spheres of human experience. For example, both sides of the distinction between *conceptual* and *perceptual* spaces in the Euclidean versus non-Euclidean geometries debate agree that our physical world is neither in Euclidean nor in non-Euclidean space, both of which are conceptual abstractions. Their dispute is merely as to which of the sets furnishes the proper method for calculating spatial phenomena. Thus all the geometrical spaces are grounded on the same experience of physical space, which they interpret and idealize differently while seeking to simplify and systematize it by means of the various postulates which define them. The fact that both theories depart from the same experience of physical space makes it possible for us to evaluate each by assessing how its postulates relate to or make possible our handling of spatial experience or real space. And this does make it possible or even easy for anyone to reject non-Euclidean spatial theory on the basis of its epistemological implications. It is important to note, in agreement with Wiredu, that what makes this possible is the universality of our mental activities of reflective perception, abstraction, and inference as well as our physical constitution. All these universal conditions allow us to form a notion of physical space by fusing together the data derived from visual, tactile, and motor sensations. That fusion is largely accomplished by ignoring the differences between their several deliverances and by correcting the appearances to one sense by another in such a manner as to give the most trustworthy perception of the object.

But what does it mean, in Wiredu's own definition, to *understand* a proposition like "Oxen are cucumbers" or "Twins are birds" in the manner sketched above? Wiredu would argue that there is no bar to the understanding of the sayings, because they are expressed in human language as such. But "the fact of language" is not an experience. It is a capacity which enables us to *experience* languages in their diverse and varyingly complex and complexly variant forms. We therefore do not experience language in the same sense that we experience physical space. Although the ability to speak and to sense are, excepting cases of congenital and acquired impairments, both physical human endowments centered on the universal human somatic nature, there is no guarantee that whatever is speakable is physically reducible. And neither does the ability to sense *per se* imply the ability to speak. The universality of physically reducible concepts is by no means a feature peculiar to them, but may be explained as arising out of the methodological character of the assumptions on which they rest. Thus, while the ability to sense gives us access to fairly objective data about physical reality, the ability to speak does not guarantee the objectivity of its contents with the same degree. This feature of language is made more complex by the fact that not all concepts are derived from experience in the narrow physicalist sense of the term. Wiredu's reductionist theory does not cover such nonphysically reducible concepts.

The intercultural untranslatability of the Nuer sayings was not due to the irrationality of the Nuer, but to the erroneous assumption that they were making conjunctive statements of physical or metaphysical identity. Not that the Nuer do not or cannot make use of the mental activities of reflective perception, abstraction, and inference on which the principle of Noncontradiction is based, but rather that they do not always apply the law of conjunction in only one sense as the analytic overtones in the debate tended to restrict the meanings of the sayings in their English translations. Either they appear to have more uses for the conjunctive copula "is" than the law of conjunction allows for analytically minded speakers of the English language, or the English language was not culturally inclined to express the Nuer sayings in ways other than the structurally conjunctive. Another way of expressing this disjunction is in the following question form: Are the Nuer exceptions to the theory of the universality of the principle of Noncontradiction, or are their sayings an indication that concepts, and the belief system in which they are grounded, are sometimes more complex than we can reduce to physically universal statements? Without being defensive of the Nuer sayings, an acceptable answer seems to head in the direction of the concept of physically irreducible cultural entities suggested by Chomsky, Feigl, Sellars, and Margolis.

In the end, we need to state where this engagement with Wiredu's reductive physicalism leaves us. Our position, at least we believe, lies somewhere midway between, on the one hand, those who say that because we can identify cases of intercultural conceptual untranslatability and incommensurability, then all conceptual schemes must *in toto* be untranslatable and incommensurable, and, on the other hand, those who claim the converse, that because we can identify cases of intercultural conceptual translatability and commensurability, all conceptual schemes must *in toto* be translatable and commensurable. This position resembles what Margolis calls moderate conceptual incommensurability.[59]

Finally, I want to state, rather boldly, that the examples from the Nuer sayings mitigate against Margolis's claim[60] that cultural relativity is not a philosophical thesis at all in the sense that it does not involve "alethic questions—questions regarding the use of these or those truth-values—[which] are always, or always entail, legitimative questions." The point is this: if the sayings "Oxen are oxen" and "Oxen are cucumbers" can be used by the same people in a sense which does not entail claims of ontic change of "oxen" perceptively from being animals to being tubers or fruits or vegetables, then they are not identical with and cannot be reduced to the type of perspective-relative predicates like "looks red to S seen from here" as distinct from "looks blue to P seen from here" as discussed by Benjamin Whorf about cultural perspectival commitments. So, for the Nuer, the relationship between "Oxen are oxen" and "Oxen are cucumbers" is not one of perspectival relativity in the perceptive sense. Yet they are committed to both all the time. Thus, although Margolis is right in pointing out that the (mere) affirmation of different cultural commitments to separate values does not *per se* constitute a philosophical strategy, it is naive to assume that it is the only sense of cultural relativity.

The Nuer example, then, serves a double role: it enables us to refute the materialist and physicalist reductionism of Wiredu; but it also enables us to distinguish between the weak (noncognitive) sense of cultural relativity and another one—still nameless at this point—which is philosophically interesting. Consider the following statement from a college course description: "Contemporary Western thought makes two assumptions—that there is a natural set of links between various art genres or forms, and that the study of aesthetics is only relevant to these linked phenomena. . . . The purpose of this . . . course and lecture series is to counter the emphasis on Western élite categories in the study of African aesthetics." This statement describes what we call a weak sense of cultural relativity and which Margolis identifies as *first order* type, not only because its basis is the perceptive domain which can engender a perfect case for the strong sense of incommensurability, but also because it can only give us a *tabula* of features which separate Western art from African or other art traditions. And I believe that the Nuer saying that "Oxen are cucumbers" has cognitive implications in a way that the course description above has not.

To be is to be known

Wiredu's saying that "to be is to be known" is generally coherent with the theme of "truth as opinion." In view of the recent developments in Wiredu's position toward reductive physicalism as we have sketched above, we can now deduce that for Wiredu, "to be is to be known" expresses the strong thesis according to which the unity which connects the act of knowing to physical reality is the reductive disposition of each toward the other. It is based on a naturalistic thesis, and thus differs significantly from the structuralist philosophy which has references in the philosophy of consciousness developed in Germany in modern times. According to structuralist philosophy, the world as "world" exists only with reference to the knowing mind, and the mental activity of the subject, itself dependent on sociocultural and historical factors, determines the form in which the world appears. This position finely blends the ethnological structuralist position of the social anthropologist Lévi-Strauss with Karl Mannheim's sociology of knowledge. Lévi-Strauss laments (in opposition to Jean-Paul Sartre's *raison dialectique*) that

> it is forgotten that each of the tens or hundreds of thousands of societies which have existed side by side in the world or succeeded one another since man's first appearance, has claimed that it contains the essence of all the meaning and dignity of which human society is capable and, reduced though it may have been to a small nomad band or a hamlet lost in the depths of the forest, its claim has in its own eyes rested on a moral certainty comparable to that which we can invoke in our own case. But whether in their case or our own, a good deal of egocentricity and naivety is necessary to believe that man has taken refuge in a single one of the historical or geographical modes of his existence, when the truth about man resides in the system of their difference and common properties.[61]

According to Lévi-Strauss, the world is conceived as a structural unity of meanings and significations, as opposed to the medieval ontological world, which was conceived not only as consisting of a plurality of disparate events but also as a world existing independently of the knowing subject, in a fixed and definite form. In the structuralist view, everything depends on the manner of reacting to the world in all realms of experience—in folk spirit. Mannheim writes:

> Every fact and event in an historical period is only explicable in terms of meaning, and meaning in its turn always refers to another meaning. Thus the conception of the unity and interdependence of meaning in a period always underlies the interpretation of that period. Secondly, this interdependent system of meanings varies both in all its parts and in its totality from one historical period to another. Thus the reinterpretation of that continuous and coherent change in meaning becomes the main concern for our modern historical sciences . . .[62]

or, as Wiredu says it, of philosophy. These views, which cover such an immense area ranging from the sociology of knowledge to cultural anthropology and history, date back to the time of Michel de Montaigne (1533–92).[63]

Truth, therefore, is nothing more than opinion, because, according to Wiredu, it "belongs only to a comparative context wherein to be true is to coincide with a corroborative point of view."[64] Wiredu's argument can be rephrased in the following way: many times we are wrong when we make judgments on truth, especially in regard to situations different from those which we ourselves talk or judge from.

The following example, which came from a friend during a casual and non-philosophical conversation, may illustrate and clarify the point we wish to make here: Mountaineering as a sport is a relatively modern exercise in Africa, at least in Kenya, the country with which we are most acquainted. It was introduced by white foreigners who were used to the cold and snowy mountains and weather conditions in Europe. When these people came to Africa and projected their mountaineering impulses toward Mount Kenya, the second highest on the continent, they required local guides to lead them to the mountaintop. Though they accepted the temporary employment, the native climbers rejected the offer of specially designed cloaks brought by the Europeans for that kind of activity. The white man could not believe his ears, and exclaimed that it was impossible for anybody to reach those heights (17,000 ft.) barefoot and with only a thin blanket wrapped around the body as the natives were doing. My friend remarked here that because the white adventurers, used to their modern equipment for today's needs, find it impossible to climb Mt. Kenya barefoot, they think it must be equally impossible for anybody else to do the same without the "proper" equipment. When told that Kenyans living in the vicinity of the mountain had frequently gone barefoot to the mountaintop to pray, the white man remarked: "It is not true. It cannot be true." So because it is not possible for this foreigner to climb the mountain barefoot because his point of view—that is, his conditions created by the technological culture in which he permanently lives—forces him not to be able to see the other man's conditions as an alternative possibility, he thinks that what is untrue now and to him cannot be true to any other person and cannot have been true earlier either.

Wiredu would argue that it would be completely wrong for this foreigner to pretend he is able to come out of his cultural disposition so as to see this reality *as it is not* (now to him). The point is that the native, armed with all the possible equipment (facts) at his disposal, lived his own reality, in which climbing a mountain barefoot was a truth. "An expression is meaningless if it refers to no possible object or situation, etc.,"[65] but a proposition is not false simply because belief in it leads to harsh—rather than physically impossible—consequences.[66] Nor can we force this foreigner to accept the position of the native. The foreigner is differently equipped, both in clothing and intent, and, from his point of view, what he holds is equally true—but only to him and others who may have the same point of view as his. But Wiredu would add that, looked at more closely, the European regalia should offer better, superior, and more comfortable conditions of mountain climbing compared to the dangerous and unreliable traditional style.

In comparative inquiries, truth is relative—it is only opinion. Wiredu therefore defines objectivity as "conformity with the principles of rational inquiry"[67] in which the principles of rational inference must be subject to the situation within which they arise and where such identified principles are the sufficient rational tools required for the confrontation and explanation of the given reality "unto the day."

African Philosophy, Its Status and Validity

The conclusion of Wiredu on the value of traditional thought as philosophy can be inferred to be that although it would be difficult for us today to qualify traditional thought systems as philosophical, given our different (analytic and scientific) orientation in philosophy and in other fields of knowledge, there are many aspects of such thought systems which must be accepted as having been based on limited methodology and available evidence. The problem with the traditional thought habits is that they were hardly penetrated by rational methods. Traditional thought systems remained protected from critical and analytic thinking habits. These habits, Wiredu believes, are the roots of the processes of modernization and development. "Man should link the modernization of the conditions of his life with the modernization of all aspects of his thinking," he says. Africa's lagging behind the Western world in matters of development—including those of the degree to which modern science and technology are used to control, protect, and improve conditions of life—is clear evidence that Africa lags behind the West in the cultivation of rational and critical inquiry.

The urgent problem for Wiredu, therefore, is not whether or not traditional thought systems were philosophical, but the need to address some of the central ideas which may lead to the improvement of the conditions of life for Africans today. As he says, "The function of philosophy everywhere is to examine the intellectual foundations of our life, using the best available modes of knowledge and reflection for human well-being."[68] For this, Wiredu considers analytic philosophy as the therapy for African thought. Wiredu has no doubt that there must have been occasions and instances when and where traditional African thought systems performed this central function of philosophy to the satisfaction of the traditional society. This is, however, no longer sufficient, for there is a clear contrast between the traditional society and the present one. If intuition and emotion worked in the traditional society as claimed by Senghor, Wiredu would appear to say, that was fine. But can these methods of handling problems of life be really effective, today or at any other time? Wiredu rightly has his serious doubts. We cite him at length here from a passage which we believe answers not only this question but also that of the status of ethnophilosophy in general. He says:

> Admittedly, there is a place for intuition and emotion in life. Life is not all logic. But this kind of point is often covertly taken as an excuse for being unmindful of logic and rational procedures generally; as if from the fact that life is not all logic it follows that it is not logic in any part at all. On the contrary, it is as true in Africa as anywhere else that logical, mathematical, analytical, experimental procedures are essential in the quest for the knowledge of, and control over, nature and, therefore, in any endeavour to improve the condition of man. Our traditional culture was somewhat wanting in this respect and this is largely responsible for the weaknesses of traditional technology, warfare, architecture, medicine, etc. There can be little doubt that many of the hardships of traditional life were, and still are, traceable to this cause.[69]

In Wiredu's view, then, African traditional society was simple and unaware of the scientific and analytic methods of inquiry. But this does not warrant the inferential claim in ethnophilosophy that therefore the intuitionistic method used then applied to all departments of life, and worse still that it is the method which must obtain for Africans even in contemporary society. For the modern African philosopher, the urgent task of philosophy is to gain full understanding of the scientific and analytic methods of inquiry in answer to the problems of the environment in which the practice of philosophy occurs. As Horace Thayer writes, in his chapter on John Dewey, "The recurring challenge to reason is not to try to resist or transcend cultural change, but to give it intelligent direction."[70]

Hence those philosophers who are seeking to revive and reinstate the (past) traditional African philosophy as the appropriate philosophy for Africa today are not actually misunderstanding what philosophy is (as is the center of present debate); they are, however, doing disservice to Africa in trying to pretend that that philosophy is still sufficient or useful or applicable to Africa's needs, i.e., that it is able to cope with the new and modern problems and issues facing Africa today as brought in with encroaching modernization. And because this encroachment requires new methods of investigation and analysis, which must be diversified due to the complexity of the situation, ethnophilosophy just has no place in it.

Wiredu agrees with Bertrand Russell's suggestion in his (Russell's) *History of Western Philosophy* that "a philosopher, as far as truth permits, [is] an outcome of his *milieu*, a man in whom [are] crystallized and concentrated thoughts and feelings which in a vague and diffused form, [are] common to the community of which he [is] a part."[71] It is compelling, finally, to state that Wiredu does not hold a relativistic view in regard to traditional thought, although he admits there must have been, and might still be, many acceptable aspects of traditional knowledge. Wiredu believes that what is true is timelessly true, even if it addresses what is transient; hence, truth cannot be restricted merely to what appears or seems to be the case, and seeming incompatibilities regarding truth can only be relativized (benignly) to our contingent beliefs at this or that moment of inquiry. Any stronger claim of relativism must be incoherent or self-contradictory at some point in successful inquiry.

Odera Oruka vs. Wiredu on the Theory of Truth

Wiredu's theory of truth has not gone without criticism. Bedu-Addo, a classicist and scholar of the Akan language, addresses specifically Wiredu's claim that the concept *nokware* in the Akan language translates into the moral rather than the cognitive concept of truth. Bedu-Addo thus engages Wiredu in the analysis of what it means in Akan to say that a statement is or is not "true." In "On the Concept of Truth in Akan" (1985), Bedu-Addo argues that *nokware* is just one of several idioms Akan speakers use to express the idea of truth, and that it is often the context which determines when any one of these idioms is used to express either the moral or the cognitive sense of truth. On their own, these idioms, like the English word "truth," remain ambiguous as to which of the two categories of "truth" they may belong to or they may evoke. The criticism by Odera Oruka,[72] who has engaged Wiredu in numerous and consistent dialogues concerning the equation of truth and opinion, is important here because on the basis of it Wiredu saw the obligation to expand, even if only by way of clarification, on his theory of truth. Odera Oruka observes that for Wiredu, "there can be nothing true outside the whims and beliefs of the individual, no matter how wicked and stupid he may be. . . . [And] any principle of learning or education must be regarded as being purely arbitrary. Why should we have . . . rules of learning . . . when truth is but an opinion and there are as many truths as there are opinions?"[73]

In answer to this Wiredu gives three points to explain his position:

(1) That the formation of opinion is governed by rules—rules of evidence and rules of formal logic;

(2) That truth is normally the outcome of *rational inquiry*;

(3) That "truth is not relative to point of view. It *is*, in one sense, a point of view."[74]

Wiredu discusses the problem of truth on two levels. The first level is the discussion of the meaning of truth from the purely theoretical point of view. This level discusses the formal nature and principles that govern truth-claims and the making of inferences as well as their justification. As far as these are concerned, it seems, Wiredu has no objection to Odera Oruka's observations.

The snag comes, however, when Wiredu insists, as point three above shows, that his claim is not that truth is relative to point of view, but that it *is*, in one sense, *a* point of view. There appears to be an existentialist injection at this point —that is, a move on to a metaphysical plane, or what he (Wiredu) himself calls the "meta-theoretical" level where he is "not making truth-claims but only talking about them." In other words, Wiredu's discussion is about *the conditions* under which truth-claims and their contestations become sensible. He is concerned with the dialectically changing bases of rationality and the dialectical commensurability between these bases.

However, the point Odera Oruka raises is important in that it may render Wiredu's own point even clearer. Odera Oruka appears to understand Wiredu as saying that rules of logical validity are relative to the rules of logical soundness, which are in turn contingent upon varieties of experience. And since Odera Oruka uses "experience" in the personal context, his point, if correct, would signal great difficulties for Wiredu's theory of knowledge. Wiredu's point, however, is that the rules of logical soundness are controlled by principles of science which are universally applicable. These principles, Wiredu believes, arise out of a unilinear and universal historical progression of growth of knowledge. For him, then, any contestation of truth must take into account the principles in use which are produced by the proportionate relationship between anthropology and history. His point is, therefore, that contestations of truth become meaningful only under the laws of commensurability as explained by Marx in his dialectical theory of the growth of knowledge.

We had remarked earlier that Wiredu's theory of truth is reminiscent of Protagoras's famed saying on the same. Georgias of Leontini challenged Protagoras's claim by contending that because nothing is, all opinions are equally false. Protagoras, of course, based his claim on the fact of cultural diversity, similar to the present pluralist theory of rationality. He envisaged that concrete human life must be based on a body of truths concerning reality as well as human behavior. These truths must have been universal. But contact with other cultures and peoples revealed ways of life different from the usual Greek ones, and yet these people were happy too. Protagoras was led to conclude, therefore, that truths, especially those pertaining to human behavior, were variable, i.e., non-universal. Each truth had to be judged according to the amount of happiness it brought or failed to bring to the persons who believed in it. It is unclear to us what response Wiredu would give to Georgias, but he would certainly be in agreement with Protagoras in the sense in which we have interpreted him above. In other words, for Wiredu, any judgmental assertion is warranted by inquiry, as he says in point 2 above. And he also says that there is a certain correspondence between the warranted assertion and the problematic situation that give rise to inquiry. This is what Wiredu says in point 3 above, and explains at length in pages 210–212 of his book *Philosophy and an African Culture*.

Because the structure of knowing is dialectical, it moves from one point to the next, from a lower to a higher, from a less to a more comprehensive level; it is not flat. It does not comprehend its object entirely and totally at one given instance as light over a flat disc. It rather resembles the effect of the sun on the planet Earth. At every particular point of the globe, there is a specific reality particular to that point created by the relationship between the sun and the globe in its position. And each particular point throughout the entire globe has its own reality created by this relationship with the sun at one given time; one has twilight, another dawn, still another midnight, and another midday, etc. If taken singly, by themselves, each point represents a truth. But at each point's specific time, each of all the other points has its own truth, opposed to every other and to the first one. Thus while they are all true, they also equally exclude each other in that what is a truth at one point at that specific time is false to another. And since it is impossible for any finite being to be at a position to judge all these points together at one point at the same time, the only solution becomes that of a mathematical abstraction whose "relative" truth must be based on the position (point) in question in relation to the sun. From different perspectives no person can judge another.

But at any given time, to know the truth at stake, one must at least assume some position, must effect a relationship. "Is" always presupposes the imposing "I" from where it is radiated and to where it returns for concretization and expression. To be is to be known; that "something *is*" is an act of judgment, an act of self-presentation to consciousness, to a judging subject. And since an object can present itself to a consciousness only in one or more of its multiple characteristics (as a problem and object of inquiry), each one of such characteristics, because it is the result of the unity of the consciousness itself in relation to the object, is both true and false. It is true because each point of view is an expression of a unified and objective perception. And it is false because each position, compared with another, presents nonbeing, that which denies the actual reality. This, as Wiredu calls it, is the point of relativity or opinion. Truth is a point of view.

If to be is to be known, that is, if self-presentation of an object to consciousness is closely connected with the general unity of that specific consciousness, then logically what can be expressed of the object depends on the nature of every consciousness under consideration. In the claim that "to be is to be known," on which the discussion of truth is consequently based, Wiredu investigates the general forms of knowledge as the manifestation-presence of being to the human being. Every knowledge is a fact of *consciousness*, the latter being indicated as the *act of being present* of a thing, an object, an event, or a content and where *being present* means the actualized or realized relationship between an object and the active knowing faculty. It is only in these terms that we can talk of something as "is." To be is therefore to have this *coexistence* of object and intellect.

Expressed in this way, Wiredu's position on "to be is to be known" appears to have close affinity to some aspects of recent European continental philosophy, notably gnosiology, which developed in the fifties and sixties as the continental approach to the philosophical study of knowledge. But we have seen that Wiredu espouses a strong reductive physicalism. But here, in a strange turn, they appear as strange bedfellows in their critique of the correspondence theory of truth which posits a separation of the knowing mind from its object in a manner that neither physicalism nor gnosiology seems to accept. The difference, of course, is that gnosiologists are phenomenological while Wiredu remains empiricist. In contrast to epistemology in the definition and thinking of analytic philosophers, gnosiology developed in continental Europe along phenomenologico-metaphysical lines at the height of the revision of Kantian epistemology. According to Ugo Viglino, a passionate exponent of the gnosiological school, "The stone that flings down to the ground unnoticed, the light that escapes at an incredible speed on the other side of the globe in human absence, the fetus that is forming in the maternal womb, etc., are all *happening* without *being seen*; they are *advents* without *adverts*, the *not-yet-found*."[75] Consciousness, as an act in the process of knowing, means the act of "showing oneself" of whatever is happening. For the object, "to be [there] is the same thing as 'to *show* itself'."[76] To be is to be known. It is only in the light of being known that the verb "is" can be predicated of something.

The discussion of truth as opinion also appears at times to follow this phenomenologico-metaphysical exposition. Viglino writes:

> Radically, the problem of truth, if by this is meant the questioning of its *being* or *not being* (that is, whether there *is* any truth at all), is not the issue. [For] there is truth so long as there is being and its manifestation. The problem of truth is [thus] not whether or not there is truth in general, but the *way* in which it is there; in other words, the question to be asked is: in what proportion and manner does the manifestation and communication of being come in the world and in man?[77]

Obviously, this question transcends the traditional way of approaching truth as *adaequatio rei et intellectus* or *conformitas intellectus ad rem*. But if "truth" means presence and communication of being, then all the existential forms within which this manifestation and communication happen belong to the domain of truth. Truth, according to this view, cannot be limited to a value of empirical propositions only. Rather, it is a condition and quality of experience in a wider sense. Thus truth is found in sense experience, in feelings of pleasure and pain, and more generally in the attitudes which determine or accompany our choices in the diverse and complex forms of practical life.

According to gnosiologists, truth is understood to be a quality of the dialectical relationship between the *res* and the *intellectus* rather than only a value of statements which reflects the degree of exactitude with which the *intellectus* represents (in the sense of the Latin verb *adaequō*) something about the *res*. Gnosiologists contend that the sense of truth as a value of propositions, also called truth as "just what is the case," is only part of a more complete meaning of truth. It is only part because, for them, the focus of the idea of truth as "just what is the case" is limited to the representational act of the mind as expressed in propositions. This sense of truth is based on an assumed possibility to separate the *intellectus* from the *res* as a condition for evaluating the "adaequation" of the *intellectus* to the *res*. In this attempt to isolate the *intellectus* from the *res*, gnosiologists argue, positivist epistemologists assume that there still remains, after the separation, a *res*, an abandoned object, an *in se* free of the representational act of the *intellectus*, and whose unrepresented (that is, unknown) self can be used to check the adequacy of the representational act of the *intellectus*. The gnosiological observation is that not only does the positivist assumption entangle in a quagmire, but also that such positivist sense of truth is hard to sustain since it lacks a ground of objectivity, which it requires for its procedure. The point is that the *in se* cannot be a validating factor since it remains unknowable and without sense when separated from the *intellectus*. The *in se*, therefore—and here Wiredu agrees with Kant—does not make any sense insofar as it does not constitute the domain of truth, of the known. But neither is the *intellectus* anything meaningful without the *res*. Without content or object, the *intellectus* remains the not-yet, the pure void. Hence truth is generated only as a result of the relationship between the two and must be intended as the existential moment of the dynamic relationship of the two parts of the cognitive structure—the *res* and the *intellectus*—as possibilities of experience and thought.

Wiredu thus recognizes that there are two domains of truth. The primary domain is that of truth-claims in the cognitive sense, such as "it is true that Omondi is a man." This is also called truth as "just what is the case," as in the proposition "it is the case that Omondi is a man." This kind of truth is truth of fact. The secondary domain of truth is that which concerns itself with the metaphysical level of reference. At this level man concerns himself with "truthfulness," rather than with truth as "just what is the case" or as *adaequatio rei et intellectus*. It is this second domain with which Wiredu is deeply concerned, and he claims that it is with this second domain that the talk of the ordinary man is primarily preoccupied.

Because of the primary moral concern with truth at the ordinary man's level, Wiredu says that "It emerges, then, that *nokware* [an Akan word meaning "truth"] translates 'truthfulness' rather than 'truth' in the cognitive sense"[78] to imply that the common man's preoccupation with truth is in the secondary domain, where "to be truthful is to let your speech reflect your thought." For example, when asked what he thought was the cause of a fierce outbreak of fire in his neighborhood, a resident of a crime-infested shantytown answered, "The wrath of God has descended upon the town due to its evils." But asked the same question, a modern government official sent to the town to investigate the incident answered, "Someone is suspected of having set his neighbor's house on fire following a quarrel, but given the strong winds in the area and the palm-leaf roofing of the houses, the fire spread quickly to over two thousand houses in that estate." Now these two people, according to Wiredu's theory, and indeed according to that of Hebga, are both correct. The claims of the government agent do not necessarily and should not be forced to disprove the claims of the villager; after all, they are not mutually exclusive. Within these limits, both Hebga and Wiredu are correct. The two people in our example, the villager and the government agent, are talking from two distinct contexts, and what they are expressing is equally "true" in each respective context. They simply cannot be compared. The government agent has, however, only part of the whole truth from the point of view of the villager. The villager is ready to accept the finding of the government investigator if he can prove it. The villager too recognizes that at the level of the question "Who lit the fire?" the discourse is about matters of physical fact—provable, true or false. "But when this has been achieved," Wiredu says, "it still remains to give an account of the vital importance of truth." This is the position of the villager and which Wiredu calls the moral domain of truth.

But Wiredu does not, however, accept this kind of cheap relativism. For him, the fact that the ordinary man concerns himself with moral truths rather than with truths of fact is the result of his lagging behind in the development of rational methods and the design of effective means for the control of conditions of life. In this regard, Wiredu does not entertain any ambiguity concerning the relations between the two forms of truth or knowledge. Empirical knowledge, which concerns itself with truths of fact, must take precedence over certain types of belief. Likewise, analytic knowledge must take precedence over intuitive knowledge. Wiredu, in other words, believes in the universality and commensurability of rationality.

In the case of our example above, therefore, Wiredu would place the position of the government agent above that of the villager as it alone (of the two) is capable of leading to greater measures of safety. Why so? Because it is a position which arises out of a careful rational analysis of available evidence. Belief, Wiredu insists, must be sustainable only where it is in agreement with the universal canons of rational inquiry.[79] This, he says, is what distinguishes his view from relativism. Beliefs, he appears to say, must be rationally justified—that is, they must be born out of rational inquiry. But in the various spheres of traditional thought and action, many beliefs were taken for granted, even when the practical consequences drawn from them consistently proved to be detrimental and contrary to the requirements of rational inquiry. But the ordinary people still held onto their beliefs, not because they chose to do so despite their knowledge of the unreasonableness of the beliefs, but rather because they operated outside the sphere of the full requirements of rational inquiry. Like Horton and his cohorts, Wiredu believes that traditional thought tries no alternatives. This is what he says in comparison of such two cases:

> A man pushing a doctrinaire line against all good sense, for instance, does not in the standard case say "I know that the policy I am pursuing is not reasonable but I don't care." What usually happens is that his sensitivity to the finer points of observation and ratiocination is dulled by, say, some emotional habits; his perception is perverted, and consequently he actually and honestly sees his line as the best.[80]

For Wiredu, then, opinions are not cases of a stalemate in opposition. Rather, they should be the starting point for further inquiry, which, for Wiredu, is dialectical.

However true it may be, all this only means that man is constitutionally placed within the domain of truth, like a living organism is placed within an atmosphere that surrounds it on all sides and which forms its circumventing horizon or world of "experience," its world of action. But this does not mean that man lives only within truth, and less still that it is this "atmosphere" that primarily matters for him.

Man lives a life of objective limitation and subjective creativity. Within his objective limitation man concerns himself with the most momentary problems of his day-to-day living—with facts and things to be judged good, bad, or just, with exact calculations, analyses, satisfactions, and comprehension of facts and history to enhance creative and protective activities. And all this is not consciously carried out with the objective of conformity to the primary and vast moral goal. Of course the moral globality may be important in determining the nature of choice and cultural structure just as much as the atmospheric environment influences the structure and development of organic biology for adaptation. But taken singly, each of these constitutions presents an independent whole that embodies facts with which our everyday language is concerned in the sense in which our assertions are judgeable as either affirmative or negative propositions. Conditional and hypothetical propositions are derived as much from the domain of facts as from that of moral or cultural determinative circumstances. We cannot, therefore, pay less attention to the problems of truth as related to the domain of facts.

Recapitulation on Wiredu

Wiredu's position regarding the status of ethnophilosophy has been explained by him with unsurpassed clarity. That explanation includes also his critique of Hountondji's anti-ethnophilosophy school. Even clearer are Wiredu's views on the role of philosophy in contemporary Africa. "Our societies are being rapidly changed by industrialization," he says, "and if we wish to understand this change and control its direction, [then] we must adopt new ways of thinking, a new outlook upon man, society, and nature." Because of his strong Deweyian views on the role of reason, Wiredu is uncompromising about the unhelpfulness of the traditional mind in dealing with modern problems. Ties between the past and the present can only be instituted by the modern philosopher, who may apply his analytic methods to discuss conceptual values of the traditional world. And he has himself frequently done this already.[81]

There have been objections, however, albeit informally, to the view that traditional thought has little, if anything at all, to contribute to contemporary African philosophy. The person best known for this objection to Wiredu is Henry Odera Oruka. But Odera Oruka has not made his objection by addressing Wiredu's views directly. His position was developed independently of Wiredu's views in this connection, and may have been equally inspired by Hountondji's extremist rejection of ethnophilosophy. Odera Oruka's view, known as African philosophic sagacity, has since picked up much popularity, especially among African philosophers, as an even more moderate position than Wiredu's on the issue of ethnophilosophy. However, since the publication of *Philosophy and an African Culture*, Wiredu himself has consistently shown more interest in traditional thought. His interest has particularly been directed at the analysis and discernment of different concepts and conceptual categories in traditional thought by means of analytic skills.

H. Odera Oruka: On African Philosophic Sagacity

So far what we have said about the various attempts to define African philosophy covers only two of the trends identified by Odera Oruka. According to him, there are four such trends discernible from the general body of literature and the arguments surrounding this topic.

The first one is what he calls, after Hountondji, the *ethnophilosophy* trend, and covers, among others, the writings of Tempels, Griaule, Kagame, and Mbiti, whom we have discussed in chapters two to five above. This trend, as we have seen, was initiated by Tempels and has been kept alive by a group of disciples from both within and outside Africa, with a large number coming mainly from clerical circles.

The second trend, according to Odera Oruka, is that of *professional philosophy*. We have presented various writings from this trend in the present chapter. Included here are the writings of people who, being professionally trained in philosophy, have taken up the discussion of African philosophy from the strict and critical philosophical point of view. While a few points characterize this group— such as rejection of Tempels and his school, a call for the universality of the philosophic method, etc.—belonging to the group is judged by the strictly analytic theoretical and argumentative manner in which they handle their issues with little or no reference to ethnographic data. Odera Oruka himself belongs to this group. One wishes a better name could be found for this school that would avoid the false impression that the actors in the other trends, notably ethnophilosophy, are not professional philosophers. While nonprofessionalism could be said of Odera Oruka's fourth trend actors, it cannot be attributed to, say, Kagame or Mulago or many of those trained African philosophers who practice phenomenological analysis of African concepts in either metaphysical or theological perspectives.

The third trend, identified by Odera Oruka as *Africa's modern political and ideological thought*, focuses on the production of Africa's postcolonial ideological discourse. This trend includes the thoughts and writings of leading Africans about Africa's social, cultural, political, and economic problems in the traditional, colonial, and postcolonial periods. Odera Oruka includes in this category the works of such people as Léopold Sédar Senghor, Kwame Nkrumah, Julius Nyerere, Amilcar Cabral, Kenneth Kaunda, Oginga Odinga, and Abdel Nasser. This list could of course grow either longer or shorter depending on the concessions one is ready to make regarding the definition of the subject matter (such as philosophy, or ideology) or any other criterion of classification that would allow, for example, the inclusion of someone like, say, Mudimbe, or Chinua Achebe, or Wole Soyinka, or Ngugi wa Thiongo, or Wiredu, Hountondji, or even Odera Oruka himself, in either this or any other category. Their intellectual practices, like the works and concerns of Senghor, Nkrumah, Nyerere, or Odinga, address issues arising directly from the political, ideological, and cultural conditions of Africans in the precolonial, colonial, and postcolonial spaces of their experiences. Odera Oruka needs a more elaborate definition and separation of his categories (trends) which would allow a more adequate system of categorization that would take care of the intellectual productions of so many African thinkers with different intellectual orientations and foci.

Apart from these three, Odera Oruka identifies a fourth trend, which he calls *African philosophic sagacity*, the theory of which is based on the epistemological value of wisdom or sagacity. The general background to this trend is traceable to the attempt to find African traditional thinkers whose thought can be accepted as characteristically philosophical. This challenge was given to Tempels by his critics so as to strengthen his hypothesis about the existence of African philosophy. The fourth trend is therefore another follow-up to Tempels's theory and is specifically a critique of Marcel Griaule's definition of an African philosopher as seen by him in the person of the old sage Ogotemmêli. It is Odera Oruka's position regarding the content and value of this trend which has earned him a place of significance within the African philosophy debate. Although I have tried to relate his major claims to the arguments developed by Mudimbe and by Hallen and Sodipo, especially in regard to the issues of pluralism and commensurability of rationality, knowledge, and truth and language, this is sometimes possible only by putting extensions on his theses, as he does not participate in the nuances. The value of his contribution should therefore be more visible as part of the now rife debate on representations and the role of narrative and metaphor.

The general claim of this trend toward African philosophy as African philosophic sagacity is that in Africa, contemporary or traditional, there were and must still be wise men and women who, despite their lack of modern and formal education, convey critical thinking that is essentially philosophical and distinct from the type of general narrative description of cultural traditions, customs, and laws as portrayed by the old sage Ogotemmêli of the Dogon.

In Griaule's monumental *Conversations*, Ogotemmêli is initially meant to shine as a paradigm of Tempels's hypothesis of African philosophy, its philosopher par excellence. But he comes out of it a mere recipient and recitor of the collective lores, feelings, and insights of the Dogon people in general, as is supposed to be the case with anybody of similar age and sharp memory of the teachings passed down by the forefathers of the tribe. Professors J. O. Sodipo and Barry Hallen of Ife University in Nigeria have largely supported Griaule's view.[82] Their work has focused, as did that of Griaule, on the selected wise men and women regarded as the keepers of traditional knowledge. In the work of Hallen and Sodipo, such wise men and women are the *onisegun*—masters of medicine, herbalists or native doctors—the professional group that retains the philosophy of the people. Odera Oruka rejects this view on the grounds that it is merely representative of the group or tribe as a whole and therefore embodies little more than cultural prejudices—not a philosophy. According to Odera Oruka, philosophic sagacity should go beyond this ability at recitation of the common lores.

However, in their work *Knowledge, Belief and Witchcraft*, Hallen and Sodipo claim to do a slightly different thing. Rather than merely report or re-present the teachings of the *onisegun* in the narrative form as Griaule did for the Dogon, Hallen and Sodipo claim to have engaged the *onisegun* in *discussions* as colleagues. From these discussions, they claim (p.10), they were able to expose analytically the *onisegun*'s conceptual distinctions between different philosophically relevant notions, such as "true"/"false," "know"/"believe," etc. Their task, however, is centrally a comparative evaluation or analysis of these notions as they are used both by the *onisegun* and by Western philosophers.

Now this scheme raises at least one question which appears to justify Odera Oruka's objection to it in that although the *onisegun* are purportedly speaking as "philosophical colleagues," the conceptual scheme of their language remains part of the general and ordinary conceptual scheme within which the *onisegun* work. Their relevance stems in fact from the degree to which their advice to the ordinary people fits into the generally accepted scheme of explanations and justifications. This is the role of medicine men and medicine women in many other cultures. The *onisegun* discourses are therefore largely part of the ordinary traditional discourse. Nevertheless, Hallen and Sodipo have taken a bold step beyond these discourses in that they have analyzed the various epistemological conceptual categories in ordinary traditional discourses. And this method, of course, although becoming increasingly popular as a new direction in the practice of philosophy in Africa, removes focus from the *onisegun* and their equivalents in other cultures to the academic philosopher himself.

Secondly, discussions do not always differ distinctly from interviews. A probing discussion is capable of soliciting a predetermined direction of responses just as effectively as can leading questionnaire questions. Many skeptical people would perhaps benefit more if the material or data gathered through such methods as discussions or interviews were accompanied by direct transcripts of the encounters. Odera Oruka has fortunately now done this.[83]

Odera Oruka's argument in favor of the sages is nearly identical with Taaita Towett's earlier argument on the same issue.[84] Like Towett, Odera Oruka argues that writing, literacy, or modern formal education is not a prerequisite for the definition or making of a philosopher. Socrates, who is referred to and used as an example by both, never wrote any of the doctrines "attributed" to him as his philosophy. And among the pile of written philosophical literature there is no single methodology identifiable as belonging specifically to philosophy. Towett therefore considers as satisfactory the definition of a philosopher as "he who devotes all or most of his time and thought to philosophy."[85] And philosophy is in turn defined as "love of wisdom and search for knowledge and truth. It is the means by which we believe or accept and interpret all that which man is capable of thinking or discussing." In other words, according to Towett, philosophy is any body of reasons by which we make our beliefs logical and systematic. Within these bounds, Odera Oruka contends, as does Towett, that there must have been African philosophers engaged in the formulation of culture philosophy. These sages, Odera Oruka says, are sage-philosophers. To him,

> Philosophic sagacity is the reflection of a person who is (1) a sage and (2) a thinker. As a sage the person is versed in the wisdoms and traditions of his people, and very often he is recognized by the people themselves as having this gift. . . . Being a sage, however, does not necessarily make one philosophic. . . . But as thinkers, they are rationally critical and they opt for or recommend only those aspects of the beliefs and wisdoms which satisfy their rational scrutiny.[86]

Such sages transcend the communal wisdom of their own people. They stand out as being different from them. They reform and sometimes utterly oppose the existing traditions. The reformulation of the traditional values in a theoretical manner by an individual, says Odera Oruka, can indeed be truly philosophical. Such an individual goes beyond mere sagacity since he bases his judgments, including judgments on the values and beliefs of his own culture, on pure reason.

Odera Oruka gives an example to illustrate his point about the difference between Ogotemmêli's cultural wisdom and that of a philosophic sage. He says:

> For Ogotemmêli, woman's difference from man is taken as a curse and punishment from God. And it is clear that such ideas are no more than a recitation of the communal myths of the tribe.
>
> [But] Mbuya [who was a renowned sage among the Luo community in Kenya], for example, knows, as Ogotemmêli does, what his community thinks about *woman*. But he nevertheless makes his own rational assessment about a woman.

Odera Oruka goes on to quote Mbuya:

> 'A man has the physical capacity to run faster than a woman. But on the other hand a woman has the physical capacity to undergo the pains of carrying and bearing a baby which a man lacks. So we cannot correctly say one is superior or inferior to the other. . . . In truth the two sexes are naturally equal or balanced.'

"This sort of argument is independent of the communal chorus of general Luo beliefs about woman,"[87] Odera Oruka declares, rather wishfully.

Paul Mbuya's views on woman may of course lead to deep and refined notions, not only about woman as such, but on humans in general. But as it stands, his statement is only a metaphysical statement about man (as gender) thrown out without much of the usual elaboration that often goes with philosophic exposition. In other words, it is a statement of common sense, but hardly anything more. He merely states the factual differences as he has observed them. The question which one feels should be asked here is, therefore, whether or not for any statement or opinion to be philosophic all that is needed is for it to be clever or non-mediocre. Mbuya's statement on woman is by no means stupid or mediocre. It is an intelligent statement of a man who observes and notices events and facts around him, probably with some alertness and acumen which the majority of the people in his community lack. Such individuals are, of course, rare, and this is evidenced by the short list not only of philosophers but also of other kinds of outstanding people who have made significant inventions or discoveries or moved history in any other way. The majority of mankind is concerned with the practical problems of everyday living and do not care for theoretical inquiries.

So we like our tea with sugar without ever questioning the chemical combinations that constitute sugar and which make its dissolution in certain liquids possible; nor do we inquire, before taking tea, about the chemical-biological stimulations within the human body that make the sensation of taste possible. Yet we share such experiences equally with chemists and biologists. However, even if research and training have made the latter the professionals that they are, they initially began with some "curiosity" triggered by some "cleverness" in observation and attention compared to the majority of other individuals. But we would not call these people philosophers. Nor would they become scientists by merely declaring that what we perceive when we taste sugar is called sweetness. In other words, there are individuals in every society who are gifted in various forms of intellectual alertness, with extraordinary capability of dealing with various types of problems, but who are not philosophers. This is the type of wisdom and power of judgment demonstrated by King Solomon in handling the case of the disputed child as recorded in the book of Kings of the Old Testament.

Cleverness is thus not *ipso facto* a philosophic attribute. While, therefore, Mbuya's statement on woman is surely a commonsense saying within the sociocultural environment of Mbuya's life and in relation to the majority of his contemporaries at that particular time, this alone does not suffice to give it a philosophic attribute. Mbuya may have been a philosopher, and indeed there may be many other such deep thinkers as Mbuya, but the sample quotation given by Odera Oruka to support this vital point is rather weak.

Towett also cautions against this assumption. According to him, only the *interpretation* of a point of view about the essence and about the realities of life or of certain aspects of it falls within the domain of philosophy. But all those other interpretations of the universe or of part of it which we make thanks to observation or to mathematical formulas do not make part of philosophy.[88] Towett seems to be making a point that has also been made by Wiredu in this connection, namely, that while theoretical abstractions are often to be encountered not only in philosophical treatises but also in everyday thought or common sense, the difference between philosophical treatises and everyday thought lies in the greater elaboration and the technical sophistication of the former. What Mbuya says above rests on a fairly theoretical and abstract statement: that there is a sense in which all people are equal despite gender differences. But the other statements which count as the elaboration of this primary assertion are not theoretical statements. They are statements of fact which appeal to direct experience and common sense. For this reason, both Towett and Wiredu would reject them as not belonging to the domain of philosophy.

A major critic of this trend has been Peter Bodunrin. According to him, "It is one thing to show that there are men capable of philosophical dialogue in Africa and another to show that there are African philosophers in the sense of those who have engaged in organized systematic reflections on the thoughts, beliefs, and practices of their people."[89] Because philosophic sagacity is brought out by way of interviews and questionnaires, Bodunrin believes that the end result of such an undertaking becomes essentially a joint product of both the sage concerned and his interviewer, the trained philosopher. Odera Oruka reacts to this objection by saying that "Most philosophers come to create new ideas or styles of philosophy only as a result of responding to the ideas or works of some other philosophers or persons."[90]

Surely, this is quite correct. As Hegel once said, philosophizing is like swimming; you don't do it on dry land. It needs a fertile and relevant ground. One may learn about swimming from books or in a typical classroom, but it is only in water that one tests the acquired and natural talents of agility that go with swimming. The same applies to philosophy. Philosophy does not create ideas and concepts in use. We may have many of these concepts and ideas embedded in us by tradition, experience, education, and even bias, but it is only through dialogue with other philosophies and theories that we get to the real philosophic track, that is, to the theoretical exposition of our experiences. Natural talents and wisdom are important assets but, left to themselves, they are not a philosophy. However, as human endowments they are certainly important and prerequisite for philosophical practice.

Thus while Odera Oruka's reply to Bodunrin and the examples he cites to support his argument are unquestionably exact, they do not quite clarify the issue. In the example of Marx's or Russell's dependence on Hegel's philosophy, the former two developed their own thought systems from a tradition or legacy created and established by the latter rather than from him directly and personally. This tradition played for them the role of a dominant intellectual atmosphere within which many more philosophical students and scholars of the time gained experience. The outcome of such an experience cannot be fairly compared with an experience that often ensues from person-to-person dialogue between two or more individuals, and especially when such dialogue is held in interview form like the one Odera Oruka had with Mbuya.

This type of interview is often conducted by means of questionnaires aimed at "uncovering" answers supposedly belonging to the person interviewed. This method used alone, however, raises questions about the originality of the answers so obtained. While it is quite satisfactory in cases of direct questions such as "Where is Nairobi?" or "What is a locomotive?" it is often not a satisfactory method where the object of discussion is a concept. For conceptual questions, answers may easily be determined *a priori* by the manner in which the questions are set and designed. Although the answers may come directly from the person interviewed, they may still fall within the bounds of the world conception of the person who framed them.

An example which is quite close to this in the history of philosophy is Socrates with his maieutic method. For Socrates, this method was important, not because it turned all the participants in the dialogues into philosophers, but because, for him, the point of departure was opinion, the personal *doxa*, which is open to further logical development and thorough examination. To Socrates this personal *doxa* is a (normal) human orientation already underway. A dialogue is in fact possible only between men who have opinions, not between those who have only their sensations. The truth is interior to us and can be reached only through dialogue and communication. Socrates set out to demonstrate this to people, and by that to show them the way to a virtuous life.

In our own time, this Socratic view is found in a modified form in the existentialist philosophy of Martin Heidegger. But neither in Socrates nor in Heidegger is it explicitly held that man is a philosopher by virtue of his ability to decipher reality around him, but rather, because of his ability to do so, that we can philosophically analyze and interpret reality by observing these natural (though special) activities of his. The discovery of the value and method of dialogue was a philosophical result of Socrates' own personal meditations and contemplations, which were mainly based on a critical rethinking of the Sophist tradition. But this did not *ipso facto* make all the people with whom he held dialogues in the marketplace philosophers. Thus, even in Socrates there is a distinction between what pertains to the human and natural *doxa* and what results from elaborate examination of the contents of *doxa*. In other words, the Socratic dialogues indicate that philosophy is something different from just a body of opinions. The point here is that a philosopher must build up a kingdom—whether on sand, cardboard, or rock—whose main strength is the *search for truth* rather than just truth alone. In this lies also the strength of philosophy as a discipline: on the dialectical nature of its specific truths or answers. The comparison of African traditional sages with Socrates is therefore a rather unfair undertaking. And this is true whether we talk of the "small world of technical philosophy" or the "wide world of general philosophy."[91]

Whatever the role of Socrates' interlocutors, however, the dialogues often amounted to confirmations of principles in Socrates' own philosophical framework. Thus even the theory of reminiscence served more to prove Socrates' doctrine of the immortality of the soul and its superiority over the body than that all people were equally clever and knew the truth. For Socrates, the ability to know the truth, as well as the capacity to diligently search for it, is the human element that must be cultivated and directed toward the truth, because the *logos* shines in all, but only as a faculty.

This is not to discredit the interview or dialogue method. But we must be aware that there is a distinct difference between what we normally understand as interview and as philosophical dialogue. An ordinary type of interview usually has a specific answer to uncover regarding some specific question(s). In a philosophical interview, however, the setting of the question may be specific but the interviewer must try by all means to refrain from dominating the scene. In a philosophical interview the interviewer must give in to the direction of the interlocutor, and often the course of the interview may change frequently according to the answers given to questions and further related questions that the answers may solicit, sometimes leading away from what may have been the original objective of the interviewer. In such a case, the interlocutor takes over the intiative in the encounter, and may successfully expound his own independent thought undeterred by the interests of the interviewer. The interview may thus develop into a typical and proper dialogue, regardless of the agreements or disagreements of views between the dialoguers. While this kind of interview may be closer to a philosophical dialogue and be able to bring out the individual thoughts of the sages interviewed, we need to be aware of the dangers involved, for the outcome may not always be successful.

The crucial and perhaps most useful point is that despite his disentanglement from the popular representations of Greek cultural knowledge and beliefs, Socrates, as Plato reproduces him, remained deeply Greek or Athenian. His style was a reproduction of the popular dialogical practice, and his thematic preoccupations an exposition of the interrogations that were probably common to intellectual orientations of many other persons. In Socrates, then, the traditional merged with its own ruptures, in a way. By seeking justification for popularly held beliefs, and by subjecting them to interrogations that would bring out of them durable and respectable principles, Socrates built the foundations for what was to be a tradition of discourse. Thus, in this way the broad and stricter senses of philosophy shade into each other as suggested by Meinrad Hebga in his new sense of ethnophilosophy, and by reference to the relationship of mutual influence between the communal philosophy or tradition and the thinking of sage philosophers. Currently, in fact, there is a resurgence of suggestive writing which recommends that the production of African philosophy should spring from and form its own discursive formation free of the epistemological canons of the West. The point, in other words, is what we can or should do with the kind of knowledge produced by the traditional cultural actors.

The other arguments which have been connected with this debate—the importance or non-importance of writing in philosophy, whether or not Africans have discursive reason, etc.—are rather peripheral to Odera Oruka's central issue. Socrates is often referred to as one of the greatest philosophers although he never used writing as a method of imparting his knowledge or thought. There is no denial that writing, taken merely as a medium of communication, is surely not essential to philosophizing. But it is also true that reading and writing are presently the most effective media for expanding and communicating our ideas. The value of reading and writing in the domain of scholarship cannot be exaggerated.

It is plausible, however, to accept that there could have been individuals in traditional Africa comparable to Socrates in intellectual nobility and greatness despite the absence of the written tradition. But this is just a *possibility*, and quite an abstract one at that, because we have no evidence such as we have in the case of Socrates. The examples we cite today to support this claim—wise men like Paul Mbuya and others—do not quite fit as proper examples, not only because we pick them up *a posteriori* to our belief, but also because we have not shown satisfactorily what is "philosophical" in them beyond what is merely "human." To do this, we must be able to provide longer texts of discussions with these sages which will reveal to us points of passage from the level of mere wisdom and cleverness to that of philosophical debate proper. Odera Oruka is in the process of doing this, and his findings are already available in print. Further research is being conducted in search of just these points of passage, which, we believe, most probably exist.[92]

This question of writing is merely one of methodology. Africans could have preserved their wisdom in many possible forms. They did it orally, keeping their wisdom alive through powerful memories passed from one generation to the next by means of tales, fables, proverbs, and theater narrations. This oral literary form of human expression and communication was used for capturing, preserving, and imparting knowledge about man and his world, his fears and hopes, his ideals, values, and history. All these form an essential component of human culture. Nevertheless, neither the form nor the content of traditional African wisdom is "philosophical" in any exceptional way. And neither the oral nor the written form of preserving knowledge constitutes in any distinctive way the definition of Africanity.

Our position here has the Bodunrin–Odera Oruka debate in mind. According to Bodunrin, lack of a written tradition has led to Africa's late start in philosophy. In objection to this, Odera Oruka concludes that since the oral tradition has been characteristic of the traditional African past, then Bodunrin must be implying that "to be authentically philosophical, Africans must be unAfrican," that is, they must drop their oral tradition and adopt the written one, which is both foreign and unAfrican. While we clearly cannot tell whether these inferences are correct (because the axioms on which they are based are questionable), it is our belief, nonetheless, that the question of African philosophic sagacity is indispensable to a complete historical account of the development of African civilization. The form or style of literary expression is basically, by itself, indifferent to philosophy. Yet this must not be taken to imply that since Africans had no writing as part of their traditions, they need not write at all.

The idea that critical thinking can develop within an oral tradition finds a strong objection in the work of Jack Goody, *The Domestication of the Savage Mind*. According to Goody, "One of the features of oral communication in pre-literate societies lies in its capacity to swallow up the individual achievement and to incorporate it in a body of transmitted custom that can be considered as the approximate equivalent to what Tylor called 'culture' and Durkheim 'society' . . . which both writers regarded as *sui generis*."[93] Although this observation by Goody justifies the starting point of Odera Oruka's hypothesis—that what is known as culture must be the outcome of the thought of individuals, however far they may be removed in history—it also points out the weakest point of the sage philosophy theory in that it makes the sage philosophers an anonymous species within cultural constructs. The sage philosophers appear as logical constructs rather than as real persons. For Goody, "the difference between oral and literate cultures . . . bears upon the question of the individual's role in the creative process and hence the whole problem of the intellectual—the individual signature is always getting rubbed out in the process of generative transmission."[94]

According to Goody, it is wrong to assume that the method in which knowledge is processed and transmitted remains indifferent to the nature and structure of that knowledge, as appears to be presupposed in Odera Oruka's rejoinder to Bodunrin. In Goody's view, method and content of knowledge are "two aspects [which] are very closely intertwined so that a change in one is likely to effect a change in the other."[95] Goody's chapter on "Literacy, Criticism and the Growth of Knowledge" is partly a response to Horton and argues that the differences which the latter characterizes as distinctive of open and closed systems of thought can be related to differences in the systems of communication and, specifically, to the presence or absence of writing. Goody's specific proposition is that:

> Writing, and more especially alphabetic literacy, made it possible to scrutinise discourse in a different kind of way by giving oral communication a semi-permanent form; this scrutiny favoured the increase in scope of critical activity, and hence of rationality, skepticism, and logic to resurrect memories of those questionable dichotomies.[96]

For Goody, then, the growth of knowledge is essentially dependent on the ability to review the content of knowledge in a continuous fashion—that is, in his words, the ability to return to static texts. This ability requires a method which objectifies knowledge beyond the historical fluidity of oralism. It makes possible what Jewsiewicki called the usable past and what Mudimbe calls an autonomous gnostic or epistemic tradition complete with its own history. And Mudimbe rightly believes that time has not yet run out for African philosophers to identify, apply, and problematize the basic African epistemic frameworks and principles in analyses of discourses and in a manner that will make oral traditions useful to the present. In other words, the growth of knowledge, as the result of the deliberate intellectual pursuit of explanation and understanding, cannot be sufficiently dependent on the natural methods of preservation and transmission such as the oral tradition. Oralism must be seen as a natural method whose functions and aims need to be fortified through new methods to guarantee the reliability and vigor of the pursuit for knowledge. The point made by Goody is not, as Odera Oruka says of his other critics, that "a tradition without writing is incapable of philosophy." Rather, the point is that writing is an important vehicle for the systematization and growth of knowledge. Even the pre-Socratic Greek philosophers, such as Thales, Anaximander, Heraclitus, are people whose thoughts or tales would have remained indistinguishable parts of Greek mythology in the absence of the systematizing reformulations which they received in the hands of later formal philosophers like Aristotle. The important point, however, is that the thoughts of the pre-Socratics, like those of the traditional sages, do not make significant points to anybody today outside their theoretical reformulations by systematic scholars like Odera Oruka or Aristotle or Hegel. In this respect, the availability of original texts, together with their (original) reformulations and discussions among a large number of interested parties, contributes better to a larger variety of opinions (explanations and interpretations), and hence to greater search and debate. And philosophy, at least in its Socratic definition, is greatly punctuated by the characteristics of debate and search. So, although it is true that search and debate do not *per se* preclude oralism, it is also true that many of us today would probably not have been able to comment on the utterances of the pre-Socratics with any sense of confidence if they had not been preserved in writing either in their original presentation or in their reformulations. So also, how will many African students of philosophy today and tomorrow comment on traditional discourses or return to the traditional epistemological loci if these have been lost in the irretrievable past?

I find Kwasi Wiredu's view on the subject of writing philosophy compelling. Wiredu considers the defense of oral literary form as counterproductive to the notion of African philosophy in the sense of a tradition. According to him, to talk of "African philosophy" or "Western philosophy" is to suppose a tradition. His argument is that the philosophy of a people is always a tradition; and a tradition presupposes a certain minimum of organic relationships among (at least some of) its elements. If a tradition of modern philosophy is to develop and flourish in Africa, there will have to be philosophical interaction and cross-fertilization among contemporary African workers in philosophy. It is of course a little ironic that while he continues to defend the oral literary form as a sufficient philosophical tool, Odera Oruka sees the need to transcribe the orally produced thoughts of sage philosophers as the means that makes them part of an organic complex—the tradition of African philosophy. In postmodern terms, it is the transcription which transforms the thoughts of the sages into texts and into the core of the emergent tradition of philosophical discourse in Africa.

A brief point about the importance of sage philosophy. In the introduction to his book *Sage Philosophy*, Odera Oruka writes:

> This importance [of sage philosophy] can be seen in two aspects: first, the thoughts of the given and named individual sages express and defend themselves as philosophical counsellings on various issues of nature and human life. Anybody concerned with looking for answers or advice on the fundamental moral and metaphysical questions will find much material in the thoughts of the sages to utilize. Secondly, their thoughts form significant raw data for technical philosophical reflections by the professionals.[97]

Of the first importance one needs to state quickly that no reasonable claim states that whatever is rational or reasonable and practicable is by that strength alone philosophical. Odera Oruka himself points out the failure of Plato's *Republic*, which nonetheless remains, for many, a philosophical classic. Experience reveals much practical reasoning at the traditional level which identifies more with belief systems than with investigative inquiries. Of the difference between the two, the late Okot p'Bitek once wrote the following:

> Philosophy is the rational investigation of the truths and principles of being, knowledge or conduct. It must be contrasted with belief; which is an opinion or conviction; confidence in the truth or existence of something not immediately susceptible to rigorous proof. To say that one believes, for instance, in God is to have confidence in the existence of God, although without absolute proof that one is right in doing so.[98]

Of the second importance, one would suggest further explication and proper definition of the role of the trained philosopher in the reformulation of traditional discourses, a question of recent but ever growing concern and interest for many African philosophers. The reformulation of traditional discourse by trained African philosophers is the project which Crahay had suggested in 1965 as being capable of generating a properly African philosophical discourse. In other words, the traditional discourse which must be retrieved from the sages and sage philosophers must be the runway from which the "*décollage conceptuel*" ought to take place. It is also the project reformulated by Mudimbe in *The Invention of Africa*. The reference to Socrates, however, has a historical-cultural significance. The emergence of Socrates signifies a break from tradition and the common world of myth as vigorously symbolized in the thought of some selected wise men—the pre-Socratics. This pre-Socratic thought lacks any significant form of discourse.

It is a set of mythological narratives. Its importance is that it provides the setting for the discourse which begins with the emergence of the sophist school, of which Socrates was a member.

The significance of the Socratic or sophist tradition is that it organized, systematized, and formalized the discourse on tradition and traditional discourse into a subject of formalized and organized debate. The main purpose of this debate was to establish an understanding of the nature of knowledge, but it also demonstrated how frequently tradition and various types of opinion were based on insufficient reason. Socrates, in other words, was bent on contrasting the bases of tradition with properly researched knowledge. The purpose of philosophy, then, was not so much to contradict the oracles as it was to question and examine their bases with the aim of establishing truth as opposed to unwarranted opinion. To do this, philosophy relied significantly on analysis, definition, and explanation.

In this view, the thrust and strength of philosophy lies in the sustenance of explanation as part of the quest to establish understanding, and this can be done either analytically, as Socrates does it in the Dialogues or as Odera Oruka does in his discussion of Wiredu's "Truth as opinion," or synthetically, as Hegel explains history in *The Phenomenology of the Spirit* or as Sartre analyzes ontological freedom in *Being and Nothingness*. In this view, the pre-Socratics have no place in philosophy, just as many of our sages also have no place in philosophy. For what we call sustenance of explanation is not the ability of an individual to hold a discussion or interview for a reasonable length of time on one or a number of topics, but rather a consistent attitude toward and practice of explanation. And this requires a reasonably high degree of abstraction and conceptual analysis and relation.

In this respect, philosophy is more than just "personal opinion" as a variance from traditional norms. Rather, it ought to be seen as an attempt to transcend personalism through its discussions at a purely theoretical level.

There is a congenial combination of Crahay and Horton here in a way. In Crahay's view, the act of philosophizing indicates a conceptual "takeoff" (Fr. *la décollage conceptuel*) from mythology to the level of abstraction and theoretical discourse. Horton makes the same distinction between "theoretical explanations" and divination.

Lastly, it must be pointed out that Afrocentric interests are not a sufficient reason for asking readers to accept African wise men and women as philosophers as Odera Oruka appears to plead or do in his uncritical endorsement of Martin Bernal's Afrocentric argument.[99]

Philosophic Sagacity Is not Culture Philosophy

Apart from philosophic sagacity, Odera Oruka believes that it is also meaningful to talk of "culture philosophy." This is quite different from philosophic sagacity and is constituted in large part by the theoretical elements that correlate with overt cultural behavior. These theoretical elements tend to explain *why* any given people are required to follow some given traditions. The theoretical elements which explain overt cultural behavior, in Odera Oruka's view, are what constitute "culture philosophy." One major difference between philosophic sagacity and culture philosophy is that the former remains essentially the work of the individual thinker whether or not his or her views agree with the cultural traditions of the community. Culture philosophy, on the other hand, remains largely an anonymous body of ideas because it is common to all those who share the given cultural experience. Another difference between the two is that philosophic sagacity explains facts and events by analysis of ideas and how these may or may not be relevant or meaningful as cultural beliefs; culture philosophy, on the other hand, tends to explain facts and events by referring to other facts, taboos, or events that are believed to be connected with the ones explained. Thus while for the latter it is the *belief* that is central to explanations, for the former it is mainly theoretical elaboration.

Culture philosophy is therefore a communal body of knowledge shared by most members of a given cultural group, albeit at different levels of detail depending on individual ability of memory and retention. The practical life of custom, taboos, and rituals is all derived from it. And those who teach it, people like Ogotemmêli, qualify only as cultural sages, not as sage-philosophers. Although they are free to modify the form of presentation, they usually lack the creative hand in bringing about the substance or knowledge they themselves teach. They merely see to it that the society lives according to the teachings of the wiser men and women who actually thought out and framed certain laws and manners as worth living by. Thus the cultural sages are not the same as sage-philosophers or as philosophers who may not be sages at all, for they merely handle, keep, and transmit what comes down as a popularized version or form of the philosophical acumen.

There are therefore, according to Odera Oruka, two distinct manners or levels in which we talk of the "philosophy" of any given culture. The first one is developed and formulated by influential individual members of a community. Its purpose is mainly for social control. So it is taught to the people in the form of normative assertions. In time, its theoretical parts disappear as people concentrate on its practical and normative aspects. These normative aspects then acquire their own identity as a body of rules or beliefs such as taboos. The majority of members of any community come to know only such rules as they are required to follow. Such a body of rules and beliefs is what Odera Oruka calls culture philosophy.

Conclusion

Experience and African Philosophy

AFTER WIREDU'S EVALUATION of ethnophilosophy on the basis of John Dewey's theory of the historical and empirical vocation of reason, one would expect that the question about the influence of experience upon methods of philosophizing had been answered. But this has not been the case. For despite Wiredu's clarity on this issue, there have still been persistent voices insisting that a return to the traditional past is the only way to identify different thought systems, philosophy included. We have, following Wiredu, called these voices the "nationalist school."

There are significant parallels between the debates over the criteria for African philosophy and the debate over rationality in Anglophone philosophy. To the nationalist school the traditional past should be the only object for philosophic interrogation. But the school goes further than simply expressing this position. It argues that all philosophies share some features of the traditional culture of the communities in which they were formulated. Hence philosophers are obliged to describe such features. This is the position held by Meinrad Hebga in his defense of ethnophilosophy. He argues that all philosophies are ethnological in many fundamental ways, and that African ethnophilosophy is no exception. What is perturbing about Hebga's defense of ethnophilosophy, however, is that it puts emphasis on the impact of historical and cultural experience on the content of thought but does not give adequate consideration to the questions of method and unanimity, which are the main targets of critique in African ethnophilosophy. The fundamental question not resolved by the nationalists is whether each culture is unique and African cultures are fundamentally different from other cultures, or whether there are modes of thinking and philosophizing shared by all.

The question of how to define the criteria of rationality has become a central theme in Anglophone philosophy. It also now occupies debates among social anthropologists and sociologists and philosophers of science. On one side are the foundationalists, who argue that formal rational procedures are the defining feature of science, which supersedes common sense and is universal. On the other side are the pluralists, who argue in favor of the diversity of human experience and systems of representation. These include the criteria for the definition of knowledge and for making judgments. A resolution to this debate argues that diverse modes of thought are found in all cultures but are distributed in historically and socially distinct ways. Hence "modalities of experience must be given equal weight in coming to an understanding of the world."[1] Jackson and Karp describe this position as a philosophical approach in which "modalities of experience should not be reified and debated as competing epistemologies. Rather they should be seen as descriptive of the varying ways human beings experience the world according to widely varying needs and interests."

For the foundationalists the universal criteria of rationality lie outside of history and are not affected by experience. For the pluralists history and experience determine the "logos" and define rationality. The position which states that our sense of the world and of personhood varies according to the varieties of experience takes a middle ground between the foundationalists and the pluralists by arguing that what are called products of the rational mind are not really conflictual with what are oppositionally referred to as the disorderly life of the body and the emotions. Rather, this third position argues, such products carry equal weight as they are modes of thinking which illustrate the variant modalities of experience. This position avoids the Cartesian dichotomy which posits the *cogito* as separate from, opposed to, and more reliable than bodily experiences. This position argues for a historical and contextual approach to the definition of knowledge and rationality.

This debate has its parallels with the theses of the nationalist school, whose fundamental claims can be expressed as follows: first, that every philosophical system is rooted in some specific epistemologically determinative experience, and second, that there should be no epistemologically determinative experience for anybody other than the traditional cultural roots of their communities. As a result, they argue, any philosophy must be fundamentally different from any other in form and content. This position reproduces the most extreme form of the pluralist argument in the rationality debate.

For the nationalists, African philosophy must be seen to be different from other philosophies: Chinese, Indian, Western, etc. Each group has and must have its own philosophy, which reflects and is rooted in its own traditions, for any thought system which is not part of its traditions does not constitute experience. To the members of this school, acculturation is simply impossible. The nationalist position denies any possibility of examining "the varying ways human beings experience the world according to widely varying needs and interests."

Although there is much sense in holding this position, the kind of reasoning that it portrays belongs to the realm of common and natural inclination. In his *Experience and Education* John Dewey states that

Mankind likes to think of extreme opposites. It is given to formulating beliefs in terms of Either-Ors, between which it recognizes no intermediate possibilities. When forced to recognize that the extremes cannot be acted upon, it is still inclined to hold that they are all right in theory but that when it comes to practical matters circumstances compel us to compromise.[2]

When applied to the nationalist position, this quotation shows that the nationalist school bases its reasoning on the "Either A or not-A, but not both A and not-A" logic of the excluded middle. The mistake in this view is that it conceives culture (which is the realm of primary experiences) as an empirical reality in the sense of something external, as a body of fact which can only be recognized or perceived by people in their respective situations. Second, this view appears to hold that people are so "chained" to their respective culturally determined experiences that perception of other experiences is impossible. To this view, the role of the philosopher cannot be other than that of the spectator who passively observes and records what is happening and what has happened, for he does not add anything new to the object by his mental activity. In other words, his essential role is to give his cultural values a hermeneutical interpretation.

This position returns us to ethnophilosophy. The nationalists fail to distinguish between ethnophilosophy and philosophical knowledge. Yet the difference between philosophical knowledge and ethnophilosophy lies in the distinction between a critical, methodical, and systematic knowledge proceeding from the full but purified nonprogrammatic contact with the "object" and the spontaneous responses to life situations or experiences. The object of philosophical knowledge is always thematic in itself only insofar as its end is seen only in relation to the need and desire for knowledge. Philosophy does not approach Being primarily as a prerequisite for the accomplishment of a practical end. It takes its object in itself. Philosophical cognizance is opposed to the pragmatic deformation of knowledge in that it seeks to understand the object in its own deep sense. The prerequisite for all philosophical knowledge is a full interest in the object as such and in the knowing contact with it. Hence it is not limited by immediate practical intentions.

What Wiredu says in regard to the functional role of philosophy in general and of African philosophy in particular serves also to clarify the question about experience and its relation to philosophical activity. The question about the nature of experience can be quite wide and complex, for experience, as Dewey says, can be nonrational and irrational, but it can also be funded with intelligence and controlled inference. We therefore find it expedient to say that we are concerned here only with such experience as may be significant to philosophical activity.

Experience is the result of the complex relationship between thought or reason and the external situation. What makes up the external situation may vary from abstract social conjectures about given economic relations such as "exploitation of the masses" to political repression or to more complex events such as apartheid and other forms of discrimination.

However, that such "external" situations become experience depends on application of procedures and results of intelligent activity. Such application allows us to make inferences such as "That society is individualistic," or "This government is oppressive." And many times the inferences do not describe any observable objective reality, but yet are regarded as doing so by those who formulate them. They are the pretensions of many writers on such varied subjects as, for example, "the oppressive dimensions of technology," "imperialism and neocolonialism," "oppression of the masses," etc. These expressions describe *representations* of the social phenomena they refer to. They become assertions within the wider context of experience, derived out of specific problematic situations and guided by the same situations. Very significantly, such assertions are results of inquiry, of a comparison of the situations they describe with alternative ones. Thus by inquiry not only do we reconstruct the situation of experience into one of conceptual relations, but we also form new theories which we posit as its solutions.

There are two important implications of what we have said above. First, that such assertions as the ones we have exemplified above are what constitute the world of experience for philosophers. Philosophers do not concern themselves with empirical assertions straightforwardly. The basic assertions for philosophers are assertions which result from an interpretation of the empirical reality of events and facts as well as of representations, both general and private. As such they tend to be personal rather than unanimous and collective representations of reality. Frequently, in fact, they co-exist with rival assertions, both cultural and personal. Second, they are not the only assertions that can be made of the given situations. Inquiry may be directed to any aspect of empirical reality as an intelligent inquirer may deem of priority and/or importance. You would wonder, for example, why some African writers waste so much effort waging literary wars against neocolonialism instead of talking more constructively about the rampant practices of corruption, nepotism, tribalism, mismanagement, oppression, authoritarianism, population growth, or even about the creative imaginations in everyday narratives and metaphors. Yet we are saying that there is no objective criterion for determining what should or must constitute the area of urgent attention for everyone or for persuading anyone that these practices and events constitute problems at all. There can be no objective agreement. As a result, human experience must be recognized as a variety of independent, self-consistent worlds of discourse, each the result of the interaction between subject and object. Every experience can only claim a relative validity in comparison to others.

Philosophy is experience. It is a personal point of view insofar as it is mine, and because philosophy consists not in persuading others but in making our own minds clear. Yet, if in so doing we present the grounds upon which philosophy rests, then philosophy becomes more than merely personal. This does not mean, on the other hand, that every philosophy is relative and therefore free of criticism and rejection. Michael Oakeshott writes that "A form of experience is fallacious and can be rejected in so far as it fails to provide what is satisfactory in experience. . . . To refute is to exhibit the principle of the fallacy or error in virtue of which a form of experience falls short of complete coherence; it is to discover both the half-truth in the error, and the error in the half-truth."[3] Any attempt to popularize philosophy by prescribing the nature it should take in regard to form or content thus at once debases it; a general demand for philosophy is a general demand for its degradation.

There is no single philosophical tradition that was tailor-made and produced like an industrial product. There is no justifiable reason, therefore, why one individual or group should try to tailor-make African philosophy by prescribing what ought to be its content, method of reasoning, and standards of truth. Like other philosophical systems and traditions, African philosophy must also be born out of its own peculiar cultural circumstances combined with a living and constructive zeal amongst individual African intellectuals to understand and explain the world around them. These cultural circumstances must be seen to include many African constructions of their reality, their forms of modern living, their needs, problems, and methods of acquiring meaningful knowledge. Also, the dialectical method must be put into operation. In other words, African philosophy will thrive only when and if we continue to articulate and clarify our experiences of these historical and cultural conditions in philosophical premises in the manner of dialogue and discussion. Debate and the desire to get our concepts properly understood are two vehicles of intellectual inquiry that have helped in the establishment of philosophy as a special intellectual activity; and we have no reason to exempt African philosophy from them. Such intellectual inquiry is, however, possible only where we will all be open to the historical processes affecting and conditioning our needs, experiences, and general historical choices. This move toward a new culture is inevitable, and many African intellectuals, especially in philosophy, need to shed the antiquarian complex that is suffocating progress in many aspects of their thinking. So while we say yes to African personality, we ought also to say yes to technological modernism; yes to the African conscience, but also yes to universal science.

Notes

All translations from non-English titles throughout the text are mine unless stated otherwise. Where quotations are from existing translations, I have cited the English titles in the notes.

1 Logocentrism and Emotivism

1. HARLAND, R., *Superstructuralism: The Philosophy of Structuralism and Post-Structuralism* (Routledge, London and New York, 1987), p. 123.

2. HEGEL, G. W. F. von, *Lectures on the Philosophy of World History*, 1975; revised edition, 1989, p. 177.

3. Ibid., pp. 152 and 153.

4. Ibid., p. 176.

5. Ibid.

6. Ibid., p. 135.

7. POLANYI, M., *Personal Knowledge: Towards a Post-Critical Philosophy*, (Harper Torchbook edition, Harper & Row, New York, 1964), p. 287.

8. See DU BOIS, "The Conservation of Races," American Negro Academy Occasional Papers, No. 2, 1897. Reprinted in FONER, P. S. (ed.), *W. E. B. Du Bois Speaks: Speeches and Addresses 1890–1919* (Pathfinders Press, New York, 1970), p. 78.

9. See, for example, McCLENDON, J. H., "The Afro-American Philosopher and the Philosophy of the Black Experience: A Bibliographical Essay on a Neglected Topic Both in Philosophy and Black Studies," in *Sage Race Relations Abstracts*, Vol. 7, No. 4, November 1982, p.2, and HARRIS, L., *Philosophy Born of Struggle: Anthology of Afro-American Philosophy from 1917* (Kendall/Hunt Publishing Co., Dubuque, Iowa, 1983), p. xii.

10. HARRIS, *Philosophy Born of Struggle*, p. xii.

11. This is not to discredit the African reaction to European invasion as can be cited from cases throughout the African continent.

12. CARRILHO, M., *Sociologia della negritudine* (Liguori Editore, Napoli, 1974), pp. 29–30. Carrilho is here echoing the central theme of Fanon's *Black Skin, White Masks*.

13. COOK, M., "Les Precurseurs négro-américains de la Négritude," in *Le Soleil*, Numero sur la Négritude, No. 305, Dakar, 8 May 1971, p. 12.

14. Blyden first used this phrase, considered by many to be the English variable (sometimes the word "Black" is substituted for "African") of *négritude*, coined by Aimé Césaire about 1934–35 and used publicly for the first time in his book *Cahier d'un retour au pays natal* in 1939, in 1893 at a congress in Freetown. Shortly after, the phrase was used by Henry Sylvester Williams of Trinidad at a conference in London in 1900 to protest the selling of African native land by Europeans. This conference does not go down as one of the pan-African congresses, but nonetheless it was their precursor and had nearly identical characteristics. But due to his staunch anti-white attitude, Blyden withheld his support from the congress after

denouncing the participation of Du Bois. See DU BOIS, *A Voice from Bleeding Africa* (Monrovia, 1856), *A Vindication of the Negro Race* (New York, 1897), and "The Negro in Ancient History" in *The Methodist Quarterly* (New York, 1869).

15. As the French philosopher and writer Jean-Paul SARTRE was to describe it later in his celebrated preface "Orphée Noir" to Léopold S. SENGHOR's *Anthologie de la nouvelle poésie nègre et malgache de langue française* (Presses Universitaires de France, Paris, 1948).

16. FILESI, T., *Movimenti di emancipazione coloniale a nascita dei nuovi stati in Africa* (Casa Editrice Dott. Francesco Vallardi, Milano, 1971), p. 27.

17. Blyden, quoted by LYNCH, H. R., "A 19th century progenitor of Pan-Africanism and Negritude: Edward Wilmot Blyden," in *The New African* (London), Vol. 7, No. 2, 1968, pp. 4–8.

18. Marcus Aurelius Garvey was arrested and charged with public offenses and incitation of the public to commit racist acts. He was then sentenced to four years in prison in 1924. Awarded a parole after two years, he went to London where he died a poor man in 1940.

19. McKAY, C., *Banjo*, Editions Rieder, Paris, 1929. *Banjo* was first published in its original English version by Harper & Brothers of New York in the spring of 1929. Its French translation was published by Rieder in Paris later that same year. However, its impact was greater among the young founders of the negritude movement studying in France at the time— people such as Léopold Sédar Senghor, Aimé Césaire, and Léon Damas, for example—than in the United States. My reading and quotation are from the French translation; the translation back into English here is mine.

20. See BRAMBILLA, C., *La Négritudine* (Edizioni Nigrizia, n.d.), p. 27.

21. CLIFFORD, J., *The Predicament of Culture: Twentieth-Century Ethnography, Literature, and Art* (Harvard University Press, Cambridge, Massachusetts, 1988), p. 177.

22. DEPESTRE, R., *Bonjour et adieu à la négritude* (Robert Laffont, Paris, 1980), pp. 144–45.

23. MENIL, R., *Tracées: Identité, négritude, esthétique aux Antilles* (Robert Laffont, Paris, 1981).

24. CLIFFORD, *The Predicament of Culture*, p. 178.

25. Ibid., pp. 28–29.

26. Ibid., p. 120.

27. Ibid., p. 56.

28. DELAFOSSE, M., *Les Nègres* (Rieder, Paris, 1927).

29. HARDY, G., *L'Art nègre* (Laurens, Paris, 1927).

30. FROBENIUS, L., *Kulturgeschichte Afrikas* (Zurich, 1933). French translation: *Histoire de la civilisation africaine* (Gallimard, Paris, 1936).

31. Author of many ethnological books on West African peoples and cultures; together with Maquet, Balandier edited the well-known *Dictionnaire des civilisations africaines*.

32. DIOP, C. A., *The African Origin of Civilization* (Lawrence Hill & Company, Westport, Connecticut, 1974), pp. 151–52.

33. OLELA, H., "The African Foundations of Greek Philosophy," in WRIGHT, R. A. (ed.), *African Philosophy: An Introduction* (University Press of America, Lanham, Maryland, 1984), p. 80.

34. Ibid.

35. Ibid., p. 81.

36. Ibid., p. 82.

37. See CLARK, R. T. R., *Myth and Symbol in Ancient Egypt* (Thames and Hudson, London, 1959), pp. 64–66. Quoted in OLELA, "African Foundations . . . ," p. 85.

38. OLELA, "African Foundations . . . ," pp. 87–88.

39. Ibid., p. 86.

40. Ibid., p. 89.

41. See chapter 3 below (section on Marcel Griaule).

42. OLELA, "African Foundations . . . ," p. 89.

43. JAMES, G., *The Stolen Legacy* (Philosophical Library, New York, 1954), pp. 75–76. Quoted by OLELA in "African Foundations . . . ," p. 89.

44. BOWERSOCK, G. W., "Black Athena I. The Fabrication of Ancient Greece 1785–1985, by Martin Bernal," book review in *The Journal of Interdisciplinary History*, Vol. 19, No. 3, pp. 490–91.

45. LEFKOWITZ, M., "Not Out of Africa: The Origins of Greece and the Illusions of Afrocentrists," in *The New Republic*, 10 February 1992, pp. 29–36.

46. BRAMBILLA, *La Négritudine*, p. 33.

47. Enlightenment (Fr. *philosophie des lumières*; Germ. *Aufklärung*; Sp. *illustration*; It. *illuminismo*) is the European intellectual movement that flourished in the 1700s, characterized by a full (perhaps even exaggerated) confidence in the capacity of reason to break through the darkness and mystery of the unknown that cloud the human spirit.

48. CÉSAIRE, A., *Cahier d'un retour au pays natal* (Edition of Présence Africaine, Paris, 1956), p. 49.

49. CRANE, C. B., *Alain Locke and the Negro Renaissance*, Ph.D. thesis, University of California, San Diego, 1971, p. 210.

50. See also WASHINGTON, J., *Alain Locke and Philosophy: A Quest for Cultural Pluralism* (Greenwood Press, New York, 1986), p. 217.

51. SENGHOR, L. S., in "Message de Goethe aux Nègres nouveaux."

52. SENGHOR, L. S., "L'Esthétique négro-africaine," in *Diogène* (Paris), October 1956, pp. 202–03.

53. SENGHOR, L. S., "La Civilisation négro-africaine," in *Les plus beaux écrits de l'Union Française et du MAGHREB* (La Colombo, Paris, 1964), pp. 70–71.

54. See GOLDWATER, R., *Primitivism in Modern Art* (enlarged edition, The Belknap Press of Harvard University Press, Cambridge, Massachusetts, 1986), pp. 104–42 (originally published by Random House, 1938). Note the following quotation he takes from August Mache to support his point: " 'To hear the thunder is to feel its secret. To understand the speech of forms is to be nearer the secret, to live. To create forms is to live. Are not children creators who build directly from the secret of their perceptions, rather than the imitators of Greek form? Are not the aborigines artists who have their own form, strong as the form of the thunder?' "

55. MUDIMBE, V. Y., "African Gnosis, Philosophy and the Order of Knowledge: An Introduction," in *The African Studies Review*, Vol. 28, Nos. 2/3, June/September 1985, p. 206.

56. KOBLER, J. F., *Vatican II and Phenomenology* (Martinus Nijhoff Publishers, Dordrecht, 1985), p. 71.

57. Ibid., p. 79.

58. MUDIMBE, "African Gnosis," p. 204.

59. The following bibliography is indicative of the volume of phenomenological works done especially under the influence of Vatican II:

POSTIOMA, Adalberto da, "Elementi costitutive per una filosofia africana," in *Filosofia e vita*, No. 3, 1964, pp. 68–77.

———, *Filosofia africana*, Edizioni Missionari Estere Cappuccini, Milano, 1967.

———, "Esiste una filosofia africana?" in *Filosofia e vita*, No. 1, 1969, pp. 64–74.

——, "Idee religiose e idee filosofiche nell'Africa d'oggi," in *Filosofia, religione e religioni*, numero speciale di *Filosofia e vita*, Nos. 2–3–4, 1966, pp. 305–56.

——, "Per una filosofia africana," in *Filosofia e vita*, No. 3, 1963, pp. 79–85.

——, "Premesse filosofiche africane e cristianesimo," in *Filosofia e vita*, No. 2, 1964, pp. 63–71.

——, "Presenza africana nella filosofia universale," in *Filosofia e vita*, No. 1, 1969, pp. 68–76.

BIMWENYI, O., "Le Dieu de nos ancêtres," in *Cahiers des religions africaines*, Vol. 4, 1970, pp. 137–51 and Vol. 5, 1971, pp. 59–112.

——, "Le Muntu à la lumière de ses croyances en l'au-delà," in *Cahiers des religions africaines*, Vol. 2, 1969, pp. 73–94.

BUAKASA, G., "Philosophie et religion bantoues," in *Femmes, Vie, Monde*, Vol. 19, 1964, pp. 9–11.

FOUDA, B., *La Philosophie africaine de l'existence*, Ph.D. thesis, Lille, Faculté des Lettres, 1967.

GUISIMANA, B., "L'homme selon la philosophie pendé," in *Cahiers des religions africaines*, Vol. 2, 1968, pp. 65–72.

——, "Nambi selon la philosophie pendé," in *Cahiers des religions africaines*, Vol. 4, 1970, pp. 31–40.

HAULE, C., *Bantu "Witchcraft" and Christian Morality: The Encounter of Bantu Uchawi with Christian Morality, an Anthropological and Theological Study*, Suppl. 16 of *Neue Zeitschrift für Missionswissenschaft*, 1969.

ILOGU, E., "Christianity and Ibo Traditional Religion," in *International Review of Missions*, Vol. 54, 1965, pp. 215, 335–342.

MBITI, J. S., *African Religions and Philosophy* (Heinemann, London, 1969).

——, *Concepts of God in Africa* (S.P.C.K., London, 1970).

MBONYIKEBE, D., "Ethique chrétienne et valeurs africaines," in *Cahiers des religions africaines*, Vol. 3, 1969, pp. 149–59.

OLELA, H., *The Rationale for an African Philosophy: A Critical Examination of the African Cosmological Views with Some Reference to Luo Beliefs*, Ph.D. thesis, The Florida State University, Tallahassee, 1971.

ONGONG'A, J. J., *The Luo Concept of Death: A Study of Beliefs and Ceremonies of Death in the Light of Christian Message*. Ph.D. thesis, Pontificia Università Urbaniana, Rome, 1979.

60. SARTRE, Preface to SENGHOR, *Anthologie*, p. xliii.

61. FRANKLIN, A., "La Négritude: Réalité ou mystification? Réflexions sur l'orphée noir," in *Les Etudiants noirs parlent* (Présence Africaine, Paris, 1953).

62. SENGHOR, "Sorbonne et Négritude," speech given at the Sorbonne in 1961, in *Liberté 1* (Seuil, Paris, 1964), pp. 135–36.

63. FANON, F., *Peau noire, masques blancs* (Seuil, Paris, 1952), pp. 135–36.

64. SARTRE, in FANON, F., *The Wretched of the Earth* (Penguin Books, London, 1978), pp. 11–12.

65. Ibid., p. 19.

66. Ibid., p. 20.

67. FANON, *The Wretched of the Earth*, pp. 88–89.

68. Ibid., p. 188.

69. For a biographical account of Fanon, see GENDZIER, I. L., *Frantz Fanon: A Critical Study* (Grove Press, New York, 1973); PERINBAM, B. M., *Holy Violence: The Revolutionary Thought of Frantz Fanon* (Three Continents Press, Washington, D.C., 1982); and HANSEN,

E., *Frantz Fanon: Social and Political Thought* (Ohio State University Press, Columbus, 1977); for a shortened summary see the latter's "Freedom and Revolution in the Thought of Frantz Fanon," in *Universitas: An Inter-Faculty Journal* (Ghana), Vol. 5, No. 2 (New Series), May/November 1976, pp. 19–40.

70. HANSEN, E., "Freedom and Revolution in the Thought of Frantz Fanon," in *Universitas*, p. 21.

71. MARX, K., "Theses on Feuerbach," in FEUR, L. (ed.), *Basic Writings on Politics and Philosophy: Karl Marx and Friedrich Engles* (Anchor Books, New York, 1959), p. 245 — Thesis XI.

72. FANON, *The Wretched of the Earth*, p. 252.

73. See FANON, F., *Black Skin, White Masks* (Grove Press, New York, 1967), p. 17.

74. GENDZIER, *Frantz Fanon*, p. 23.

75. FANON, *Black Skin, White Masks*, pp. 216–17.

76. HEGEL, G. W. F., *The Phenomenology of Mind*, translated by J. B. Baillie, 2nd, revised edition (Allen and Unwin, London, 1949), p. 233; quoted in FANON, *Black Skin, White Masks*, p. 218.

77. HANSEN, "Freedom and Revolution . . . ," in *Universitas*, p. 28.

78. JAHN, J., *Muntu: An Outline of the New African Culture* (Grove Press, New York, 1961), p. 141.

79. Ibid., pp. 142–43.

80. Ibid., p. 143.

81. ABRAHAM, W. E., *The Mind of Africa* (University of Chicago Press, Chicago, 1962), p. 42.

82. See MBITI, J. S., *African Religions and Philosophy* (Heinemann, London, 1969), p. 11.

83. DEREN, M., *Divine Horsemen, the Living Gods of Haiti* (London and New York, 1953).

84. JAHN, *Muntu*, p. 110.

85. If it does not amount to advancing a theory too far, we may say that it is also due to these philosophical movements, dominant on the European continent at the time and to which British philosophers generally remained indifferent, that the emergence of African philosophy came first in the French colonies and has remained more lively and dominant there. These movements also influenced the difference in attitude and point of focus between the Continental (mostly French) and British anthropologists. It would be enough to compare Marcel Griaule, Germaine Dieterlen, or Louis V. Thomas with, let us say, Meyer Fortes, E. E. Evans-Pritchard, A. R. Radcliffe-Brown, etc. While the former group is analytical and spiritualistic in the line of Cartesian reason, the latter is predominantly descriptive and bent toward a social relations aspect of culture in the empiricist tradition.

86. MUDIMBE, V. Y., *The Invention of Africa* (Indiana University Press, Bloomington/Indianapolis, 1988), p. 154.

87. HARRIS, L., "Philosophy Born of Struggle: Afro-American Philosophy since 1918," in ORUKA, H., and MASOLO, D. A. (eds.), *Philosophy and Cultures* (Bookwise Publishers, Nairobi, 1983), p. 104. Other titles from the Afro-American camp of this stuggle are, to mention just a few, PERRY, R. L. M., *Sketch of Philosophical Systems, Suffrage* (American Publication Company, Hartford, Connecticut, 1895); FONTAINE, W. T., "Toward a Philosophy of American Negro Literature," in *Présence Africaine*, Vol. 53, No. 7, 1958; WEST, C., "Philosophy and the Afro-American Experience," in *The Philosophical Forum*, Vol. 9, Nos. 2/3, Winter–Spring 1977–78; JONES, W. R., "The Legitimacy and

Necessity of Black Philosophy," in *The Philosophical Forum*, Vol. 9, Nos. 2/3, Winter–Spring 1977–78.

88. MUDIMBE, "African Gnosis . . . ," p. 205.

2 Tempels and the Setting of Ethnophilosophy

1. TEMPELS, P., *La Philosophie bantoue* (Présence Africaine, Paris, 1965, 3rd ed.), p. 13. Unless otherwise stated, all quotations are my translations from this edition.

2. Ibid., p. 14.

3. Ibid., p. 15.

4. Ibid., p. 16.

5. Ibid.

6. Sometimes the use of these concepts reveals a grave misunderstanding of the religious beliefs and practices here in question.

7. TEMPELS, *La Philosophie bantoue*, pp. 22–23.

8. Ibid., p. 25.

9. Ibid., p. 32.

10. Ibid., p. 44.

11. Ibid., pp. 49–50.

12. Ibid., p. 50.

13. Ibid., p. 52.

14. Ibid., p. 54.

15. Ibid., pp. 57–60.

16. Ibid., p. 80.

17. Ibid., p. 81.

18. Ibid., p. 122.

19. Ibid., p. 115.

20. Ibid.

21. See ibid., p. 61.

22. This passage, which is quoted by F. Eboussi-Boulaga in his article "Le Bantou problématique," is taken from the first edition of Tempels's *La Philosophie bantoue* (Elizabethville, Lovania, 1945), pp. 53–54. See EBOUSSI-BOULAGA, "Le Bantou problématique," in *Présence Africaine*, Vol. 66, 1968, p. 28.

23. See TEMPELS, 1st ed. (1945), p. 148.

24. For a more complete treatment of this sociohistorical ill-fate of Tempels's *La Philosophie bantoue*, see EBOUSSI-BOULAGA, "Le Bantou problématique," pp. 21–32.

25. ROELENS, V., "A propos de '*La Philosophie bantoue*'," in *Grand Lacs*, Vol. 62, No. 7, 1947, pp. 358–60.

26. See CÉSAIRE, A., *Discours sur le colonialisme* (Reclame, Paris, 1950). In this line we may also mention the article of Abbe B. Kiambi, "L'Être chez les bantous," in *Revue du clergé africain*, Vol. 21, No. 5, 1966, pp. 428–35. Kiambi holds that it is nonsense for Tempels to have presumed that the Bantu notion of force replaces exactly the scholastic notion of being; because this implies that the Bantu have an intelligence essentially different from that of Europeans. See Kiambi, p. 432, quotation from E. Boelaert.

27. TEMPELS, *La Philosophie bantoue*, pp. 35–36.

28. HALLETT, G., "The Theoretical Content of Language," in *Gregorianum*, Vol. 54, No. 2, 1973, p. 310.

29. Ibid.

30. SMET, A. J., *Histoire de la philosophie africaine contemporaine: courants et problèmes* (Kinshasa-Limete, Faculté de Théologie Catholique, 1980), p. 111.

31. Ibid., p. 112.

32. TEMPELS, *La Philosophie bantoue* (Elizabethville, 1945), p. 135.

33. TEMPELS, P., *Bantu-filosofie* (Antwerp, 1946), p. 103.

34. HORTON, R., "African Traditional Religion and Western Science," in *Africa*, Vol. 37, Nos. 1/2, 1967, pp. 50–71 and 155–87.

35. SMET, A. J., "L'Oeuvre inédite du Père Placide Tempels," in *Revue africaine de théologie*, Vol. 1, No. 2, 1977, pp. 219–33.

36. TEMPELS, *Bantu-filosofie*, pp. 23–24; cited by SMET in *Histoire de la philosophie africaine contemporaine*, pp. 118–19.

37. In 1948, as the newly-founded publishing house Présence Africaine (Paris) prepared to release its version of Tempels's *La Philosophie bantoue*, the directors of Présence Africaine solicited notes of opinion, called testimonies (Fr. *témoignages*), on the book from leading French-speaking intellectuals as part of the prelude to the launching of the book. These notes or testimonies were later published in the journal *Présence Africaine* (No. 7, 1949, pp. 252–278) under the title "Témoignages sur *La Philosophie bantoue* du Père Tempels"; the authors included Gaston Bachelard, Albert Camus, P. H. Chombard de Lauwe, Marcel Griaule, Jacques Howlett, Louis Lavelle, F. H. Lem, Gabriel Marcel, Paul Masson-Oursel, G. Mounin, Madeleine Rousseau, Adolphe Saar, Abdoulaye Sadji, Ch. Traore-Leroux, and Jean Wahl.

38. SMET, *Histoire de la philosophie africaine contemporaine*, p. 118.

39. HEIDEGGER, M. *Being and Time*, translated by John Macquarrie and Edward Robinson (Harper & Row, New York and Evanston, 1962), p. 35.

40. The Foundationalist school is a name widely given today to identify the group of scholars, mainly philosophers of science, who believe in the rational foundations of knowledge and regard the search for these foundations as the primary duty of philosophy. They believe these foundations are universal because they are based on the empiricistic notion of a unified objective world which is knowable only through application of universal epistemological principles as defined by Western science. Although philosophical study of science has been in existence for more than two thousand years, the recent orientations in philosophy of science are mainly an evaluation of the revolutionary impact of the Enlightenment. The prominence of the Foundationalist school is closely related to this. It emerged in the early 1960s as a resistance to the claims advanced forcefully by Thomas Kuhn (1964), and later by Richard Rorty (1980) and P. Feyerabend (1975, 1978) and supported by the famous anthropological studies by Evans-Pritchard and Lienhardt, that Western science itself is a product of social paradigms. The Foundationalists have recently come out particularly strongly in defense of the categories and principles of Western scientific thought against pluralist definitions of rationality which argue in favor of inclusion of the so-called nonscientific modes of thought into the ranks of rationality. The Foundationalist school includes such people as Ian Hacking, Martin Hollis, Steven Lukes, Robin Horton, and Dan Sperber, among others.

41. Tempels's work raised much professional debate among his European readers as one would have normally expected. Of those who disagreed with his attribution of philosophy to Africans, see notably the following: SOUSBERGHE, L. de, "À propos de *La Philosophie bantoue*," in *Zaire*, No. 5, 1951, pp. 821–28; FABRO, C., "Controversie sul pensiero dei primitive," in *Euntes Docete*, No. 1, 1948, pp. 50–62; CHARLES, P., "Note relative à l'ouvrage du R. P. Tempels intitulé 'La Philosophie bantoue,' " in CHARLES, P., *Etudes missiologiques* (Desclée de Brouwer, 1956), pp. 266–72; LAYDEVANT, F., "Philosophie des bantous: à propos du P. Tempels," in *Africae Fraternae Ephemerides Romanae*, Nos. 24–25, 1947, pp. 55–

57. A better and more constructive criticism is that of CRAHAY, F., "Le Décollage conceptuel: conditions d'une philosophie bantoue," in *Diogène*, No. 52, 1965, pp. 61–84. Apart from these critical writings and comments on the work, Tempels also received sympathetic recognition from a group of leading Francophone intellectuals who thought that the missionary's work had made a breakthrough into the "soul" of the Bantu and Africans in general. These people include those who wrote under the title "Témoignages" in *Présence Africaine* in preparation for the publication of the Présence Africaine edition of Tempels's book in 1948 (see above, note 37). A number of African philosophers, especially Hountondji, have bitterly criticized the views expressed in the "Témoignages" as being very insincere and misleading and utterly incongruent with the true and critical philosophical activities in which these very authors were individually engaged and which are opposed to the noncritical and collective body of knowledge which Tempels had attributed to Africans as their "philosophy."

3 Systematic Ethnophilosophy

1. The credibility of Ogotemmêli's conversations has, however, been highly doubted, with claims that *Dieu d'eau* was a hoax, that Ogotemmêli, acting under instructions from the traditional Dogon experts, deliberately put up a rehearsed show for Griaule. But importance is still accredited to the work, which, on this ground, is still accepted.

2. See BALANDIER, G., "Tendances de l'ethnologie française," in *Cahiers internationaux de sociologie*, No. 27, 1960, pp. 11–22; and SAREVSKAJA, B. I., "La Méthode de l'ethnographie de Marcel Griaule et les questions de méthodologie dans l'ethnographie française contemporaine," in *Cahiers d'études africaines*, Vol. 4, No. 16, 1963, pp. 590–602.

3. See RICHARDS, A. I., "African Systems of Thought: An Anglo-French Dialogue," in *Man*, No. 2, 1967, pp. 286–98; DOUGLAS, M., "If the Dogon," in *Cahiers d'études africaines*, No. 28, 1967, pp. 659–72; and GOODY, J., "Review of Conversations with Ogotemmêli by M. Griaule," in *American Anthropologist*, Vol. 69, No. 2, 1967, pp. 239–41.

4. CLIFFORD, *The Predicament of Culture*, p. 88.

5. GRIAULE, M., *Dieu d'eau, entretiens avec Ogotemmêli* (Fayard, Paris, 1966), p. 15.

6. Ibid., pp. 15–17.

7. Ibid., p. 45.

8. Ibid.

9. Ibid., pp. 55–56.

10. Ibid., p. 69.

11. See ibid., pp. 70–73 (the eleventh day).

12. Ibid., p. 75.

13. Ibid., p. 77.

14. Ibid., pp. 79–80.

15. Ibid., pp. 95–100.

16. Ibid., p. 95.

17. Ibid., p. 101.

18. Ibid., pp. 104–05.

19. See ibid., pp. 115–16.

20. Ibid., p. 122.

21. Ibid., p. 125.

22. Ibid., p. 159.

23. See ibid., pp. 127–28.

24. See LETTENS, D. A., *Mystagogie et mystification: Evaluation de l'oeuvre de Marcel*

Griaule (Presses Lavigerie, Bujumbura, Burundi, 1971) and Michel-Jones, F., *Retour au Dogon: figure du double et ambivalence*, (Le Sycamore, Paris, 1978).

25. GRIAULE, *Dieu d'eau*, p. 177.

26. GRIAULE, M., "Preface," in DIETERLEN, G., *Essai sur la religion bambara* (Presses Universitaires de France, Paris, 1951), pp. vii–viii.

27. GRIAULE, *Dieu d'eau*, p. 201.

28. See above, p. 75.

29. GRIAULE, "Preface," in DIETERLEN, p. viii.

30. I have referred to "philosophy of nature" as a wisdom or system of thought that tries to interpret and give meaning to all things, visible and invisible. It represents a holistic view of the world and of the universe in its structure and essential abstract elements. The conception of beings and life is synthetic and unifying. The essence of all things is one. The world of this thought is large, but in basic elements it remains one. It is in this sense that we have here spoken of a "philosophy of nature" because it embraces and reduces everything to a unity. It is a global or cosmic lore typical of popular mythological wisdom such as that recited by Ogotemmêli. I do not intend to violate the celebrity of the philosophy of nature of our day in the line of Einstein and his school. My branding of Ogotemmêli's narration as a "philosophy of nature" has been done simply for convenience of language and should be taken to mean "worldview."

31. GRIAULE, *Dieu d'eau*, p. 161.

32. Ibid., pp. 161–63.

33. DIETERLEN, G., *Les Âmes des Dogons*, Université de Paris, Travaux et mémoires de l'Institut d'Ethnologie, 40, Paris, 1941, p. vi.

34. Ibid.

35. Ibid., p. vii.

36. Ibid., pp. 10–11.

37. See ibid., p. 18. See also GRIAULE, *Dieu d'eau*, pp. 159–63.

38. DIETERLEN, *Les Âmes des Dogons*, p. 73.

39. Ibid., p. 73.

40. Ibid., pp. 73–74.

41. Ibid., p. 75.

42. GRIAULE, *Dieu d'eau*, p. 124.

43. GRIAULE, M., *Masques Dogons*, Université de Paris, Travaux et mémoires de l'Institut d'Ethnologie, 33, Paris, 1938, pp. 160–64.

44. GRIAULE, *Dieu d'eau*, pp. 160–61.

45. DIETERLEN, *Les Âmes des Dogons*, pp. 75–76.

46. Ibid., p. 76.

47. Ibid., p. 76.

48. See ibid., p. 93.

49. See ibid., p. 95.

50. See GRIAULE, *Dieu d'eau*, pp. 127–28.

51. Ibid., p. 163.

52. DIETERLEN, *Les Âmes des Dogons*, p. 126.

4 Language and Reality

1. For a full list of these classes, see KAGAME, A., *La Philosophie bantu-rwandaise de l'être*, Académie Royale des Sciences Coloniales (Classes des Sciences morales et politique. Memoires in 8° Nouv. Serie XII, i), Brussels, 1956, p. 41.

2. Ibid., pp. 74–77.
3. Ibid., p. 119.
4. Ibid., p. 108.
5. See ibid., pp. 112ff.
6. Ibid., p. 121.
7. Ibid., p. 298.
8. Ibid., p. 120.
9. Ibid., p. 148.
10. Ibid., p. 150.
11. See ibid., pp. 196–203.
12. For the full account on this section, see ibid., pp. 152–203.
13. See ibid., pp. 207–210.
14. Ibid., p. 215.
15. Ibid., p. 240.
16. Ibid., p. 249.
17. Ibid., p. 250.
18. Ibid., p. 267.
19. Ibid., p. 320.
20. Ibid., p. 344.
21. See ibid., pp. 281–82.
22. See ibid., pp. 350–55.
23. Ibid., p. 119.
24. HARRIES, L., "*Philosophie bantu-rwandaise de l'être,* by Alexis Kagame," book review in *Africa* (London), No. 27, 1957, p. 305.
25. Ibid.
26. Ibid.
27. KAGAME, *La Philosophie bantu-rwandaise de l'être,* p. 39. See also KAGAME, A., "L'Ethno-philosophie des 'Bantu,' " in KLIBANSKY, R. (ed.), *La Philosophie contemporaine* (Chronique), Vol. 4 (La Nuova Italia, Firenze, 1971), p. 594.
28. KAGAME, *La Philosophie bantu-rwandaise de l'être,* pp. 121–22.
29. For a fuller discussion of this issue, see MASOLO, D. A., "Alexis Kagame and African Socio-linguistics," in FLOISTAD, G. (ed.), *Contemporary Philosophy: A New Survey,* Vol. 5, *African Philosophy* (Martinus Nijhoff, Dordrecht, 1987), pp. 181–205.
30. VENDLER, Z., *Linguistics in Philosophy* (Cornell University Press, Ithaca, New York, 1967), p. 9.
31. WITTGENSTEIN, L., *Philosophical Investigations, I* (Basil Blackwell, Oxford/London, 1968), p. 90.
32. MARTINET, A., "Structure and Language," in EHRMANN, J. (ed.), *Structuralism* (Anchor Books, New York, 1970), p. 2.
33. KAGAME, A., *La Philosophie bantu comparée* (Présence Africaine, Paris, 1976), p. 122.
34. Ibid, p. 120.
35. LYONS, J., *Introduction to Theoretical Linguistics* (Cambridge University Press, 1974), p. 407.

5 Cultures without Time? Mbiti's Religious Ethnology

1. MBITI, J. S., *An Introduction to African Religion* (Heinemann, London, 1975), p. 12.
2. Ibid.

3. Ibid., p. 14.

4. Ibid., p. 19.

5. MBITI, J. S., *African Religions and Philosophy* (Heinemann, London, 1969), p. 2.

6. Ibid., p. 29.

7. Ibid., p. 32.

8. Ibid., p. 33.

9. Ibid., pp. 35–36.

10. Ibid., pp. 39–41.

11. Smith, E. W., *African Ideas of God* (Edinburgh House, London, 1950), p. 59.

12. Ibid., p. 58.

13. MBITI, *African Religions and Philosophy*, p. 59.

14. Ibid., pp. 75–76.

15. See IDOWU, E. B., *Olodumare: God in Yoruba Belief* (Longmans, London, 1962), pp. 55–106.

16. MBITI, *African Religions and Philosophy*, p. 78.

17. Ibid., p. 81.

18. Ibid., p. 16.

19. Ibid., p. 17. Mbiti adopts the Swahili words *zamani* and *sasa* for the English "past" and "present" respectively.

20. Published by Oxford University Press, 1971. Because of the length of this title, we will hereafter refer to it as *New Testament Eschatology*.

21. MBITI, *New Testament Eschatology*, p. 2.

22. Ibid., p. 28.

23. See ibid., pp. 32–50.

24. See ibid., pp. 51–56.

25. Ibid., p. 57.

26. Ibid., p. 132.

27. Ibid., p. 133.

28. See ibid., p. 139.

29. See ibid., pp. 153–56.

30. MBITI, *African Religions and Philosophy*, p. 32.

31. See, for example, GYEKYE, K., "*African Religions and Philosophy* by J. S. Mbiti," book review in *Second Order, an African Journal of Philosophy*, Vol. 4, No. 1, January 1975, pp. 86–94.

32. MBITI, *African Religions and Philosophy*, p. 15.

33. GYEKYE, book review in *Second Order*, p. 90.

34. Ibid., p. 92.

35. MBITI, *African Religions and Philosophy*, p. 17.

36. Ibid.

37. Ibid., pp. 17–19.

38. Ibid., p. 19.

39. Ibid., p. 18.

40. LÉVY-BRUHL, L., *Primitive Mentality* (Beacon Press, Boston, 1923), pp. 123–24; 445–46.

41. RIGBY, P., *Persistent Pastoralists: Nomadic Society in Transition* (Zed Books, London, 1985), pp. 67–91.

42. Ibid., p. 71.

43. See EVANS-PRITCHARD, "Nuer Time Reckoning," in *Africa*, Vol. 12, 1939, pp. 189–216; BEIDELMAN, T. O., *Moral Imagination in Kaguru Modes of Thought* (Indiana University Press, Bloomington, 1986); and BOHANNAN, P., "Concepts of Time among the

Tiv of Nigeria," in *South Western Journal of Anthropology*, Vol. 9, 1953, pp. 251–62 and reprinted in MIDDLETON, J. (ed.), *Myth and Cosmos* (University of Texas Press, Austin, 1963; 2nd ed., 1980).

44. BOHANNAN, "Concepts of Time among the Tiv of Nigeria," in MIDDLETON (ed.), *Myth and Cosmos*, p. 326.

45. LÉVY-BRUHL, *Primitive Mentality*, pp. 445–46; and MBITI, *African Religions and Philosophy*, p. 22.

46. LENIN, V. I., *Materialism and Empirico-Criticism* (Progress Publishers, Moscow, 1947), pp. 177–79.

47. LEACH, E. R., *Rethinking Anthropology* (Athlone, London, 1961), p. 132.

48. HORTON, R., "African Traditional Thought and Western Science," in *Africa*, Vol. 37, Nos. 1/2, p. 176; and RIGBY, *Persistent Pastoralists*, p. 89, footnote 6.

49. RAY, B. C., *African Religions* (Prentice-Hall, Englewood Cliffs, New Jersey, 1976), pp. 40–42.

50. RIGBY, *Persistent Pastoralists*, p. 75.

51. ALTHUSSER, L., "The Errors of Classical Economics: An Outline for a Concept of Historical Time," in ALTHUSSER, L., and BALIBAR, E., *Reading Capital* (New Left Books, London, 1970).

52. See also Kwame Appiah's argument against Mbiti on time in APPIAH, K., "Stricture on Structures: On Structuralism and African Fiction," in GATES, H. L. (ed.), *Black Literature and Literary Theory* (Methuen, London, 1984), pp. 142–44.

53. MBITI, *African Religions and Philosophy*, pp. 15–16.

54. KATO, B. H., *Theological Pitfalls in Africa* (Evangel Publishing House, Kisumu, 1975), p. 51.

55. Ibid., p. 55.

56. MBITI, *African Religions and Philosophy*, p. 10.

57. Ibid., p. 16. See also KATO, *Theological Pitfalls*, p. 56.

58. TEMPELS, P., *La Philosophie bantoue*, 1st French ed. (Ed. Lovania, Elisabethville, 1945), p. 34.

59. See MBITI, *African Religions and Philosophy*, p. 16, footnote 1.

60. See ibid., p. 17.

61. See ibid., p. 107. See also KATO, *Theological Pitfalls*, p. 57.

62. KATO, *Theological Pitfalls*, p. 62.

63. Ibid., p. 63.

6 Mysticism, Science, Philosophy, and Rationality: The Analytic View

1. See WINCH, P., "Understanding a Primitive Culture," in *American Philosophical Quarterly*, No. 1, 1964, pp. 307–24, also reprinted in WILSON, B. R. (ed.), *Rationality* (Harper and Row, New York, 1970); HORTON, R., "African Traditional Thought and Western Science," in *Africa*, Vol. 37, Nos. 1 & 2, 1967, pp. 50–71; 155–187.

2. TAMBIAH, S. J., *Magic, Science, Religion, and the Scope of Rationality* (Cambridge University Press, Cambridge, 1990), p. 115.

3. POLANYI, M., *Personal Knowledge: Towards a Post-Critical Philosophy* (Harper Torchbooks, Harper and Row Publishers, New York, 1964), p. 287.

4. Ibid., p. 287.

5. OVERING, J., "Introduction," in OVERING, J. (ed.), *Reason and Morality* (Tavistock Publications, London, 1985), p. 2.

6. HOLLIS, M., *Models of Man* (Cambridge University Press, Cambridge, UK, 1977), p. 150.

7. Ibid., p. 151.

8. TAMBIAH, *Magic, Science, Religion*, p. 115.

9. HACKING, I., "Language, Truth and Reason," in HOLLIS, M. and LUKES, S. (eds.), *Rationality and Relativism* (The MIT Press, Cambridge, Massachusettes, 1982), p. 52.

10. WINCH, P., *The Idea of a Social Science and Its Relation to Philosophy* [1958] (Routledge and Kegan Paul, London, 1971), p. 100.

11. Ibid., pp. 100–101.

12. See MANDT, A. J., "The Inevitability of Pluralism: Philosophical Practice and Philosophical Excellence," in COHEN, A., and DASCAL, M. (eds.), *The Institution of Philosophy: A Discipline in Crisis?* (Open Court Publishing Company, La Salle, Illinois, 1989), pp. 77–101.

13. MUDIMBE, V. Y., *The Invention of Africa* (Indiana University Press, Bloomington and Indianapolis, 1988).

14. Two anthropological publications which critically examine the crisis of philosophical assumptions of anthropological practice are: *Writing Culture: The Poetics and Politics of Ethnography*, edited by James Clifford and George E. Marcus (University of California Press, 1986); and *Anthropology as Cultural Critique: An Experimental Moment in the Human Sciences*, by George E. Marcus and Michael M. J. Fischer (The University of Chicago Press, 1986).

15. WIREDU, K., "Mysticism, Philosophy and Rationality," in *Universitas*, Vol. 2, No. 3, 1973, pp. 97–106.

16. HORTON, R., "African Traditional Thought and Western Science," in *Africa*, Vol. 37, Nos. 1/2, 1967.

17. Ibid, p. 157.

18. Ibid, p. 159.

19. Ibid, pp. 159–60.

20. See APPIAH, K., "Old Gods, New Worlds: Some Recent Work in the Philosophy of African Traditional Religion," in FLOISTAD, G. (ed.), *Contemporary Philosophy*, Vol 5: *African Philosophy* (Martinus Nijhoff Publishers, Dordrecht/Boston/Lancaster, 1987), p. 223.

21. Ibid., p. 226.

22. HORTON, "African Traditional Thought," p. 160.

23. WIREDU, K., *Philosophy and an African Culture* (Cambridge University Press, Cambridge, UK, 1980), pp. 37–50.

24. APPIAH, "Old Gods, New Worlds," pp. 222–23.

25. GOODY, J., *The Domestication of the Savage Mind* (Cambridge University Press, Cambridge, UK, 1977), p. 43.

26. Ibid.

27. KUHN, T., "Logic of Discovery and Psychology of Research?" in LAKOTOS, I., and MUSGRAVE, A. (eds.), *Criticism and Growth of Knowledge* (Cambridge University Press, Cambridge, UK, 1970), pp. 9–10.

28. KUHN, T., *The Structure of Scientific Revolutions* [1962] (The University of Chicago Press, 1970), pp. 37–38.

29. POLANYI, M., *Personal Knowledge*, p. 275. Note, however, that Polanyi's support of Kuhn is only in concept and argument but is not chronological, as Polanyi's *Personal Knowledge* was nearly four years older than Kuhn's *The Structure of Scientific Revolutions*.

30. Ibid., p. 276.

31. Ibid.

32. EVANS-PRITCHARD, E. E., *Witchcraft, Oracles and Magic among the Azande* (Oxford University Press, Oxford, 1937), pp. 314–15. In this respect, there is also something very unsystematic about "scientific" discoveries and revolutions. Many of them are unplanned for or chance results which are realized in the course of more restricted puzzle-oriented experiments. This shows, according to Kuhn, that the independence of scientific discoveries from socially defined attitudes and constructions is a false impression about Western science. Scientific knowledge is not free of value judgments. Other recent philosophers of science who have defended this thesis include Richard W. Miller (*Fact and Method*, Princeton University Press, 1987), Sandra Harding and Merrill Hintikka (*Discovering Reality: Feminist Perspectives on Epistemology, Metaphysics, Methodology, and Philosophy of Science*, D. Reidel, 1983), Evelyn F. Keller (*Reflections on Gender and Science*, Yale University Press, 1986), Lynn H. Nelson (*Who Knows: From Quine to a Feminist Empiricism*, Temple University Press, 1990), Helen E. Longino (*Science as Social Knowledge: Value and Objectivity in Scientific Inquiry*, Princeton University Press, 1990) and Nancy Tuana (*Feminism and Science*, Indiana University Press, 1989). Apart from Miller, the other authors listed here, all women philosophers, discuss the value content of scientific knowledge mainly from a gender perspective which argues that science cannot be objective as it is defined solely according to Eurocentric and phallocentric perceptions of reality. Science defines knowledge according to *dead white men*; and any knowledge which is biased on the basis of race and gender cannot claim objectivity.

33. EVANS-PRITCHARD, E. E., *Nuer Religion* (Oxford University Press, London, 1956), p. 128.

34. EVANS-PRITCHARD, E. E., *Theories of Primitive Religion* (Clarendon Press, Oxford, 1980), p. 89.

35. *Nuer Religion*, p. 128.

36. *Witchcraft, Oracles and Magic among the Azande*, p. 313.

37. *Theories of Primitive Religion*, p. 90.

38. Ibid., pp. 89–90.

39. HALLEN, B., and SODIPO, J. O., *Knowledge, Belief and Witchcraft: Analytic Experiments in African Philosophy* (Ethnographica, London, 1986), p. 18.

40. Ibid., p. 22.

41. Ibid., p. 49.

42. Ibid., pp. 60–64.

43. Ibid., p. 76, including footnote 23.

44. FIRTH, R., "Twins, Birds and Vegetables," in *Man*, Vol. 1, No. 1, 1966, pp. 1–17.

45. See LIENHARDT, G., "Modes of Thought," in EVANS-PRITCHARD, E. E., et al., *The Institutions of Primitive Society* (Blackwell, Oxford, 1954), pp. 95–107.

46. FIRTH, "Twins, Birds and Vegetables," p. 1.

47. Ibid.

48. Ibid., p. 2.

49. Ibid., p. 3.

50. Ibid.

51. Ibid., pp. 7–8.

52. BODUNRIN, P. O., " 'Theoretical Identities' and Scientific Explanation," in *Second Order*, Vol. 4, No. 1, 1975, pp. 56–65.

53. LITHOWN, R. J. M., "Bodunrin on Theoretical Identities: A Critique," in *Second Order*, Vol. 5, No. 2, 1976, pp. 76–84.

54. MASOLO, D. A., in FLOISTAD, G. (ed.), *Contemporary Philosophy, a New Survey*, Vol. 5, *African Philosophy* (Martinus Nijhoff, Dordrecht, 1987), pp. 181–205.

7 *Excavating Africa in Western Discourse*

1. EBOUSSI-BOULAGA, F., "Le Bantou problématique," in *Présence Africaine*, No. 66, 1968, pp. 7–8.
2. TEMPELS, P., *La Philosophie bantoue* (Lovania, Elizabethville, 1945), pp. 20–21. All references made to Tempels's *La Philosophie bantoue*, unless otherwise indicated, are to the first edition, 1945. The translations are mine.
3. EBOUSSI-BOULAGA, "Le Bantou problématique," p. 9.
4. See CÉSAIRE, A., *Discours sur le colonialisme* (Reclame, Paris, 1950).
5. EBOUSSI-BOULAGA, "Le Bantou problématique," p. 10.
6. Ibid., p. 11.
7. TEMPELS, *La Philosophie bantoue*, p. 29.
8. EBOUSSI-BOULAGA, "Le Bantou problématique," p. 12.
9. TEMPELS, *La Philosophie bantoue*, p. 29.
10. EBOUSSI-BOULAGA, "Le Bantou problématique," pp. 13–14.
11. Ibid., p. 14.
12. Ibid.
13. See TEMPELS, *La Philosophie bantoue*, p. 40.
14. Ibid., p. 44.
15. EBOUSSI-BOULAGA, "Le Bantou problématique," p. 15.
16. Ibid., p. 17.
17. BERGSON, H., *La Pensée et le mouvant: essais et conférences* (Presses Universitaires de France, Paris, 1946), p. 60.
18. EBOUSSI-BOULAGA, "Le Bantou problématique," p. 17.
19. Then we must say that, according to Eboussi-Boulaga, Mabona is a Greek and all the Bambara are Greeks and their thought is Greek philosophy.
20. EBOUSSI-BOULAGA, "Le Bantou problématique," p. 18.
21. Ibid., p. 6.
22. Ibid.
23. Ibid., p. 19.
24. TEMPELS, *La Philosophie bantoue*, p. 96.
25. EBOUSSI-BOULAGA, "Le Bantou problématique," p. 20.
26. See TEMPELS, *La Philosophie bantoue*, pp. 8–9.
27. EBOUSSI-BOULAGA, "Le Bantou problématique," p. 24.
28. TEMPELS, *La Philosophie bantoue*, p. 136.
29. EBOUSSI-BOULAGA, "Le Bantou problématique," p. 26.
30. TEMPELS, *La Philosophie bantoue*, p. 149.
31. EBOUSSI-BOULAGA, "Le Bantou problématique," p. 32.
32. Emphasis mine.
33. EBOUSSI-BOULAGA, "Le Bantou problématique," p. 4.
34. Ibid., pp. 33–34.
35. Ibid., p. 37.
36. Ibid., p. 38.
37. TEMPELS, *La Philosophie bantoue*, p. 139.
38. EBOUSSI-BOULAGA, "Le Bantou problématique," p. 38.
39. EBOUSSI-BOULAGA, F., *La Crise du Muntu. Authenticité africaine et philosophie* (Présence Africaine, Paris, 1977), p. 17.
40. Ibid., p. 18.

41. Ibid.
42. Ibid., p. 20.
43. Ibid., p. 23.
44. Ibid., p. 28.
45. Ibid., p. 30.
46. See HOUNTONDJI's definition of ethnophilosophy in "Remarques sur la philosophie africaine contemporaine," in *Diogène*, No. 71, 1970, pp. 122–23, and in *African Philosophy: Myth and Reality* (Indiana University Press, Bloomington, 1983), p. 34.
47. EBOUSSI-BOULAGA, *La Crise du Muntu*, p. 36.
48. Ibid.
49. Ibid., pp. 68–69.
50. Ibid., p. 85.
51. See ibid., pp. 85–86.
52. Ibid., p. 88.
53. Ibid., p. 89.
54. EBOUSSI-BOULAGA, "Le Bantou problématique," p. 25. See also TEMPELS, *La Philosophie bantoue*, p. 6.
55. EBOUSSI-BOULAGA, *Le Crise du Muntu*, p. 120.
56. Ibid., p. 177.
57. Ibid., p. 99.
58. Ibid., p. 140.
59. Ibid., p. 138.
60. TOWA, M., *Essai sur le problématique philosophique dans l'Afrique actuelle* (Ed. Clé, Yaoundé, 1971), p. 17.
61. Ibid., pp. 17–19.
62. Emphasis mine.
63. TOWA, *Essai . . .* , p. 23.
64. FOUDA, B. J., *La Philosophie africaine de l'existence* (Faculté des Lettres, Lille, 1967) (a doctoral thesis in philosophy).
65. TOWA, *Essai . . .* , p. 27.
66. See ibid., p. 28.
67. Ibid., p. 29.
68. Ibid., p. 30.
69. Ibid., p. 31.
70. Ibid., p. 39.
71. Ibid., p. 40.
72. Ibid., p. 41.
73. Ibid., p. 42.
74. Ibid., p. 45.
75. Ibid., pp. 56–57.
76. My emphasis.
77. See TOWA, *Essai . . .* , p. 62.
78. Ibid., p. 63.
79. Ibid., p. 64.
80. Ibid., p. 68.
81. Ibid., p. 24 and pp. 27–28.
82. For Franz Crahay "African philosophy" begins with the writings of Senghor, Alioune Diop, Sekou Toure, and Kwame Nkrumah. But Maurier is opposed to both the foregoing positions. For Maurier, although these works, which are properly political, constitute a research

that profoundly supposes African human realities and on this level interest the philosopher, they cannot be said to truly constitute a philosophy. "The economic and political points of view, though important," writes Maurier, "hold a predominant place in the damage of research on basic causes. They affirm more than they criticize traditional values. But they are precious as a desire for the liberation of man, and prevent the philosopher from withdrawing by hiding himself in the sterile and air-conditioned comfortable ivory tower." See MAURIER, H., *Philosophie de l'Afrique noire* (Anthropos Institut, St. Augustin, Bonn, 1976), pp. 15–16.

83. SELVAGGI, F., *Scienza e Metodologia* (Università Gregoriana, Roma, 1962), p. 195.

84. Ibid., p. 178.

85. TOWA, *Essai . . .* , p. 263. Many African philosophers hold this view today (see, for example, Lansana Keita's "Contemporary African Philosophy: The Search for a Method," in *Praxis International*, Vol. 5, No. 2, July 1985, pp. 154–156), but it is perverse. Philosophical doctrines do not lose or gain their credibility and worth on the basis of whether or not they are convertible to practice.

86. TOWA, *Essai . . .* , p. 35.

87. Ibid., p. 45. On making African philosophy empiristic, Towa needs to have known that Nyerere tried to build the sociopolitical structures of *ujamaa* on the basis of what was believed (by him as well as by Senghor and Nkrumah) to be the traditional African communalistic attitude of mind. On the *democratic* and *scientific* nature of the "new" societies, Towa needs to have explored fully the meaning of such terms when used in the context of the social forms he ascribes them to. Not only is it difficult to talk of scientific truths of social processes, but their practical establishment calls for dictatorial rather than democratic rulerships. The envisaged democratic ideal of such formations is usually rendered so far off by actual experiences and processes that it comes out only as a good idealistic conjecture rather than an objective scientific description of relations in reality. Is this so difficult to see? How do we otherwise explain the collapse of Nyerere's *ujamaa* and Mao's China?

88. Ibid., p. 47.

89. MARX, K., *L'Idéologie allemande* (Ed. Sociales, Paris, 1968), p. 75; quoted in TOWA, *Essai . . .* , p. 52.

90. IRELE, A., in "Introduction," in HOUNTONDJI, *African Philosophy: Myth and Reality*, p. 26. Emphasis mine.

91. SELVAGGI, *Scienza e Metodologia*, p. 176.

92. HEBGA, M., "Plaidoyer pour les logiques de l'Afrique noire," in aa.vv., *Aspects de la culture noire* (Fayard, Paris, 1958), p. 105.

93. KARP, I., and BIRD, C. S. (eds.), *Explorations in African Systems of Thought* (Indiana University Press, Bloomington/Indianapolis, 1980), pp. 1–10.

94. HEBGA, "Plaidoyer . . . ," p. 105.

95. Ibid., p. 106.

96. Ibid., p. 109.

97. HEBGA, M., in a private unpublished note on the concept of "ethno-philosophy." This note was contained in Hebga's letter to me in 1978. In a later article, "Eloge de l'ethnophilosophie" (in *Présence Africaine*, No. 123, 1982, pp. 20–41), Hebga makes a fervent defense of ethnophilosophy against those who claim that ethnophilosophy fails to qualify as philosophy proper because it is not self-critical. Hebga argues that philosophical literature can generally be classified into two types, the direct synthetic discourse and the analytic-critical commentaries. With the first type Hebga identifies most of those works which are accepted as classics in Western philosophy, such as the works of Plato, Pascal, Hobbes, Hegel, and so on. These works, Hebga argues, are no less mythical and ethnophilosophical than are the great African myths such as the Bambara epics. Yet, he says, Franz Crahay and his anti-eth-

nophilosophical disciples choose to accept the former as philosophical masterpieces and not the latter. In this way, Hebga defends also Odera Oruka's "philosophical sagacity," which we shall consider below in chapter 8. Hebga's point is propositionally significant to contemporary currents in the writing of cultures.

98. HEBGA, "Plaidoyer . . . ," pp. 110–111.

99. Ibid., p. 112.

100. Ibid., p. 116.

101. RODNEY, W., "Technological Stagnation and Economic Distortion in Pre-Colonial Times," in GUTKIND, P. C. W., and WATERMAN, P. (eds.), *African Social Studies* (Heinemann, London, 1977), p. 110.

102. Ibid., p. 111.

103. Though such a question is not explicitly formulated by Towa, we can analyze it backwards from the essay as: Will Africa reach the equality that it so badly needs through the claim of a proper philosophy—"ethnophilosophy"?

104. MUDIMBE, V. Y., *The Invention of Africa: Gnosis, Philosophy, and the Order of Knowledge* (African Systems of Thought series, Indiana University Press, Bloomington/Indianapolis, 1988).

105. JEWSIEWICKI, B., "African Historical Studies: Academic Knowledge as 'Usable Past' and Radical Scholarship," in *The African Studies Review*, Vol. 32, No. 3, December 1989, pp. 1–76.

106. MUDIMBE, *The Invention of Africa*, p. x.

107. FOUCAULT, M., *The Order of Things* (Tavistock Publications, London, 1970), p. 345.

108. Ibid., p. 36.

109. MUDIMBE, *The Invention of Africa*, p. x.

110. Ibid., p. 27.

111. FOUCAULT, M., *Language, Counter-Memory, Practice* (Cornell University Press, Ithaca, New York, 1977), p. 207.

112. MUDIMBE, *The Invention of Africa*, p. 28.

113. Ibid., p. 154.

114. See LÉVI-STRAUSS, C., *The Savage Mind* (The University of Chicago Press, Chicago, 1966), p. 22; and MUDIMBE, *The Invention of Africa*, p. 31.

115. MUDIMBE, *The Invention of Africa*, p. 199; see pp. 187–200.

116. VANSINA, J., *Oral Tradition as History* (University of Wisconsin Press, Madison, 1986); VANSINA, "Is Elegance a Proof? Structuralism and African History," in *History in Africa*, Vol. 10, 1983, pp. 307–48; see also KARP and BIRD (eds.), *Explorations in African Systems of Thought*, pp. x–xi.

117. ORUKA, H. O., "Sagacity in African Philosophy," in *International Philosophical Quarterly*, Vol. 23, No. 4, 1983, pp. 383–93.

118. HALLEN, B., and SODIPO, J. O., *Knowledge, Belief and Witchcraft: Analytic Experiments in African Philosophy* (Ethnographica, London, 1986), pp. 5–13.

119. FOUCAULT, *The Order of Things*, p. xv.

120. MUDIMBE, *The Invention of Africa*, p. 34.

121. Ibid., pp. x–xi.

122. Ibid., p. 200.

123. Ibid., p. 34.

124. See HEBGA, "Plaidoyer . . . ," pp. 104–16.

125. WOLFRAM, S., "Basic Differences of Thought," in HORTON, R., and FINNIGAN, R. (eds.), *Modes of Thought: Essays on Thinking in Western and Non-Western Societies* (Faber and Faber, London, 1973), pp. 357–74.

126. Ibid., p. 364.
127. OVERING, J. (ed.), *Reason and Morality* (ASA Monographs 24, Tavistock Publications, London/New York, 1985), p. ix.
128. See GYEKYE, K., *An Essay on African Philosophical Thought: The Akan Conceptual Scheme* (Cambridge University Press, Cambridge, UK, 1987), pp. 51–57.
129. Ibid., chapter 2, pp. 59–186.
130. OCHOLLA-AYAYO, A. B. C., *Traditional Ideology and Ethics among the Southern Luo* (The Scandinavian Institute of African Studies, Uppsala, 1976), p. 42.

8 *"Tradition" and "Modernity": The Role of Reason*

1. HOUNTONDJI, P., "Remarques sur la philosophie africaine contemporaine," in *Diogène*, No. 71, 1970, pp. 122–23.
2. HOUNTONDJI, P., "Le Problème actuel de la philosophie africaine," in KLIBANSKY, R. (ed.), *La Philosophie contemporaine*, Vol. 4 (La Nuova Italia, Firenze, 1971), p. 616 (Chronique).
3. HOUNTONDJI, "Remarques . . . ," p. 123.
4. Ibid., p. 128.
5. In his work, Franz Crahay had said that the works of people like Tempels, Kagame, Mbiti, Mulago constituted what he called "first language"—sometimes also called "first order philosophy"—i.e., mere descriptions of experiences. Proper philosophy, according to Crahay, is and must be constituted by a "second language" which characterizes a "takeoff" from the first one. He gave the following conditions for a proper African philosophy:

(i) The Bantu must have specialists, individual philosophers.
(ii) Bantu philosophy must relate itself to some specific tradition or school within Western philosophy as Indian thought has done.
(iii) Bantu philosophy must utilize original linguistic resources and mental categories specific to Africa.
(iv) Bantu philosophy must discard myth and become both reflective and in consonance with scientific truths in physics, biology, chemistry, etc.
(v) African intellectuals must refrain from adopting and assimilating foreign theories without critical approval.

It is difficult to comment on these conditions fully in a note. To say the least, however, the first and last conditions look rational though debatable. The second, third, and fourth are highly controversial.
6. HOUNTONDJI, "Remarques . . . ," p. 128.
7. Ibid., p. 134.
8. See ibid., p. 135, footnote 18.
9. Ibid, p. 135.
10. Ibid, p. 139, footnote 25.
11. Ibid., p. 139.
12. HOUNTONDJI, P., *African Philosophy: Myth and Reality* (English translation of *Sur la "Philosophie africaine,"* 1977) (Hutchinson, London, and Indiana University Press, Bloomington, 1983), p. 84.
13. Ibid., p. 87.
14. Ibid., pp. 87–88.
15. Ibid., pp. 97–98.
16. Ibid., p. 98.

17. ALTHUSSER, L., *Philosophy and the Spontaneous Philosophy of the Scientists and Other Essays* (Verso, London, 1990), p. 106 (emphases in the quotation are from the text).

18. ALTHUSSER, L., "From *Capital* to Marx's Philosophy," in ALTHUSSER, L., and BALIBAR, E., *Reading Capital* (New Left Books, London, 1970), pp. 41–42.

19. HOUNTONDJI, *African Philosophy: Myth and Reality*, p. 99.

20. Ibid.

21. Ibid., p. 101.

22. ALTHUSSER, L., *Philosophy and the Spontaneous Philosophy of the Scientists*, p. 107.

23. Ibid.

24. HOUNTONDJI, *African Philosophy*, p. 175.

25. See MUDIMBE, V. Y., "African Gnosis, Philosophy and the Order of Knowledge," in *African Studies Review*, Vol. 28, Nos. 2–3, June-September 1985, p. 207.

26. See BODUNRIN, P. O., "The Question of African Philosophy," in *Philosophy: The Journal of the Royal Institute of Philosophy*, No. 56, 1981, pp. 161–79.

27. See KEITA, L., "Contemporary African Philosophy: The Search for a Method," in *Praxis International*, Vol. 5, No. 2, July 1985, pp. 145–61.

28. See KA MANA, "Les philosophies négro-africaines face au problème du développement," in *Zaire-Afrique*, No. 120, December 1977, pp. 591–608.

29. See IRELE, A., "Introduction," in HOUNTONDJI, *African Philosophy*, p. 29.

30. WIREDU, K., *Philosophy and an African Culture* (Cambridge University Press, London, 1980), p. 29.

31. Ibid., p. 66.

32. Ibid., p. 211.

33. Ibid., p. 212.

34. HABERMAS, J., *Knowledge and Human Interests* (Beacon Press, Boston, 1971), p. 313.

35. WIREDU, *Philosophy and an African Culture*, p. 65.

36. Quoted in SLOTKIN, J. S. (ed.), *Readings in Early Anthropology*, Viking Fund Publications in Anthropology, No. 40 (Aldine Publishing Co., Chicago, 1965), p. 173.

37. WIREDU, *Philosophy and an African Culture*, pp. 114 and 124ff.

38. Ibid., p. 115. Emphasis mine.

39. See in particular WIREDU, K., "Are There Cultural Universals?" in *Quest: An African International Journal of Philosophy*, Vol. 4, No. 2, December 1990, pp. 5–19.

40. See SCHILLER, F. C. S., *Studies in Humanism* (Macmillan and Co. Ltd., London/New York, 1907).

41. See Wiredu's argument against the traditional methods of knowledge, in *Philosophy and an African Culture*, pp. 12–13.

42. CHILDE, V. G., *Society and Knowledge* (Allen and Unwin, London, 1956), p. 106.

43. Ibid., p. 107.

44. Ibid.

45. Ibid., p. 110.

46. Ibid., p. 118.

47. WIREDU, "Are There Cultural Universals?"

48. Ibid., p. 5.

49. QUINE, W. V. O., *Word and Object* (MIT Press, Cambridge, Massachusetts, 1960), p. 74.

50. WIREDU, "Are There Cultural Universals?" p. 11.

51. CHOMSKY, N., *Language and Mind* (Harcourt, Brace, New York, 1972, revised edition), p. 9.

52. MARGOLIS, J. Z., *Persons and Minds* (D. Reidel, Dordrecht, Holland/Boston, U.S.A., 1978), p. 18.

53. Ibid., emphasis is in the text.

54. Ibid., pp. 14–15.

55. WIREDU, "Are There Cultural Universals?" p. 7.

56. See WIREDU, K., "On Defining African Philosophy," in NAGL-DOCEKAL, H., and WIMMER, F. M. (eds.), *Postkoloniales Philosophieren: Afrika* (Oldenbourg Verlag, Wien/München, 1992), p. 54; and MARGOLIS, J. Z., *Persons and Minds*, p. 19.

57. MARGOLIS, *Persons and Minds*, p. 20.

58. See, for example, SELLARS, W., "Philosophy and the Scientific Image of Man," in *Science, Perception, and Reality* (Routledge and Kegan Paul, London, 1963).

59. MARGOLIS, J. Z., *The Truth about Relativism* (Blackwell, Oxford, UK/Cambridge, Massachusetts, 1991), p. 6.

60. Ibid., p. 14.

61. LÉVI-STRAUSS, C., "History and Dialectic," in DE GEORGE, R. T., and DE GEORGE, F. M. (eds.), *The Structuralists from Marx to Lévi-Strauss* (Anchor Books, New York, 1972), p. 213.

62. MANNHEIM, K., *Ideology and Utopia: An Introduction to the Sociology of Knowledge* (Routledge and Kegan Paul, London, 1968), p. 61.

63. See *Essays of Michel de Montaigne*, trans. by Charles Cotton (Doubleday, New York, 1947), pp. 4–10.

64. WIREDU, *Philosophy and an African Culture*, p. 121.

65. Ibid., p. 103.

66. Ibid., chapter 5, on "Marxism, Philosophy, and Ideology."

67. Ibid., p. 122.

68. Ibid., p. 62.

69. Ibid., p. 12.

70. THAYER, H. S., "John Dewey 1859–1952," in SINGER, M. G. (ed.), *American Philosophy* (Cambridge University Press, London, 1985), p. 78.

71. WIREDU, *Philosophy and an African Culture*, 143–44, quoting from the Preface of Bertrand RUSSELL's *History of Western Philosophy* (Allen and Unwin, London, 1961).

72. ORUKA, H. O., "Truth and Belief," in *Universitas* (Ghana), Vol. 5, No. 1, November 1975, pp. 177–84. Odera Oruka recently published another discussion on this topic: see ORUKA, H. O., "For the Sake of Truth," in *Quest*, Vol. 11, No. 2, 1988, pp. 3–21. Although this later article is a much more sophisticated discussion on "truth" than his previous article, Odera Oruka does not appear to have changed what I consider to be his basic misunderstanding of Wiredu's use of the word "opinion." As a result, the article in *Quest* is only a reaffirmation of the positions expressed in the earlier one in *Universitas*.

73. ORUKA, "Truth and Belief," p. 182.

74. WIREDU, *Philosophy and an African Culture*, p. 176.

75. VIGLINO, U., *La Conoscenza: Problematicità e valore* (Pontificia Università Urbaniana, Rome, 1969), pp. 247–49. My translation.

76. Ibid., p. 250.

77. Ibid., p. 379.

78. WIREDU, K., "The Concept of Truth in the Akan Language," paper read at the Nigerian Philosophical Association's International Symposium on *Philosophy in Africa*, Ibadan, February 1981, p. 1; here quoted from BEDU-ADDO, J. T., "Wiredu on Truth as Opinion and the Akan Language," unpublished paper, p. 6.

79. See WIREDU, K., "In Behalf of Opinion: A Rejoinder," in *Universitas* (Ghana), Vol. 5, No. 2, 1976, p. 199.

80. Ibid.

81. See, for example, his "Morality and Religion in Akan Thought," in ORUKA, H. O., and MASOLO, D. A. (eds.), *Philosophy and Cultures* (Bookwise Publishers, Nairobi, 1983), pp. 6–13.

82. A comprehensive report of the Sodipo-Hallen research is contained in HALLEN, B., and SODIPO, J. O., *An African Epistemology: The Knowledge-Belief Distinction and Yoruba Thought* (University of Ife, 1981), presented to the Nigerian Philosophical Association Conference, Ibadan, February 1981.

83. See ORUKA, H. O. (ed.), *Sage Philosophy: Indigenous Thinkers and Modern Debate on African Philosophy* (E. J. Brill Publishers, Leiden, The Netherlands, 1990).

84. See TOWETT, T., "Le Rôle d'un philosophe africain," in *Présence Africaine* (Deuxième Congrès des Ecrivains et Artistes Noirs), Numéro spécial 27–28, August-November 1959, pp. 111–12.

85. Ibid., p. 111.

86. ORUKA, H. O., "Sagacity in African Philosophy" (unpublished paper), pp. 6–7; this paper is a modified and expanded version of "Four Trends in Current African Philosophy," in *Filosofiska Tidscrift* (Uppsala), Vol. 1, No. 2, February 1981, pp. 31–37.

87. Ibid., p. 1. All quotations are taken from the unpublished version.

88. See TOWETT, "Le Rôle d'un philosophe africaine," pp. 113–14.

89. BODUNRIN, "The Question of African Philosophy," p. 70.

90. ORUKA, "Sagacity in African Philosophy," p. 13.

91. NJOROGE, R. J., and BENNARS, G. A., *Philosophy and Education in Africa* (TransAfrica Press, Nairobi, 1986), pp. 5–6.

92. Two research projects in this field are: OSEGHARE, A. S., *The Relevance of Sagacious Reasoning in African Philosophy* (Ph.D. thesis, University of Nairobi); and HOFFMAN, G. R., *Faktoren und gegenwartige Tendenzen der Entwichlung nicht Marxistischer philosophie in Afrika* (Ph.D. dissertation, Leipzig, 1984).

93. GOODY, J., *The Domestication of the Savage Mind* (Cambridge University Press, London, 1977), p. 27.

94. Ibid.

95. Ibid., p. 36.

96. Ibid., p. 37.

97. ORUKA, *Sage Philosophy*, p. xvii.

98. P'BITEK, O., "Reflect, Reject, Recreate," in *East Africa Journal*, Vol. 9, No. 9, April 1972, p. 30.

Conclusion: Experience and African Philosophy

1. JACKSON, M., and KARP, I., "Introduction," in *Personhood and Agency: The Experience of Self and Other in African Cultures* (Uppsala Studies in Cultural Anthropology, Acta Universitatis Upsaliensis, Uppsala, 1990), p. 17.

2. DEWEY, J., *Experience and Education* (Collier Books, New York, 1963), p. 17.

3. OAKESHOTT, M., *Experience and Its Modes* [1933] (Cambridge University Press, New York, 1985), p. 4.

Bibliography

ABRAHAM, W. E., *The Mind of Africa*, University of Chicago Press, Chicago, 1963.

ALTHUSSER, L., "From *Capital* to Marx's Philosophy," in ALTHUSSER. L., and BALIBAR, E., *Reading Capital*, New Left Books, London, 1970.

———, "The Errors of Classical Economics: An Outline for a Concept of Historical Time," in ALTHUSSER, L., and BALIBAR, E., *Reading Capital*, New Left Books, London, 1970.

———, *Philosophy and the Spontaneous Philosophy of the Scientists and Other Essays*, Verso Publishers, London, 1990.

APPIAH, K. A. "Stricture on Structures: On Structuralism and African Fiction," in GATES, H. L. (ed.), *Black Literature and Literary Theory*, Methuen, New York, 1984.

———, "Old Gods, New Worlds: Some Recent Work in the Philosophy of African Traditional Religion," in FLOISTAD, G. (ed.), *Contemporary Philosophy: A New Survey: Vol. 5, African Philosophy*, Martinus Nijhoff Publishers, Dordrecht, Netherlands, 1987.

———, *In My Father's House: Africa in the Philosophy of Culture*, Oxford University Press, New York and Oxford, 1992.

ARENS, W., and KARP, I. (eds.), *Creativity of Power: Cosmology and Action in African Societies*, Smithsonian Institution Press, Washington, D.C., 1989.

BAHOKEN, J. C., *Clairières métaphysiques africaines. Essai sur la philosophie et la religion chez les Bantu du Sud—Cameroun*, Présence Africaine, Paris, 1967.

BALANDIER, G., *Sociologie actuelle de l'Afrique noire*, Presses Universitaires de France, Paris, 1955.

———, *Afrique ambiguë*, Plon, Paris, 1957.

———, "Tendences de l'ethnologie française," in *Cahiers internationaux de sociologie*, No. 27, 1960.

———, *Anthropologie politique*, Presses Universitaires de France, Paris, 1967.

BALANDIER, G., and MAQUET, J. (eds.), *Dictionnaire des civilizations africaines*, Fernand Hazan Editeur, Paris, 1968.

BEDU-ADDO, J. T., "Wiredu on Truth as Opinion and the Akan Language," in BODUNRIN, P. (ed), *Philosophy in Africa: Trends and Perspectives*, University of Ife Press, Ile-Ife, Nigeria, 1985, pp. 68–90.

BEIDELMAN, T. O., *Moral Imagination in Kaguru Modes of Thought*, Indiana University Press, Bloomington, 1986.

BERGSON, H., *La pensée et le mouvant: essais et conférences*, Presses Universitaires de France, Paris, 1946.

BERNAL, M., *Black Athena: The Afroasiatic Roots of Classical Civilization*, Rutgers University Press, New Brunswick, New Jersey. Vol. I: *The Fabrication of Ancient Greece 1785–1985* (1987); Vol. II: *The Archeological and Documentary Evidence* (1991).

BIMWENYI, O., "Le Dieu de nos ancêtres," in *Cahiers des religions africaines*, Vol. 4, 1970, and Vol. 5, 1971.

———, "Le Muntu à la lumière de ses croyances en l'au-delà," in *Cahiers des religions africaines*, Vol. 2, 1969.

BODUNRIN, P. O., " 'Theoretical Identities' and Scientific Explanation: The Horton-Skorupski Debate," in *Second Order*, Vol. 4, No. 1, 1975, pp. 56–65.

———, "The Question of African Philosophy," in *Philosophy: The Journal of The Royal Institute of Philosophy*, No. 56, 1981.

———, "The Question of African Philosophy," in WRIGHT, R. A. (ed.), *African Philosophy: An Introduction*, University Press of America, Lanham, Maryland, 1984, pp. 1–23.

BODUNRIN, P. O. (ed.), *Philosophy in Africa: Trends and Perspectives*, University of Ife Press, Ile-Ife, Nigeria, 1985.

BOHANNAN, P., "Concepts of Time Among the Tiv of Nigeria," in *South Western Journal of Anthropology*, Vol. 9, 1953; also in MIDDLETON, J. (ed.), *Myth and Cosmos*, University of Texas Press, Austin, 1963 (2nd edition, 1980).

BOWERSOCK, G. W., "Black Athena, I. The Fabrication of Ancient Greece 1785–1985, by Martin Bernal," book review in *The Journal of Interdisciplinary History*, Vol. 19, No. 3.

BRAMBILLA, C., *La Négritudine*, Edizioni Nigrizia (undated).

BUAKASA, G., "Philosophie et religion bantoues," in *Femmes, Vie, Monde*, Vol. 19, 1964.

CAETA, C. G. (ed.), *Christianity in Tropical Africa: Studies Presented and Discussed at the Seventh International African Seminar at the University of Ghana, April 1965*, Oxford University Press, 1968.

CAPUTO, J. D., *Radical Hermeneutics*, Indiana University Press, Bloomington/Indianapolis, 1987.

CARRILHO, M., *Sociologia della negritudine*, Liguori Editore, Napoli, 1974.

CÉSAIRE, A., *Cahier d'un retour au pays natal* [1939], Edition de Présence Africaine, Paris, 1956.

———, *Discours sur le colonialisme*, Reclame, Paris, 1950.

CHARLES, P., S. J., "Note relative à l'ouvrage du R. P. Tempels, intitulé 'La Philosophie bantoue,' " in CHARLES, P., S. J., *Etudes missiologiques*, Desclée de Brouwer, Paris, 1956.

———, *Etudes missiologiques*, Desclée de Brouwer, Paris, 1956.

CHILDE, V. G., *Society and Knowledge*, Allen and Unwin, London, 1956.

CHOMSKY, N., *Language and Mind* (revised), Harcourt, Brace, New York, 1972.

CLARK, R. T. R., *Myth and Symbol in Ancient Egypt*, Thames and Hudson, London, 1959.

CLIFFORD, J., *The Predicament of Culture: Twentieth Century Ethnography, Literature, and Art*, Harvard University Press, Cambridge, Massachusettes, 1988.

CLIFFORD, J., and MARCUS, G. E. (eds.), *Writing Culture: The Poetics and Politics of Ethnography*, University of California Press, Berkeley, 1986.

COHEN, A., and DASCAL, M. (eds.), *The Institution of Philosophy: A Discipline in Crisis?* Open Court Publishing Company, La Salle, Illinois, 1989.

COOK, M., "Les précurseurs négro-américains de la Négritude," in *Le Soleil*, Numero sur la Négritude, No. 305, Dakar, 1971.

COULSON, A. (ed.), *African Socialism in Practice: The Tanzanian Experience*, Spokesman Publishers, Nottingham, (1979) 1982.

CRAHAY, F., "Le Décollage conceptuel: conditions d'une philosophie bantoue," in *Diogène*, No. 52, 1965.

CRANE, C. B., *Alain Locke and the Negro Renaissance*, Ph.D. thesis, University of California, San Diego, 1971.

DAVIDSON, B., *Black Star: A View of the Life and Times of Kwame Nkrumah*, Panaf Books, London, 1973.

——, *Panaf Great Lives: Kwame Nkrumah*, Panaf Books, London, 1974.

DELAFOSSE, M., *Les Nègres*, Rieder, Paris, 1927.

DEPESTRE, R., *Bonjour et adieu à la négritude*, Editions Robert Laffont, Paris, 1980.

DEREN, M., *Divine Horsemen: The Living Gods of Haiti*, London/New York, 1953. Reprint, Delta, New York, 1970.

DERRIDA, J., *De la grammatologie*, Minuit, Paris, 1967.

——, *La Voix et le phénomène*, Presses Universitaires de France, 1967.

DEWEY, J., *Experience and Education*, Collier Books, New York, 1963.

DIETERLEN, G., *Les Âmes des Dogons*, Institut d'Ethnologie, Paris, 1941.

——, *Essai sur le religion Bambara*, Presses Universitaires de France, Paris, 1951.

DIOP, C. A., *Nations nègres et culture*, Présence Africaine, Paris, 1954.

——, *Antériorité des civilisations nègres*, Présence Africaine, Paris, 1967.

——, *L'Unité culturelle de l'Afrique noire*, Présence Africaine, Paris, 1967.

——, *The African Origin of Civilization: Myth or Reality* (edited and translated by Mercer Cook), Lawrence Hill & Company, Westport, Connecticut, 1974, and Présance Africaine, Paris, 1974.

DOCHERTY, T., *After Theory: Post Modernism/Post Marxism*, Routledge, London, 1990.

DOUGLAS, M., "If the Dogon," in *Cahiers d'études africaines*, No. 28, 1967, pp. 659–72.

DU BOIS, W. E. B., *A Voice from Bleeding Africa*, Monrovia, 1856.

——, *A Vindication of the Negro Race*, New York, 1897.

——, *W. E. B. Du Bois Speaks: Speeches and Addresses 1890–1919* (P. S. Foner, ed.), Pathfinders, New York, 1970.

EBOUSSI-BOULAGA, F., "Le Bantou problématique," in *Présence Africaine*, No. 66, 1968, pp. 4–40.

——, *La Crise du Muntu. Authenticité africaine et philosophie*, Présence Africaine, Paris, 1977.

——, *Christianisme sans fétiche. Révélation et domination*, Présence Africaine, Paris, 1981.

EHRMANN, J. (ed.), *Structuralism*, Anchor Books, New York, 1970.

EVANS-PRITCHARD, E. E., *Witchcraft, Oracles and Magic among the Azande*, Oxford University Press, London, 1937.

——, "Nuer Time Reckoning," in *Africa*, Vol. 12, 1939.

——, *Nuer Religion*, Oxford University Press, London, 1956.

——, *Theories of Primitive Religion* [1965], The Clarendon Press, Oxford, 1980.

FABIAN, J., "Philosophie bantoue: Placide Tempels et son ouvre vus dans une perspective historique," in *Etudes Africaines du C.R.I.S.P.*, Nos. 108–109, Bruxelles, 1970.

————, *Time and Other: How Anthropology Makes Its Object*, Columbia University Press, New York, 1983.

————, *Power and Performance*, The University of Wisconsin Press, Madison, 1990.

FABRO, C., "Controversie sul pensiero dei primitivi," in *Euntes Docete*, No. 1, 1948, pp. 50–62.

FANON, F., *Black Skin, White Masks*, Grove Press, New York, 1967.

————, *The Wretched of the Earth*, Penguin Books, London, 1978.

FILESI, T., *Movimenti di emancipazione coloniale e nascita dei nuovi stati in Africa*, Casa Editrice Dott. Francesco Vallardi, Milano, 1971.

FIRTH, R., "Twins, Birds, and Vegetables: Problems of Identification in Primitive Religious Thought," in *Man*, Vol. 1, No. 1, 1966.

FLOISTAD, G. (ed.), *Contemporary Philosophy: A New Survey*, Vol. 5: *African Philosophy*, Martinus Nijhoff, Dordrecht, 1987.

FONER, P. S. (ed.), *W. E. B. Du Bois Speaks: Speeches and Addresses 1890–1919*, Pathfinders Press, New York, 1970.

FONTAIN, W. T., "Towards a Philosophy of American Negro Literature," in *Présence Africaine*, Vol. 53, No. 7, 1958.

FORTES, M., and Dieterlen, G. (eds.), *African Systems of Thought*, Oxford University Press, London, 1965.

FOUCAULT, M., *Madness and Civilization*, Random House, New York, 1965.

————, *The Order of Things*, Tavistock Publications, London, 1970; Pantheon, New York, 1973.

————, *Discipline and Punish*, Pantheon, New York, 1977.

————, *Language, Counter-Memory, Practice*, Cornell University Press, Ithaca, New York, 1977.

————, *Power/Knowledge: Selected Interviews and Other Writings 1972–1977*, Pantheon, New York, 1980.

————, *The Archeology of Knowledge*, Pantheon, New York, 1982.

FOUDA, B. J., *La Philosophie africaine de l'existence*, doctoral dissertation, Lille, Faculté des Lettres, 1967.

FROBENIUS, L., "The Origin of African Civilization," in *Annual Report of the Board of Regents of the Smithsonian Institution*, Washington, D.C., 1899.

————, *Kulturgeschichte Afrikas*, Zurich, 1933.

————, *Histoire de la civilisation africaine*, Gallimard, Paris, 1936.

FROELICH, J. C., *Animismes, les religions païennes de l'Afrique de l'ouest*, Orante, Paris, 1964.

————, *Nouveaux dieux d'Afrique noire*, Orante, Paris, 1969.

GADAMER, H. G., *Wahrheit und Methode*, J. C. B. Mohr, Tubingen, 1965.

————, *Truth and Method* (trans. of *Wahrheit und Methode*), Seabury Press, New York, 1975; Crossroad, New York, 1982.

GATES, H. L. (ed.), *Black Literature and Literary Theory*, Methuen, New York, 1984.

GEERTZ, C., *The Interpretation of Cultures*, Basic Books, New York, 1973.

GELLNER, E., *Legitimation of Belief*, Cambridge University Press, London, 1974.

GENDZIER, I. L., *Frantz Fanon: A Critical Study*, Grove Press, New York, 1973.

GOETHEM, E. van, "Le Dieu des Nkundo," in *Aequatoria*, No. 1, 1950, pp. 4–14.

GOLDWATER, R., *Primitivism in Modern Art* [1938], The Belknap Press of Harvard University Press, Cambridge, Massachusetts, 1986.

GOODY, J., "Review of Conversations with Ogotemmeli by M. Griaule," in *American Anthropologist*, Vol. 69, No. 2, 1967.

———, *Literacy in Traditional Societies*, Cambridge University Press, Cambridge, UK, 1968.

———, *The Domestication of the Savage Mind*, Cambridge University Press, London, 1977.

———, *The Interface Between the Written and the Oral*, Cambridge University Press, New York, 1987.

GRIAULE, M., *Masques Dogons*, Institut d'Ethnologie, Paris, 1938.

———, *Dieu d'eau: entretiens avec Ogotemmêli*, Chêne, Paris, 1948; Fayard, Paris, 1966.

———, "Philosophie et religion des noirs," in *Présence Africaine*, Nos. 8–9, 1950, pp. 307–12.

———, "Le Savoir des Dogon," in *Journal de la société des africanistes*, No. 22, 1952, pp. 27–42.

———, *Conversations with Ogotemmêli* (trans. of *Dieu d'eau*, 1948), Oxford University Press, London, for the International African Institute, 1965.

GRIAULE, M., and DIETERLEN, G., *Le Renard pâle*, Institut d'Ethnologie, Paris, 1965.

GUTKIND, P. C. W., and WATERMAN, P., *African Social Studies*, Heinemann, London, 1977.

GYEKYE, K., "Al-Ghazali on Causation," in *Second Order*, Vol. 2, No. 1, 1973.

———, "African Religions and Philosophy by J. S. Mbiti," book review in *Second Order*, Vol. 4, No. 1, 1975.

———, *An Essay on African Philosophical Thought: The Akan Conceptual Scheme*, Cambridge University Press, London, 1987.

HABERMAS, J., *Knowledge and Human Interests*, Beacon Press, Boston, 1971.

HACKING, I., *Why Does Language Matter to Philosophy?* Cambridge University Press, New York, 1973.

———, "Language, Truth and Reason," in HOLLIS, M., and LUKES, S. (eds.) *Rationality and Relativism*, The MIT Press, Cambridge, Massachusettes, 1982.

HALLEN, B., and SODIPO, J. O., *Knowledge, Belief and Witchcraft: Analytic Experiments in African Philosophy*, Ethnographica, London, 1986.

HALLETT, G., "The Theoretical Content of Language," in *Gregorianum*, Vol. 54, No. 2, 1973, pp. 307–36.

HANSEN, E., *Frantz Fanon: Social and Political Thought*, Ohio State University Press, Columbus, 1977.

HARDY, G., *L'Art nègre*, Laurens, Paris, 1927.

HARLAND, R., *Superstructuralism: The Philosophy of Structuralism and Post-Structuralism*, Routledge, London, 1987.

HARRIES, L., "*Philosophie bantu-rwandaise de l'Être* by Alexis Kagame," book review in *Africa* (London), No. 27, 1957, p. 305.

HARRIS, L., "Philosophy Born of Struggle: Afro-American Philosophy since 1918," in ORUKA, H. O., and MASOLO, D. A. (eds.), *Philosophy and Cultures*, Bookwise Publishers, Nairobi, 1983, pp. 99–112.

———, *Philosophy Born of Struggle: Anthology of Afro-American Philosophy from 1917*, Kendall/Hunt Publishing Co., Dubuque, Iowa, 1983.

———, *The Philosophy of Alain Locke: Harlem Renaissance and Beyond*, Temple University Press, Philadelphia, Pennsylvania, 1989.

HAULE, C., *Bantu "Witchcraft" and Christian Morality: The Encounter of Bantu Uchawi with Christian Morality, an Anthropological and Theological Study*, Suppl. 16 of *Neue Zeitschrift für Missionswissenschaft*, 1969.

HAUTAMAKI, A., *Points of View and Their Logical Analysis*, Acta Philosophica Fennica, Vol. 41, Helsinki, 1986.

HEBGA, M., "Plaidoyer pour les logiques de l'Afrique noire," in aa.vv., *Aspects de la culture noire*, Librairie Arthème Fayard, Paris, 1958, pp. 104–16.

———, "Acculturation et chances d'un humanisme africain moderne," in *Présence Africaine*, No. 68, 1968, pp. 164–74.

———, *Emancipation d'églises sous-tutelle. Essai sur l'ère post-missionnaire*, Présence Africaine, Paris, 1976.

———, "Eloge de l'ethnophilosophie," in *Présence Africaine*, No. 123, 1982, pp. 20–41.

HEGEL, G. W. F. von, *Lectures on the Philosophy of World History: Introduction*, Cambridge University Press, Cambridge, UK, 1975. Revised edition, 1989.

HEIDEGGER, M., *Being and Time*, Harper and Brothers, New York, 1962.

HILDEBRAND, D. von, *What Is Philosophy?* Franciscan Herald Press, Chicago, 1973.

HOFFMAN, G. R., *Faktoren und gegenwartige Tendenzen der Entwichlung nicht Marxistischer philosophie in Afrika*, doctoral dissertation, Leipzig, 1984.

HOLLIS, M., *Models of Man*, Cambridge University Press, Cambridge, UK, 1977.

HOLLIS, M., and LUKES, S. (eds.), *Rationality and Relativism*, The MIT Press, Cambridge, Massachusettes, 1982.

HORTON, R., "The Kalabari World View: An Outline and Interpretation," in *Africa*, Vol. 32, No. 3, 1962, pp. 197–220.

———, "African Traditional Religion and Western Science," in *Africa*, Vol. 37, Nos. 1 & 2, 1967, pp. 50–71 and 155–87.

———, "African Traditional Thought and Western Science," in WILSON, B. R. (ed.), *Rationality*, Harper & Row, New York, 1970, pp. 131–71.

———, "Spiritual Beings and Elementary Particles—A reply to Mr. Pratt," in *Second Order*, Vol. 1, No. 1, 1972, pp. 21–33.

———, "Lévy-Bruhl, Durkheim and the Scientific Revolution," in HORTON, R., and FINNEGAN, R. (eds.), *Modes of Thought*, Faber and Faber, London, 1973, pp. 249–305.

———, "Paradox and Explanation: A Reply to Mr. Skorupski," in *Philosophy of The Social Sciences*, Vol. 3, No. 3, 1973, pp. 231–56; and Vol. 3, No. 4, 1973, pp. 289–314.

———, "Understanding Traditional African Religion: A Reply to Professor Beattie," in *Second Order*, Vol. 3, No. 1, 1976, pp. 3–29.

———, "Traditional Thought and the Emerging African Philosophy Department: A Comment on the Current Debate," in *Second Order*, Vol. 6, No. 1, 1977, pp. 64–80.

———, "Tradition and Modernity Revisited," in HOLLIS, M., and LUKES, S. (eds.), *Rationality and Relativism*, The MIT Press, Cambridge, Massachusettes, 1982, pp. 201–60.

HORTON, R., and FINNEGAN, R. (eds.), *Modes of Thought*, Faber and Faber, London, 1973.

HOUNTONDJI, P., "Remarques sur la philosophie africaine contemporaine," in *Diogène*, No. 71, 1970, pp. 120–40.

———, "Le Problème actuel de la philosophie africaine," in KLIBANSKY, R. (ed.), *La Philosophie contemporaine*, Vol. 4, La Nuova Italia, Firenze, 1971, pp. 613–21.

———, "Le Mythe de la philosophie spontanée," in *Cahiers philosophiques africains— African Philosophical Journal*, No. 1, 1972, pp. 107–42.

———, *Sur la "philosophie africaine." Critique de l'ethnophilosophie*, François Maspero, Paris, 1977.

———, *African Philosophy: Myth and Reality*, Hutchinson, London, and Indiana University Press, Bloomington, 1983.

———, "Occidentalism, Elitism: Answer to Two Critiques," in *Quest: An African International Journal of Philosophy*, Vol. 3, No. 2, December 1989, pp. 3–30.

HOWLETT, J., "La Philosophie africaine en question," in *Présence Africaine*, No. 91, 1974, pp. 14–25.

IDOWU, E. B., *Olodumare: God in Yoruba Belief*, Longmans, London, 1962.

———, *African Traditional Religion: A Definition*, 1973.

IRELE, A., "Introduction" to HOUNTONDJI, P., *African Philosophy: Myth and Reality*, Indiana University Press, Bloomington, 1983.

JACKSON, M., *Paths Toward a Clearing: Radical Empiricism and Ethnographic Inquiry*, Indiana University Press, Bloomington, 1989.

JACKSON, M., and KARP, I., "Introduction," in JACKSON, M., and KARP, I. (eds.), *Personhood and Agency: The Experience of Self and Other in African Cultures*, Uppsala Studies in Cultural Anthropology, Acta Universitatis Upsaliensis, Uppsala, 1990, pp. 15–30.

JAHN, J., *Muntu: An Outline of the New African Culture*, Grove Press, New York, 1961.

JAMES, C. L. R., *Nkrumah and the Ghana Revolution*, Lawrence Hill, West Port, Connecticut, 1977.

JAMES, G., *The Stolen Legacy*, Philosophical Library, New York, 1954.

JEWSIEWICKI, B., "African Historical Studies: Academic Knowledge as 'Usable Past' and Radical Scholarship," in *The African Studies Review*, Vol. 32, No. 3, 1989, pp. 1–76.

JONES, W. R., "The Legitimacy and Necessity of Black Philosophy," in *The Philosophical Forum*, Vol. 9, Nos. 2–3, Winter–Spring 1977–78.

KA, MANA, "Les Philosophies négro-africaines face au problème du développement," in *Zaire-Afrique*, No. 120, December 1977, pp. 591–608.

KAGAME, A., *La Philosophie bantu-rwandaise de l'être*, Académie Royale des Sciences Coloniales, Bruxelles, 1956.

———, "L'Ethno-philosophie des 'Bantu,' " in KLIBANSKY, R. (ed.), *La Philosophie contemporaine*, Vol. 4, La Nuova Italia, Firenze, 1971, pp. 589–612.

———, *La Philosophie bantu comparée*, Présence Africaine, Paris, 1976.

KARP, I., and BIRD, C. S. (eds.), *Explorations in African Systems of Thought*, Indiana University Press, Bloomington, 1980; Smithsonian Institution Press, Washington, D.C., 1987.

KATO, B. H., *Theological Pitfalls in Africa*, Evangel Publishing House, Kisumu, 1975.

KEITA, L., "Contemporary African Philosophy: The Search for a Method," in *Praxis International*, Vol. 5, No. 2, July 1985, pp. 145–61.

KIAMBI, A. B., "L'Être chez les bantous," in *Revue de clergé africain*, Vol. 21, 1966, pp. 428–35.

KINYONGO, J., "Philosophie en Afrique: conscience d'être," in *Cahiers philosophiques africains—African Philosophical Journal*, Nos. 3–4, 1973, pp. 13–25; 127–28, 149–58.

———, "Essai sur la fondation épistémologique d'une philosophie herméneutique en Afrique: les cas de la discursivité," in *Présence Africaine*, No. 109, 1979, pp. 12–26.

———, "La Philosophie africaine et son histoire," in *Les Etudes philosophiques*, No. 4, 1982, pp. 407–18.

KLIBANSKY, R. (ed.), *La Philosophie contemporaine* (4 vols.), La Nuova Italia, Firenze, 1971.

KOBLER, J. F. (ed.), *Vatican II and Phenomenology*, Martinus Nijhoff, Dordrecht, 1985.

KOFFI, N., "L'Impensé de Towa et de Hountondji," paper presented at the International Seminar on African Philosophy, Addis-Ababa, December 1976.

———, "Les Modes d'existence matérielle de la philosophie et la question de la philosophie africaine," in *Koré, Revue Iviorienne de Philosophie et de Culture*, Nos. 5,6,7, and 8, 1977.

KOFFI, N., and ABDOU, T., "Controverses sur l'existence d'une philosophie africaine," in SUMNER, C. (ed.), *African Philosophy*, Chamber Printing House, Addis-Ababa, 1980.

KUHN, T., "Logic of Discovery and Psychology of Research? Reflections on My Critics," in LAKATOS, I., and MUSGRAVE, A. E. (eds.), *Criticism and the Growth of Knowledge*, Cambridge University Press, Cambridge, UK, 1970.

———, *The Structure of Scientific Revolutions* [1962], The University of Chicago Press, Chicago, 1970.

LAKATOS, I., and MUSGRAVE, A. E. (eds.), *Criticism and the Growth of Knowledge*, Cambridge University Press, Cambridge, UK, 1970.

LALEYE, I. P., *La Conception de la personne dans le pensée traditionnelle yoruba*, Lang, Berne, 1970.

———, *La Philosophie? Pourquoi en Afrique? Une phénoménologie de la question*, Lang, Berne, 1975.

———, *Pour un anthropologie repensée*, La Pensée Universelle, Paris, 1977.

———, "Philosophie et réalités africaines," in *Langage et philosophie*, a publication of the Faculté de Théologie Catholique, Kinshasa, 1981, pp. 39–52.

———, "La Philosophie, l'Afrique et les philosophes africains: triple malentendu ou possibilité d'une collaboration féconde," in *Présence Africaine*, No. 123, 1982, pp. 42–62.

LANGER, S. K., *Philosophy in a New Key*, New American Library, New York, 1948.

LAYDEVANT, F., "Philosophie des bantous: à propos du P. Tempels," in *Africae Fraternae Ephemerides Romanae*, Nos. 24–25, 1947, pp. 55–57.

LEACH, E. R., *Rethinking Anthropology*, Athlone, London, 1961.

LEEUW, G. van de, *La Religion dans son essence et ses manifestations*, Paris, 1945.

LEFKOWITZ, M., "Not Out of Africa: The Origins of Greece and the Illusions of Afrocentrists," in *The New Republic*, 10 February 1992, pp. 29–36.

LENIN, V. I., *Materialism and Empirico-Criticism*, Progress Publishers, Moscow, 1947.

LETTENS, D. A., *Mystagogie et mystification: évaluation de l'oeuvre de Marcel Griaule*, Presses Lavigerie, Bujumbura, Burundi, 1971.

LÉVI-STRAUSS, C., *Structural Anthropology*, Basic Books, New York, 1963.

———, *The Savage Mind*, The University of Chicago Press, Chicago, 1966.

———, "History and Dialectic," in De GEORGE, R., and De GEORGE, F. (eds.), *The*

Structuralists from Marx to Lévi-Strauss, Anchor Books, New York, 1972, pp. 209–37.

LÉVY-BRUHL, L., *Les Fonctions mentales dans les sociétés inférieures*, Paris, 1910.

——, *La Mentalité primitive*, Paris, 1922.

——, *Primitive Mentality*, Beacon Press, Boston, 1923.

——, *L'Âme primitive*, Presses Universitaires de France, Paris, 1927.

——, *Le Surnaturel et la nature dans la mentalité primitive*, Paris, 1931.

——, *Les Carnets de Lucien Lévy-Bruhl*, Presses Universitaires de France, Paris, 1949.

——, *Notebooks on Primitive Mentality*, Torchbook Edition, Harper & Row, New York, 1978.

Lewis, C. I., *Mind and the World Order: Outline of a Theory of Knowledge*, C. Scribner's Sons, New York and Chicago, 1929.

——, *An Analysis of Knowledge and Valuation* (1st ed.) Open Court Publishers, La Salle, Ill., 1946.

——, *Our Social Inheritance*, Indiana University Press, Bloomington, 1957.

LIENHARDT, G., *Divinity and Experience: The Religion of the Dinka*, Oxford University Press, Oxford, UK, 1961.

LUFULUABO, F. M., "Vers une théodicée bantoue," in *Eglise vivante*, November–December 1961, pp. 426–34.

——, "La Conception bantoue face au christianisme," in *Personnalité Africaine et Catholicisme*, Présence Africaine, Paris, 1962, pp. 115–30.

——, *Vers une théodicée bantoue*, Casterman, Tournai, 1962.

——, *La Notion luba-bantoue de l'être*, Louvain, 1962.

——, *Perspective théologique bantoue et théologie scholastique*, Malines, 1966.

LYNCH, H. R., *Edward Wilmot Blyden: Pan-Negro Patriot 1832–1912*, Oxford University Press, London, 1967.

LYONS, J., *Introduction to Theoretical Linguistics*, Cambridge University Press, Cambridge, UK, 1974.

MABONA, A., "The Depths of African Philosophy," in *Personnalité Africaine et Catholicisme*, Présence Africaine, Paris, 1963, pp. 29–58.

MAHIFU, W. de, "Mythe, science, philosophie et religion," in *Congo-Afrique*, No. 29, 1968, pp. 457–65.

MAKARAKIZA, A., *La Dialectique des Barundi*, Académie Royale des Sciences Coloniales, Bruxelles, 1959.

MAKINDE, M. A., *African Philosophy, Culture, and Traditional Medicine*, Ohio University Monographs in International Studies, Africa Series, No. 53, Athens, Ohio, 1988.

MANDELBAUM, M., "The History of Philosophy: Some Methodological Issues," in *The Journal of Philosophy*, Vol. 74, No. 10, October 1977, pp. 561–72.

MANDT, A. J., "The Inevitability of Pluralism: Philosophical Practice and Philosophical Excellence," in COHEN, A., and DASCAL, M. (eds.), *The Institution of Philosophy: A Discipline in Crisis?* Open Court Publishing, La Salle, Illinois, 1989.

MANNHEIM, K., *Ideology and Utopia: An Introduction to the Sociology of Knowledge*, Routledge and Kegan Paul, London, 1968.

MAO TSE TUNG, *On Practice*, Foreign Language Press, Peking, 1966.

MARABLE, M., "Kwame Nkrumah and the Convention People's Party: A Critical Reassessment," in *TransAfrica Forum*, Vol. 3, No. 4, Summer 1986.

MARCEL, G., *The Existential Background of Human Dignity*, Harvard University Press, Cambridge, Massachusettes, 1963.
MARCUS, G. E., and FISCHER, M. M. J., *Anthropology as Cultural Critique: An Experimental Moment in the Human Sciences*, University of Chicago Press, Chicago, 1986.
MARCUSE, H., *One-Dimensional Man*, Routledge and Kegan Paul, London, 1964.
MARGOLIS, J. Z., *Persons and Minds*, D. Reidel, Dordrecht, Netherlands/Boston, Massachusetts, 1978.
——, *The Truth About Relativism*, Blackwell, Oxford, UK/Cambridge, Massachusettes, 1991.
MARGOLIS, J., and MARGOLIS, E., "Black and White on Black and White," in *The Humanist*, Vol. 4, No. 1, Spring 1976.
MARKOVITZ, I. L., *Léopold Sédar Senghor and the Politics of Negritude*, Atheneum, New York, 1969.
——, *Senghor and the Politics of Negritude*, Heinemann, London, 1970.
MARTI, M. P., "Metaphysique noire et psychologie," in *Revue de psychologie des peuples*, No. 11, 1956, pp. 174–80.
MARTINET, A., "Structure and Language," in EHRMANN, J. (ed.), *Structuralism*, Anchor Books, New York, 1970.
MARX, K., *Pre-Capitalist Economic Formations*, Lawrence and Wishart, London, 1964.
——, *L'Idéologie allemande*, Ed. Sociales, Paris, 1968.
MASOLO, D. A., "African Oral Tradition: Luo Oral Literature," in *Africa*, No. 1, Rome, 1976.
——, *Some Aspects and Perspectives of African Philosophy Today*, Istituto Italo-Africano, Rome, 1981.
——, "Alexis Kagame (1912–1981) and La Philosophie Bantu rwandaise de l'être," in *Africa*, Vol. 38, No. 3, Rome, 1983, pp. 449–54.
——, "Political Ideology and Dogmatism," in WAHBA, M. (ed.), *The Roots of Dogmatism*, Ain Shams University, Cairo, 1983.
——, "Kwame Nkrumah, Socialism for Liberation: A Philosophical Review," in *Praxis International*, Vol. 6, No. 2, July 1986, pp. 175–89.
——, "Ideological Dogmatism and the Values of Democracy," in OYUGI, W. O., and GITONGA, A. (eds.), *The Democratic Theory and Practice in Africa*, Heinemann, Nairobi, 1987, pp. 24–41.
——, "Alexis Kagame and African Socio-linguistics," in FLOISTAD, G. (ed.), *Contemporary Philosophy, a New Survey*, Vol. 5: *African Philosophy*, Martinus Nijhoff, Dordrecht, 1987, pp. 181–205.
MAURIER, H., "Avons-nous une philosophie africaine?" in *Revue du clergé africain*, No. 25, July 1970, pp. 365–77.
——, "Méthodologie de la philosophie africaine," in *Culture et développement*, No. 6, 1974, pp. 85–107.
——, *Philosophie de l'Afrique noire*, Verlag St. Augustin, Anthropos Institut, Bonn, 1976.
MBITI, J. S., *African Religions and Philosophy*, Heinemann Educational Books, London, 1969.
——, *Concepts of God In Africa*, S.P.C.K. (The Society for Promoting Christian Knowledge), London, 1970.

————, *New Testament Eschatology in an African Background*, Oxford University Press, Oxford, 1971.

————, *An Introduction to African Religion*, Heinemann, London, 1975.

MBONYIKEBE, D., "Ethique chrétienne et valeurs africaines," in *Cahiers des religions africaines*, Vol. 3, 1969, pp. 149–59.

McCLENDON, J. H., "The Afro-American Philosopher and the Philosophy of the Black Experience: A Bibliographical Essay on a Neglected Topic Both in Philosophy and Black Studies," in *Sage Race Relation Abstracts*, Vol. 7. No. 4, November 1982.

McKAY, C., *Banjo*, Harper Brothers, New York, 1929; Harcourt Brace Jovanovich, New York, 1970. French edition: Rieder, Paris, 1929.

MÉNIL, R., *Tracées: Identité, négritude, esthétique aux Antilles*, Robert Laffont, Paris, 1981.

MICHEL-JONES, F., *Retour au Dogon: Figure du double et ambivalence*, Le Sycamore, Paris, 1978.

MIDDLETON, J. (ed.), *Myth and Cosmos*, 2nd ed., University of Texas Press, Austin, 1980.

MILLER, C. L., *Theories of Africans: Francophone Literature and Anthropology in Africa*, The University of Chicago Press, Chicago, 1990.

MONTAIGNE, M. de, *Essays of Michèle de Montaigne* (trans. C. Cotton), Doubleday and Company, New York, 1947.

MOSELY, A., "The Metaphysics of Magic," in *Second Order*, Vol. 7, Nos. 1–2, 1978.

MOURALIS, B., "Mudimbe et le savoir ethnologique," in *L'Afrique littéraire et artistique*, Vol. 58, No. 1, 1981, pp. 112–25.

————, "V. Y. Mudimbe et l'odeur du pouvoir," in *Politique africaine*, No. 13, 1984.

————, *Littérature et développement*, Silex-ACCT, Paris, 1984.

————, *V. Y. Mudimbe ou le discours, l'écart et l'écriture*, Présence Africaine, Paris, 1988.

MUDIMBE, V. Y., *L'Autre face du royaume. Une introduction à la critique des langages in folie*, L'Age d'homme, Lausanne, 1973.

————, *Visage de la philosophie et de la théologie contemporaines au Zaire*, Cedaf, Brussels, 1981.

————, "La Pensée africaine contemporaine 1954–1980. Répertoire chronologique des ouvrages de langue française," in *Recherche, pédagogie et culture*, Vol. 56, No. 9, 1982, pp. 68–73.

————, *L'Odeur de père. Essai sur des limites de la science et de la vie en Afrique noire*, Présence Africaine, Paris, 1982.

————, "African Philosophy as an Ideological Practice: The Case of French-Speaking Africa," in *African Studies Review*, Vol. 26, 1983.

————, "African Gnosis, Philosophy and the Order of Know ledge: An Introduction," in *African Studies Review*, Vol. 28, Nos. 2–3, June–September 1985, pp. 149–231.

————, *The Invention of Africa*, Indiana University Press, Bloomington and Indianapolis, 1988.

————, *Parables and Fables: Exegesis, Textuality, and Politics in Central Africa*, The University of Wisconsin Press, Madison, 1991.

MUDIMBE, V. Y. (ed.), *The Surreptitious Speech: Présence Africaine and the Politics of Otherness 1947–1982*, The University of Chicago Press, Chicago, 1992.

MULAGO, V., *L'Union vitale bantu chez les Bashi, les Banyarwanda, et les Barundi face à l'unité vitale ecclésiale*, unpublished dissertation, Propaganda, Rome, 1955.

———, "Dialectique existentielle des Bantous et sacramentalisme," in aa.vv., *Aspects de la culture noire*, Librairie Arthème Fayard, Paris, 1958.

———, "La Théologie et ses responsabilités," in *Présence Africaine*, Nos. 27–28, 1959.

———, *Un visage africaine du christianisme*, Présence Africaine, Paris, 1965.

———, "La Conception de Dieu dans la tradition bantoue," in *Revue de clergé africain*, Vol. 22, 1967, pp. 272–99.

———, "Le dieu des Bantu," in *Cahiers des religions africaines*, Vol. 2, 1968, pp. 23–24.

———, "La participation vitale, principe de la cohésion de la communauté Bantu," in *Pour une théologie africaine*, Yaounde, 1969, pp. 191–218.

———, *La Religion traditionnelle des Bantu et leur vision du monde*, Presses Universitaires du Zaire, Kinshasa, 1973.

———, "Discours de clôture," in *Philosophie et libération, Actes de la 2e semaine philosophique de Kinshasa, 18–22 avril 1977*, Kinshasa, 1978.

NJOROGE, R. J., and BENNARS, G. A., *Philosophy and Education in Africa*, Trans-Africa Press, Nairobi, 1986.

NKOMBE, O., "Méthode et point de départ en philosophie africaine: authenticité et libération," in *La Philosophie africaine*, Faculté de Théologie Catholique, Kinshasa, 1977, pp. 69–87.

———, "Essai de sémiotique formelle: les rapports différentiels," in *Mélanges de philosophie africaine*, No. 3, Faculté de Théologie Catholique, Kinshasa, 1978, pp. 131–48.

———, "Sagesse africaine et libération," in *Philosophie et Libération*, Faculté de Théologie Catholique, Kinshasa, 1978, pp. 61–72.

———, *Métaphore et métonymie dans les symboles parémiologiques. L'Intersubjectivité dans les proverbes tetela*, Faculté de Théologie Catholique, Kinshasa, 1979.

———, "Langage et Realité. Vers une ontologie du verbe," in *Langage et Philosophie*, Faculté de Théologie Catholique, Kinshasa, 1981, pp. 85–112.

NKRUMAH, K., *Neo-Colonialism: The Last Stage of Imperialism*, Heinemann, London, 1965.

———, *Consciencism, Philosophy and Ideology for Decolonization and Development with Particular Reference to the African Revolution*, Panaf Books, London, 1970.

NORDENSTAM, T., *Sudanese Ethics*, Scandinavian Institute of African Studies, Uppsala, 19—.

NOTHOMB, D., *Un Humanisme africaine*, Lumen Vitae, Bruxelles, 1965.

NYERERE, J. K., *Freedom and Unity*, Oxford University Press, Oxford, 1967.

———, *Ujamaa: Essays on Socialism*, Oxford University Press, London, 1968.

———, *Freedom and Socialism*, Oxford University Press, Oxford, 1968.

———, *Freedom and Development*, Oxford University Press, Oxford, 1973.

———, "The Arusha Declaration Ten Years After," in COULSON, A. (ed.), *African Socialism in Practice: The Tanzanian Experience*, Spokesman Publishers, Nottingham, 1979, pp. 43–71.

———, "The Rational Choice," in COULSON, A. (ed.), *African Socialism in Practice: The Tanzanian Experience*, Spokesman Publishers, Nottingham, 1979, pp. 19–26.

OAKESHOTT, M., *Experience and Its Modes*, Cambridge University Press, New York, 1985.

OCHOLLA-AYAYO, A. B. C., *Traditional Ideology and Ethics among the Southern Luo*, The Scandinavian Institute of African Studies, Uppsala, 1976.

ODERA-ORUKA, H. See Oruka, H. O.

O'GORMAN, F., *Rationality and Relativity: The Quest for Objective Knowledge*, Aldershot, Avebury, 1989.

OKERE, T., *Can There Be an African Philosophy? A Hermeneutical Investigation with Special Reference to Igbo Culture*, doctoral dissertation, Louvaine University, 1971.

——, "The Assumptions of African Values as Christian Values," in *Civilsation noire et église catholique*, Présence Africaine, Paris, 1978.

——, *African Philosophy*, University Press of America, Washington, D.C., 1983.

OLELA, H., *The Rationale for an African Philosophy: A Critical Examination of the African Cosmological Views with Some Reference to Luo Beliefs*, doctoral dissertation, The Florida State University, 1971.

——, *An Introduction to the History of Philosophy: From Ancient Africa to Ancient Greece*, Select Publishing Co., Atlanta, Georgia, 1980.

——, "The African Foundations of Greek Philosophy," in WRIGHT, R. A. (ed.), *African Philosophy: An Introduction*, University Press of America, Lanham, Maryland, 1984, pp. 77–92.

ONGONG'A, J. J., *The Luo Concept of Death: A Study of Beliefs and Ceremonies of Death in the Light of Christian Message*, doctoral dissertation, Urbaniana Pontifical University, Rome, 1979.

ORUKA, H. O., "Mythologies as African Philosophy," in *East Africa Journal*, Vol. 9, No. 10, October 1972, pp. 5–11.

——, "Truth and Belief," in *Universitas* (Ghana), Vol. 5, No. 1, 1975.

——, "Sagacity in African Philosophy," in *The International Philosophical Quarterly*, Vol. 23, No. 4, 1983, pp. 383–93.

——, *Punishment and Terrorism in Africa*, East African Literature Bureau, Nairobi, 1985 (second edition).

——, "Ideology and Truth," in *Praxis International*, Vol. 5, No. 1, 1985, pp. 35–50.

——, "For the Sake of Truth—A Response to Wiredu's Critique of 'Truth and Belief,' " in *Quest*, Vol. 11, No. 2, 1988, pp. 3–22.

——, *Sage Philosophy: Indigenous Thinkers and Modern Debate on African Philosophy*, Brill Publishers, Leiden, The Netherlands, 1990, and Acts Press, Nairobi, 1991.

——, *The Philosophy of Liberty*, Standard Textbooks Publishers, Nairobi, 1990.

——, *Ethics*, University of Nairobi Press, Nairobi, 1990.

——, "Sagacity in African Philosophy," unpublished paper, University of Nairobi.

ORUKA, H. O.; OJWANG', J. B.; and MUGAMBI, J. K. N., *The Rational Path*, Standard Textbooks Publishers, Nairobi, 1989.

ORUKA, H. O., and MASOLO, D. A. (eds.), *Philosophy and Cultures*, Bookwise Publishers, Nairobi, 1983.

OSEGHARE, A. S., *The Relevance of Sagacious Reasoning in African Philosophy*, doctoral dissertation, University of Nairobi, 1985.

OVERING, J. (ed.), *Reason and Morality*, Tavistock Publications, London, 1985.

PADMORE, G., *Pan-Africanism or Communism?* Doubleday, New York, 1971.

PARRINDER, E. G., *Religion in Africa*, Pall Mall Press, London, 1970.

——, *African Traditional Religion* (3rd ed.), Sheldon Press, London, 1974.

P'BITEK, O., *African Religions in Western Scholarship*, East African Literature Bureau, Nairobi, 1970.
——, "Reflect, Reject, Recreate," in *East Africa Journal*, Vol. 9, No. 9, April 1972.
PERBAL, A., "La Philosophie bantoue; à propos du livre du R. P. Tempels," in *Africae Fraternae Ephemerides Romanae*, Nos. 24–25, 1947, pp. 55–57.
PERINBAM, B. M., *Holy Violence: The Revolutionary Thought of Frantz Fanon*, Three Continents Press, Washington, D.C., 1982.
PERRY, R. L. M., *The Cushite or the Descendants of Ham*, 1893.
——, *Sketch of Philosophical Systems, Suffrage*, American Publication Company, Hartford, Connecticut, 1895.
PETERSON, O., *Chiefs and Gods: Religious and Social Elements in the South Eastern Bantu Kingship*, Lund, 1954.
PIVCEVIC, E., *Husserl and Phenomenology*, Hutchinson University Library, London, 1970.
POLANYI, M., *Personal Knowledge: Towards a Post-Critical Philosophy*, Harper Torchbook edition, Harper & Row Publishers, New York, 1964.
POSSOZ, E., "A la Recherche de la philosophie clanique," in *Bulletin CEPSI*, No. 3, 1946–47, pp. 84–88.
POSTIOMA, A. da, "Per una filosofia africana," in *Filosofia e Vita*, No. 3, 1963.
——, "Premesse filosofiche africane e cristianesimo," in *Filosofia e Vita*, No. 2, 1964.
——, "Elementi costitutive per una filosofia africana," in *Filosofia e Vita*, No. 3, 1964.
——, "Idee religiose e idee filosofiche nell'Africa d'oggi," in *Filosofia, religione e religioni*, numero speciale di *Filosofia e Vita*, Nos. 2–3–4, 1966.
——, *Filosofia Africana*, Edizioni Missionari Estere Cappuccini, Milano, 1967.
——, "Esiste un filosofia africana?" in *Filosofia e Vita*, No. 1, 1969.
——, "Presenza africana nella filosofia universale," in *Filosofia e Vita*, No. 1, 1969.
Pourquoi la philosophie en Afrique? numero special 3/4 des *Cahiers Philosophiques Africains—African Philosophical Journal*, Special Journées Philosophiques, Lubumbashi, 1973.
QUINE, W. V. O., *Word and Object*, the MIT Press, Cambridge, Massachusettes, 1960.
RADIN, P., *Primitive Man as Philosopher*, D. Appleton and Co., London/New York, 1957.
RAY, B., *African Religions*, Prentice-Hall, Englewood Cliffs, New Jersey, 1976.
RICHARDS, A. I., "African Systems of Thought: An Anglo-French Dialogue," in *Man*, No. 2, 1967, pp. 286–98.
RICOEUR, P., *History and Truth*, Northwestern University Press, Evanston, 1965.
——, *The Symbolism of Evil*, Harper & Row, New York, 1967.
——, *The Conflict of Interpretations*, Northwestern University Press, Evanston, 1969.
——, *The Reality of the Historical Past*, Marquette University Press, Milwaukee, Wisconsin, 1984.
RIGBY, P., *Persistent Pastoralists: Nomadic Society in Transition*, Zed Books, London, 1985.
RODNEY, W., "Technological Stagnation and Economic Distortion in Pre-Colonial Times," in GUTKIND, P. C. W., and WATERMAN, P. (eds.) *African Social Studies*, Heinemann, London, 1977, pp. 107–15.

—, *How Europe Underdeveloped Africa*, Howard University Press, Washington, D.C., 1981.
ROELENS, V. A., "A propos de 'La Philosophie bantoue,' " in *Grand Lacs*, No. 62, 1947, pp. 358–60.
ROGER, J., "La Filosofia bantu," in *Antropologia y Etnologia*, No. 7, 1952, pp. 533–51.
ROSEN, S., *Hermeneutics as Politics*, Oxford University Press, New York, 1987.
ROUSSEAU, M., "La Philosophie des Nègres," in *Musée Vivant* (Paris), Nos. 36–37, 1948, pp. 9–12.
RUCH, E. A., "Philosophy of African History," in *African Studies*, Vol. 32, 1973, pp. 113–36.
RUCH, E. A., and ANYANWU, K. C., *African Philosophy*, Rome, 1981.
SAID, E., *Orientalism*, Pantheon Books, New York, 1978.
SAREVSKAJA, B. I., "La Méthode de l'ethnographie de Marcel Griaule et les questions de méthodologie dans l'ethnographie française contemporaine," in *Cahiers d'études africaines*, Vol. 4, No. 16, 1963, pp. 590–602.
SARTRE, J-P., "Orphée noir," in SENGHOR, L. S. (ed.), *Anthologie de la nouvelle poésie nègre et malgache de langue française*, Presses Universitaires de France, Paris, 1948.
—, *Being and Nothingness*, Simon and Schuster, New York, 1956.
—, *Critique de la raison dialectique*, Gallimard, Paris, 1960.
—, *Search for a Method*, Vintage Books, New York, 1968.
—, *Black Orpheus*, Présence Africaine, Paris, 1976.
SCHILLER, F. C. S., *Studies in Humanism*, Macmillan and Co., Ltd., London and New York, 1907.
—, *Humanism* [1912], Greenwood Press, Westport, Connecticut, 1970.
SELLARS, W., "Empiricism and the Philosophy of Mind," in *Science, Perception, and Reality*, Routledge and Kegan Paul, London, 1963.
—, "Philosophy and the Scientific Image of Man," in *Science, Perception, and Reality*, Routledge and Kegan Paul, London, 1963.
SELVAGGI, F., *Scienza e Metodologia*, Universita Gregoriana, Rome, 1962.
SENGHOR, L. S., *Anthologie de la nouvelle poésie nègre et malgache de langue française* [1948], Presses Universitaires de France, Paris, 1972.
—, *Nation et voie africaine du socialisme*, Présence Africaine, Paris, 1961.
—, *Pierre Teilhard de Chardin et la politique africaine*, Seuil, Paris, 1962.
—, *Liberté I: Négritude et humanisme*, Seuil, Paris, 1964.
—, *Les Fondements de l'africanité ou négritude et arabité*, Présence Africaine, Paris, 1967.
—, *Liberté II: Nation et voie africaine du socialisme*, Seuil, Paris, 1971.
—, *Liberté III: Négritude et civilisation de l'universel*, Seuil, Paris, 1977.
SINGER, M. G. (ed.), *American Philosophy*, Cambridge University Press, New York, 1985.
SKORUPSKI, J., *Symbol and Theory* [1967], Cambridge University Press, 1976, 1983.
SLOTKIN, J. S. (ed.), *Readings in Early Philosophy*, Viking Fund Publications in Anthropology, No. 40, Aldine Publishing Co., Chicago, 1965.
SMET, A. J., "Bibliographie de la pensée africaine," in *Cahiers Philosophiques Africains—African Philosophical Journal*, No. 2, 1972, pp. 39–96.

——, *Philosophie africaine: Textes choisis*, Presses Universitaires Zaire, Kinshasa, 1972.

——, "L'oeuvre inédite du Père Placide Tempels," in *Revue africaine de théologie*, Vol. 1, No. 2, 1977, pp. 219–33.

——, "Histoire de la philosophie africaine, problèmes et méthodes," in *La Philosophie Africaine*, Faculté de Théologie Catholique, Kinshasa, 1977, pp. 47–68.

——, "Le Père Placide Tempels et son oeuvre publiée," in *Revue africaine de théologie*, Vol. 1, No. 1, 1977.

——, *Histoire de la philosophie africaine contemporaine: courants et problèmes*, Mimeograph, Faculté de Théologie Catholique, Kinshasa-Limete, 1980.

SMITH, E. W., "*La Philosophie bantoue* by Placide Tempels," book review in *Africa*, No. 16, 1946, pp. 199–203.

——, *African Ideas of God*, Edinburgh House, London, 1950.

SODIPO, J. O., "Notes on the Concept of Cause and Chance in Yoruba Traditional Thought," in *Second Order*, Vol. 2, No. 2, 1973.

——, "Philosophy in Africa Today," in *Thought and Practice*, Vol. 2, No. 2, 1975.

——, "Philosophy, Science, Technology and Traditional African Thought," in ORUKA, H. O., and MASOLO, D. A. (eds.), *Philosophy and Cultures*, Bookwise Publishers, Nairobi, 1983, pp. 36–43.

SOUSBERGHE, L. de, "A propos de 'La Philosophie bantoue,' " in *Zaire*, No. 5, 1951, pp. 821–28.

SOYINKA, W., *Myth, Literature and the African World*, Cambridge University Press, Cambridge, UK, 1976.

SUMNER, C. (ed.), *Ethiopian Philosophy*, Central Printing Press, Addis-Ababa. Vol. 1: *The Book of the Wise Philosophers* (1974); Vol. II: *The Treatise of Zär'a Yacob and of Walda Haywat* (1974); Vol. III: *The Treatise of Zär'a Yacob and of Walda Haywat* (1978); Vol. IV: *The Life and Maxims of Skandas* (1981).

——, *African Philosophy. Philosophie Africaine*, Chamber Printing House, Addis-Ababa, 1980.

TAMBIAH, S. J., *Magic, Science, Religion, and the Scope of Rationality*, Cambridge University Press, Cambridge, UK, 1990.

TAYLOR, C., *Sources of the Self: The Making of the Modern Identity*, Cambridge University Press, Cambridge, UK, 1989.

TEMPELS, P., *La Philosophie bantoue*, Lovania, Elizabethville, 1945. Présence Africaine, Paris, 1949 and (3rd edition) 1965.

——, "L'Etude des langues bantues à la lumiere de la philosophie bantoue," in *Présence Africaine*, No. 5, 1958, pp. 755–60.

——, *Bantu Philosophy* (trans. Rev. Colin King), Présence Africaine, 1959, 1969.

——, *Notre rencontre*, Centre d'Etudes Pastorales, Léopoldville, 1962.

——, *Philosophie bantu* (a new version adapted from the English translation, and with an Introduction by A. J. Smet), Faculté de Théologie Catholique, Kinshasa, 1979.

TOWA, M., *Essai sur la problématique philosophique dans l'Afrique actuelle*, Clé, Yaoundé, 1971.

——, *Léopold Sédar Senghor: négritude ou servitude?* Clé, Yaoundé, 1971.

——, *L'Idée d'une philosophie africaine*, Clé, Yaoundé, 1979.

TOWETT, T., "Le Rôle d'un philosophe africain," in *Présence Africaine*, Nos. 27–28, 1959, pp. 108–28.

TSHIAMALENGA, N., "La Philosophie de la faute dans la tradition luba," in *Cahiers des religions africaines*, Vol. 8, 1974, pp. 167–86.

———, "Que'est—ce que la 'philosophie africaine,' " in *La Philosophie africaine*, Faculté de Théologie Catholique, Kinshasa, 1977, pp. 33–46.

———, "Langues bantu et philosophie. Le cas du ciluba," in *La Philosophie africaine*, Faculté de Théologie Catholique, Kinshasa, 1977, pp. 147–58.

———, *Denken und Sprechen: Ein Beitrag zum linguistischen Relativitäts Prinzip am Beispiel einer Bantusprache (Ciluba)*, Inaugural-Dissertation, Johann Wolfgang Goethe Universität, 1980.

VAN PARYS, J. M., "Etat actuel de l'activité philosophique en Afrique," in *Langage et société*, Faculté de Théologie Catholique, Kinshasa, 1981.

VANSINA, J., "Is Elegance a Proof? Structuralism and African History," in *History in Africa*, Vol. 10, 1983, pp. 307–48.

———, *Oral Tradition as History*, University of Wisconsin Press, Madison, 1986.

VENDLER, Z., *Linguistics in Philosophy*, Cornell University Press, Ithaca, New York, 1967.

VIGLINO, U., *La Conoscenza: problematicità e valore*, Pontificia Università Urbaniana, Rome, 1969.

WASHINGTON, J., *Alain Locke and Philosophy: A Quest for Cultural Pluralism*, Greenwood Press, New York, 1986.

WEST, C., "Philosophy and the Afro-American Experience," in *The Philosophical Forum*, Vol. 9, Nos. 2–3, Winter–Spring 1977–78.

WILSON, B. R. (ed.), *Rationality*, Harper & Row, New York, 1970.

WINCH, P., *The Idea of a Social Science and Its Relation to Philosophy* [1958], Routledge and Kegan Paul, London, 1971.

———, "Understanding a Primitive Society," in *American Philosophical Quarterly*, No. 1, 1964, pp. 307–24. Reprinted in WILSON, B. R. (ed.), *Rationality*, Harper & Row, New York, 1970.

WIREDU, K., "Mysticism, Philosophy and Rationality," in *Universitas* (Ghana), Vol. 2, No. 3, 1973, pp. 97–106.

———, "In Behalf of Opinion: A Rejoinder," in *Universitas* (Ghana), Vol. 5, No. 2, 1976.

———, *Philosophy and an African Culture*, Cambridge University Press, Cambridge, UK, 1980.

———, "Morality and Religion in Akan Thought," in ORUKA, H. O., and MASOLO, D. A. (eds.), *Philosophy and Cultures*, Bookwise Publishers, Nairobi, 1983, pp. 6–13.

———, "The Concept of Truth in the Akan Language," in BODUNRIN, P. (ed.), *Philosophy in Africa: Trends and Perspectives*, University of Ife Press, Ile-Ife, Nigeria, 1985, pp. 43–54.

———, "Replies to Critics," in BODUNRIN, P. (ed.), *Philosophy in Africa: Trends and Perspectives*, pp. 91–104.

———, "Are There Cultural Universals?" in *Quest: An African International Journal of Philosophy*, Vol. 4, No. 2, December 1990, pp. 5–19.

———, "On Defining African Philosophy," in NAGL-DOCEKAL, H., and WIMMER, F. M. (eds.), *Postkoloniales Philosophieren: Afrika*, R. Oldenbourg Verlag, Wien und München, 1992, pp. 40–62.

WITTGENSTEIN, L., *Philosophical Investigation, I*, Basil Blackwell, London, 1968.

WOLFRAM, S., "Basic Differences of Thought," in HORTON, R., and FINNEGAN, R. (eds.), *Modes of Thought: Essays on Thinking in Western and Non-Western Societies*, Faber and Faber, London, 1973, pp. 357–74.

———, "Facts and Theories: Saying and Believing," in OVERING, J. (ed.), *Reason and Morality*, Tavistock Publications, London, 1985, pp. 71–84.

WRIGHT, C., *Realism, Meaning and Truth*, Basil Blackwell, Oxford, 1990.

WRIGHT, R. A. (ed.), *African Philosophy: An Introduction*, University Press of America, Lanham, Maryland, 1984.

Index

Abazimu: Bantu concept of immortality, 90
Abraham, William E., 38
Africa. See African philosophy; History; Religion; specific groups
African Inland Mission (A.I.M.), 109
African philosophy: debate on reason and rationality in, 1–15, 124–28, 145–46; politics of rationality, 15–24; Jahn on structural levels of, 39; history of and debate on reason and rationality in, 40–45; critiques of Tempels, 67; role and impact of Ogotemmêli and Griaule on, 68–83; Kagame on language and Being, 84–102; Mbiti on African religious concepts and, 104; language, truth, and reason in, 128–45; Eboussi-Boulaga on African exponents of, 158–64; Hountondji's definition of, 195; Wiredu on truth and, 204–32; Wiredu on value of traditional thought, 223–25; Odera Oruka on sage philosophers, 233–46; emergence of in French colonies, 257n; Crahay on conditions for, 271n. See also Ethnophilosophy; Philosophy
Afrocentricity: Bernal on two projections of, 23; sage philosophers and, 245
Agikuyu: concept of time, 114
Ahantu: as category of localization, 91
Akamba: concept of time, 109–10, 114, 121; spirit world of, 111
Akans: concept of God, 112; concept of truth, 225
Althusser, Louis, 117, 199, 200, 201
Amagara: Bantu concept of Being, 89
Amma (God): in Dogon cosmology, 70, 78, 80
Anaxagoras, 122
Anaximander, 75
Anthropocentrism: Mbiti on African cosmology, 119–21
Anthropology: views of reason and culture, 6; ahistoricist school of, 7; monotheism and

evolutionist, 122; Mudimbe on imperialism and, 182–83, 188; influence of Lévi-Strauss on Mudimbe, 185; difference in focus of French and British, 257n
Antiabsolutism: dialectical Marxist orientation in contemporary philosophy, 202
Anyanwu, Kane C., 28
Appiah, Kwame, 130, 134
Aristotle, 20, 55, 76, 145, 154
Art: influence of African on European in 1920s, 15–16
Azande: Polanyi on reason and, 6–7; beliefs about witchcraft, magic, and oracles, 125

Bacon, Francis, 201
Bahoken, Jean-Calvin, 28, 39, 104, 119
Balandier, Georges, 18
Bambara: Olela on history and cosmology of, 20; concept of nothingness, 88
Bantu: Tempels on ontology of, 47–52; Kagame on language and Being, 84–102; Eboussi-Boulaga's critique of Tempels, 149–55
Beattie, John, 130
Bedu-Addo, 225
Beidelman, T. O., 115
Being: Tempels on Bantu concept of, 57–58; Kagame on Bantu language and, 84–102; Eboussi-Boulaga's critique of Tempels, 149–55
Bena: concept of God, 106
Bergson, Henri: Tempels's theory of vital force, 48–49, 56, 152
Berkeley, George, 209, 212–13
Bernal, Martin, 21–23, 41, 245
Binu: cult of, 74–75, 76
Bird, C. S., 173
Black Athena (film), 23
Blyden, Edward Wilmot, 11–12, 13, 184, 253–54n